D1593508

GLASS AND GAVEL

GLASS AND GAVEL

The U.S. Supreme Court and Alcohol

Nancy Maveety

ROWMAN & LITTLEFIELD
Lanham • Boulder • New York • London

Published by Rowman & Littlefield
An imprint of The Rowman & Littlefield Publishing Group, Inc.
4501 Forbes Boulevard, Suite 200, Lanham, Maryland 20706
www.rowman.com

Unit A, Whitacre Mews, 26-34 Stannary Street, London SE11 4AB

British Library Cataloguing in Publication Information Available

Library of Congress Cataloging-in-Publication Data

Names: Maveety, Nancy, author.
Title: Glass and gavel : the U.S. Supreme Court and alcohol / Nancy Maveety.
Description: Lanham : Rowman & Littlefield, 2019. | Includes bibliographical references and
    index.
Identifiers: LCCN 2018033786 (print) | LCCN 2018035893 (ebook) | ISBN 9781538111994 (Elec-
    tronic) | ISBN 9781538111987 (cloth : alk. paper)
Subjects: LCSH: Liquor law—United States--History. | Judges—Alcohol Use—United States. |
    United States. Supreme Court—Officials and Employees—Alcohol use.
Classification: LCC KF3919 (ebook) | LCC KF3919 .M27 2018 (print) | DDC 344.7305/41—dc23
LC record available at https://lccn.loc.gov/2018033786

♾ ™ The paper used in this publication meets the minimum requirements of
American National Standard for Information Sciences Permanence of Paper
for Printed Library Materials, ANSI/NISO Z39.48-1992.

Printed in the United States of America

"How beverage alcohol is produced, distributed, consumed, and regulated . . . offers a key to the nature of a society and how it changes over time."

—Jack S. Blocker, "Tidy Pictures of Messy Behavior"

CONTENTS

ACKNOWLEDGMENTS

The inspiration for this book came from conversations with a colleague—fellow political scientist and cocktail enthusiast—about presidential and congressional drinking. Our shared fascination was rewarded, when that year's "Tales of the Cocktail" featured a seminar on the signature drinks of certain chief executives. "You know what would be fun," I ventured as we savored a seminar sample, "is a cocktails book of the justices of the Supreme Court." I thought of the Marshall Court's convening for judicial conference in area taverns (boardinghouses, really), and about various famous alcohol-related cases in the annals of constitutional law. The idea of a full-blown Supreme Court history of alcoholic beverages has got real potential, I pondered aloud, and my first future reader looked intrigued. So, thank you, Brian, for helping to spark *Glass and Gavel*.

Until I started the research for this book, I didn't fully appreciate the sheer volume of interesting work on the social and political history of alcohol in the United States. We are all familiar with the period of Prohibition, but alcohol's rather central presence in the life of the American republic both predates and continues on after that infamous era of the intersection of alcohol and American law. I am indebted to these historians who laid the foundations for my enterprise. And in immersing myself in the saga of fashionable cocktails and liquors, and who might have been drinking what during a particular Supreme Court era, I drew on the burgeoning literature on the history of the cocktail.

These scholar mixologists, and the vintage cocktail manuals whose reissuance they have championed, have been invaluable guides.

I benefited from the assistance and support of many sources in my writing of this book. A research grant from the Lurcy Fellowship at Tulane University enabled my travel to consult archival materials that enriched my account of the justices and their legal and personal relationships with beverage alcohol. Special recognition must go to the staffs of the Supreme Court Historical Society and the National Archives in Washington, DC, and the Louisiana Research Collection in New Orleans, LA. My good friend Karin provided early research assistance, which included fieldwork at the Round Robin Bar of the Willard Hotel and the Off the Record Bar at the Hays Adams Hotel—two venerable Washington, DC, political watering holes whose history and contemporary profiles I explored thanks to her efforts. Many friends and colleagues have been sounding boards and unofficial contributors, but I especially appreciate my colleagues at the Tulane Law School who read and commented on various draft chapters during and after the annual faculty workshop. Manuscript preparation assistance, including help with securing ever-important publication permissions for the book's illustrations, came from Tasia Kastanek and Zhen Lin. Last but not least, I thank my editor, Jon Sisk, for believing in this project when it was still in its initial stages and for his enthusiasm and encouragement all along the way.

My most devoted advocate, of this book and its value and in all of our life projects together, is Tom. To you and your orchestration of many a Celebration of the Anniversary of the Repeal of Prohibition, this book is dedicated.

PREFACE AND INTRODUCTION

A Cocktail [Book] of Decisions

Alcohol—its enjoyment and its regulation—has shaped American political life and law since the colonial era. Alcohol—its use and its restriction—has affected both American society and political culture. Americans' very definition of who we are finds expression in that very American creation: the cocktail. Presidential cocktail imbibing marks not only American social history, but the distinctive personality of each political era as well—Cheers to the Chief, in the inimitable words of one recent account of the topic.

There is a rich trove of popular histories of America and its drinking that tell the story of alcohol in American life and experience. The provocatively titled *Alcoholic Republic* is just one of a number of scholarly but accessible works that situate American political development firmly inside the tavern. (Literally.) Another such book, *Mint Juleps with Teddy Roosevelt,* bills itself as "the complete history of presidential drinking," tantalizingly promising in its Amazon.com and Google Books advertising copy: "Stroll through our country's memorable moments . . . and discover the role that alcohol played in all of them."[1] More effusively, Susan Cheever's 2015 *Drinking in America: Our Secret History* declares, "The interesting truth, untaught in most schools and unacknowledged in most written history, is that a glass of beer, a bottle of rum, a keg of hard cider, a flask of whiskey, or even a dry martini was often the silent, powerful third party to many decisions that shaped the American story."[2]

Even the story of our Constitution and its law has been influenced by the changing role of alcohol and alcoholic beverage drinking in the United States, from the founding to the present day. While the period of Prohibition is perhaps the most familiar, with its textual and tangible effects the most noticeable, it is hardly the only time period in which governmental balance of powers and individual liberties have been seen through a wine glass darkly, so to speak. Liquor has long been the evil twin of the American sense of American enterprise, and both regulating it and evading that regulation have been pursued with great glee throughout our history.

Still, the very centrality of alcohol to the Prohibition era fueled a special cultural obsession with *explaining* it, with trying to *distinguish* it. (Or extinguish it, as a bad memory.) What is harder to accept, or even to fathom, is that the period 1920–1933 was less unique than extreme, its sour legacy often exaggerated for effect. Indeed, both drinking and punishing it are more entwined in the American experience than the morbid interest in all things speakeasy would lead one to think.

Ironically enough, that interest—whether sullen and sour, or more frankly fetishistic—has had one very salubrious impact: it sparked a veritable industry of authenticity, alcohol-wise. Although causes of cultural trends are notoriously slippery, whatever the reasons, fixation on the Flappers and their flasks proceeded fairly effortlessly to the contemporary fascination for and appreciation of "period cocktails." *That* has spawned a serious and well-researched literature of cocktail histories—of vintage spirits and their use, of drink recipes and their particular historical context, of the historical periods that birthed the classics of American drinking.

A seemingly mundane thing—the cocktail—thus becomes the icon or totem of a particular time period, transporting us there and to its sensibilities as we imbibe. How can this "cocktale" not also evoke a particular *political or legal* time? Our institutions of public memory have certainly made the connection: presidential predilections regarding alcohol (that favorite topic) found their way into a recent exhibit at the National Archives, "Spirited Republic: Alcohol in American History," where FDR's cocktail shaker and service were displayed not as historical ephemera but telling documentation. For the cultural studies

branch of social history, no artifact is too trivial or prosaic to lack significance and meaning. For the social history of alcohol in American life
and law, political and popular culture are inextricably linked.

"Intoxicating liquor" is one of the few things so plainly material to
merit explicit mention, not once, but twice, in the amendments to the
U.S. Constitution. Mentioned, but so often unmentionable in polite
company. For this reason, liquor's popular depictions often best narrate
how attitudes toward alcohol have profoundly affected American political culture and values. As the lurid posters of the Women's Christian
Temperance Union and Anti-Saloon League, the dreamy pictorial advertisements for all manner of distilled spirits that have graced the
nation's magazines, the stern but stylish midcentury graphics for the
Yale University Studies on Alcohol "Alcoholism Is an Illness" campaign,
and a current tourist postcard of the lovingly re-created old mahogany
Main Bar at the "new" Old Ebbitt Grill[3] all amply illustrate: the visual
slideshow of liquor in American life is the story of a particularly intense
love-hate relationship.

Yet only fuzzily remembered or documented within that troubled
romance is the entity of the U.S. Supreme Court. This is as grave an
omission as the olive from the martini, for the court and its justices have
been caught with glass as well as gavel in hand. Less flippantly put, the
U.S. Supreme Court has regularly and frequently been at the center of
the tricornered relationship between drinking, public life, and constitutional law and liberties. The court has defined, refined, and, at times,
embodied that relationship. From the tavern as a judicial meeting
space, to the bootlegger as both pariah and patriot, to the individual
freedom issue of the sobriety checkpoint—there is the Supreme Court:
adjudicating, but also partaking in the temper(ance) of the times.

American political culture and the court have hardly been neglected,
of course. Social and popular histories of the Supreme Court have eagerly personalized and contextualized the court, its eras, and its justices.[4] Popular history and cultural studies of the Supreme Court have
even united to involve the justices themselves. For instance, a June
2016 program for the National Museum of American History, "Legal
Eats: Food and the Culture of the U.S. Supreme Court," featured Justices Ruth Bader Ginsburg and Sonia Sotomayor participating in "a
conversation" about "the unique food traditions of the Supreme Court."
The Smithsonian webpage on the event provided this tantalizing copy:

> Throughout American history, the Justices of the nation's highest
> court have come together to deliberate legal matters . . . but they
> have also found time to break bread. Since the early 19th century
> when they took all their meals together while living in a boarding
> house, the Justices have continued to reinforce cordiality and coop-
> eration through shared food traditions, such as eating lunch together
> on Court and Conference days.

And drinking together, Justice Ginsburg would add during a remarks
segment of the program, referencing the custom of her court's members sharing wine and dinner before attending the president's State of
the Union Address.

Examination of the court and its times (and the court in its time) has
a long tradition as a device to understand the institution and its decisions. Such an approach is not surprising, nor gimmicky: it is simply one
way that we make sense of our political institutions and connect them to
our own lives. And when the Constitution, and the eras of the Constitution and of constitutional law are found in the decisions of the Supreme
Court, as they are, then popular and social and historical contextualiza-
tion of the court becomes elucidation of constitutional meaning.

So . . . alcohol, the justices, and their decisions: how to connect
them? If the Constitution itself sights alcohol in its crosshairs, then can
we turn the scope around and let alcoholic beverages and their cultural
regimes of enjoyment and regulation provide a fresh and telling perspective on the Supreme Court, as an institution and a decision maker,
in both political and legal time? Of course we can, and such a perspective yields not the "alcoholic republic," but *Glass and Gavel: The U.S.
Supreme Court and Alcohol*, whereby *Supreme Court eras and constitutional interpretations are inspected through that period's culture of
drinking and attitudes toward controlling it.* The examination of alcohol
in American public life exposes rich traditions and cultural practices;
this book's premise is that the examination of alcohol in the public *and
legal* life of the justices of the Supreme Court promises to do the same.

My aim is to show how much of our constitutional law—Supreme
Court rulings on the powers of government and rights of individuals—
has been shaped by our American love/hate relationship with the bottle
and the barroom, while at the same time re-creating some of the flavor
of that relationship, in its phases and changes, throughout Supreme
Court time. Figuratively and sometimes literally, soaked in booze are

we all—the justices of our court no less. It is high time they were invited to the national cocktail party.

Popular history struggles to exist in the space between lighthearted entertainment and legitimate scholarship. Cocktail tales labor under the special burden of the titillating nature of alcohol itself: the alcoholic beverage is somehow frivolous as a topic and specious as a motif. How then can the cocktail and its judicial intersections possibly be a valid enterprise, except as a novelty act? I would argue that we still have much to appreciate about the social use and misuse of alcohol in our politics, society, and law. Moreover, as a judicial scholar and political scientist by training, I know we still have much to investigate about the factors, internal and external to the court, that affect judicial decision making. Far from suggesting, *pace* Jerome Frank, that the judge decides what he or she drank for lunch (although there are a few to whom the trope might apply), I am arguing that alcohol can be considered a fact or part of a fact pattern that stimulates a judicial response—a vote in a case, an opinion written. Hence, *for each era of the court, alcoholic beverages and drinking presented very specific judicial and occasionally jurisprudential challenges. These required resolution, shaped the court's outputs, and—most significantly—had to be and were reconciled with the legal doctrines of the day.*

There is abundant evidence of serious academic attention to the nexus between constitutional law and alcohol, liquor, and a satisfactory policy of its social ordering. The fiftieth anniversary of the Repeal of Prohibition and the adoption of the Twenty-First Amendment was the occasion for a group of scholars to gather to discuss and consider the consequences of the liquor ban and its repeal at a conference entitled "Prohibition Fifty Years Later: Implications for Law, Alcohol, and Order," and to generate a published volume of the same name.[5] In 1994 one of the few book-length doctrinal treatments of Prohibition's influence on criminal law decision making was released. The author of this study stresses "the importance of the [prohibition] experiment for the development of legal thought"[6] —an importance that has largely been overlooked.[7] Not only that, this legal study urges a revision of the conventional wisdom regarding the Supreme Court of the 1920s and 1930s. That conventional wisdom has seldom been kind. Still, there is an important truth lurking within the debate over that historical court's checkered reputation. The Supreme Court's apparent sensitivity to the waxing and waning popularity of Prohibition's enforcement suggests that what we know—or think we know—about the *various eras of the Supreme Court can be usefully illuminated by examining judicial decisions about regulating—as well as enjoying—the alcoholic beverage.* But to truly do so, we need to widen the scope of our judicial inquiry beyond the era of the Prohibition and Repeal Amendments, beyond what existing legal studies have addressed. We need, in other words, to sketch a history of the Supreme Court's decision making that partakes of the same historical sweep as the literature on drinking in America.

The historical eras of the Supreme Court roughly track the American political cultural and social developments that surround the judicial institution. Political scientists are in dispute as to how this happens, whether through new court appointments or individual judges' permeation by public sentiment or judicial concern for institutional legitimacy in the face of popular pressure. Whatever the actual process or processes, the court's eras are the political society's, too, albeit with less than perfect correspondence. One of the central conventions of marking the court's eras—of marking judicial time—is to personalize them, by the name and the tenure of the chief justice. This is a well-established way of thinking historically about the court and American society. "Both academics and laypersons," says legal scholar Melvin Urofsky, "tend to periodicize the Court by reference to the chief justice; we talk of the 'Marshall Court' or the 'Taney Court' or the 'Warren Court' and at least in some instances, the appellation is correct. John Marshall and William Howard Taft, for example, did lead their colleagues and put the impress of their own jurisprudential views on the decisions of their courts." Yet the meaningfulness of such naming varies, as "historians recognize that there is a continuity on the Court of the associate justices, whose terms are not coterminous with those of their chiefs . . . [and who sometimes] really provide the intellectual and political leadership" that mark a court era."[8] More than that, the mortality (or service record, at any rate) of any one chief justice does not usually perfectly match a political era. Most chief justices live too long, and encompass more than one era of changing attitudes, or serve too briefly, and partake of only a piece of an era or an age. We use the chief-justice-name+Court nomenclature nevertheless, knowing this, and attending to the legal policy making of each court era accordingly.

Do our chiefs, then, each match up with a distinctive era of American imbibing? Not perfectly, certainly, for the popularity of this or that intoxicating beverage—or of *any* intoxicating beverage, for that matter—may span or subdivide eras on the bench. ("Booze hounds" can quote chapter and verse on that. The temporal shelf life of the mint julep is long; that of the Mamie Taylor or the Zombie, relatively brief by comparison.) But it is still true that for each era of the Supreme Court, we can mark the time period and the passage of sociocultural time by what people—including justices—were (or were not) imbibing. A period cocktail per court, in other words, adds a nip of verisimilitude (and, on occasion, a nip of elite hypocrisy) to the analysis. Thus, I begin each judicial chapter with a historically accurate and verifiably accordant drink recipe. Where a chief justice is personally associated with a particular beverage, I of course choose this as his era's emblem. Where such a specific association cannot be assigned or defended, I draw on the rich history of fashions and fads in spirits and wines, both in the nation's capital and in the country as a whole, to make my choice. It is defensible, I think, to identify certain cocktails as totems of their times.

What we drank, how and when we drank it (or didn't), who drank (or didn't), are all matters of the historical record. What this book tries to do is place that well-documented beverage story within a historical periodization of the Supreme Court, supplementing both with the decisional record of each period. The book's purpose is to illustrate the connection or nexus between alcohol in American public and political life and the activities of the U.S. Supreme Court. To do this, I combine an examination of the justices' participation in the sociocultural usages of alcohol across the court's (and the republic's) history with a survey of the content and impact of the court's decisions on alcohol regulation. The objective is a profile of the cocktail of judicial decisions—and the cocktails of the times—that demarcate liquor and drinking's status in American life and influence on American legal life.

But a survey of the eras of the Supreme Court does more: it shows that just as the culture of alcohol was the template for judicial decisions about it, the court's decisions also helped *construct* the era's culture of alcohol—by creating legal space for a culture of its enjoyment, or by endorsing a culture and legal regime of its regulation. To paraphrase Chief Justice Charles Evans Hughes, constitutional law is what the court says the Constitution is. What the justices say and do with respect to alcohol, then, tells us something important about their times, our times, and our "constitutional cocktail"[9] of limited governmental powers and individual rights.

PROLOGUE

Early Times and the Early Supreme Court

The Bill of Rights, which declares that among the inalienable rights possessed by the citizens is that of seeking and pursuing their safety and happiness, and that the absolute and arbitrary power over the lives, liberty, and property of freemen exists nowhere in a republic, not even in the largest majority, would be but an empty sound if the legislature could prohibit the citizen the right of owning or drinking liquor, when in so doing he did not offend the laws of decency by being intoxicated in public.

So pronounced the opinion of the U.S. Supreme Court in the 1915 decision of *Adams Express Co. v. Kentucky*. That opinion was quoting another, contemporaneous decision by the State Supreme Court of Kentucky. That land of Early Times Kentucky Whiskey® was apparently once a bastion of the constitutional liberty in drink. Yet the county of distillation for Kentucky's other famous liquor product, Bourbon whiskey, was—until very recently—so dry that tourists on local distillery tours were denied the option of tasting a sample.

The early years of the American republic set the stage for the American alcohol experience, in life and the law. This prologue presents those years as a prelude to our study—an aperitif, as it were. It may be taken, as is the aperitif beverage, to prepare the palate for what is to come. Thirsts already whetted may skip ahead to the first chapter dedicated to a single judicial era and its constitutional cocktail.

Any prelude to a study of alcohol and the Supreme Court must begin by mentioning the three short-tenure chief justices who launched the institution of the federal judiciary. These three were John Jay (1789–1795), John Rutledge (1795), and Oliver Ellsworth (1796–1800). They were all well-known and well-regarded men of their time, patriots and federalists, appointed to give distinction to a new and fledging judicial branch. To this end their tenures were of limited effect. Not only that, their courts rendered no decisions that were liquor related. The relevance of their early court era lies in the role that alcohol and drinking were already playing in American public life—a role that subsequent Supreme Courts would build upon, once they had some actual cases to decide.

Each of the early chiefs presided over a court that had little to do while in session in the national capital, so the justices spent most of their time on the road, "riding circuit." This practice amounted to each justice riding from tavern boardinghouse to tavern boardinghouse in his assigned geographic jurisdiction of states, holding ad hoc appellate court sittings with local federal district judges. Sometimes the sittings were in the tavern itself, due to the want of suitable quarters for a courtroom. The weary traveling jurists could at least soothe themselves at each posting, but it did not prevent them from quitting (or sickening and dying) in quick succession.[1]

Jay, the very first chief justice of the United States, was the first and most prominent of the three authors of *The Federalist Papers*—although he wrote the fewest of them. Jay functioned more as the marquee name around which to organize this tract written to convince the people of the American states (and, in particular, Jay's pivotal home state of New York) to ratify the new Constitution. Interestingly, even *The Federalist* makes mention of alcohol: in number 12, Alexander Hamilton argues that among the laudable powers of the new national government is the authority to levy excise taxes on "ardent spirits," providing needed and fairly apportioned revenue. Hamilton goes on, in this aside to the general topic of the practical power of one national government:

> That article [of ardent spirits] would well bear this rate of duty, and if it should tend to diminish the consumption of it, such an effect would be equally favorable to the agriculture, to the economy, to the

morals, and to the health of the society. There is nothing so much a
subject of national extravagance as this very article.

Jay's few and initial entries, by contrast, are concerned more blandly
with security against the hostility of foreign nations. But he too had
temperance leanings—at least, if the religious scruples that would come
to inform Jay's later abolitionist activism are taken into account. Still, it
is important to recognize that the "temperance" of some of the founding fathers was just that: *tempering* one's indulgence, and largely directed at drams of hard liquor or "ardent spirits."

As for what this meant for Jay himself, he was a known connoisseur
of wines who, during his diplomatic mission as the Continental Congress minister to Spain, "made it a point to sample every possible
brand" of Spanish wine he came across.[2] *The Spirits of America* also
suggests that Jay was fairly good-spirited in his moderation. As its author recounts, "John Jay seldom went to a social gathering of any sort
without taking up a position at the punch bowl, acting as unofficial
greeter as he served cup after cup of liquid fire to himself and others."[3]
Punch, in its classic four-part formula of "one strong, one weak, one
sour, one sweet," was the favorite mixed drink of the precocktail seventeenth and eighteenth centuries.[4] Brandy and rum were its most common "strong" ingredients, and its strength as a libation presumably varied with its preparer. As did its respectability. An early advocate for the
medical benefits of sobriety, Dr. Benjamin Rush—Declaration of Independence signer and physician-contemporary of Jay's—produced a
chart detailing "the effects of liquor on the bodies and minds of men"
and "the progress of temperance and intemperance." (His "Moral and
Physical Thermometer" of 1791 has become the stuff of legend, now
more ironically than otherwise. But while he was largely a voice in the
wilderness in his own time period, he greatly influenced the antialcohol
movement of the nineteenth century.) Punch was right on the border-
line. Rush classified weak or mild punch along with wine or strong beer,
with effects including "cheerfulness, strength, and nourishment, when
taken only in small quantities." But once punch crossed into the strong
category, Rush saw the deleterious consequences of its intake as "idle-
ness and gaming, sickness and debt." One trusts that Jay took care with
his imbibing.

Once appointed to the court in 1789, Jay spent a good portion of his chief justiceship serving as a special ambassador in Great Britain, negotiating the post–Revolutionary War resolution. This no doubt took place over glasses of port, given English predilections at that time—whether Jay joined in with gusto or not, we cannot know. Subsequent to the ratification of the Jay Treaty, he resigned from the bench in 1795 after his election as governor of his home state of New York. President Washington then named as his successor John Rutledge, who had briefly served as an associate justice before quitting in somewhat of a huff. Rutledge lives more in infamy than the other early chiefs, in that his appointment was never confirmed by the Senate, due to his contentious public stance on the aforementioned Jay Treaty. He ended his days in despondency and, it was said, drink. Less than one year later, in 1796, Washington nominated Oliver Ellsworth in replacement as chief. Ill throughout his service, Ellsworth spent a good deal of his short tenure as part of a diplomatic mission to France—where one hopes he enjoyed more than dry, consular conversation.

Although there were no alcohol-related decisions from the bench under these protochiefs, there was plenty of alcohol being quaffed. Ironically, intoxication and public service were inextricably linked long before the highest federal court could ever rule on the matter of alcohol and the law. This linkage came in the Congress's attack on the competence of Federalist Judge John Pickering. Already impaired in health and basic functioning when President Washington appointed him to the federal district court in 1795, Pickering would become the first federal judge to be impeached in the new United States—indeed, the first federal official to be impeached and so removed. Charged with bad moral character due to drunkenness, Pickering's case and subsequent removal from the bench in 1804 occasioned a raging political controversy over whether he had committed the "high crimes or misdemeanors" required by Article II, section 4 of the U.S. Constitution.

A less dramatically alcohol-inflected early judicial episode was the Supreme Court's very first meeting. This occurred in 1790 in New York City, where the U.S. government resided before the building of the federal city capital in Washington. Concluding their inaugural sitting after having no cases to hear, the Jay Justices went to a local tavern for dinner where they made thirteen different toasts, including one to the Constitution and one to the new judicial institution.[5] It is not recorded what Chief Justice Jay led his associates in imbibing, but a survey of tastes of the time helps us to speculate.

Rum was the colonial spirit of choice; it was part of colonial life—and became a large part of colonial complaint as well. It was British tariffs on molasses (1733) and sugar (1764) imported from the Caribbean that helped fuel colonial resentment against imperial rule. Both were used to distill rum, with many such distilleries located in Massachusetts and Rhode Island. Resentment over British interference with the production of a beloved local elixir birthed the Boston Caucus, whose members made the Green Dragon tavern on Union Street the "headquarters" of the American Revolution.[6] Similarly, the City Tavern in Philadelphia became the unofficial location of the Continental Congress, where "sophisticated libations such as Madeira wine, slings, toddies, and flips" could be had.[7] Peter Thompson's 1999 account of tavern going and public life in eighteenth-century Philadelphia, *Rum Punch and Revolution,* identifies the City Tavern as "lavishly built through subscriptions by 'gentleman proprietors' and, as such, a first step in the splintering along class lines of a formerly unitary tavern culture in the colonial period."[8] Perhaps it is not surprising, then, that thirteen years later, City Tavern was the site of the relatively elite gentlemen delegates' behind-the-scenes deliberations over the pending constitution in the summer of 1787.[9] Still, the more typical interclass jostling of colonial Philadelphia tavern life "made a valuable contribution to the 'small politics' of everyday life" and "supported 'a polity in which the ruled feel that their rulers are accessible.'"[10] Tavern keepers tended to be proindependence as a result of the many taxes they had been subjected to over the years, with almost every aspect of the tavern subject to regulation, or a license—whether from Parliament or colonial, and later, new state legislatures.[11]

Targets of governmental regulation or no, taverns *as meeting places* incubated the revolution and its cry for liberty. Jefferson's Declaration of Independence was likely composed in a tavern, "glass of madeira at his side."[12] And, as the *Rum Punch and Revolution* author concludes, "revolutionary era Philadelphians 'continued to believe that speech and action in public—*especially in taverns*—held singular significance as likely indicators of the true value of men and ideas'" (emphasis added).[13]

So what were these "public men" imbibing along with their revolutionary sentiment? *Imbibe!* calls the **flip** "the mighty quaff of Colonial days—when Flips were made from quarts of ale and gills of strong rum, thickened with eggs and sugar and poured back and forth from pitcher to pitcher in the traditional rainbow arc."[14] *And a Bottle of Rum* seconds this, while also detailing the many and varied rum concoctions the colonial tavernkeeper could be expected to offer.[15] Toddy hot in the winter (especially the apple version, made with cider brandy and baked apple) and sling cold in the summer[16] was one of the invariables of American drinking from the middle of the eighteenth century until the end of the nineteenth, says *Imbibe!*[17] A list of spirit-based recreational drinks of America published in the *Pennsylvania Gazette* of 1788 mentions toddy, grog, sling, and bitters—or stomach elixir.[18] In health or for ill health, there was an alcoholic tonic.

Liquors of all kinds figured in all parts of the American experience. While the rum-related "triangle trade"—involving New England rum to Africa, slaves from there to the Caribbean, and sugar from the West Indies to North America—was perhaps an overblown myth,[19] rum was nevertheless one of New England's major trading commodities,[20] and British interference with it engendered colonial resentment. Significantly, the British taxes also diverted domestic production into other alcoholic substances, namely, grain whiskey. But rum remained the king of colonial mixology—as it had also been central to trade and congress with the Indian tribes. It was a devious device, as Benjamin Franklin mused in his *Autobiography*: "If it be the Design of Providence to extirpate these Savages in order to make room for Cultivators of the Earth, it seems not improbably that Rum may be the appointed Means." Elixir or poison, rum may have had few contenders, but some few it nonetheless did. French brandy and Dutch gin (or Genever) were known, and consumed, but their imported status and higher price limited their widespread appeal. Many New Englanders (like John Adams) and upstate New Yorkers (like Chief Justice John Jay) favored fermented, hard cider—with applejack (or cider brandy) being its distillate, usually and sometimes inadvertently made through the freezing of a cider barrel. (Rather a regular risk in those frigid winter climes.) Domestic and honorable, cider was the pre-Revolutionary daily beverage of choice, from Virginia northward, and "probably" accounted for more of the total alcohol ingested than rum.[21] Peach brandy was the analogous Southern fruit specialty of the colonial period. Philadelphia famously produced porter, which found favor with many in the 1770s, including George Washington. The Continental Army general and first president was truly a man of varied and catholic tastes when it came to alcoholic beverages: Barbados rum was served at his inaugural ball,[22] and unaged, clear rye whiskey was produced by Washington (among other colonial luminaries) in his career as a distiller after he retired from the presidency.[23] Madeira was the favorite of every gentleman of the early Republic; port was the fortified wine preferred in England but was much less available in the Americas and, besides which, had a loyalist tinge. Indeed, one of the objectives of the Sugar Act of 1764 had been to tax the more favored sweet wine so as to direct the American palate from madeira to port, to direct the proceeds of the colonials' purchasing away from Portuguese coffers and into English ones.[24] Smuggled madeira was drunk instead.

Such a range of other alcoholic products notwithstanding, rum consumption in the late eighteenth century also fell victim to changing tastes, and to an animated American nationalism. As *And a Bottle of Rum* puts it:

> American consumers had come to regard rum as an artifact of the ancient regime, a product associated with the imperious British. . . . Prior to the Revolution, drinking rum was a sign of the growing affluence and independence of the colonists. It demonstrated they were prosperous enough to purchase rum made abroad—and later to manufacture their own rum from raw materials acquired through trade. . . . But following the war, rum took on a whiff of national weakness and vulnerability, and became an emblem of financial imprisonment.[25]

Such powerful political symbolism attaching to an alcohol would occur again and again in American life and culture.

So "if rum was the spirit of the past, what was the spirit of the future? Without question, it was whiskey."[26] Domestic grain whiskey began its rise to prominence well before independence, as essential to the political economy of the Back Country. Given the logistic difficulties of dispatching surplus grain to market, farmers distilled it as a commodity for easier and more profitable trade. When the Royal Navy blockade of American ports during the Revolutionary War made both rum and molasses imports from the West Indies scarce, whiskey filled the demand for spirits. One of the biggest whiskey consumers of the time period was the Continental Army, which provided soldiers a daily liquor ration of four ounces.[27] After the war, Maryland and Pennsylvania would become national centers of rye production; frontier Kentucky, of corn whiskey—or "Bourbon," taken from the name of the county where it was first produced.[28]

Whiskey, like rum, also played a key part in the politics of the young nation. The provocation was a 1791 congressional statute taxing distilled spirits. The Excise Act was passed to help service the war debt of the new country, and its tax on spirits domestically produced and from domestic ingredients was the lowest rate, but these local whiskeys were still taxed. As *Drinking in America: A History* explains, "Alexander Hamilton, the new nation's first secretary of the treasury, rightly foresaw a bonanza in revenues on distilled liquor, although there are also hints in the documents that temperance sympathies in men like Hamilton and Madison helped place whiskey on the taxable list."[29] The desirability of such a tax was discussed even under the Articles of Confederation that preceded the Constitution of 1789; Hamilton had urged its adoption as an excise in *Federalist* 12 as among the benefits of the stronger federal government. But these federalist niceties mattered little to the objecting small farmers, for the 1791 tax applied even to small amounts produced for noncommercial, personal consumption purposes. It also smacked of the same liberty-curtailing interference that the British had inflicted, and against which the colonists had made revolution. Opposition protests escalated into the Whiskey Rebellion of 1792–1794. Protesters in Pennsylvania used violence and intimidation to prevent federal officials from collecting the tax; after some failed efforts at negotiation, President Washington ordered an army of militiamen to suppress the insurgency. The rebels all went home before the arrival of the troops, and there was no confrontation—they "vaporized like rye mash when the heat was applied."[30] But the incident illustrated two important but somewhat discordant things: the unquestionable enforcement power of the new national government, and a culture of defiance of the law, for the excise tax remained difficult to collect from small distillers in the hinterlands of western Pennsylvania and the backwoods of Kentucky. The Whiskey Rebellion not only showed the importance of distilling to the frontier economy of the time, it also "high-lighted conflicts between regions and classes in the early U.S."[31]

Nor would it be the last time that bootlegging would function as patriotic resistance.

That friend of liberty and fine French wine, Thomas Jefferson, would see the whiskey tax repealed when he and his Republican Party took office in 1801. His own opposition was fueled in large part by his ideological opposition to Hamilton's Federalist Party policies. This brings us to one final, partisan connection between drinking and early republican period politics: that found in the formation of the Demo-cratic-Republican clubs, which grew out of the patriotic Cincinnati So-ciety of Continental Army veterans. The clubs denounced what they saw as the new and tyrannously centralizing Federalist values, and were the origin of both the Democratic Party and the Tammany Hall political machine. As the author of *America Walks into a Bar* writes: "The Dem-ocratic Party was conceived in a tavern and spent many of its first years there—drinking and recording its traditional sixteen toasts at each meeting." This was for the sixteen states of the union in 1799, the date of the Tammany Society's founding.[32]

If years later, some opponents would still call the Democratic Party the party of "Rum, Romanism, and Rebellion," this only illustrates the power of the political metaphor of liquor. Even so, and while pleasingly alliterative, the particular metaphoric association is anachronistic, for by the time of its application in the presidential contest of 1884, rum had long ceased to be any politico's spirit of choice. "Demon rum" had, however, acquired the meaning of a general (and generally disparaging) reference to liquor or intoxicating spirits.

What's past is only prologue, for there was clearly more drinking than law about it in the eighteenth-century republic. The early times of the three early chief justices do reveal a nexus between alcohol and politics in America—even between specific alcohols and specific politics. But it would not be until the era of the great jurist Chief Justice John Marshall that the link between the Supreme Court and drinking would really develop. Not only is his court the first to register constitutional law's attention to alcohol, Marshall is the first and perhaps the greatest epi-cure of drink to sit as its chief.

I

THE MARSHALL ERA OF PUNCH AND THE PUBLIC HOUSE

The first Supreme Court decision involving alcoholic drink occurs in 1817,[1] some fifteen years into the tenure of Chief Justice John Marshall. It concerned the imposition of a federal license duty on stills for the production of spirituous liquors, the result of an act of Congress in 1813 to help defray the cost of the War of 1812. In the case, the U.S. government sought to recover the licensing fee from defendant Tenbroek, charging that the lower court had acted in error in not applying it to him. The controversy turned on the distinction between distillation and rectification (or purification) of spirits, and the Marshall Court agreed with the defendant that the latter was a distinct process to which the duty did not apply. The opinion in *U.S. v. Tenbroek* is interesting in that Justice Gabriel Duvall, writing for the court, evinces a detailed knowledge of the chemistry of stills and their products.[2] Chief Justice Marshall's first, and apparently only, opinion concerning an alcohol-related regulation would not come for another fifteen years. Yet compared to the dearth of decisions under the chief justices who preceded him, Marshall presided over an era whose handful of decisions presaged important legal debates—while also presiding during an era of unabashed joviality.

Accordingly, then, our first chapter concerns the *Marshall Court* era (1801–1835). This chapter will set the format that all subsequent chapters will follow. It begins with a brief, encapsulating introduction. It then identifies the signature cocktail for the era, explaining why this particular alcoholic beverage is chosen. A sketch of the alcohol culture of the times follows, attending to both the culture of enjoyment and the liquors that were part of it, and the corresponding culture of regulation. Next, a detailed summary of the alcohol-related decisions of the Supreme Court during the era is presented. Decisions are grouped by topic or theme but discussed chronologically within these categories, to give a sense of the development of legal doctrine and the justices' general thinking about drinking. The chapter closes with a brief conclusion that distills the essence of the era's contributions, both libational and doctrinal.

Terminology matters to specialists, but because this book is attempting to boundary cross, it takes some liberties. First, I am using the term "cocktail" somewhat loosely, to refer to the concoctions, beverages, or brews that captivated the tastes of an era. I do realize that "cocktail" has a very specific definition for mixology; where relevant to developments with respect to imbibing in a given era, I will point this out. Second, although constitutional jurisprudence and judicial decision making is my scholarly expertise, my discussion of Supreme Court cases will make every effort to wade through and pare down the technicalities and legalese. Of course, I am concerned with how the alcohol decisions fit within the legal policy making of the various court eras, but I try to establish those connections as painlessly as possible for nonlawyers and non–political scientists. I care about what most of my general readers likely also care about: attitudes toward liquor in American life, through the lens of American constitutional law. Often, the justices making those pronouncements provide the fun for all of us, in the very language of their opinions. I quote from them when it is too tempting not to. Lastly, I am an academic but not an academic historian. I use archival artifacts but not the archivist's painstaking methodology: I pick and choose what adds richness to my story but I make no claims to be exhaustive in uncovering the documentary evidence of our alcohol-laced past. All I will say in my own spirited defense is that mine is a more popular than a professional historical exercise. Many elements make up each court era and its cocktail hour, from political institutions' decisions and policies to society's cultural phenomena to ordinary people's daily lives. My chapters partake of all this material, as I could find and assemble it. I encourage those who thirst for more details to belly up to the Supreme Court bar on their own.

Punch and the American Revolution tie the first chief justice to the first great chief justice, as does the challenge of establishing the supremacy of the new national government under the Constitution and the authority of its Supreme Court. Only John Marshall rose to this challenge, and this is how history remembers him—for seminal state-building decisions such as *Marbury v. Madison* (1803) and *McCulloch v. Maryland* (1819). But both John Jay and John Marshall were accomplished statesmen of the early republic, and that early republic was a punch-drinking time. *Imbibe!* identifies the era of punch as the 1670s through the 1850s, a long tenure indeed.[3] Its classic composition of "one strong, one weak, one sour, one sweet" admitted an infinite variety of tasty combinations, using a variety of liquors and ingredients. Punch is usually thought of as a protococktail, as it lacks one of the cocktail's essential items: aromatic bitters. But this should in no way suggest that it is an inferior concoction. To the contrary, its refinement lies in its balance of flavors, so recipes were jealously guarded things.

Though Jay's particular preferences are lost in obscurity, the drink of John Marshall's era is unquestionably **Quoit Club Punch**, a rum-brandy-madeira based mixture lightened with lemons and ice and sweetened with sugar. This specific recipe was drunk at Marshall's own Quoit Club in Richmond, Virginia, as cocktail historian David Wondrich relates in *Punch: The Delights (and Dangers) of the Flowing Bowl*. The Quoit Club was just as it name indicates: a gentlemen's private social club whose principal—but well lubricated—activity was the lawn sport of quoits. Marshall spent a fair amount of time here, as his circuit duties as a member of the Supreme Court included his home turf of Virginia. Wondrich offers this account of the chief justice, his club, and his beverage:

> The thirty members of the Richmond, Virginia, Quoit Club, founded in 1788, met every other Saturday from May until October "under the shade of some fine oaks," as one visitor recalled, at Buchanan's Spring, right outside of town. There they would throw the heavy, ring-like quoits at posts, eat barbecue and drink themselves silly on Mint Julep, Toddy and this, the club's Punch, which was prepared with great skill by Jasper Crouch, their black cook. The club's most

famous member was one of its founders, John Marshall, chief justice
of the United States Supreme Court.[4]

Marshall himself was a convivial tippler and positively bibulous by
modern standards. Like most gentlemen of his time and stature, most
of his consuming of intoxicants occurred in the social confines of the
private club. Those clubs were the descendants of the English seven-
teenth-century coffeehouse and tavern discussion societies that migrated from taking a private room in a public establishment for their activities, to securing their own building, membership, and dining and
drinking facilities.[5] Mary Newton Standard in *John Marshall and His
Home* refers to Marshall's Richmond "barbeque club" where quoits
were played after (noon) dinner, "at which julep, punch and toddy were
allowed, though wine was prohibited except on special occasions."[6] On
one occasion in the late 1820s "a basket of champagne" was obtained by
fining two members for discussing the subject of politics, a conversa-
tional topic that was forbidden at the club. Interestingly, the champagne was drunk from tumblers, as the club possessed no proper stemware for wine. The same source also recounts the Quoit Club "bowl of
mint julep" incident, occurring in 1829. This oft-told anecdote cheerily
recounts the chief justice warming up to a mighty toss of the quoit after
a healthy swig from the julep bowl.[7] Claire Cushman's more recent
Courtwatchers attributes the story to portrait painter Chester Harding,
who says Marshall was seventy-five at the time.[8] By all accounts, Marshall appears to have been good company, sober or warmed up. So
cherished was Marshall's company by his fellows that after his death,
one of the club members, Senator Benjamin Watkins Leigh, moved that
the club never fill the vacancy but always leave the number of members
one less than it had been.[9]

Cushman's *Courtwatchers* confirms that Marshall had a taste for
spirits and frequented Richmond taverns when at home. He shared his
Revolutionary-generation contemporaries' fondness for madeira, an ingredient in the Quoit Club punch mentioned above. He likewise shared
his contemporaries' predilection for integrating alcohol use into all aspects of daily life. Cushman, again, notes that alcohol was far from a
purely recreational pastime for the chief, who arranged for vintage wine
to be shipped to Washington each term in bottles labeled "The Supreme Court" *and* insisted that all the justices join in a glass of madeira

at dinner together as a kind of professional requirement.[10] Gregarious and personable, John Marshall projected these qualities onto the justices' shared social and work spaces. Part of his greatness as chief justice was the aplomb with which he combined what judicial scholars call "social" and "task" leadership on the bench—getting things done but getting them done smoothly and affably. His personality was certainly a factor in his success, but so was one key feature of the Marshall justices' service: their *shared* and, to twenty-first-century eyes, boozily social workspace.

Another unmistakable aspect of imbibing in the Marshall era—aside from its copiousness—was how much it was part of the work life of the court. For most all of Marshall's tenure, all the justices lived and worked together in a Washington, DC, boarding house, with their conferences about the cases they had heard occurring in the boardinghouse tavern or common rooms. In Marshall's time, the boardinghouse was both respite and workplace, as well as bane of the federal judicial existence. This was because judicial circuit riding was (and would be, for quite a long time) a feature of Supreme Court service, and the traveling justices sitting for intermediate federal court appeals were expected to hole up at the country's taverns. These were often not very inviting, where the bed might well be straw-stuffed and shared and the board was typically pork products and some sort of grog. Immersion in the context of the common man's experience was inevitable. Enthusing about the practice in 1826, one member of Congress lauded the justices getting out and communing with the people: they would *and should* receive the full benefit of the conversations of learned tapsters and others, in taverns, boardinghouses, and bar rooms.[11] Not to mention a full acquaintance, salutary or otherwise, with the typical fare—liquid and solid—being served in American public settings.

While this congressman was likely putting a positive spin on a fairly uncomfortable obligation, he cannot have been unfamiliar with the tavern himself. From Fourteenth Street on down toward the Capitol and near E and F Streets was the location of the old "Rum Row." This area included the famous watering holes of the Old Ebbitt House and the Willard Hotel, plus legions of boardinghouse hotels where members of Congress resided during their months in Washington.[12] The area also thrummed with political saloons well through the nineteenth century.[13] The congressional boardinghouse settlement, where members clustered in houses by region, was a self-contained village community in the Jeffersonian period, minimizing interinstitutional interaction. Eight boardinghouses, a tailor, a shoemaker, a washerwoman, a grocery store, and an oyster house served the congressional settlement in 1801. In later years, a liquor store and taverns had been added.[14] Communal political living was thus a fact of political life in the capital's early decades. As to the justices, one source notes that they too were part of a boardinghouse community,

> Liv[ing] in the style of the brotherhood they felt themselves to be, all rooming and taking meals at a common table in the same lodging house on Capitol Hill. "The judges here live in perfect harmony . . . in the most frank and unaffected intimacy," wrote Justice Story, one of Marshall's colleagues. "We are all united as one. . . . We moot every question as we proceed, and . . . conferences at our lodgings often come to a very quick, and, I trust, a very accurate opinion, in a few hours." Not until 1845, apparently, did the judicial fraternity break up, with four justices going to live in one house and three in another.[15]

This would have been well after Marshall's time, and into his successor Roger B. Taney's era.

The place intended for the Supreme Court's building remained swamp, unoccupied and undeveloped. The expense of development was considered unwarranted, given the small size of the court establishment and the small volume of business handled by the justices during their brief two-month stay in Washington each year. The court, we are told, "made itself inconspicuous and served justice in the basement of the Capitol. 'It is by no means a large or handsome apartment, and the lowness of the ceiling, and the circumstances of it being underground, give a certain cellar like aspect, which . . . tends to create . . . the impression of justice being done in a corner.'"[16] For this source of the period, the court's relative isolation meant that the justices have "only a minor place in a study of the governmental community during [the time]. . . . In the sociological sense the justices were barely members of the Washington community." Even the organizational effect of their cohabitation was unremarkable to political historian James Sterling Young. "The unanimity of their case decisions provides little food for political analysis," he writes, beyond the observation that their single-mindedness on policy questions *conformed to the fraternal character of their lifestyle* [emphasis added]; and the justices were too secretive about their activities in their boardinghouse to afford insights about the group *in camera*. Moreover, they lived such a reclusive existence that the community record does little more than note their presence in the capital. They rarely received guests and they rarely ventured out of their lodgings after hours except to make obligatory appearances at official functions and to pay an annual courtesy call, en bloc, at the executive mansion. . . . Justice Story perhaps spoke for the group when he wrote: "I scarcely go to any places of pleasure or fashion . . . [and] have separated myself from all political meetings and associations . . . since I am no longer a political man."[17]

On this reading, separation of powers was "separation of persons" and each of the branches became "a self-contained, segregated social system within the larger governmental establishment."[18] In the case of the Supreme Court, "the maintenance of 'social distance' vis-à-vis members of the 'political' branches accorded with both the recognized proprieties of judicial conduct and, presumably, the interest of the judiciary in maintaining its own independence."[19] So argues Young in his *The Washington Community, 1800–1828,* which makes a fairly thorough study of the collegial domestic arrangements of Washington's early political class.

Other scholars of the period paint a somewhat different picture of the working life of the court. G. Edward White, in his *Marshall Court and Cultural Change,* says that the justices' correspondence suggests a more active social life than the somewhat monastic existence Young depicts, with regular attendance at dinners and balls and with Marshall himself seldom turning down an invitation. A letter of 1830 to his wife, Polly, refers to "how gay and sprightly the wine made me" at one dinner party.[20] White also confirms the justices' living together in boardinghouses, from 1815 to 1830, with "the particular boarding house var[ying] from year to year, and during the summer months the justices would correspond with one another about arrangements."[21] Indeed, after the burning of the Capitol in 1814, the court was forced to convene entirely in a private home for the next two years, only returning to their somewhat refurbished basement room in 1819. White retells of the Marshall justices living under the same roof, taking their meals together, and working within the same small building.[22] He, however, does not assume that the high degree of seeming judicial unanimity during this time necessarily stemmed from cohabitative conviviality.

It is certainly true that upon assuming the chief justiceship, Marshall had instituted the single, institutional opinion of the court as the Supreme Court's legal voice. Prior to that, the justices had written serial and separate opinions that taken together decided the cases brought to them. Marshall's thinking was that a single opinion "of the court" would enhance its authority and prominence as the third federal branch. It is also true that Marshall often wrote these opinions speaking for the court, and that the opinions were frequently unanimous. Other justices, nonopinion authors, were given discretion to record their opinions, but seldom did so. White construes justices who declined to publish their concurrences or dissents as being freed from being formally accountable for their votes, with silence allowing a certain amount of latitude for ambiguity: it could be reluctantly going along, or passively objecting.[23] Unanimity, under this interpretation, looks less than enthusiastic or even voluntary. When, after 1829, the court modified its living custom, with Justices McLean and Johnson neither taking their meals nor sleeping in the judicial boardinghouse quarters, more frequent dissents did appear.[24] This suggests that cohabitation did have a force, but one that was easily and perhaps eagerly averted once boardinghouse life ceased.

Still, "Marshall clearly associated collective residence in a boardinghouse with the production of collective opinions of the court and was therefore willing to work to ensure the boardinghouse setting." He regularly informed himself about prospective boardinghouse arrangements for the next term.[25] The clientele at Mrs. Dunn's on North Capitol Street was known to be "exclusively judicial," and "became a favorite."[26] In a letter of 1831 to Story, Marshall speaks of "Brown's Hotel" as a place he favored, where the justices had boarded for several years, but that Justice Baldwin showed a decided preference for "Mrs. Peyton's."[27] Why is lost to posterity, but by this time, Brown's had become Brown's Indian Queen Hotel, at 6th and Pennsylvania; its proprietor, Jesse Brown, would ensure that large complimentary decanters of brandy wine and whiskey were placed at each table setting. A subsequent letter of Marshall's confirmed that their next winter's arrangement would be to quarter with "Ringold,"[28] known to be the Ringgold

House at 1801 F Street. John Marshall Memorial Park, on Pennsylvania between 4th and 5th Streets, "marks the historic site of a boarding house where Marshall and his fellow Supreme Court Justices drafted many of their landmark opinions." So claims the Memorial Park Foundation website, in any case. All the boardinghouse establishments would have provided similar accommodations, with private rooms for each justice, a common dining room that would double as a conference chamber, and plain, solid victuals accompanied by various alcoholic beverages.

Young's study also reports the prevalence of wine—meaning madeira or some such fortified type—at the early nineteenth-century boardinghouse table. His account comes in the context of frayed tempers due to the long, close quarters in the congressional boardinghouse, as this anecdote reveals: "In a sudden affray at the table in Miss Shields' boardinghouse, Randolph, pouring out a glass of wine, dashed it in Alston's face. Alston sent a decanter at his head in return, [and] there was much destruction of glassware."[29] Such liquor-fueled hijinks notwithstanding, "after-dinner parlor assemblages in the boarding houses were 'caucuses'"—or, in the Supreme Court's case, conferences—"in fact even if they were not so in name. Common rooms or parlors were where members assembled after dinner to play cards, tell tales, talk over the events of the day, 'and then for politics,'" Young writes.[30] By contrast, boardinghouses were frowned on in executive society as déclassé at best, with a boardinghouse executive residing in a separate suite of rooms and dining separately, when he did board. Rather, the basic unit of executive society was the family household. This too would be the court's form of living once the justices moved on from rooming together—with their homes in the capital also constituting their workspaces, before the twentieth-century erection of their building with its judicial offices.[31]

Whatever the nature or influence of the court's collective boarding, alcohol was clearly a lubricant to the coassociation. A famous anecdote about Marshall gives this strong impression, and is quoted here, at length:

> Vinous drink had no greater devotee than Chief Justice John Marshall. At the boarding house in Washington where the Supreme Court justices lived, the boarders permitted wine only in wet weather, for the sake of their health. Upon occasion, the Chief Justice

would command Justice Story to check the window to see if it were raining. When informed that the sun shone brightly, Marshall would observe, "All the better, for our jurisdiction extends over so large a territory that the doctrine of chances makes it certain that it must be raining somewhere." The chief justice, observed Story, had been "brought up upon Federalist and Madeira, and he [was] not the man to outgrow his early prejudices."[32]

Ben Perley Poore's *Reminiscences*, a period source, also comments on the convivial communal lifestyle of the Marshall justices: they were "a rather jovial set," for "the best madeira was that labeled 'the Supreme Court' as their Honors, the Justices, used to make a direct importation every year, and sip it as they consulted over the cases before them, every day after dinner, when the cloth had been removed."[33]

Of Marshall's era, and the early nineteenth century generally, it is worth noting that there were numerous occasions at which it was conventional to drink alcoholic beverages, of a variety of kinds. *The Alcoholic Republic* names several: drams (or small shots of straight liquor) in the morning, the "elevens" when gentlemen adjourned from business for a hot toddy (whiskey, sugar, and hot water) or a hot sling (with gin substituted), the Virginia gentry's 1 p.m. julep prior to dinner in the afternoon.[34] Many of these practices applied to men, and to men of a certain class standing only, but alcohol was used by women, children, and the elderly—perhaps less socially than therapeutically, but used nonetheless. In terms of raw consumption, by the 1830s, average per capita alcohol intake was over 7 gallons.[35] Indeed, Marshall's era coincides with the highest average annual consumption of absolute alcohol, about 7.1 gallons per person, sustained over several decades from 1810 to 1830. The notion that alcohol was good for the health remained firmly fixed in this period. Ardent spirits were basically part of the diet, taken at breakfast, midmorning, and midafternoon, during and after dinner to aid digestion, and as a "strengthening" nightcap before bed. One recipe for a healthful such evening potion called for whiskey, maple syrup, nutmeg, and boiling water, then dashed with rum. Even nondrinkers kept a supply of spirits on hand for guests—it was considered polite.[36]

In terms of drinking behaviors, also noteworthy about this era is the first usage of the word "cocktail." The word refers to a "bittered" sling: a sling—liquor, water, and sugar—to which some kind of aromatic bitters are added. Bitters themselves had an esteemed medicinal heritage in Europe, dating from the Medieval era discovery and early practice of distillation and infusion of various roots and herbs in alcohol. But the genius of combining them with spirits like whiskey and gin was, if not an American invention, then an American advancement. The earliest, explicit cocktail references seem to have been an 1803 newspaper entry and, then, in 1806 a more substantial and politically resonant reference in a Whig newspaper. Detailing a bar bill incurred by a Republican candidate plying voters, the editor listed among the rum grogs and gin-slings, "25 dozen cocktails" which he described as a drink of spirits, sugar, and bitters that after being swallowed, "a person . . . is ready to swallow anything else"—presumably, any political malarkey.[37]

Various contemporary cocktail anthologies—*Imbibe!* for one, but also *And a Bottle of Rum*—provide alternative etymological accounts of the origins of the term "cocktail,"[38] but concur with the 1806 account of its first documented U.S. usage. Both emphasize that a cocktail by definition always contains bitters. There were various popular brands of bitters in the nineteenth century, originally designed to be taken on their own—as stomach tonics, pick-me-ups, and invigorators. The cocktail, too, was initially a morning therapeutic, or a before-bedtime prescription. From its earliest days—say, the 1810s and 1820s—the cocktail was overwhelmingly a room-temperature "tonic," while the julep (which also has roots in this early period) was a "cooling drink," meant to be sipped and with ice.[39] Once rum fell from popular favor and before the reign of whiskey, Holland gin (a malty, sweet style, as opposed to the modern, London dry style) and brandy were the two most popular spirits used for the early, bittered-sling cocktails, as both spirits were for the contemporaneous (unbittered) slings. Punch did not disappear in the early years of the cocktail, but rather migrated from Marshall's familiar bowl to the individual portion of the small bar glass.

While alcohol was greatly more a part of court life than the court docket under Marshall, important law with liquor as its subject had begun to make an appearance. Two substantively minor cases occur in the era's early decades; these were mentioned at the outset of this chapter. By comparison, *Brown v. Maryland* in 1827 was of great consequence for several reasons. First, the decision was Chief Justice Marshall's first, and apparently only, opinion concerning an alcohol-related regulation. Second, the ruling was one of the few, but eventually growing number of, nonunanimous decisions issued by the Marshall bench. Finally, the holding was the first to properly feature a nexus between alcohol and *constitutional law*, and it also nicely conforms to the national supremacist jurisprudence for which the Marshall era is best known.

The state of Maryland had required a license for importers and sellers of "foreign articles, or commodities, of dry goods, wares, or merchandises, or of *wine, rum, brandy, whiskey, and other distilled spirituous liquors*" (emphasis added). Not surprisingly, given Marshall's fierce protection of federal authority over interstate commerce, his decision invalidated the state license fee as violating the commerce clause of Article I, as well as the constitutional proscription against a state "lay[ing] any impost or duty" on foreign imports. The decision in *Brown* would be an important precedent for the future—not just for the understanding of federal commerce versus state tax powers, but for its understanding of "imports." In affirming that the states had no constitutional authority to lay duties on foreign imports, Marshall proceeded to define imported goods. He essentially circumscribed when an article entering a state's commerce became something a state could legislatively act upon, thus ensuring that "imported" products, while they retained the identity as imports, were beyond the state's control. His definition not only removed import items from state jurisdiction, it led to a doctrine that insulated foreign and out-of-state imports from state action under the states' legitimate powers, such as tax or police powers. *Brown* would thus have far-reaching implications for the out-of-state importation of alcohol as a consumable. Even though the particular case facts concerned dry goods and not liquor per se, the ruling's ramifications for the transit of liquor and a state's regulation of what came across its borders were portentous.

The case also elicited one of the rare Marshall era dissents recorded; interestingly, it also occurred while the justices were still cohabiting in the same boardinghouse. Even the dissenter, Justice Smith Thompson, noted the unusualness of the lack of unanimity, opening his opinion with this candid mea culpa:

> It is with some reluctance and very considerable diffidence that I have brought myself publicly to dissent from the opinion of the Court in this case, and did it not involve an important constitutional question relating to the relative powers of the general and state

governments, I should silently acquiesce in the judgment of the Court although my own opinion might not accord with its.

His argument was that the license fee and the selling were purely local, state acts and thus fully within the tax and commerce powers constitutionally ascribed to states. While Thompson lost the argument, the presence of his dissent was a signal of the significance of *Brown* as a constitutional ruling on federalism. More obscure than landmark rulings like *McCulloch v. Maryland* or *Gibbons v. Ogden* (1824), Marshall's alcohol ruling was nevertheless the occasion for a similarly important jurisprudential statement about the breadth of federal power over all of commerce.

There was only one other alcohol-related ruling during the Marshall era, but it too signaled an important beginning. In 1829, near the end of the tenure of the Marshall Court, the justices decided the first of what would be many Supreme Court cases concerning the regulation of alcohol commerce with the Indian tribes. The subject of Indian alcohol consumption would consume much judicial ink over the decades, as the court struggled with defining the relative powers of the national government and the states over the Indian territories. Indian law, from its constitutional outset, concerned foreign relations: between the U.S. government and the Indian nations. Native Americans would not be considered U.S. citizens until the twentieth century, and "Indians" moved from being foreign nationals and enemies to wards and finally to semiautonomous tribal entities. All along the way, alcohol was a presence.

Beginning in acts of 1802 and followed up in 1820 and 1834, Congress enacted legislation regulating alcohol trade in Indian country. The goal was to keep spirituous liquors out of Indian territories, punish Indian traders for violations, and outlaw distilleries on tribal lands. The sentiment behind the law was less noble experiment, or oppressive paternalism, than self-protection: from colonial times, there was white European fear about the ferocity and danger presented by the "likker'd up" Indian. Of course, this had never prevented European settlers' use and abuse of liquor in their treaty negotiations with the native populations. The decision in *American Fur Co. v. U.S.* (1829) did not engage the legitimacy of the alcohol regulation per se but, rather, addressed the narrower question of the proper application of the statutory penalties by the trial court. The case's importance lies not in its actual content, but in its chronology: the Indian law dimension of regulating traffic in alcohol shows just how early the national prohibition effort began in the United States. Admittedly, the regulation in *American Fur* was targeted to a specific group—and proceeded from less than salubrious motives. Additionally, there had been even earlier local-level laws limiting access to or use of intoxicating drink, including colonial era laws prohibiting African slaves from entering taverns at all.[40] But the federal efforts to ban Indian alcohol, first addressed by Marshall's Court, show the early and uneasy coexistence of prohibition with a generalized culture of drinking.

Of that generalized culture, and Marshall's time period in particular, *Drinking in America: A History* speculates as to whether "democratic ideology itself was not an unimportant factor in American drinking habits. The rise of the individualist ideology and dramatic increase in drinking were parallel phenomena."[41] Jeffersonian and Jacksonian democracy's rugged individualism, the staff of liberty, and the jug was at a distance from the more abstemious, more discerning virtue of the classically republican Founding Fathers.[42] Yet this early nineteenth-century culture of carousing, whether accurate or overgeneralization, was to have its comeuppance: the American Society for the Promotion of Temperance was founded in Boston, Massachusetts, in 1826. The beginnings of a counsel of moderation—meaning the measured use of non-distilled alcoholic beverages—was coming to American society with the great religious revival of the early to middle decades of the nineteenth century.[43] By the end of Marshall's era in 1835, a growing competition between the forces of prohibiting and the forces of tippling was making itself felt. As it happened, the new moderate approach to alcohol in American life would be, in some senses, emblematized by the person of the next chief justice: Marshall's successor, Roger Brooke Taney.

CONCLUSION

The nexus between alcohol and the Supreme Court in Marshall's era finds its way less into the court's decision making than into the Marshall justices' reflection of the consumption patterns and proclivities of the time. That Marshall's Court conferenced in a public house, a tavern boardinghouse, complete with spirited libations, is clearly an artifact of another, more alcohol-inclusive age.

2

THE LONG TANEY ERA OF THE MINT JULEP

John Marshall's long and productive tenure as chief justice solidified the importance of his office as leader of the High Bench, just as his decisions enshrined the Supreme Court as a powerful third branch of the national government. His institutional importance is undeniable. But the era over which he presided in terms of alcohol, its enjoyment, and its integration into the court's very work life was already changing by its end. Though he left a profoundly influential jurisprudential legacy, he was powerless to preserve his social culture of alcohol and its part in the boardinghouse workspace of the court. The kind of gentlemanly table drinking, of punch and madeira, conversing over diverse and intellectual legal projects, that characterized Marshall's time and social class was gone. There was both more drinking in America and more challenges to it, in the next Supreme Court era of Chief Justice Roger Brooke Taney.

The *Taney Court* (1836–1864) has the distinction of seeing the first Supreme Court case involving drunk driving—specifically, the liability issues surrounding the drunken operation of a stagecoach, in *Stockton v. Bishop* in 1846.[1] The Taney era is also a long one, spanning the American westward expansion, the rise of party machines and popular politicking, and the onset of the Civil War. Taney was a Marylander born on a tobacco plantation in Calvert County, appointed by President Andrew Jackson after a distinguished legal career that included a stint as Jackson's attorney general. Tennessean Andrew Jackson has quite a reputation for hard drinking, as does the popular image of his rowdy, orange punch-fueled first inauguration party at the White House. Despite this, by the time Jackson ascended to the White House, he was already past his carousing prime and would in fact take, in 1837, the American Temperance Society pledge to abstain from hard liquor.[2] Taney's time and indeed Taney's personal circumstances illustrate the coincidence of these cultural trends: heavy drinking of spirits, mostly whiskey, alongside a temperance sentiment growing in various pockets of New England and the Midwest. Of course, that the most common temperance pledge of the time was the "short" one, that allowed the use of hard cider, beer, wine, and liquors for "medicinal" purposes, speaks volumes as to the period's dominant attitudes.

As discussed in the previous chapter, domestically produced grain whiskey, distilled from corn and/or rye, had supplanted imported liquors in the American economy and day-to-day palate. While the certifications with which we are now familiar—bourbon, rye, sour mash, Tennessee style—had yet to be fully standardized, whiskeys were the spirits most available and on offer in a range of largely male, social and political drinking settings. With that, some whiskey drink must belong to this era—and there is no more totemic whiskey drink of the era than the **mint julep**, which reigned supreme at the bar for a good fifty years or more. It is also a highly appropriate beverage choice that unites the Taney period's seemingly incompatible cultural trends, for the julep was considered potently tasty as well as singularly healthful.

Imbibe! dates the heyday of the Julepian art to be from the 1810s to the Civil War.[3] The julep is essentially a type of sling, composed of liquor, water, and sugar, to which mint has been added. What raised the mint julep to a new level or category of drink was the use of ice and/or iced water in its preparation. Innovations in the preservation and, later, the production of ice changed the simple sling—of which the julep is the pinnacle in achievement—forever. The icy, minty concoction was particularly popular among the antebellum plantation set, and especially appreciated as a cooling beverage in the steamy American South. Taney's Maryland was considered part of "the julep belt" that stretched from Virginia through Georgia and all the way to Kentucky, and Maryland's regional spirit in the nineteenth century was rye.[4] Juleps were initially made with brandy, as were a majority of early cocktails in America, but later incorporated the more prevalent (and popular medicinal use of) whiskey as well. The inclusion of mint reflected the belief that this additive had properties that protected against both disease and the ill effects of the southern region's heat. As Barr's *Drink: A Social History of America* encapsulates it, "the mint julep uniquely combined medicinal virtue with the intoxicating effects of alcohol and the capacity for refreshment."[5]

If Jackson was a sometime temperate, Taney was not much of a drinker at all, due to his own ill health for much of his life. His biographer Lewis says that Taney lacked a "robust physique" and often had to "recuperate in bed" after a hard case at law.[6] (He nevertheless lived to the ripe old age of eighty-seven.) The toddy, a warmed-up sling, was frequently prescribed to revitalize invalids. As a cooling version of the toddy, the mint julep provided myriad kinds of relief—including for stomach disorders, which especially plagued Taney. So he might have taken either, in a therapeutic context. Continuing in this vein, Barr comments that "southerners continued [from the late eighteenth century through the nineteenth] to drink spirits mixed with herbs or roots on the grounds that these 'bitters' served as a necessary prophylactic against the fevers of the region. The most famous of these compounds was the mint julep."[7] Conveniently, *Imbibe!* provides a recipe for the "Prescription Julep," "a little piece of medical humor from 'A Winter in the South,'" a serial *Harper's Monthly* ran in 1857. That version utilized "white sugar, spring water, strong cognac, spirits of rye, mint leaves as desired, and as much powdered ice as necessary." The mock doctor's prescription concluded: "Repeat dose three or four times a day until cold weather."[8]

The mint julep also clearly had a more ribald side. It was famous—or infamous—among the drinks served at the political socializing hub that was the Willard Hotel in Washington, DC, during the 1830s and 1840s.[9] Henry Clay—a founder of the Whig Party of the period, which ironically is traditionally associated with early temperance movements—is credited with having introduced the mint julep to Washington, in the Willard's Round Robin Bar.[10] (It remains immortalized there, as an emblem of the Taney time period, as the entry for one-term president John Tyler (1841–1845), on "The Residence of Presidents Cocktail Menu," at today's reinstallation of the Round Robin Bar of the Willard Hotel.) The drink was brought to fame by celebrity bartender Orsamus Willard, who perfected it at the hotel lobby bar of New York

City's The City Hotel and thereby popularized the use of ice in drinks.[11] Whoever deserves credit for introducing it as a bar drink, it caught on wildly in the ensuing decades. Fanny Trollope mentions the mint julep as restorative for heat and fatigue, in an 1849 memoir.[12] Visiting America in 1842, Charles Dickens describes a massive julep wreathed in flowers that he shared one evening with Washington Irving.[13] Charles Hammack's Washington, DC, saloon offered, in its drinks list from 1863, eight juleps among the smashes, cocktails, and cobblers.[14] Even as the Civil War raged and the South burned, the mint juleps still flowed in Washington's Willard Hotel. No less an authority than author Nathaniel Hawthorne advised visitors to that informal center of operations in the capital to "adopt the universal habit of the place, and call for a mint julep . . . for the conviviality of Washington sets in at an early hour, and, so far as I had an opportunity of observing, never terminates at any hour."[15]

Unfortunately for the story, there does not seem to be much evidence that Taney was a real mint julep man. (Although Carl Swisher's 1935 biography of him entitles its first chapter "The Heritage of a Southern Gentleman.") While he was far from a teetotaler, his delicate health—which included stomach and digestive trouble, as well as rheumatism—caused him to refrain from all but the most modest alcoholic beverages.[16] In this, he was somewhat atypical for his upbringing. Lewis's biography mentions the morning eggnog(s) that Taney's planter father insisted upon before fox hunting—just as the biography also mentioned that Taney avoided partaking as it gave him a headache.[17] *Forgotten Maryland Cocktails* confirms the importance of eggnog to Maryland drinking culture, and says that for those of wealth or on the coast, the preferred spirit for it was brandy, rum, or some form of fortified wine.[18] *Imbibe!* reports a recipe for a Baltimore Egg Nogg that includes brandy or rum, plus madeira,[19] and another recipe that substitutes sherry for the brandy/rum. Like the julep, the eggnog also had a palliative side. Bartender Jerry Thomas, whose 1862 recipe book was a mixology benchmark, notes that eggnog "makes an excellent drink for debilitated persons, and a nourishing diet for consumptives."[20] Taney biographer Lewis does mention Taney recording in a letter that he had been taking milk and lime water during a health retreat[21]—a far cry from a good-sounding beverage, but suggesting medicinal quaffing of some nature on Taney's part.

If Taney distanced himself from the eggnog-and-fox-hunting aspect of the landed gentry lifestyle, madeira and sherry are items Taney himself identifies imbibing: for instance, in a letter from 1862, Taney mentions drinking "a glass of old sherry" to the health of the recipient.[22] His own habits were moderate for his times, but the presence of that kind of moderation was a part of his times, as evidenced in the voluntary societies then forming, that condemned drunkenness but were otherwise rather lenient about the use of alcohol.[23] Temperance would soon acquire a harder edge, and its temperance societies would push closer and closer to abstinence as both a personal and a policy goal. The first concrete example of such good intentions was Maine's 1851 law, "An Act for the Suppression of Drinking Houses and Tippling Shops."[24] What is noteworthy about this early prohibition law, and some of its contemporaries in sister states, is how easily and enthusiastically it was apparently evaded before it was allowed to expire.

Liquor and drinking, then, were enduring and situational parts of Taney's life, throughout his long life. There is, for instance, the story of a welcome home/political reception for Taney at which the period-typical hard cider was served and many toasts of (unspecified) wine were drunk.[25] Cider, as well as the (holiday) seasonally prominent apple brandy toddy, reflected the importance of apples as a fruit crop in the Chesapeake.[26] Another account of another occasion of multiple toasts being drunk occurred at a political banquet.[27] The toast, and drinking in rounds of treats, was very much part of male drinking rituals at this time, and very much a part of male political life. Taney, during his time as part of the Jackson cabinet, was certainly surrounded by hard drinking contemporaries: the aforementioned Clay for one, as well as political opponent Daniel Webster.[28] In addition to Taney's various personal encounters with liquor in American life, his era also included several, more general liquor-related developments. One, the term "bourbon" for Kentucky grain whiskey was coined during the 1850s.[29] Peck's *The Prohibition Hangover* says that it was traders in New Orleans, where the whiskey was shipped in wooden storage barrels down the Mississippi, who started calling it bourbon after the Bourbon County (KY) name stamped on the barrel lids.[30] Another development, occurring in 1863 at the very end of Taney's tenure, was the formation of the first liquor industry lobby, the U.S. Brewers Association, who launched a vigorous legislative campaign that succeeded in substantially reducing taxes on beer.[31] The lager beer being brewed on an increasingly industrial scale by German immigrants was becoming the "people's beverage" by the middle decades of the 1800s; the German brewers presented their product as wholesome and its regulation as altogether a different matter than that of distilled spirits.

Widespread and more populist and diversified alcohol consumption thus characterizes Taney's era. Taney's own, one big indulgence was cigars.[32] One historian specifically notes a court session during which Taney "*as usual* was smoking a black Spanish cigar" (emphasis added).[33] How often that cigar was accompanied by a sherry or a julep or some wholesome nogg, we cannot say. But though disinclined to much participate in it, Taney was clearly part of a drinking era in the American political culture—albeit one of somewhat less genteel customs than Marshall's earlier time.

There was one way, however, in which Taney shared a trait with his predecessor chief justice, and that was by continuing to reside in Washington boardinghouses. Like Marshall, Taney at first boarded in the district during the portion of the year that was the court term. He then returned to his home and wife in Baltimore when the Supreme Court was not in session and when he was not on circuit duty in Virginia or Delaware. Boarding arrangements for the justices were taken care of by the clerk of court, with the justices boarding together in the same establishment except for Justice Wayne during the early Taney period. The boardinghouse continued to supply their conference room,[34] and the justices still made a point of dining together when they could, although they sought greater individual privacy than in Marshall's day. Taney usually shared a sitting room with one other justice and had their meals brought to them there. Later, as living conditions in Washington improved, more of the justices brought their wives and households to the capital.[35] But the justices still spent a good deal of time on the road and in boardinghouse-tavern situations there. Circuit duty, by the mid-nineteenth century, was an increasing burden, what with the growth in the Supreme Court's docket and the geographic expansion of the country. In the West and the South, in particular, the size of the circuits had become unmanageable for the existing conditions of travel. Justices occasionally skipped U.S. Supreme Court terms, staying out on the road in order to cope with the backlog of appeals.[36]

As the chief with other administrative duties to attend to, Taney's circuit was small and compact enough to minimize such arduousness. His main complaints concerned his lodging in the capital. We know that in 1839 Taney lodged at Elliott's on Pennsylvania Avenue, from where he wrote a letter to his son-in-law exhorting him to send a box of black cigars. Of the several boardinghouses "that catered to their [judicial] trade," there was Dawson's on Capitol Hill, the accommodations of the Misses Polk, and Missus Turner's on Pennsylvania Avenue—where Taney resided in 1841 and where he reported disliking the dining room and its food. [37] After his wife's death, Taney moved permanently to a small row house a short walk from the Capitol, with his spinster daughter Ellen looking after him. [38]

Taney's Court also continued, like Marshall's, to hold session in the room directly beneath the old Senate chamber, described by contemporary sources as "a triangular, semi-circular, odd-shaped apartment, with three windows and a profusion of arches in the ceiling" that was nevertheless "a cramped crypt, a potato hole of a place." The courtroom had been refurbished since Marshall's time to give each justice a mahogany desk and comfortable leather-backed armchair. A correspondent attending a Taney case reported that the chamber presented itself better than before, "a great deal of the furniture is new, the carpets are rich and beautiful; the desks and chairs of the judges of a pattern unsurpassed for beauty and convenience and the whole appointment of the room in excellent taste." Taney took a detailed interest in such matters of interior decoration, reports his biographer Lewis. [39] One assumes the chief justice's care was for the stateliness of the judicial institution, but his concern for the decorations may also have been inspired by an oddish practice of the time period. It was then the fashion, in the capital, to turn out for major court arguments as for the opera—including for ladies, who dressed in splendid attire and waving millenary plumes for the occasion. One described instance was the famous *Charles River Bridge* case of 1837, which offered hours of grandiose and (hopefully) scintillating argument. [40] Victorian era oratory was a more fulsome and dramaturgical exercise than contemporary ears are used to, but lectures and other examples of it were what the public craved in entertainment during the period. The appearances of acclaimed Supreme Court advocates had an aura more akin to the stage than a courtroom.

During session, the court convened at 11 a.m. and sat until 3 p.m., then the closing time for government offices. The customary Washington dinner hour was 4 p.m., with tea and crackers or bread served at eight o'clock in the evening.[41] In the first term after the election of 1860, the court moved to the old Senate chamber (the Senate having decamped to the Capitol's north wing). This was a larger and grander setting for the judicial branch, in quarters that were light and commodious. But the move nevertheless brought nostalgia, and in the new space a contemporary observer noted that the justices seemed to shrink.[42] Cushman's *Courtwatchers* notes another peculiarity: that to refresh themselves during the long argument sessions, now from 11 a.m. to 5 p.m., the justices would retire in pairs behind a curtain that screened the back of the bench and accommodated small tables on which the messengers would serve them luncheon from the kitchen of the Senate restaurant. The rattle of the knives and forks could at times be heard. Rumor has it that one day a justice popped open a bottle of champagne and the cork flew out over the bench.[43] Whether this particular incident occurred in Taney's time, or somewhat after, is not clear. Taney Court conference deliberations, however, were still held after dinner in a private room in a boardinghouse, "which was pleasanter and more conveniently located than the dingy conference room given them in the capitol building."[44] This would have been during the 1840s, and for some time after. So while the chronology of some details is fuzzy, what is clear is that the Taney era was a time of transition, both in terms of court living patterns and court workspace. What comes across is a somewhat more formal, more institutionalized, and less casually chummy body than that under John Marshall.

Taney faced the unenviable challenge of succeeding that great jurist and personage. While he lacked the easy companionable charm of Marshall, there is no evidence that he was not a respected and effective court leader. Taney was esteemed for his astute legal mind, his serious demeanor, and his own devotion to enhancing the legitimacy of the Supreme Court. Of Taney the jurist, American statesman and lawyer Dean Acheson had this to say:

> Judicial self-restraint was Taney's great contribution to the law and custom of the Constitution. . . . The giant stature which Taney assumes in the history of the Supreme Court is due chiefly to his insistence that the judge, in applying Constitutional limitations, must

restrain himself and leave the maximum of freedom to those agencies of government whose actions he is called upon to weigh.[45]

Judicial restraint, a philosophy of judicial deference to the reasoning and judgment of the legislature and the executive, is a way of husbanding judicial power, reserving it for unavoidable constitutional disputes and therefore depoliticizing it. As its chief, then, Taney "deliberately sought to keep the Court out of party controversies and . . . he was largely successful in doing so."[46]

Until the 1857 *Dred Scott* case, that is. The decision was a violation of the cardinal principles of judicial restraint, by inserting the court into the sectional controversy surrounding the extension of slavery into the territories and, potentially, to new states to be admitted to the Union. Unhelpfully, and unnecessary to decide the actual case or controversy, Taney's opinion chose to take a stance on free-soil abolitionism that included a vehement statement that no person of African descent brought to labor in America could ever be a citizen of the United States, with a citizen's rights and privileges. The opinion in *Dred Scott v. Sanford* was "celebrated in the South and excoriated in the North,"[47] and succeeded only in inflaming tensions over the issue of slavery. Fairly or unfairly, the decision overshadows the Taney Court's legacy,[48] including the Supreme Court's substantial contributions to various areas of law under Taney's leadership.

One such area was the constitutional balance between national and state powers in regulating commerce. Chief Justice Marshall had laid out a legal doctrine of the plenary power of Congress over interstate commerce, reducing the states' authority to legislate by shrinking the scope of commerce that was wholly internal or intrastate. *The License Cases* of 1847 required the Taney Court to weigh in on this somewhat asymmetrical balance, in particular, with respect to alcohol regulation. While Marshall's more nationalist court had been inclined to view the matter of commerce "among the several states" as entirely subject to congressional authority, Taney and his court saw somewhat more room for state action in the realm of commercial activities—and over the regulation of alcohol more specifically.

The Taney justices agreed that licensing of liquor sales was among the police powers of states, but there were still six separate opinions constituting "the court's" decision in *The License Cases*. Constitutional law scholar Carl Brent Swisher argues that "chaos" pervaded the judicial minds when it came to the issue of the "original package doctrine." That legal rule, dating from the Marshall era precedent of *Brown v. Maryland,* concerned when an item introduced into a state through foreign or interstate commerce lost its character as an imported good subject to exclusively national regulation.[49]

When that imported good was a cask or bottle of liquor, as it was in *The License Cases,* the stakes of this state-versus-national power struggle over commerce were even higher. This was because some state laws of the 1830s and 1840s had begun to exhibit the temperance or proto-prohibitionist sentiment that would first come to full fruition in the Maine prohibition law of 1851. *Thurlow v. Massachusetts,* one of the cases in the 1847 group, featured one such temperance-motivated statute coming out of New England. It required a license for any retail of spirits for consumption on the spot, as well as prohibiting the sale for the purpose of carrying away less than twenty-eight gallons of spirits. (That the law did not function nearly as intended was somewhat beside the point.) The question in *Thurlow,* and by extension the other cases, was at what point did state restriction of domestic sales of liquor interfere with Congress's authorization of the importation of that same liquor, and thus interfere with Congress's control over interstate and foreign commerce? Marshall's approach in *Brown* had been to suggest that imported goods were not subject to the state's jurisdiction, that they could not be acted upon by a state without intruding on congressional power. Losing their "original packaging"—their crating or mass shipment container and being repackaged for unit or single serving sale—might be one sign that they had transferred into the state's local or internal commerce, over which *it* had authority. It was this perspective that Taney would adopt in parsing the effect of the three state laws at issue, and the interpretation he would attach to Marshall's *Brown v. Maryland* decision. Interestingly, Taney himself had been the advocate for the state of Maryland in the Marshall Court—duly acknowledging such in his *License Cases* opinion.

So what motivated Taney in his decision: his constitutional reading of federalism or an antiliquor sentiment? The advocate in the *Thurlow* case spoke to both. He expended a good deal of rhetoric defending the state's police powers, when used in their legitimate arena, as well as defending them against a general national policy seeking to generate revenue from the importation and sale of liquor. "It has never been maintained," he lectured,

> that a free use of wines and spirits has any tendency to promote public prosperity, nor is it denied that an excessive use is manifestly prejudicial. There can be no doubt, that where abstinence or severe temperance prevails accumulation is increased and the means of subsistence enlarged.

Counsel's language in the Massachusetts case showed the strength of temperance feeling in parts of the country during the Taney era. This passage is pointedly illustrative: "If excessive indulgence in the use of intoxicating drinks be an evil, and no one will question it, it is the right of the legislature to guard against it by wise and prudent regulations. . . . If the evil be such as to demand stringent provisions, reaching to exclusion, there is no constitutional objection to such legislation."

All three cases, of state laws "passed for the purpose of discouraging use of ardent spirits," rested on such premises about alcohol, as much as they rested on a characterization of state versus federal power.

What Taney had to say about the matter, in his opinion addressing the three cases, was less inflamed, but no less pro-state regulation. He first offered this concession to the forces of free trade, in alcohol or any other commercial item:

> It has, indeed, been suggested that, if a state deems the traffic in ardent spirits to be injurious to its citizens, and calculated to introduce immorality, vice, and pauperism in to the state, it may constitutionally refuse to permit its importation, notwithstanding the laws of congress; and that a state may do this upon the same principles that it may resist and prevent the introduction of disease, pestilence, and pauperism from abroad. But it must be remembered that disease, pestilence, and pauperism are not subjects of commerce, although sometimes among its attendant evils. They are not things to be regulated and trafficked in, but to be prevented, as far as human foresight or human means can guard against them. But *spirits and distilled liquors are* universally admitted to be subjects of ownership and property, and are therefore subjects of exchange, barter, and traffic, *like any other commodity* in which a right of property exists. (emphasis added)

Despite this acknowledgment of alcohol as a traded good, Taney held that the particular laws of Massachusetts and Rhode Island did *not* interfere with the trade in ardent spirits while they remained a part of foreign commerce, "in the hands of the importer for sale, in the cask or vessel in which the laws of Congress authorize it to be imported." These two state laws, rather, acted upon retail or domestic traffic within the states' borders. They were thus legitimate exercises of state power. He then went further. These laws, Taney pronounced,

> may, indeed, discourage imports, and diminish the price which ar-
> dent spirits bring . . . [but] if any State deems the retail and internal
> traffic in ardent spirits injurious to its citizens, and calculated to
> produce idleness, vice, or debauchery, I see nothing in the constitu-
> tion of the United States to prevent it from regulating and restraining
> the traffic, or from prohibiting it altogether, if it thinks proper. Of
> the wisdom of this policy, it is not my province or my purpose to
> speak. Upon that subject, each State must decide for itself.

Taney did not, however, apply this analysis to New Hampshire's liquor law; he used a different one. New Hampshire's prohibition law also affected sales of spirits (gin, in this instance), but spirits that were still in their original import barrel and being so transferred between merchants in an interstate act of trade. The spirits in question were not technically foreign imports anymore, yet neither were they out-of-state goods specifically covered by any act of Congress explicitly sanctioning their importation. They were, admittedly, items within interstate com- merce, and thus within Congress's power to regulate under the Consti- tution's commerce clause. But "as yet," Taney cautioned, "Congress has made no regulation on the subject." Taney's reasoning for his nu- anced—or hairsplitting—holding was this:

> the validity of a State law making regulations of commerce . . . cannot
> be made to depend upon the motives that may be supposed to have
> influenced the legislature, nor can the court inquire whether it was
> intended to guard the citizens of the State from pestilence and dis-
> ease. . . . Upon this question the object and motive of the State are of
> no importance, and cannot influence the decision. *It is a question of
> power.* (emphasis added)

And in the absence of congressional action on the interstate commerce in alcohol, as Taney saw it, the states *had* the power to make whatever regulations on it or affecting it *they* saw fit.

Taney and his judicial colleagues disagreed over this "question of power," just as they disagreed as to the meaning and utility of the original versus nonoriginal packaging distinction in *The License Cases*. Taney himself seemed torn between embracing state antialcohol efforts and reading the entire controversy as a Solomonic exercise in adjudicating federalism—tempted by the former, but resolutely returning to the latter. In the end, the resolution of the cases created more doctrinal problems than it solved. Their collective incoherence notwithstanding, the opinions in *The License Cases* mark the first real occasion that a Supreme Court decision helped to *construct* an era's culture of alcohol: by creating (some) legal space for a culture of its enjoyment, while at the same time unmistakably endorsing a culture and legal regime of its regulation.

Aside from this major if somewhat garbled ruling, the alcohol-related decision record in the Taney era is relatively sparse and uninteresting—not dissimilar to Taney's own personal record when it came to relishing beverage alcohol. In the majority of the Taney Court's booze cases, alcohol was an incidental fact in an otherwise unrelated dispute at trial, with the Supreme Court functioning in an error-correcting, appellate review capacity and not as a constitutional court. One partial exception is the admiralty law case of *The Genoese Chief* (1851). In this Taney opinion, Taney's Court made clear that Congress's admiralty and maritime power extended to the regulation of navigable interior waters such as lakes and, therefore, the federal district court had jurisdiction to resolve the dispute at issue—which had arisen out of a collision between two vessels, and the putatively negligible actions of a wheelsman, who "may have been incapacitated by liquor." Like the drunken stagecoach driver being sued in *Stockton v. Bishop* in 1846, the ship's sloshed helmsman in *Genoese Chief* was an early harbinger of what would be a much-litigated Supreme Court subject: drunk driving and the law.

The long Taney era was the cusp of many changes, on the court and in law, society, and politics. Alcohol in American life and law was no exception, for during the long Taney era, contrasting ideas about liquor's place in American culture grew up and flourished side by side.

One noteworthy innovation of the times was the use of the term "saloon," which comes into common parlance by the early 1850s. Incongruous, perhaps, given what the biographical record seems to reveal about Taney personally: one pictures him in a saloon environment with the greatest discomfort, despite the glad-handing in which he must have engaged throughout his precourt political career. Yet it is Taney's era that witnessed the nascent beginnings of the saloon in all its glory, and infamy. By the end of the nineteenth century, the saloon culture would produce politicking, unruliness, and excessive consumption united in the same space, along with a golden age of cocktails and luxury barrooms . . . and, almost simultaneously, a virulent antisaloon reaction movement.

But just as Taney can be only tangentially connected to his long era's totemic drink, he hovers in between the two sides of his era's culture of alcohol use, fully embracing neither. Chief Justice Taney was something of a man caught in the middle: of the attitudes and practices of his elite class, of a sectional conflict, of the developmental transition of a country and its commercial rules and regulations. Incidentally but richly symbolically, Taney was the first chief justice to give judgment in modern trousers instead of knee britches.[50] His official bust in the Supreme Court building, however, still depicts him as a classical hero, as those punch-drinking republicans Jay and Marshall had been sculpted, in toga-style drapery. An ancient *and* a modern was Taney, yet somehow uncomfortably neither.

CONCLUSION

Taney was not much of a drinker, but his was a drinking age, with the saloon culture establishing its cultural foothold in the urban metropolis, the frontier, and the capital itself. The Taney Court's only significant alcohol-related ruling was the opening foray into what would be both a major constitutional dispute—the federal–state balance of powers over commerce, and the subject of repeated litigation and legislation—states' efforts to restrict or condition the availability of alcohol.

3

THE CHASE ERA

Taxing Times

The *Chase Court* (1864–1873) has a fairly brief tenure and, at first blush, would seem to pose some difficulties. Salmon P. Chase, an Ohioan appointed by Abraham Lincoln, is reported by presidential cocktail scholar Mark Will-Weber to have been a nondrinker; Chase's Ohio roots and prototemperance time period lend credence to this reading of his personal traits. The Niven biography of Chase confirms it: Chase abstained from and even abjured the consumption of alcohol—on religious and moral grounds, as part of the abolitionist reform package to which he adhered and, likely too, after the bad examples of the self-destruction of his alcoholic brothers (which included "scrapes at riverfront grog shops" in Cincinnati) as well as that of a former law partner.[1] Happily, dear reader, both Chase and his court era rise above such negative unidimensionality.

The intersecting complexities of the Chase era require that this chapter deviate slightly from the template and discuss the political and social context of Chase's time and alcohol's place in it before presenting his era's cocktail. This will allow the historical and contextual discussion to foreground the various factors that go into choosing it and defending its inimitable suitability for an era whose chief justice was—most of the time—a teetotaler.

To begin with, Salmon Chase was one of the most politically ambitious individuals to ever wind up on the Supreme Court—surpassing even Charles Evans Hughes, who resigned as associate justice to run for president (unsuccessfully) and was later reappointed as chief justice. His court colleague Associate Justice Samuel F. Miller had this to say about Chase: "Religious by training and conviction and outward discipline, endowed by nature with a warm heart and a vigorous intellect, but all these warped, perverted, shriveled by the selfishness generated by ambition." Yet, as Chase biographer Niven concludes,

> paradoxically, it was this driving ambition that made Chase the appropriate person to represent the Court . . . at a critical time in its history. . . . [H]is commanding figure, his imperious nature, his political connections and interests . . . were of great importance to the image of a Court that the *Dred Scott* case had sullied. . . . His confident even aggressive personality meant that the Court would be heard on public policy decisions that would shape the future of the still distracted nation.[2]

Dred Scott's Taney may have been a political career man, but this was all before his appointment to the High Court—as his disastrous calculation in that case would seem to suggest. Chase was *always* a politician—even, and some would say, especially while leading the court.[3] As chief justice, Chase continued to speak out on long-held beliefs, such as in equal suffrage and the natural rights of man, "a divisive political issue that was legitimately in the province of the legislative and executive branches [and] may have been ill-considered."[4] Committed to furthering certain issues as he was, Chase also knew well how to wield the social side of chief justiceship: as chief, he presided over an atmosphere with his judicial colleagues that was "clubbable and rather closed in that they socialized with each other."[5] He worked collegiality, just as he had worked politics all his life.

Chase's political and judicial career spans one of the more tumultuous times in American history. He began his political life as a Whig, and had an early setback in his political career as a city councilman in Cincinnati. This was in 1840. During discussions of granting licenses to taverns dispensing liquor, he was "quite vehement on the evils of drink and urged vigorously the refusal of the license" though he did reluctantly vote for some of them. Then, at a later meeting, and misjudging the strength of the growing temperance movement in the state, he flatly refused to grant any more; when it got out that he was a temperance man, a heavy vote was cast against him and he was defeated for reelection.[6] To put Chase's enthusiasm into perspective, the temperance movement had begun in the first decades of the nineteenth century in Calvinist New England; the Massachusetts Society for the Suppression of Intemperance had organized in 1812. It gained force as part of the second Great Awakening and religiously inspired social reform movements in the 1830s and 1840s. Prohibition, however, was far from a nationwide movement. As one study summarizes, "Dry Republicans, sensing that the Republican Party would never travel far down the temperance path, splintered into a separate political party in 1869. The Prohibition Party crested in 1884 on the nation's second wave of temperance enthusiasm, when many states enacted antiliquor laws. Just as in the 1850s, however, most of these laws were soon repealed or diluted."[7] Chase's state and later national political career was coincident with the first wave of temperance, which was less tidal than tide pool.

After his local office holding as a Whig, Chase became politically active in the Liberty and Free Soil Parties; he was the author of what would be the ringing campaign phrase, "Free Soil, Free Labor, Free Men!"[8] He then served as a senator from Ohio (1849), as a "Free" Democrat. By 1855, he was seeking the People's or Republican Party's nomination for governor of Ohio. He won, narrowly, in a divided field, and immediately began scheming for a run for the presidency in 1860.[9] Unsuccessful, he then joined Abraham Lincoln's cabinet as secretary of the treasury. After intracabinet machinations and maneuvers fizzled and he was relieved of his status, Chase aspired to appointment to a judicial post—a factor in his planning being that the post could be a useful base for his continuing presidential ambitions, but also that "his moral and idealistic views on the equality of man [could be] enshrined in the supreme law of the land."[10] Once securing his chief justiceship, his political ambitions still did not cease, for Chase would be a major candidate for the Democratic presidential nomination in 1868.

Sobriety seemed the one constant of Chase's eventful political life. His appointing president, Abraham Lincoln, was a fairly abstemious chief executive—although Lincoln's personal history included a father who was a distillery hand in Kentucky and Abe's own operation of grocery store–grog shops as a young man in Indiana.[11] Still, Lincoln was an early advocate of temperance—the personal pledge variety, not the legislated imposition of teetotalism—and spoke before one such gathering in 1842.[12]

Despite the importance of personal sobriety, to both Chase and Lincoln, neither ran an alcohol-free political salon or White House. The post–Civil War period would loosen the spigot even further.[13] A contemporary period work of political fiction, *Alice Brand* (1875), depicts the Washington, DC, political society receptions of the time period, including one hosted by the chief justice and "Mrs. Chase"—although at this point in time, his hostess would have to have been his daughter Kate, as he had already buried his third wife. The author's description of the Chase reception leaves somewhat oblique the matter of alcohol service, but in some of the novel's other political reception settings, the practice of serving brandy and champagne to guests at a supper party from a sideboard in a separate room is spelled out. Such sideboard service was typical, as Americans did not generally drink wine—or any alcohol—with their meals, having never developed the custom as in Europe.[14] Another source qualifies this characterization but nevertheless concurs regarding the overall liquidity of period hospitality: "Victorians equated wine—alcohol—with hospitality. Bubbling champagne [and a host of other wines, including sherry] formalized the act of entertaining [and] . . . raised the status of the events at which they were served—note their display in decanters and on dinner tables in private homes."[15] A biography of Kate Chase confirms her identity as a leading Washington hostess, and also corroborates the extravagant partying of Washington society after the Civil War.[16]

Like Taney, Chase was a temperate man ever surrounded by liquor and drinking, in all aspects of political society. Unlike Taney, Chase fully embraced and utilized it all as a device for power politicking. The biographer Niven comments that all of Chase's entertaining while governor was "politically motivated," and says that while he found balls and formal soirees "provocative and dangerous,"[17] he clearly used entertaining for political business purposes. While chief justice, Chase gave "a series of receptions to which Washington's society turned out en masse." His daughter Kate functioned as hostess, including at formal dinner parties Chase gave for his judicial colleagues, to smooth out frictions between them. Justice Samuel Miller found Justice Stephen J. Field irritating and excitable, for example, due to the latter's "drinking habits."[18] Chase, too, could be offended by intemperance—once visibly

Figure 3.1. Kate Chase as the "leading hostess" of Washington, DC, during the tenure of her father, the Chief Justice. *Source: Courtesy of the Library of Congress Online Prints and Photographs Division, LC-DIG-cwpbh-00855.*

shocked at witnessing Daniel Webster at a social engagement knock back a healthy slug of whiskey, mistaking it for madeira. "Put off by the great man's human indulgences," Chase was perhaps personally more comfortable at the dry dinners and salons that he was known to have attended.[19] Yet this did not prevent him from lodging and attending political meetings at the infamous Willard Hotel, obviously not a dry-friendly establishment as the "center of activity" of political life in 1861.[20] Nor did Chase's sobriety absent him from the atmosphere of drinking and carrying on at Chicago bars during the Republican Convention of 1860, where Chase was one of the candidates. Ultimately, this passage from biographer Niven, describing Chase's time as a cabinet member living in Washington, seems to encapsulate Chase's stance on his alcoholic times: "Chase entertained a great deal, quite apart from his expected formal dinners and receptions. . . . Congressmen [and various others] enjoyed the bountiful meals he provided. *A teetotaler and nonsmoker himself, wine, liquor, and cigars were always available*" (emphasis added).[21]

In his later years as chief, enjoying the luxuries of the postwar boom's nouveau riche, Chase partook of the dinners President Grant gave "and the many multicourse extravaganzas deemed so essential at the dinner parties and receptions that the wealthier congressmen and the diplomatic corps hosted."[22] This would have been around 1869, and in the deluxe environs of Republican-dominated Washington. Ironically, the very extravagance Chase so enjoyed, and that he deployed so adroitly, may have been his ultimate undoing. After his first heart attack and convalescing after a stroke, Chase rebounded only to suffer a fatal relapse, when "forgoing a lifelong habit of abstinence from alcoholic beverages, he had topped off a hearty meal of fish, oysters, beef steak, mushrooms, corn on the cob, and baked apples with a glass of *sherry* and one of champagne" (emphasis added).[23]

Chase's mortal quaff of sherry inspires the choice of the totemic cocktail for his era, for sherry was the base ingredient for one of the most popular alcoholic beverages of Chase's era. The first guide to mixed drinks, prepared by celebrated bartender Jerry Thomas, was published in 1862. (*How to Mix Drinks: A Bon Vivant's Companion* was its title.) Thomas, his cocktails (including among the entries many true "bittered slings," but also "cobblers," "noggs," and "smashes"), and his concept of the American bar would go on to international fame, serving as a model for the installation at the Paris Exposition of 1867 and the headliner at the Vienna Exposition in 1873.[24] An intriguing reference from the mid-1850s illustrates the widespread appeal of one Thomas drink in particular: "At one San Francisco saloon, 'we find the governor of the state seated by a table, surrounded by *judges of the supreme and superior courts*, sipping *sherry cobblers*, smoking segars'"(emphasis added).[25] *Imbibe!* continues in this vein, enthusing that "the average drinking man of 1863" would choose the **sherry cobbler** (sherry, sugar, citrus—usually orange—served over ice) as "the one drink" from a state-of-the-art list of beverages of the era "to stand the test of time."[26]

Like the mint julep, its rough contemporary, the sherry cobbler popularized the use of ice in drinks and also introduced the novelty of the drinking straw.[27] Also like the julep, it was a popular drink in the political barroom setting. Dickens rhapsodized about both concoctions during his 1842 tour of the United States, just as he confirms that cocktail drinking was an established and beloved American activity, where a man "would follow up his meals with two hours at the bar, smoking, drinking, and indulging in what Dickens perceived to be the national pastime—talking politics."[28] But the sherry cobbler would ultimately eclipse the mint julep in consumer favor. That cobbler was an American and worldwide hit (yes, at the aforementioned Paris expo in 1867) from the 1850s through the 1880s, and it was popular with men as well as women. *Domesticating Drink* notes the gender span of its appeal, with "dining rooms in fashionable hotels serv[ing] mixed drinks—juleps, cobblers, and the like—to women throughout the nineteenth century."[29] If "such mixed drinks as claret cup, sherry cobbler, and milk punch made with sherry had particular associations with women,"[30] this only reinforces the sherry cobbler's prominence in the postwar American culture of alcohol enjoyment and its penetration into multiple drinking venues and populations.

It was nevertheless a fancy drink, a tipple of the nicer classes. For working-class men, and some women, beer drinking was the practice. Beer consumption, which had already been on the rise with the arrival of German immigrants and their bottom fermenting lager beer (whose production was better adapted to the American climate than the traditional top fermenting English ales brewed in colonial homes and taverns), really took off after the Civil War.[31] This was in part because beer distribution was begun as part of Union Army rations, replacing the old liquor allotment, and had stimulated beer's popularity and sales. Beer was cheap, and beer had yet to receive the full force of temperance condemnation. Beer also had a lobby: the U.S. Brewers Association established in 1863, who were singing the praises of their trade in liquid bread to, among other audiences, America's elected politicians.[32]

But the battle between liquor and beer for American hearts and minds was only beginning. The trauma of the Civil War essentially killed off the temperance movement for a time, as "booze helped to drown out . . . 'the soul-searing moans of the wounded and dying that echoed through the still night air.'"[33] Not only were soldiers turning to distilled liquor for solace, whether as traditional spirits or the newer marketed form of patent medicines (also liberally laced with opium), the federal government was as well. With the onset of the war between the states, the Union government enacted a series of laws taxing liquor, beginning with an 1862 act passed to help finance the Civil War debt,[34] followed by subsequent excise tax statutes in 1866 and 1868. Yet these were not "sin taxes," inspired by latent antialcohol feelings. Rather, revenue needs had driven the policy, one that "for the first time, [made] the liquor industry an important part of the American economy . . . [and] the distillers . . . full investors in democracy."[35] But the taxes' ineffectiveness was shortly seen, for they dramatically reduced sales— and the accompanying federal revenue, as well as increasing fraud and illegal stockpiling. Unsurprisingly, 1869 saw a reduction in the Civil War–period taxes on spirits, and with that, a resultant increase in legal sales and revenue. At the same time, the federal government introduced mandatory stamps for bottled liquor to prevent counterfeiting and tampering—as well as to better regulate proper payment of alcohol duties.[36]

The issue of the alcohol tax would be a major part of the Chase Court's docket of cases related to alcohol. In terms of constitutional law decisions, the most famous during the Chase era were the *License Tax Cases* in 1866. These upheld the right of the federal government to collect alcohol tax revenue on liquor illegally sold in dry jurisdictions— but not to authorize such sale under state law or immunize a seller from state prosecution. No claim can be made, Chase intoned, "that the [federal] licenses thus required gave authority to exercise trade or carry on business within a State." This revenue-oriented sophistry was again upheld in *Pervear v. Massachusetts* in 1866.

The same kind of odd conciliation between national supremacy and state sovereignty also held sway in Indian law. In 1865 in *U.S. v. Holliday* the Chase Court weighed in, as had its predecessors, on the Indian alcohol trade issue, drawing a distinction between federal commerce power to regulate alcohol for Indians who were "government wards," and state police powers to regulate alcohol for Indians whose tribal ties had been "dissolved."[37] But the Chase Court was firm in upholding federal power to ban alcohol sale to Indians "under charge of an Indian agent," even when the traffic or transaction took place on state territory and not a reservation.

Two property forfeiture cases, involving alcohol revenue statutes and the seizure of barrels of spirits on which taxes had not been paid, were basically part of the court's routine appeals work but did elucidate the constitutional proposition that "Congress possesses the power to levy taxes, duties, imposts, and excises, and it is as clear that Congress may enact penalties and forfeitures for the violation of such laws as it is that Congress may levy the taxes or duties or pass laws for their collection, safe-keeping, and disbursement."[38] Justice Stephen Field, with whom the chief justice and Justice Miller joined, nevertheless dissented from what he found to be a high-handed use of the forfeiture power, which deprived the legal purchaser of the barrels because their warehouseman and producer had failed to comply with revenue provisions. As Field complained,

> We thus have this singular and, I venture to say, unprecedented fact, in the history of judicial decisions in this country, that the property of a citizen honestly acquired, without suspicion of wrong in his vendor, is forfeited and taken from him because such vendor, at some period whilst owning the property, conceived the intent to defraud the government of the tax thereon, although such intent was never developed in action, and for the execution of which no step was even taken.

The fairness of such strict liability aside, liquor was property—an ordinary, and eminently, taxable item in commerce once again.

A second forfeiture case, one year earlier, contained the amusing factual record of an attempt to mix fraudulently acquired spirits with other spirits, to conceal their identity and prevent their seizure. The ruse in *In re The Distilled Spirits* (1870) was ultimately successful, for as the court concluded, "The case being one of a loss of identity of the original offending spirits, we submit that neither the new species nor any part of it is liable to forfeiture, and this whether the mixture was innocently made or for the purpose of destroying the identity."

In contrast to these miscellaneous alcohol tax cases, *Low v. Austin* in 1871 was one of the Chase era's most important alcohol-related rulings, in terms of long-term jurisprudential significance. It officially pronounced the "original package doctrine," deriving it from the Marshall era decision *Brown v. Maryland* (1827), which had concerned a state licensing fee for the selling of imported goods that the Marshall Court invalidated as an unconstitutional duty on imports.[39] In *Low*, Justice Field's unanimous opinion for the Chase Court also invalidated California's general property tax imposed on champagne imported from France but still being stored in its original containers in a warehouse. Reiterating that no state tax could be imposed on imports, Field laid out guidelines for when items—including liquors—lost their character as imports and were thus subject to state taxation or regulation. Those that "remained in the original unbroken packages in which they were imported" and "remained the property of the importer . . . retained their character as imports." The fact that the ad valorem tax was being assessed on wine as the commodity was of no consequence to the decision, yet the doctrine would have tremendous consequence for the unfettered importation of alcohol across state lines—including across dry state lines.

Low cleaned up and clarified the ambiguity that remained in the law of liquor transit as a result of the mixed messaging of the Taney Court's multiple *License Cases* opinions. *Low*'s significance can be seen relatively immediately—albeit indirectly—in a contemporaneous Chase Court case that was something of an addendum to the better-known *Slaughterhouse Cases* of 1873. That decision, interpreting the Reconstruction Amendments to the Bill of Rights, limited national protection of individual rights by upholding a New Orleans ordinance, regulating the slaughterhouse and butchering trade, which had been challenged as abridging the personal right to labor freely. The scope of both state police powers, on behalf of citizens' health, safety, and welfare, and the Fourteenth Amendment's guarantee to all persons the "privileges and immunities" of citizens of the United States were at issue. *Slaughterhouse* was a major constitutional ruling, with serious implications for civil rights policy. In the same year, the Chase Court held in *Bartemeyer v. Iowa* (1873) that the right to sell intoxicating liquors was *not* one of the privileges and immunities of citizens that the states were forbidden to abridge, allowing the state's alcohol prohibition law to stand.

Yet the *Bartemeyer* decision was far from open and shut. For one thing, the *Bartemeyer* court could not resist engaging in hypotheticals, pregnant with implications. As Justice Miller pressed in his opinion for the court, *if* a case were presented in which a person owning liquor at the time a law was passed by the state absolutely prohibiting any sale of it, "it would be a very grave question whether such a law would not be inconsistent with the provision of that amendment which forbids the state to deprive any person of life, liberty, or property without due course [process] of law." While the facts of the case did not themselves raise that grave constitutional question, *Bartemeyer* had a bit more up its sleeve, juridically speaking.

Coming as it did on the heels of the *Slaughterhouse Cases*, *Bartemeyer* found Justice Miller rather pointlessly going over the privileges and immunities clause grounds that the earlier decision had made frivolous, by rendering the clause null and void. "Clearly Bartemeyer, the liquor dealer in Iowa, had been 'deprived' of his right to sell alcohol, but Miller chose for the most part to just ignore this claim."[40] Justice Bradley, however, in a more searching concurring opinion, took on the livelihood deprivations in the two cases more directly. He emphasized that no invasion of property existing at the date of the alcohol law's passage had been asserted and, thus, no question of depriving a person of property without due process of law could arise. He then added this:

> a legislature may prohibit the vending of articles deemed injurious to the safety of society, provided it does not interfere with vested rights of property. When such rights stand in the way of the public good they can be removed by awarding compensation to the owner. When they are *not* in question, the claim of a right to sell a prohibited article can *never* be deemed one of the privileges and immunities of the citizen. (emphasis added)

Trafficking in spirits is totally different, Bradley instructed, "from the right not to be deprived of property without due process of law, or the right to pursue such lawful avocation as a man chooses to adopt." The deprivation of liquor as livelihood, in other words, was indisputably legitimate.

Concurring Justice Field, who had dissented in *Slaughterhouse* and declared that the right to pursue a calling *did* constitute a liberty or property protected by the due process clause of the Fourteenth Amendment, also needed to explain why he opposed the Louisiana law but not the Iowa one. He found his rationale in the Iowa law's legitimate health measure and the police power of the state as paramount.[41] Was Field not a committed nationalist, and an advocate of the liberty of contract from governmental interference? (More to the point, was he not also a drinking man?) He was, but he was able to square his *Bartemeyer* position with his overarching ideology (and imbibing preference) for one reason, it seems. The clue lies in the final sentence of his 1871 *Low v. Austin* opinion: "Imports, therefore, whilst retaining their distinctive character as such, must be treated as being *without the jurisdiction of the* taxing *power of the state*" (emphasis added). Intoxicating liquor, then, was caught in the web of a federal–state balance of government powers. What *Bartemeyer* and Field were acknowledging was that once liquor *did* become subject to state jurisdiction, there was little barrier to state regulation of it, fiscal or otherwise. But *only once so subject*, and divining *this* would consume many pages of many subsequent volumes of *The Supreme Court Reports*.

So the Chase Court, while generally committed to supporting actions of national power, including on behalf of alcohol, was not averse to carving out some space for states to pursue their own independent courses of action regarding its control. It would fall to later courts to harmonize these legal directives, but Chase's Court did take the major step of providing a new, clear rule for federally sanctioned alcohol importation versus state-mandated alcohol restriction. Ultimately, the Chase Court's original package doctrine would privilege the cross-state importation of liquors, wines, and other beverages sought by thirsty consumers for their personal use. It was less doctrinal breakthrough than recognition of regulatory reality.

Chase Court realism regarding alcohol is symbolized, sartorially speaking, by Chase's being the first official bust to show a chief justice in realistic jacket and collar, cravat or tie—although Chief Justice Chase is given an extra swath of billowy, toga-like fabric across his suit coat, for good measure and auld lang syne romance. But in contradistinction to

Taney's era, modern times were truly coming: Chase's Court was the first to sit for an official photograph, in 1865, and alcohol had moved front and center to its full integration into American life as a valuably taxable and tradable commodity.

CONCLUSION

Teetotaler and temperance sympathizer, Chase nevertheless comes of political age in a capital awash in liquor. The incipient cocktail age and the postwar government's alcohol-tax revenue strategy make the Chase judicial era (both at the sideboard and on the bench) a wet one—but more by default than uniform and unbridled zeal. *Bartemeyer* sowed the constitutional seed for what would ultimately grow into a very different mind-set regarding any "right" to drink, even as the doctrine spelled out in *Low* would protect imported liquor from a state's censorious attention. The tension between wet and dry interests was coming into the law, just as it was affecting politics and society.

4

THE WAITE ERA OF THE GRAND POLITICAL SALOON

The Waite Court and the chief justiceship that followed it, that of Melville Fuller, are sometimes lumped together by judicial historians as one long era of pro-business, pro-laissez-faire, inegalitarian and insensitive legal policy making. Whether this elision of difference is totally fair or not, there is one way in which the Waite and Fuller eras were of a piece: both are testimonials to elegant and adventurous cocktail drinking.

The *Waite Court* (1874–1888) sees another Republican Ohioan serve as chief (again, like Chase, relatively briefly), this time appointed by Ulysses S. Grant. Grant is the president who conjures the very image of drinking liquor as political suasion. Indeed, the term "lobbying" is said to date from the era of his presidency, when Grant would install himself in the lobby of the Willard Hotel, drinking, smoking, and willing to entertain political requests.[1] Upon first examination, Morrison Waite's predilections might seem inclined to temperance or even abstinence, given his devout religiosity (Episcopalian) and his abolitionist Whig background. But he did not revel in the politics of any of these issues, as did his predecessor Chase, and was known as socially skilled, which does not suggest an unbending personality but rather an ability to partake from time to time. The Magrath biography confirms this, noting that Waite "liked his expensive tastes—oysters, clams and lobsters were lifelong favorites, and New York's Park and Tilford received regular orders for sherry, claret and sauterne."[2] Magrath speaks at length about

Chief Justice Waite's lubricated social intercourse with Associate Justice John Marshall Harlan: "All the brethren joined in the whist parties, which, enlivened by a few rounds of bourbon, were a favored recreation." And in a letter commenting on a photo Waite sent to Harlan, Harlan remarked: "You look natural and life-like as you would look if I were to say that a gallon of old Bourbon was on the way from Kentucky for you."[3] Hard-drinking times seem to have abounded on the Waite Court, with Justice Stephen J. Field (a noted tippler) also making reference in a letter to Harlan's thirty-two-year-old whiskey, and to being "indisposed" for a Saturday court consultation early on in Waite's tenure.[4] *Courtwatchers* provides the coup de grace, recounting a story of a famous advocate arguing a case before the bench in 1877 while "look[ing] to be full of liquor."[5]

Full of what might a drinker be in the 1870s and 1880s, perchance? During this era the famous Manhattan cocktail is introduced—around 1875, allegedly in honor of or connected with the gubernatorial election of (ultimately unsuccessful) Democratic presidential aspirant Samuel J. Tilden. This classic cocktail's name comes from its locus of origin: the private Manhattan Club of New York City, founded after the Civil War and a silk-stockinged version of Democratic Party societies such as Tammany Hall.[6] The dedicated cocktail glass, or small cup-bottomed coupe, is also adopted at this time—by 1876 according to *Imbibe!*[7] But despite the importance of both the Manhattan and the coupe to American mixology, it is DC's claim to cocktail fame, the **Rickey**, or "air conditioning in a glass," that is the totem of the Waite era, because of the beverage's strong association with the political saloons that dominated the political culture of Waite's time.

It was one of a variety of tall drinks that claimed a place at the bar during the period. The Rickey was invented in the 1880s, by Shoomaker's bartender George Williamson, who named it after his boss, Col. Joseph Rickey, a Democratic lobbyist from Missouri.[8] According to the undocumented *Wikipedia* entry on the drink, "In 1883, Colonel Joe Rickey was purported to have invented the 'Joe Rickey,' after a bartender at Shoomaker's in Washington, D.C., added a lime to his 'mornin's morning,' a daily dose of Bourbon with lump ice and Apollinaris sparkling mineral water"—essentially a highball without the sugar element. *Imbibe!* supplies more detail on the "Joe Rickey," including that "Shoo's" was "famed for the quality of its whiskey and the political wattage of its clientele [with] some calling it the 'third room of the Congress,'" and that the drink made it into the *Washington Post* in 1889.[9] A copy of Rickey's own handwritten recipe for a Syracuse newspaper in 1895 is reprinted in *Imbibe!*,[10] which reflects the incursion of gin (the Old Tom, sweet-style) into the drink by this later time. It also includes this caution: "Don't drink too many."

The Democratic provenance of both period innovations, the Manhattan and the Rickey, should perhaps give us pause in selecting either as the totemic cocktail for the era of Republican-appointee Waite. Moreover, given his known personal tastes (which ran to the posh), Waite himself likely favored a claret cup (which dates from 1875–1880 and is made with Bordeaux, amontillado, lemon slice, gomme syrup, and club soda) on hot days. This popular but tonier cooler (and cousin to the Chase era sherry cobbler) thus merits an honorable mention for the era—with the recognition that far more Rickeys than claret cups were quaffed in the nation's and the capital's barrooms during Waite's tenure.

Part of the problem with choosing a cocktail emblem for the Waite Court is that there was so much beverage alcohol to choose from in his day. (And Waite appeared to be no slouch in doing the choosing.) Some of it masqueraded as medicine, not recreation. The period saw, for instance, the widespread use of cordials and "stomach elixirs," alcoholic patent medicines and other health tonics—some made from cannabis or including opium (the latter marketed as a tincture of laudanum). Lydia E. Pinkham's Vegetable Compound was the leading product in the alcohol curatives industry of the late nineteenth century. Sold as a remedy for "female complaints," it was 20.7 percent alcohol.[11] It was a popular therapeutic and sedative tonic in an era when bars were closed to women and their social drinking was relatively rare; it was also easily prescribed by a physician and legally sold by pharmacists, grocers, and dentists. Prescriptions could also be had for more typically liquor items, such as liqueurs and brandies. Disastrously, however, the phylloxera blight, a virus attacking grape vines that had spread through European vineyards in the 1870s, succeeded in dethroning French grape brandy from its American toddy/cocktail spotlight—"to be replaced by American whiskey in the mixing glass and Scotch whisky in the clubroom."[12] And laudanum at the pharmacy.

When more metaphorical "medicine" was needed, various cocktail preparations debuted in these later decades of the nineteenth century. One was the sour—again, initially with brandy, then with whiskey— which began in the late 1860s (by the 1880s it was ubiquitous) its near century-long reign as one of two liquor drinks with "day-in, day-out popularity."[13] The other such beverage was the highball, of which the era's Rickey is a type. The inimitable Jerry Thomas refined and codified both drinks: first, the traditional sour, adapting it from its hoary punch origins (one strong one weak, one sour one sweet). This is his original, and swanky, period recipe:

Whiskey Sour

(Use small bar-glass.)
Take 1 large tea-spoonful of powdered white sugar dissolved in a
little Seltzer or Apollinaris water
The juice of half a small lemon
1 wine-glass of Bourbon or rye whiskey
Fill the glass full of shaved ice, shake up and strain into a claret
glass. Ornament with berries.

Soda was originally used, but eventually abandoned over time. Instead, it was prominent, and remains so, in the classic highball, of which the Collins is the base for many variations. First appearing in the second, 1876 edition of Thomas's *Bar-Tender's Guide*, his Tom Collins Gin instructed:

(Use large bar-glass.)
Take 5 or 6 dashes of gum syrup
Juice of a small lemon
1 large wine-glass of gin
2 or 3 lumps of ice
Shake up well and strain into a large bar-glass. Fill up the glass
with plain soda water and drink while it is lively.

That Waite's time period was the reign of many choice beverages seems especially indisputable when one consults a publication from 1888, commemorating and documenting a Constitutional Centennial breakfast held for the Waite Court by the Philadelphia Bar at the city's American Academy of Music: the reprinted breakfast menu—the "Bill of Particulars" for a meal commencing at eleven o'clock in the morning—includes multiple courses paired with Chablis, Amontillado, Sauterne, Chateau Lafitte, and Roederer and Mumm's champagnes. High life indeed.

Despite all this liquid connoisseurship, the temperance movement was steadily gaining momentum and legislative victories during Waite's time, with state-level prohibitions on the sale and distribution of liquor having again gone into effect. An even more significant benchmark was the election in 1876 of the first officially teetotaling president. With Rutherford B. Hayes's assumption of the office in 1877, First Lady "Lemonade Lucy" Hayes decreed that no alcohol would be served at the White House. The year 1876 also marked the first occasion a national constitutional amendment outlawing distilled liquor was introduced in Congress. Referred to committee and never heard from again,[14] it nevertheless signaled a mustering of the dry forces.

The period's seemingly contradictory enthusiasm for both dry laws and drinking can be explained by the fact that most antiliquor legislation of the time attempted to control the liquor industry itself, not personal consumption.[15] Also clear was that legal and social condemnation fell most heavily on the prevalent drinking customs and locales of new immigrants like the Irish, Germans, Poles, and Italians. "Much of the country's liquor trade," a temperance minister of the 1880s complained, "is in the hands of a low class of foreigners, whose names topped the doors of most saloons, beer gardens, and low groggeries."[16] In short, to attack the liquor trade was to single out the noxious influences of foreigners and ethnic minorities, and vice versa. After all, saloons in this era were not only the plush parlors and grand settings for high-level political wheeling-dealing. They were also rough-and-ready outposts for the humble and their affairs: centers of immigrant community life, rough-and-tumble refuges from the cramped hardship of the urban slums, and nerve centers for the operation of political parties' ward politics. Those ward politics, and the immigrant voters they drew upon, threatened elite, nativist control; so antialcohol legislation aimed at the dispensaries also targeted the political threat of "ethnic" politics. But there was also a feeling, and one that would strengthen in the coming decades, that the typical saloon environment was itself unsavory: dirty, foul, and encouraging of unseemly if not unspeakably wicked behaviors.[17]

Enforcement nevertheless remained difficult for dry states, because of liquor being shipped across state lines. The Waite Court offered dry states some hope in *Mugler v. Kansas* (1887), which supported the state police powers in banning liquor production and sales and allowed states to seize liquor and liquor-related facilities without having to pay compensation. "It is the duty of the courts to adjudge," Justice Harlan announced, and the Supreme Court clearly saw the public welfare and public morals justification for the Kansas prohibition law—though Harlan ominously intoned that the justices would not accept every statute "ostensibly" so passed.[18] Since even the Kansas statute prohibiting the manufacture and sale of intoxicating liquors included an exception for "medical, scientific, and mechanical purposes," Harlan's opinion was making the point that only reasonable police power regulations would be upheld by the justices. Almost on cue, *Mugler* was followed up the next year (1888) with *Bowman v. Chicago and Northwestern Railroad*, in which the Waite Court barred Iowa from banning interstate shipments of alcohol so long as the product remained in its original package. That original package doctrine, originating in the Marshall era's *Brown v. Maryland* as a way of balancing federal commerce and state tax powers,[19] had come fully into its own. Enunciated and affirmed by the Chase Court, in Stephen J. Field's unanimous decision in *Low v. Austin*, the doctrine had been upheld by the Waite Court, with Justice Field again writing, in an 1880 ruling, *Tiernan v. Rinker. Tiernan* found Texas's protectionist taxing of imported but not domestically produced liquors in violation of federal authority over interstate commerce (but did not find in favor of the appellant in the case, who was selling both). A similarly nationalist, antilocal protectionism ruling occurred in *Walling v. Michigan* (1886), which invalidated a tax on out-of-state liquor wholesalers that did not also apply to in-state liquor wholesalers. Liquor commerce and liquor consumption thus existed in the not inconsiderable space the Waite Court created between the state's police and tax powers.

But *Mugler*'s coexistence with a vigorous original package doctrine must also be understood in light of the Waite Court's reaffirming of another, and different, Chase era decision, that in *Bartemeyer v. Iowa* (1873). *Boston Beer Co. v. Massachusetts* in 1877 held that, as a police power measure, a state law prohibiting the manufacture and sale of intoxicating liquors was not repugnant to any clause of the Constitution—did not, for instance, impair the obligation of contract. Still, Justice Bradley's majority opinion added this important caveat:

"We do not mean to say that property actually in existence, and in which the right of the owner has become vested, may be taken for the public good without due compensation. But we infer that the liquor in this case, as in the case of *Bartemeyer v. Iowa*, was not in existence when the liquor law of Massachusetts was passed. Had the plaintiff in error relied on the existence of the property prior to the law, it behooved it to show that fact. But no such fact is shown, and no such point is taken." Ten years later, *Mugler* would clarify that abating a nuisance—illegalizing the production of a commodity injurious to public health and welfare—was not a state taking property, but a state legitimately conditioning the use of property. Small comfort, perhaps, for the owner of an industrial brewery rendered of little value by a state dry law.

The Waite Court's community interest view of private property was being applied to liquor-related property interests even as an increasingly probusiness, antiregulation jurisprudence was making its intrusion into constitutional law. *Boston Beer* demonstrates the emerging influence of this latter, personal-liberty-as-liberty-of-contract approach, one that would come to define and defend the late nineteenth and early twentieth-century era of "laissez-faire" political economy in the United States. Although the Waite Court was ultimately unsympathetic to the appeal, Bradley's words acknowledged how the beer company "boldly takes the ground that, being a corporation, it has a right, by contract, to manufacture and sell beer forever, notwithstanding and in spite of any exigencies which may occur in the morals or the health of the community, requiring such manufacture to cease." Bradley's 1877 opinion temporarily deflected this horror. "We do not so understand the rights of the plaintiff. The legislature had no power to confer any such rights," he sniffed.

Indian law and alcohol was also a topic for Waite's Court. *U.S. v. 43 Gallons of Whiskey* (1876) ruled that federal Indian Prohibition could extend to ceded lands adjacent to Indian lands, with the same factual issues coming again for settlement and affirmation in 1883. The unsettlingly racialist ruling of *U.S. v. Joseph* (1876) found the Waite Court adding this insight to the constitutional debate about regulating the Indian alcohol trade: the Pueblo Indians were considered "too civilized" to be subject to the ordinary, federal Indian alcohol trade regulations.[20] The specific question for the Waite justices was whether "all laws now in force regulating trade and intercourse with the Indian tribes, or such provisions of the same as may be applicable, shall be, and the same are hereby, extended over the Indian tribes in the Territories of New Mexico and Utah." As the *Joseph* opinion explained, in answering: "They [the Pueblo] are Indians only in feature, complexion, and a few of their habits; in all other respects superior to all but a few of the civilized Indian tribes of the country, and the equal of the most civilized thereof." Wards of the federal government in other ways perhaps, the Pueblo were decreed competent to decide for themselves with respect to liquor.

Overall, in its alcohol-related cases and in general, the Waite Court attempted a jurisprudential balancing regime—the stress of which combined with the court's increasingly unmanageable caseload likely killed its chief justice. A political compromise appointee to begin with, Waite was overmatched by the overwhelmingness of his duties. *Courtwatchers* notes that he suffered a temporary breakdown in 1885, during which Associate Justice Miller had to assume his duties.[21] Returning to work after six months, Waite would collapse in the office from exhaustion and die a few days later, in 1888.

The Waite Court caseload had begun to experience the unremitting backlog that would bedevil the Supreme Court until more intermediate appellate courts were created and staffed, to process the legions of routine appeals from trial decisions in the country's growing number of commercial disputes. That backlog of routine appeals included numerous cases in which spirituous liquor was a commodity in question—or part of some otherwise routine economic (for example, taxation) or contractual (for instance, insurance liability) matter. The "flavor" of the times is variously displayed in the mundanity of the Waite Court's docket—the patent dispute regarding a new process for brewing beer that animated the 1887 case in *New Process Fermentation Co. v. Maus*, or the 1876 importation duty case of *Debary v. Arthur*, which upheld a construction of the federal statute in question that assigned an additional per bottle duty to champagnes, that is, to sparkling wines and not to other nonfortified wines. The latter case is especially interesting because of the class-based familiarities and preferences the decision's language amply displays. The duty was appropriate, said Grant-appointee and opinion of the court author Justice Ward Hunt, because "Champagne is a beverage singularly grateful to the taste, and is indulged in by those who are supposed to be able and willing to pay the tax upon it. It is an article of high luxury, and, upon the soundest principles of economy, should pay a high tax, that articles of necessity may, if possible, go untaxed."

The "articles of necessity" in question were other, "ordinary" wines, that could be imported in casks—as opposed to only in bottles, as champagne must be since its final fermentation takes place in the bottle— and thus not be subject to the per bottle duty. A relatively more serious of the routine cases, involving forfeiture of property involved in illegal activities, was *Dobbins Distillery v. U.S.* in 1877. The lessee of the property was operating in violation of various revenue laws, and the court held that its forfeiture was appropriate whether or not the owner knew his lessee was using the property to defraud the public: "if fraud is shown . . . the land is forfeited just as if the distiller were the owner."[22] Such statutory construction of revenue and customs laws was significant, because its draconian character would be appropriated into the forfeiture provisions of national prohibition laws like the Volstead Act.

With all its ups and downs, personal and juridical, the Waite era begins what H. L. Mencken dubbed the "Golden Age of American drinking." The saloon had become the archetypal American drinking place, and its singular function was concentrated in a single large space serviced by a long bar. As one source depicts the institution: "The counter itself was often decorated in an ornate style, with carved facings, a brass footrail, and spittoons of the same material tastefully disposed about its base. An alluring display of bottles and, from 1879 onwards, a cash register, backed by a wall of mirrors, drew the eye of the drinker toward the obliging bar staff."[23] In addition to the prominent and proliferating grand (and not so grand) political saloons, with Waite's era also begins a golden age of fancy hotel bars, the period of roughly 1865–1900.[24] Holland House, on 5th Avenue in New York City, typified this elegance, with its celebrated Bamboo Cocktail of sherry, dry vermouth, and orange bitters. Also reportedly a birthplace of the Waite era Manhattan cocktail,[25] Holland House was sadly one of the first of the grand hotel/restaurant bars to shutter with the onset of Prohibition in 1920.[26]

CONCLUSION

"Golden age" of elegant barrooms or pinnacle of the political saloon, Waite's era was a boozy one. Waite's personal and professional behaviors certainly included alcohol consumption, and his court's decisions reflected an increasing variety of regulatory questions involving alcohol. But as to both a signature cocktail and a signature jurisprudence, the Waite judicial era is somewhat inconclusive. Sour or highball, federal or state power, property as public interest or private right? Waite always tried to execute a balancing regime of both; in the end, it killed him.

5

THE FULLER ERA
A Gilded Age of Cocktails

The *Fuller Court* (1888–1910) finds Illinois Democrat Melville Fuller leading the Supreme Court, appointed by noted beer drinker (and "Bourbon" Democrat[1]) Grover Cleveland. Fuller maintained a close relationship with President Cleveland and corresponded with him for years, though it is unlikely he shared that man's preference in beverage. Beer and its manufacture were nonetheless in a period of phenomenal growth during the Fuller era, abetted by the waves of German, Czech, Polish, and other central European and predominantly Catholic immigrants to the United States. But anti-immigrant nativist sentiment was already dovetailing with antisaloon and antialcohol moralizing,[2] such that the ordinary workingman's opportunities to enjoy a cold one would progressively shrink during Fuller's time. For the time being, safe from the abolitionists' zeal, however, was the partaking of a wide range of refreshment in this gilded era's elite and opulent saloons and private drawing rooms.

Many and contentious were the social, legal, and judicial administration issues confronting the new chief justice. In spite of these challenges, and no intellectual giant himself, Fuller nevertheless brought to the court a gift for efficient management and a talent for moderating discord. As part of his effort to foster harmonious working relations among the justices, Fuller introduced the practice of requiring each justice to shake hands with the other justices each morning in the conference room.[3] As the U.S. Supreme Court website elaborates,

"The 'Conference handshake' has been a tradition since the days of Chief Justice Melville W. Fuller in the late 19th century. When the Justices assemble to go on the Bench each day and at the beginning of the private Conferences at which they discuss decisions, each Justice shakes hands with each of the other eight. Chief Justice Fuller instituted the practice as a reminder that differences of opinion on the Court did not preclude overall harmony of purpose."

Fuller must go down in court annals as one of the great home entertainers as chief justice, eclipsing even the efforts of Salmon and Kate Chase. Chief Justice Fuller was similarly the beneficiary of a spouse's gifts as hostess and frequently entertained his court colleagues at dinner. Cushman in *Courtwatchers* mentions a dinner at his home in 1890 for the newly appointed Justice Brewer, to which members of the Senate Judiciary Committee were also invited.[4] Indeed, the Fullers made a practice of giving a dinner for each new justice appointed to the court, such that such sociability was a custom. Moreover, during his chief justiceship, Fuller's Washington home became an extension of the court facilities. As biographer Ely details,

> During his tenure the Court met in the historic old Senate chamber in the south wing of the Capitol. Despite some attractive decor, these quarters became increasingly inadequate for the efficient conduct of judicial business. The robing room, in actuality a private sitting room, was across a hall from the courtroom. Thus the justices had to parade across a public corridor to enter and leave the courtroom. There were no chambers for the justices, so they maintained offices in their homes. Although Congress provided a conference room, the facilities were not suitable.[5]

Fuller was especially unhappy with the poorly ventilated room "and the Saturday conferences of the justices were often held at Fuller's home," including frequent evening meetings.[6] More than likely, these were all catered affairs. *Courtwatchers* observes that until 1910, attendants regularly entered the court conference room to serve drinks[7]—presumably, more during the time of Waite than Fuller, as the latter moved so many conference deliberations to his home,[8] but the idea of refreshment during discussion seemed a well-established one.

Fuller had married into wealth and was a prominent Chicagoan, residing in an elegant mansion on Lake Avenue given to his wife by her father in 1869. The residence was surrounded by large lawns, with a greenhouse on the property, a paintings collection, and an extensive library. His lifestyle and his general political attitudes were similar to those of the educated elites of his day. He was conservative as to policies effecting social leveling and profoundly probusiness; his court was a staunch supporter of the "liberty of contract" doctrine that insulated the labor market from any governmental intervention on behalf of equity or workers' protections. (*Lochner v. New York* in 1905 is the most famous and famously controversial of these decisions.) But he was far from a Simon Legree, at least in personality, for what also comes across with Fuller is an amiable gentility, an urbane sense of sophistication. He loved attending the theater[9] and was a member of a men's intellectual club, the Chicago Literary Club. As Ely notes in his biographical study of Fuller,

> The personal characteristics that enabled Fuller to make friends across party lines facilitated his rise at the Chicago bar and his selection as chief justice. He excelled in establishing harmonious personal relations with people of diverse legal and political views. Fuller was of a genial nature, with an urbane sense of humor and unfailing courtesy. He combined a scholarly manner and quick mind with generous impulses. In his law practice Fuller exemplified the virtues of loyalty, integrity, and diligence. One contemporary recalled that in court Fuller was always "a gentleman and a scholar."[10]

Despite his practice of courteous sociability, Fuller was hardly a party gadfly. His biographer Ely stresses that Fuller was essentially "domestic by nature" and "delighted in his large family and enjoyed quiet evenings reading at home."[11] He clearly enjoyed the home-based intimacies with his judicial colleagues, but balked at the many commitments that were expected of him during the capital's social season—rather unlike his predecessor, Salmon Chase, who relished such opportunities for political networking, or *his* predecessor, John Marshall, who seldom declined an invitation. *Courtwatchers* remarks that during the 1890s, the dinner hour in Washington was 5 p.m., and evening entertainments during the social season for a man in public life—such as a Supreme Court justice—would run until 10, 11, or 12 at night.[12] Much of this heady socializing and general gallivanting was dual purpose, personal as well as political. Fuller seems to have approached it all politely, but without the fevered instrumentalism of his scheming predecessor Chase or the enthusiastic indulgence of his high-living predecessor Waite. Fuller was different, as Ely explains:

> Washington social life placed additional demands on Fuller's time and energy. In the late nineteenth century the justices of the Supreme Court were not cloistered from Washington society, and they participated fully in official dinners and receptions. Being of a retiring nature, Fuller found the social dimensions of the chief justiceship an unpleasant chore, and he declined as many social engagements as possible. Fortunately, Mrs. Fuller was a charming hostess who entertained graciously. [13]

Fuller's hallmark of home hosting, then, for the court and to reciprocate other invitations, depended on his wife. With her death in 1904, he largely withdrew from formal social activities—"initiating, some say, the process that eliminated Supreme Court justices from Washington society." [14] (But not, necessarily, from the Washington cocktail party circuit, as future courts and justices will ably demonstrate.)

Fuller's Washington was clearly one resplendent and replete with high style entertaining and a standard of high living for its more elite denizens. Not surprisingly, his term as chief justice spanned an incredibly rich and varied time in the history of American cocktails—as gilded as the Gilded Age in which he lived. His era's totemic drink evokes not only this opulence but also the partisan vicissitudes of the turn of the twentieth century. That turn marked the invention of one of the many variants on the popular Manhattan cocktail developed during Waite's tenure. This one added dashes of Cherry Heering (or cherry brandy) and absinthe, representing the increasing period use of such luxury ingredients. Known as "McKinley's Delight," the cocktail was created in 1896 for that year's GOP convention by a St. Louis bartender. Fuller's antipathy for his own Democratic Party's candidate that election year— the populist and prohibition advocate William Jennings Bryan—was said to have fueled his secret supporting of a McKinley victory. "Fuller was privately relieved," Ely remarks, "when McKinley was elected over Bryan in 1896." [15] This charming little fact fittingly supports the choice of this ultra-esoteric **Manhattan cocktail variation** as the official alco-

holic beverage of the Fuller era. Indeed, some sources locate the origi-
nation of the Manhattan itself in the decade of the 1890s, at the old
Delmonico Restaurant in New York City.[16] More likely, it was popularized and perfected there, at that time, given that plush and elegant
hotel and restaurant bars were the fashionable drinking destination of
the period.

McKinley's Delight it is (or, as it later became known, "Remember
the Maine"[17]) in spite of the fact that Fuller's was decidedly *not* a time
when one cocktail or spirit dominated. Rather the opposite, with the
possible exception of the fortified wines known as vermouth, which
became a core (if supporting) element in mixology during this era. But
the Fuller era heralds far more than experimentation with the Manhattan's classic formula of whiskey, sweet Italian vermouth, and bitters. We
also see, for instance, the introduction of the Bronx cocktail, developed
around 1907–1908, and a 1910 version of the Brooklyn cocktail, which
added to the gin-based Bronx sweet and dry vermouth and substituted
raspberry syrup for the orange juice. Other variants of the Brooklyn,
one dating from as early as 1908, used whiskey, sweet vermouth, and
dashes of the liqueurs Maraschino and Amer Picon.[18] Scotch whiskey
from the house of Dewars was also being introduced into the United
States at this time, via its importation by aficionados such as Scottish-
born industrialist Andrew Carnegie. *Imbibe!* notes the "Scotch Highball" (and golf) craze of the 1890s and remarks that by 1900 it was the
most fashionable drink in America.[19] Scotch took a turn in a spirits-
based Manhattan variation, the Rob Roy cocktail of 1894, named after
the Scottish folk hero and concocted at New York's Waldorf Astoria
hotel bar. In 1909 the relatively exotic rum daiquiri was introduced to
Washington, DC, at the Army and Navy Club on Farragut Square, by a
naval officer who had been acquainted with the drink by its American
originator, an engineer managing a mine near Santiago, Cuba.[20] The
club would subsequently open its eponymous Daquiri Lounge.[21] Even
gin and gin cocktails were getting a makeover: *Imbibe!* notes that the
"dry" martini made with Plymouth or London style dry gin and French
(dry) vermouth (at a ratio of 1:1, it couldn't have been terribly dry)
began its rise as an American staple in the 1890s.[22] One account says
that it originated as the house cocktail of the Turf Club in New York
City, founded in the late 1880s as a private gambling club.[23] Others say
it was originally named the Waldorf Astoria cocktail after that "famous

old New York hostelry in the gay 90's" where it was first prepared.[24] Whatever the story, the martini, like the iconic Manhattan, would one day admit of an amazing number of variations—perhaps more than any other American cocktail. (For example, the Perfect Martini, various stages of Dry Martini, the Gibson, the Dirty Martini, the Sweet Martini,[25] etc.) Finally, a particularly successful iteration of the "fancy" whiskey cocktail—where a liqueur such as orange curaçao or Benedictine substituted for the sugar in the classic bittered sling of yore—spread from its New Orleans birthplace and across the nation. That recipe was for the absinthe-dashed Sazerac, which itself began its life with brandy not rye or bourbon as its main spirit.[26] There are countless other favorites one might list from this time period, *for Fuller's era is, perhaps, the creative heyday of the "cocktail" in general*: new concoctions abounded, and commentators of the era mentioned the well-established juleps, whiskey sours, rickeys, fizzes, and cobblers as well as "other wonderful compounds."[27]

A convivial man of property, Fuller himself was a social drinker. Social drinkers of middle and upper class native-born citizens, who cultivated an appreciation for fine drink, were as much a part of the period as were the growing temperance advocates who denounced them. In the words of "The Only William" Schmidt, author of *The Flowing Bowl* bar manual of 1891, "I believe in temperance . . . in the word's true meaning: tempering or moderating the enjoyment of liquors" in order to maximize their true appreciation.[28] The lucrative market for imported wines and spirits reflected a fixed custom of their enjoyment in social entertaining. As *Drinking in America* notes, "a turn of the century edition of *The Women's Dictionary and Encyclopedia* (edited in part by the original Fanny Farmer and promising its readers 'everything a woman wants to know') explained the mixing of no fewer than 58 cocktails, including Sours, Martinis, and Manhattans."[29] *Domesticating Drink* confirms that alcohol had a pervasive presence in respectable sociability and home hostessing in the late nineteenth and early twentieth centuries, judging by etiquette manuals, cookbooks, table-setting guides, and home entertainment handbooks of the time.[30] "Temperate" drinking, including for ladies, encompassed "wholesome" beverages such as mulled wine, cordials, and milk punch, as well as wine at a variety of social events from afternoon teas to wedding breakfasts, with balls and evening parties demanding punch and champagne.[31] An 1890 newspaper serial story notes that a certain Missus So-and-So "always has sherry and port on her sideboard on her reception day." Sociable, moderate consumption was not considered "drinking"—even by some drys—as temperance was vague in definition, but wine and cordials were often not considered dangerous intoxicants.[32]

Women—always escorted—were also finding their way into the more opulent saloons and hotel bars, those that "conjured up an image of elegance and taste."[33] Fancy cuisine restaurants such as Delmonico's of New York,[34] having spread from the Continent and then the London market, introduced to the well-heeled city dweller a cosmopolitan dining environment where respectable ladies could be seen drinking in public. There was in fact a fairly widespread "commercializing [of] heterosocial leisure" during the period, as seen in the growth of cabarets and dance halls, both of which served alcohol to mixed company.[35] Indeed, a popular cocktail of the time and the latter occasions, served almost exclusively to women, was the Mamie Taylor—a "cooler" or thirst-quencher, of Scotch, lime, and ginger ale.[36]

All this radical social change did not sit well with everyone, and there was clearly a link between the gender "turmoil" at the bar and the prohibition movement. As *Domesticating Drink* diagnoses it: "Women's public drinking represent[ed] the dissolution of the male sphere. Alcohol use [in public venues], like the right to vote, was no longer a uniquely masculine attribute. . . . [W]omen were begrudgingly admitted to male venues that no longer entailed [male] privilege."[37] Saloons that had been male enclaves were changing, diversifying, and were no longer the havens for elite male drinking and bonding. That behavior migrated to more private or exclusive spaces, and regulating public drinking establishments became more clearly about inculcating a public morality of rectitude in the community at large.

The proliferation of drinking in that community at large, not to mention the gender, racial, and class demographics of various and sundry drinking establishments, was thus responsible for the Fuller era also marking a revivified national prohibition movement. Technically, it was disgust with the Prohibition Party's ineffectualness that ultimately moved a group of Ohio Methodists to found what would be the stellarly effectual Anti-Saloon League, in 1893. Yet not coincidentally, it seems, the height of the working-class and immigrant saloon-based politics in the 1880s and 1890s was also the inception of a new antilabor and racist politics of liquor's suppression. Concerns about labor union activism and workforce productivity combined to shift factory and mill owners' attitudes against the low saloon and its combined dangerous and destructive tendencies.[38] In the agrarian South of the turn of the century, the continued subordination of the African freedmen sharecropping underclass was such that "among the hardest drinking but driest voting legislators were some of the Deep Southerners whose chief concern was to keep liquor away from the black [sic] lest it impair his capacity for cheaply paid work."[39] Not surprisingly then, the agenda of abolishing the "evil" saloon in America, "the symbol of masculinity emancipate,"[40] had a strongly class- and race-based cast, targeting the saloons of particular masculinities.

The Ohio Anti-Saloon League (ASL) focused on the soul- and family-destroying barroom. It reformulated the temperance movement goal as the paternalistic *abolition* of alcohol and its availability. The spaces for alcohol's enjoyment—by laboring men, ethnic immigrants, men of color—had to be curtailed for their denizens' own good, but those spaces also represented a threat to the upper orders: as places for collective and even seditious organization. The ASL, under the masterful leadership of Wayne B. Wheeler, would go on to distinguish itself as the first pressure politics interest group, stunningly successful in its focus, longevity, and legislative accomplishments, largely by mobilizing the nation's literalist Protestant churches and their congregations.[41] But all disparate dry interests were regarded as allies, from nativists and racists (like the KKK), to populists like Bryan to women's temperance crusaders and women's suffragists.[42] Motives for alcohol prohibitionism hardly mattered to the ASL, and neither did partisanship. Marshaling votes for anyone, Democrat or Republican, who would vote dry became its stock in trade, as well as providing campaign workers and financial contributions to candidates' electoral campaigns. Beginning with local option laws, the ASL's efforts proceeded to dry up several states.[43] Those most affected by—and, in some cases, most vigorously supportive of—those saloon-closure and other dry laws were ordinary people.

Sad to say, Fuller's Court shared much of the era's generalized suspicion of labor's collective action and other "radical" ideologies and its lack of sympathy for racial emancipation and equality. If Taney's Court is forever tarnished with the stain of *Dred Scott v. Sanford*, then Fuller's is with *Plessy v. Ferguson* of 1896, and its "separate but equal" doctrine of legalized racial segregation. Fuller's era also inaugurated a more doctrinaire view of the right to private property, and its immunity from all levels of state regulation in the public's interest, than had been applied under Waite. The Fuller Court decision in *Lochner v. New York* (1905) was responsible for the "liberty of contract" doctrine, a kind of laissez-faire social Darwinism of market competition and the personal liberty to "freely" contract one's labor, without government protections or intervention. The worldview of the court's controlling majority, which included the chief justice, was "rooted in the free market moralism of the Victorian age,"[44] accepting of social elitism, racial hierarchy, and women's fragility and basic inferiority. But one attitude of the day that the Fuller justices emphatically did not share was for temperance prohibitionism.

Pious homages to both state police power and its preservation of sobriety do occur. Significantly, the Fuller Court reaffirmed the Chase Court's earlier, denuded interpretation of the privileges and immunities of citizenship clause with respect to the liquor shop business. "There is no inherent right in a citizen to thus sell intoxicating liquors by retail. It is not a privilege of a citizen of the state or of a citizen of the United States," Justice Stephen J. Field intoned in *Crowley v. Christensen* in 1890. The prospective tavern owner in the case had challenged his denial of a license as the result of arbitrary discretion and a denial of due process of law, so the decision also required the Fuller Court to distinguish the Supreme Court's recent ruling in *Yick Wow v. Hopkins* (1886), which had protected a Chinese laundry owner from an arbitrary building permit regulation that harmed his business. Much as its progenitor *Bartemeyer* had had to do in echoing the reasoning of the *Slaughterhouse Cases, Crowley* stressed its lack of a racial discrimination element in contradistinction to the *Yick Wow* situation. Impermissible race-based classification was the original purpose of the Fourteenth Amendment, not state decisions that legitimately discriminated between favorable and unfavorable commercial practices—this was the collective holding of the decisions in *Slaughterhouse, Bartemeyer, Yick Wow,* and *Crowley.* This limiting of the scope of the Civil War Amendment had the effect of narrowing the remedies it provided for deprivations of personal liberty.

As if to justify such an interpretation, Field's opinion in *Crowley* featured an extended argument regarding the reasonable regulation of property being fully consistent with the right to private property—especially as applied to "the dram shop." "For the pursuit of any lawful trade or business the law imposes similar conditions," he began. He then went on:

> Regulations respecting them are almost infinite, varying with the nature of the business. Some occupations by the noise made in their pursuit, some by the odors they engender, and some by the dangers accompanying them, require regulations as to the locality in which they shall be conducted. Some by the dangerous character of the articles used, manufactured, or sold, require also special qualifications in the parties permitted to use, manufacture, or sell them. All this is but common knowledge, and would hardly be mentioned were it not for the position often taken, and vehemently pressed, that there is something wrong in principle and objectionable in similar *restrictions when applied to* the business of selling by retail, in small quantities, *spirituous and intoxicating liquors.* (emphasis added)

Field then replayed the pro-wet argument, seemingly playing devil's advocate: "It is urged that as the liquors are used as a beverage, and the injury following them, if taken in excess, is voluntarily inflicted, and is confined to the party offending, their sale should be without restrictions, the contention being that what a man shall drink, equally with what he shall eat, is not properly matter for legislation."

As Field continued, he utterly dismantled the wet position—highly ironic, in that he was a notoriously intemperate imbiber. But Field was also a perennial presidential candidate, and his ambitions as well as his class prejudices may have spoken when he wrote this:

> By the general concurrence of opinion of every civilized and Christian community, these are few sources of crime and misery to society equal to the dram-shop, where intoxicating liquors, in small quantities, to be drunk at the time, are sold indiscriminately to all parties applying. The statistics of every state show a greater amount of crime and misery attributable to the use of *ardent spirits obtained at these retail liquor saloons* than to any other source. The sale of such liquors in this way has therefore been, at all times, by the courts of every state considered as the proper subject of legislative regulation: Not only may a license be exacted from the keeper of the saloon before a glass of his liquors can be thus disposed of, but restrictions

may be imposed as to the class of persons to whom they may be sold, and the hours of the day, and the days of the week, on which the saloons may be opened. Their sale in that form may be absolutely prohibited. It is a question of public expediency and public morality, and not of federal law. The police power of the state is fully competent to regulate the business, to mitigate its evils, or to suppress it entirely. (emphasis added)

The Fuller Court reaffirmed this proregulation stance in 1904 in *Cronin v. Adams*, which concerned a Denver ordinance that banned women from service or presence in "any dram shop, tippling house, or liquor saloon." Upholding the validity of the law in its entirety, Fuller's Court seemed scornful of the claim itself. "The restrictions of the ordinance were conditions of [the plaintiff's] license," Justice McKenna complained,

and by accepting the license he accepted the conditions, and no rights of his were infringed. . . . What cause of action, then, has [he]? He is not a female nor delegated to champion *any grievance females may have* under the ordinance, *if they have any.* The right to sell liquor by retail to anybody depends upon the laws of the state, and they have affixed to that right the condition expressed in the ordinance. (emphasis added)

So much for heterosocial leisure. As in *Crowley*, in *Cronin* the regulation was directed at what the Fuller justices perceived as nuisance liquor dispensaries: lowlife dram shops, or saloons that also fronted for prostitution. As to the police powers of the state in that regard, McKenna was unequivocal. His *Cronin* opinion reprised an extensive segment from *Crowley v. Christensen*, of which the following portion is especially pertinent:

Not only may a license be exacted from the keeper of the saloon before a glass of his liquors can be thus disposed of, but *restrictions* may be imposed *as to the class of persons to whom they may be sold,* and the hours of the day and the days of the week on which the saloons may be opened. . . . It is a question of public expediency and public morality, and not of Federal law. The police power of the state is fully competent to regulate the business, to mitigate its evils or to suppress it entirely. (emphasis added)

The female exclusion aspect of the regulation merited no additional discussion or special analysis; it was presumed an appropriate "mitigation" of evil.

But one state's morality was not necessarily another's. Like the Waite Court, the Fuller Court addressed multiple cases involving dry state efforts to impede the interstate shipment of alcohol, rebuffing most of them. *Leisy v. Hardin* in 1890 reaffirmed the original package doctrine as espoused by the Waite Court in the 1888 *Bowman* case. As the Fuller Court reiterated in a related state import licensing versus federal commerce power case of 1891:

> We have lately expressly decided in the case of *Leisy v. Hardin*, that a state law prohibiting the sale of intoxicating liquors is void when it comes in conflict with the express or implied regulation of interstate commerce by congress, declaring that the traffic in such liquors as articles of merchandise between the states shall be free. (*Crutcher v. Kentucky*)

A tussle over applying the *Leisy* rule nevertheless occurred among the justices in the Vermont prohibition law case of *O'Neil v. State of Vermont* in 1892. Justice Blatchford's majority opinion upheld the conviction for "sell[ing], furnish[ing], and giv[ing] away intoxicating liquor, without authority," all contrary to the state statute. Much more significantly, Blatchford dismissed any federal concerns involving interstate commerce in the liquor, as well as a federal question raising the Eighth Amendment prohibition against "cruel and unusual punishments." Justice Field contested both in his lengthy dissent, as did Justice Harlan, joined by Justice Brewer, in his more succinct but no less outraged one. Uniting the dissents was a profound concern for the disproportionately severe sentence leveled against O'Neil by the state of Vermont. Multiple counts of trafficking in liquor through a mail-order business based in the neighboring state of New York had resulted in a judgment "by which the defendant is confined at hard labor in a house of correction for the term of 19,914 days, or 54 years and 204 days." This "inflicts punishment which, in view of the character of the offenses committed," Harlan said solemnly, "must be deemed cruel and unusual." Justice Field's dissenting critique was more passionate and rhapsodic:

> The state may, indeed, make the drinking of one drop of liquor an offense to be punished by imprisonment, but it would be an unheard-of cruelty if it should count the drops in a single glass, and make thereby a thousand offenses, and thus extend the punishment for drinking the single glass of liquor to an imprisonment of almost indefinite duration.

The tussle over the injustice visited on the plaintiff in *O'Neil* had partly resulted from a congressional statute that intervened between *Leisy* and the cases that followed it. In order to bypass *Leisy*'s rule, the Wilson Act of 1890 provided that intoxicating liquors transported into any state for sale or storage should immediately on arrival be subject to the laws of the state, and not be exempt from the laws of the importing state—thus rendering the state police power "more complete."[45] *In re Rahrer* in 1891 upheld the constitutionality of the Wilson Act but, in parsing the meaning of "on arrival," rendered the act somewhat toothless. In the *Rahrer* case, the imported liquor had arrived in the dry state, Kansas, before the act took effect, and the act had no authority retrospectively, nor authority to confer greater breadth on the Kansas law than its plain meaning conveyed. Such sophistry would continue. *In re Swan* in 1893 invalidated a constable's warrantless seizure of a barrel of "suspected" spirits, shipped from North Carolina into the semidry state of South Carolina, again refusing to find federal enhancement for the plain language of the state's own law.[46] In 1898 *Rhodes v. Iowa* held that a state could not seize liquor as a common carrier crossed the state line, while the alcohol was in transit; and in *Vance v. W.A. Vandercook Co.* (also in 1898), nor could a state stop interstate shipment of alcohol for personal use. The collective effect of these rulings robbed the Wilson Act of much of its drying effect.

The 1897 decision in *Scott v. Donald* had attempted to explain the Fuller justices' position on the matter. While noting that "the evils attending the vice of intemperance in the use of spirituous liquors are so great that a natural reluctance is felt in appearing to interfere, even on constitutional grounds, with any law whose avowed purpose is to restrict or prevent the mischief," the Fuller Court nevertheless held in *Scott* that the Wilson Act "was not intended to confer on any state the power to discriminatorily injure the products of another." The *Scott* case was interesting in that it added an Eleventh Amendment twist to the normal contest between alcohol aficionado and dry state: the state constables who had seized the contraband liquors argued that they were immune from any suit to recover damages in that they were acting as officers of the state and under color of state law—albeit an unconstitutional one. Having none of it, the Justice Shiras "condemned" the South Carolina statute that attempted to broadly impound any contraband liquors "while in transit or after arrival, whether in possession of a common carrier, depot agent, express agent or private person."

The constables' "interference . . . with the exercise of personal rights and privileges" of plaintiff Donald had extended to "a case of domestic California wine," "a case of whisky, in bottles, made in Maryland," "and another [case, presumably], consisting of one barrel of bottled beer, made at Rochester, New York." But the *Scott* opinion did more than supply this helpful inventory of period products. It was also the source of the jurisprudential statement that would thereafter govern judicial thinking as to alcohol, as a commodity like any other: "So long as state legislation continues to recognize wines, beer, and spirituous liquors as *articles of lawful consumption and commerce*, so long must continue the duty of the federal courts to afford to such use and commerce the same measure of protection, under the constitution and the laws of the U.S., as is given to other articles" (emphasis added). As long as it was legal, liquor could not be subject to treatment different than that for other commodities.[47] The *Scott v. Donald* rule remained true even after Congress passed the Pure Food and Drug Act in 1906, a Progressive reform that prevented "the manufacture, sale, or transportation of adulterated or misbranded or poisonous or deleterious foods, drugs or medicines, and liquors." Beverage alcohol—its packaging and labeling—could be regulated, for purity and safety, but no more so than any other item of consumption by the public.

The "wetness" of the Fuller era culminated in a 1905 decision, *American Express v. Iowa*, which protected interstate shippers' alcohol traffic to any consignee in a dry state. That many of these liquor transit rulings were written by then-associate and future chief justice New Orleanian man-about-town Edward White presaged a next court era as similarly wet. Lamentably, other, drier forces would prevail by the time of his elevation. Indeed, Justice Brown, dissenting in the aforementioned case of *Scott v. Donald*, had remarked:

> We cannot fail to recognize the growing sentiment in this country in favor of some restrictions upon the sale of ardent spirits; and whether such restrictions shall take the form of a license tax upon dealers, a total prohibition of all manufacture or sale whatever, or the assumption by the state government of the power to supply all liquors to its inhabitants, is a matter exclusively for the states to decide.

Within their own realms, states could be as dry as they liked—and state dryness was on the rise.

A tangible illustration of Brown's point came in another decision the same term as *American Express*. The plaintiff in *Foppiano v. Speed* (1905) had been compelled by state law to pay for a state license to sell liquors while on a ferryboat based at the city of Memphis, with the ferryboat plying between ports in the states of Tennessee and Arkansas, across the Mississippi River. Foppiano rented a bar privilege from the company owning the ferryboat and conducted the business of selling liquors over the bar on the boat pursuant to his lease. But his suit argued that while doing so, he was engaged in interstate commerce and so should not be subject to being taxed by the state. Foppiano had no doubt been encouraged in his suit by the Fuller Court line of decisions limiting the scope of the Wilson Act, as he had in previous years paid the license fee uncomplainingly. The court acknowledged the ambiguity in constitutional law and, in an excess of understatement, noted that "the general right of the states to regulate or prohibit the sale of intoxicating liquors within their borders is not denied; but how far they could prohibit the entrance of the liquors, or their sale, after having been brought into the state, has been a subject of examination and decision within late years by this court." Justice Peckham's opinion nevertheless found a way to affirm federal power over navigation while narrowly acknowledging the state's legitimate power over liquor. As he characterized the situation:

> That the navigation of the Mississippi river is free to every citizen of the United States is a fact not to be questioned at this time. . . . [But w]hen the ferryboat entered the boundaries of the state of Tennessee, and fastened up at the wharf in Memphis, and the plaintiff in error then sold liquors to customers as they asked for them, he became subject to the police laws of that state regarding the sale of intoxicating liquors.

Foppiano's error, it seemed, was dispensing drinks once the boat was tied up in port.

Federal commerce versus state police powers, one of the main tensions within the American Constitution's system of federalism, also animated the Fuller era debate over regulating the Indian alcohol trade. The Fuller Court addressed the matter in 1905[48] in *In re Heff*, which questioned the jurisdictional source and limited the coverage of a new federal alcohol regulatory effort. Arguing there was no such thing as federal police power, the putative authority behind the act, the decision exempted "allottee Indians," as nonreservation, tribally unaffiliated state citizens, from federal alcohol prohibition. As it happens, biographer Ely is able to report this episode from the oral argument in *Heff*:

> Charles Henry Butler, the court reporter, recalled one incident in 1905 that involved a young Kansas attorney who appeared before the justices "in a yellow tweed suit—no vest, flowing necktie, pink shirt and tan shoes." He represented a drugstore operator who had been arrested for selling liquor to an "allottee" Indian.
>
> In the course of argument Justice Brewer asked, "What do you think the status of an allottee is?" The attorney responded, "If you fellows up there don't know, how do you think us fellows down here should know?" Butler reported the stunned reaction of the justices: "The shocked expression on the face of dear Chief Justice Fuller will never be forgotten. Justice Holmes, shaking with laughter, buried his face in his arms on the Bench to hide his amusement, and there was a sort of dazed expression on the features of the other members of the Court. Notwithstanding this amusing gaffe, the Supreme Court decided the case in favor of the attorney's druggist client.[49]

Thespian antics aside, Indian law and liquor remained a quagmire, as illustrated by *Dick v. U.S.* in 1908. Post *Heff*, and its emancipation of the allottee Indian from federal supervision, the *Dick* court somewhat confusingly upheld treaty provisions that continued federal Indian Prohibition on allotted lands, the former Indian community lands that had since been parceled under the Dawes Act and become part of the new state of Idaho but were adjacent to Indian country and buffers between it and state lands. Indian land, *Dick* seemed to say, must remain dry by federal mandate, even when various and sundry Indians themselves were freed to drink by the Fuller Court in *Heff*.

There is one way to square the seemingly disparate Indian decisions and also relate them to the Fuller record overall regarding alcohol and the law: it is to note that, whatever the context, the right to personal use was paramount for the Fuller Court. In the great liquor marketplace that was Fuller's era, the "right to receive" remained protected from interfering state action by the commerce clause.[50] One commentator goes so far as to say that during the Fuller period, "when the popularity of the prohibition movement was growing rapidly, the Supreme Court's decisions were noticeably and decidedly inhospitable to the movement."[51] Still, the scope of untrammeled personal use was decidedly narrowing by the end of Fuller's time as chief. The case of *Cosmopolitan Club v. Virginia* in 1908 is instructive. It held that the contract between a private social club and the state did not authorize the club to disregard the valid law of the state regulating the licensing and sale of liquors, and that no violation of the contract clause resulted from the state subsequently voiding its charter for such disregard. The Cosmopolitans had been formed "to promote social intercourse, athletic and physical culture, and to encourage manly sports"; boozing was not one of their stated associational purposes. A Virginia statute of 1904, pushed by the state's growing dry movement, specifically targeted social clubs "being conducted for the purpose of violating or evading the laws of this state regulating the licensing and sale of liquors" as liable to lose their "chartered rights and franchises." Harlan's opinion for a unanimous court stressed that the statute regulating liquor was one which Virginia could rightfully enact under its power to care for the health and morals of its people, and that the club had misused its corporate franchise in evading it. It is true that in *Cosmopolitan Club*, the Fuller Court was merely upholding a state's power to regulate local alcohol matters, as it had been doing since *Crowley*. But the decision remains a compelling one, as it was one of the few occasions in which prohibitionist fervor was let loose on an institution of the elite class to which the justices belonged.

Nor was it the only encouragement Fuller's justices would give. In an inadvertent way, Fuller's Court indirectly spurred the populist segment of the prohibition movement when it invalidated (by a 5–4 vote) the federal income tax statute in 1895. Figures such as William Jennings Bryan henceforth began a decades-long crusade for a constitutional amendment to secure the generation of revenue from income taxes on the wealthy—a revenue source that would also conveniently destroy the argument for the continued availability of alcohol and the taxes upon it. When the Sixteenth or Income Tax Amendment finally passed in 1913 (during the tenure of Chief Justice White), its success only fueled the clamor for a similar constitutional amendment movement to enshrine Prohibition.[52]

⌒

   More prosaic, private law cases provide some additional, color commentary on drinking and disapproval of it in the Fuller period. Disruptive drinking, for instance, could court disciplinary action. For example, *Northern Pacific Railroad Co. v. Whalen* in 1893 was a case in law and equity, concerning a railroad company that was attempting to enjoin closure of a camp-side saloon patronized by its workers. Rejecting the motion, the court offered this tart observation:

   "No employer has such a property in his workmen or in their services that he can, under the ordinary jurisdiction of a court of chancery, maintain a suit, as for a nuisance, against the keeper of a house at which they voluntarily buy intoxicating liquors, and thereby get so drunk as to be unfit for work." Protected, in other words, was the personal right to freely achieve an on-the-job hangover. And, indeed, the image conjured by this excerpt from the bill to contain a nuisance does paint a picture of fairly debilitating debauchery:

> That the defendants, at and near Tunnel City, and along the line of the railroad so being constructed by the plaintiff [railroad], "for several months last past, have been running retail drinking and lager-beer saloons, and selling spirituous, malt, and fermented liquors to the said employees of said plaintiff; and that the said sales of said liquors to said employees have frequently and continuously caused drunkenness of said employees; and that the said drunkenness incapacitated the said employees so that they were not able to perform the labor assigned to them and the labor they were expected to do and for which they were employed; and that the said drunkenness increased the risk and danger incident to the necessary use of said explosives and machinery, and increased the danger to the employees employed in constructing the road as aforesaid, and to the officers and agents of said plaintiff."

Fuller Court protections for the workingmen's indulgence likely stemmed from its liberty of contract jurisprudence, a jurisprudence that protected the right of a worker to freely contract with an employer—but for his *laboring hours*, not his off-duty time and choice of pursuits. Thus, in *Northern Pacific*, the Fuller justices' elite but firmly pro–free market sentiments united with the common man's alcoholic interests. Yet once prominent capitalists and industrial magnates united in their support for antialcohol measures as means of bolstering a more productive workforce and more reliable profits, industrial workers would find their opportunities for heavy drinking curtailed without serious judicial objection. As one manufacturer rather crassly put it: "Until booze is banished, we can never have really efficient workmen. We are not much interested in the moral side of the matter as such. It is purely a question of dollars and cents."[53]

Of course, disapproval of drink could also take the more predictably moral cast, even when the drinking itself was hardly disreputable. A libel case decided in 1909, *Peck v. Tribune*, illustrated quite pointedly the infamy with which some individuals of the time period associated the charge of being a drinker. Justice Holmes's opinion for the court—and in support of the libel claim—summarized the facts of the dispute thusly:

> The libel alleged is found in an advertisement printed in the defendant's newspaper, The Chicago Sunday Tribune, and is as follows: "Nurse and Patients Praise Duffy's. Mrs. A. Schuman, One of Chicago's Most Capable and Experienced Nurses, Pays an Eloquent Tribute to the Great Invigorating, Life-Giving, and Curative Properties of Duffy's Pure Malt Whisky." Then followed a portrait of the plaintiff, with the words, "Mrs. A. Schuman," under it. Then, in quotation marks, "After years of constant use of your Pure Malt Whisky, both by myself and as given to patients in my capacity as nurse, I have no hesitation in recommending it as the very best tonic and stimulant for all local and run-down conditions," etc., etc., with the words, "Mrs. A. Schuman, 1576 Mozart St., Chicago, Ill.," at the end, not in quotation marks, but conveying the notion of a signature, or at least that the words were hers. The declaration alleged that the plaintiff was not Mrs. Schuman, was not a nurse, and was a total abstainer from whisky and all spirituous liquors. There was also a count for publishing the plaintiff's likeness without leave.

The court of appeals below, which had denied the claim, "pointed out that there was no general consensus of opinion that to drink whisky is wrong," but Holmes rejected this as beside the point. "If the advertisement obviously would hurt the plaintiff in the estimation of an important and respectable part of the community," he concluded, "liability is not a question of a majority vote." Yet Holmes—legal positivist that he was—did seem influenced by popular feeling of the time in one respect: he was clearly persuaded that the advertisement's copy could very well seriously hurt someone's standing "with a considerable and respectable class in the community." Uncontestable this was, even though the advertisement was reporting the individual's mere *medical* use of liquor.

Other private law and routine appeals cases shed a veritable market research light on the period's imbibing. An otherwise incidental Indian law case, *Sarlls v. U.S.* in 1894, required the court—in applying the Indian prohibition of liquor trade statute of 1832, as amended in 1864 and 1877—to decide "whether 'lager beer' is a 'spirituous liquor or wine.'" Noting first that, "All spirituous liquors are intoxicating, yet all intoxicating liquors are not spirituous. In common parlance, 'spirituous liquors' mean 'distilled liquors.' Fermented liquors, though intoxicating, are not spirituous," the Fuller Court went on . . . and on to reject "the meaning of the statute in the fact—true in a scientific sense—that alcohol is found in fermented as well as in distilled liquors, and that the purpose of the statute is to prevent the mischief occasioned by the use of intoxicating drinks." Having none of such niceties, the *Sarlls* decision laid out this alternative methodology:

"We cannot agree with this method of reading a penal statute. The purpose of such a statute is to notify the public of the legislative intent, not to furnish scientific definitions. That intent is, in most cases, to be found by giving to the words the meaning in which they are used in ordinary speech."

Adjudging beer not within the meaning of the Indian prohibition law, and the seller's conviction overturned, *Sarlls* ended with this meticulous if not prickly observation:

> Since this cause was tried, an amendatory act has been passed by congress, approved July 23, 1892, providing that the section shall read as follows: "No ardent spirits, ale, beer, wine, or intoxicating liquor or liquors of whatever kind shall be introduced, under any pretense, into the Indian country. Every person who sells, exchanges,

gives, barters, or disposes of any ardent spirits, ale, beer, wine, or intoxicating liquors of any kind to any Indian under charge of any Indian superintendent or agent, or introduces or attempts to introduce any ardent spirits, ale, wine, beer, or intoxicating liquors of any kind into the Indian country, shall be punished by imprisonment for not more than two years, and by fine of not more than three hundred dollars for each offense." This would seem to show that congress regarded the act, as it previously stood, as *not* including ale and beer in its terms. At any rate, the temptation to the courts to stretch the law to cover an acknowledged evil is now removed. (emphasis added)

So there.

Definitional action was also requested in *Erhardt v. Steinhardt* of 1894, with the court acting as a simple, error-correcting appellate body and where the question was whether the duty assigned to "Boonekamp Bitters" should be as a "proprietary preparation" or tonic remedy, or as "cordials, liquors [liqueurs], arrack, absinthe, kirschwasser, ratafia, and other similar spirituous beverages or bitters, containing spirits." Noting sensibly that while the bitters in question were similar to absinthe, and absinthe is bitter, Chief Justice Fuller held for the court:

> We are unable to conclude otherwise than that there was evidence tending to show that Boonekamp bitters were not substantially similar to absinthe, and that there was, therefore, no ground for taking the case away from the jury. The verdict that there was no such similarity determined that these bitters were properly classified under the proprietary preparation clause, and this excluded them from all other provisions. The rate of duty on the bottles was dependent on the rate of duty on the contents, and the determination as to the latter controlled.

Displaying that he was fully conversant with the general product line at issue, Fuller went on to comment:

> There was evidence tending to show that it contains rhubarb, orange peel, turmeric, and an essential oil, probably oil of anise; that it is bitter; that it is not attractive as a beverage, and hardly used distinctively as such; and that, while it is sold largely by liquor dealers, and used at bars, it is chiefly so sold for use and used in water, wines, or spirits, as a bitter, and for its cathartic, as well as tonic, qualities.

The subject matter of *Erhardt*—bitters, and the contemporarily popular absinthe—argues for the Sazerac as an honorable mention cocktail of the Fuller era. Such "fancy" whiskey cocktails—those that included the addition of a liqueur or exotic flavoring—had many avid fans during the Gilded Age of drinking, even though they date from much earlier in the saga of American cocktails. Fuller's own familiarity with the nomenclature and the qualities of the various spirits in the *Erhardt* case suggests that he might have been one of those fans.

Finally, expertise in beer brewing was solicited in the case of *Joseph Schlitz Brewing Co. v. U.S.* in 1901, which involved a claim for a drawback or refund of duties paid on foreign imported bottles and corks used in the manufacture of bottled beer, which was subsequently exported out of state. The Tariff Act of 1890 allowed such a rebate of duties paid on imported materials used by a manufacturer in making their products in order to stimulate domestic manufactures; the theory of the claimant was that *bottled* beer is really a different product from ordinary beer and requires a process of manufacture in which bottles and corks are a material ingredient. Dismissing the brewer's claim that the "steaming" process was unique to beer that would be bottled, and that closed bottles were essential to that final product, the Fuller Court was unconvinced. "In our view, the question presents no difficulty whatever," Justice Brown began, speaking for a unanimous bench. "[B]ottles and corks," he continued,

> are not "imported materials" at all, but finished products, and usable for any liquor which the importer may choose to put in them. Neither are they ingredients used in the manufacture of exported or any other kind of beer, in any proper sense of the term, but simply the packages which the manufacturer, for the purposes of export, sees fit, and perhaps is required, to make use of for the proper preservation of his product. Bottled beer is still beer, made of the same ingredients as ordinary beer, though made with greater care, and to speak of the bottles and corks as ingredients of the beer is simply an abuse of language.

A bottle was an encasement not an ingredient, he submitted, offering this learnedly vinous comparison:

beer does not materially differ from a hundred other articles which require to be incased for their proper preservation. Thus, champagne and other sparkling wines must be bottled while yet effervescing, or they will lose the tang which gives them their principal value.

The level of detail in Brown's opinion is an interesting testimonial to his and colleagues' easy familiarity with various alcoholic products,[54] and its conclusion displayed the typical legal formalism for which his era's Supreme Court is so well known. Reminiscent of the court's closing thoughts in *Sarlls*, Brown said this to close *Joseph Schlitz*: "If the law afford [Schlitz] an imperfect relief, his remedy is by application to Congress for additional legislation, and not to the judicial power for a strained interpretation of the law already in force." Alas, no such congressional aid to the brewers was forthcoming. The Fuller Court reaffirmed the bottled beer principle in *Anheuser-Busch Brewing Assoc. v. U S.* in 1908, despite the fact that the imported corks in question there had been subtly altered by a domestically applied treatment. The corks were still corks, Justice McKenna reasoned for the court, so they were still not materials used in the manufacture of beer, and so not eligible for the drawback of import duties.

Fuller's is one of the richest judicial records in the history of alcohol and the Supreme Court, and of alcoholic beverages in American life. It certainly was the richest decisional record to date in the Supreme Court's history. Fuller and his colleagues generally extended to their alcohol-related cases the same probusiness, antigovernment regulation jurisprudence that they applied in their decisions overall. The overstuffed docket of the Fuller Court, where delays in deciding cases could extend to years, meant that some liquor trafficking survived by clever technicality. But that overstuffed docket was also stuffed full of cases urging liquor's regulation, suggesting that the Fuller justices were merely stemming a tide that would one day overtake the court and its aficionados of fine drink.

CONCLUSION

In terms of the sheer number and variety of cocktails and liquors enjoyed, combined with the sheer regularity and complexity of the court's doctrinal pronouncements on alcohol, the Fuller era is the epitome of the well-stocked bar. Yet the class bias of emergent, second-wave prohibitionist efforts was clearly on display, in both the era's attitude to whom those efforts should (and should not) apply and the court's own jurisprudence of finesse as to antialcohol regulatory efforts.

6

THE WHITE ERA AND THE PROHIBITION AMENDMENT

Apres moi, le deluge. Or, more accurately, *Sous moi, arrete le deluge alcoolique*, for francophone Chief Justice White had the distinct misfortune to conclude his term by presiding over the inauguration of the American era of national prohibition. *The White Court* (1910–1921) sees Louisiana Democrat Edward Douglass White as chief justice, the first sitting associate justice to be so promoted. White, like Fuller, was initially appointed by Democratic president Grover Cleveland, but he was elevated to the chief's chair by Republican William Howard Taft. It was a strategic appointment by President Taft, who was engineering for his own fervently desired, future appointment as chief justice: Taft hoped that the aged White would not last long in his seat. He did not, but he lingered achingly longer than Taft anticipated.

Most notable about the White era of course, alcohol policy–wise, was the ratification of the Eighteenth Amendment on January 29, 1919, with the accompanying Volstead Act—passed over President Woodrow Wilson's veto[1]—enforcing nationwide Prohibition going into effect one year later, on January 17, 1920. Prohibition was the product of the unlikely union among antisaloon temperance Christians, racial and ethnic nativists, and Progressive reformers. White's Court found itself pressed on all sides by the Progressive movement. Not only did the Progressives' economic reforms challenge the probusiness/antigovernmental regulation legal doctrines of the Supreme Court, but the Progressive social agenda also included the vigorous endorsement of all manner of social improvements, with antialcohol prohibition being a keystone. There was a strong tinge of the racialist theory of eugenics to some of the Progressives' social engineering, and in this they were joined by post-Reconstruction Southern white elites, whose views of the urgency of liquor's restriction were decidedly colored by race and race fears. When Alabama congressman Richmond Hobson introduced his 1914 alcohol prohibition bill, he prefaced it with remarks about liquor's especially deleterious effects on the behavior of "the Negro," its capacity to produce feeblemindedness and perversion in women, and its generally unsavory impact on the vigor of (Anglo-Saxon) male and female reproductive systems.[2] While this bill was narrowly defeated in the House, things would be quite different just a few years later. The decades-long strategy of the Anti-Saloon League was paying off, and the 1916 elections sent so many dry organization–endorsed candidates to the House and Senate "that action on a prohibitory national amendment was virtually assured."[3]

The strictures of World War I gave the prohibition crusade a further opportunity to demonstrate its dedication to national unity and discipline.[4] Prohibition came specifically to the District of Columbia in November 1917, with the Hobson-Sheppard Act outlawing all alcohol save for personal use or prescribed by a doctor. (A follow-up act in 1919 closed the former loophole.) With wartime alcohol prohibition already in effect, state ratification of the Prohibition Amendment pressed forward with alarming alacrity. Still, Washington remained "wet," as it would throughout White's and the entire Prohibition era, with speakeasies and bootlegging operating fairly unmolested. George Cassiday would be known as the bootlegger to Congress, first the House and then the Senate.[5] President Warren G. Harding's Washington has been described as "awash in alcohol from the moment of his inauguration"[6] —from his storied White House poker-and-whiskey-highball games, to the "infamous den of iniquity," the Little Green House on K St. The contradictions and tensions of the Fuller and early White periods, over liquor's restriction versus its enjoyment, gave way to the full-blown hypocrisy of the 1920s.

The political contradictions of the pre-Prohibition segment of the White era, regarding alcohol, are nicely captured by this flowery testimonial from one Mississippi politician:

You have asked me how I feel about whiskey. Well, here's how I stand on the question. If when you say whiskey, you mean that devil's brew; the poison spirit, the bloody monster that defiles innocence, dethrones reason, destroys the home, and creates misery and poverty . . . if you mean that evil drink that topples the religious man from the pinnacle of righteousness, gracious living, and causes him to descend to the pit of degradation, despair, shame, and helplessness, then I am certainly against it with all my heart.

But if when you say whiskey, you mean the oil of conversation, the philosophic wine, the ale consumed when good fellows get together that puts a song in their hearts and laughter on their lips and the warm glow of contentment in their eyes . . . if you mean the drink whose sale put untold millions of dollars into our treasury . . . then certainly I am in favor of it. This is my stand, and I will not compromise.[7]

The White justices, too, fell into this uneasy duplicity: upholding with little objection most of the dry laws they reviewed, but remaining men of spirits in private.

White's era should be thought of as the last gasp of the epoch of elegant cocktailing. The courtly, heavyset White was himself a man from another time, socially as well as politically. He was a member of the landed, monied elite of the old South, scion of a Creole family of French Louisiana who had supported the Confederacy during the Civil War. His habits, including his drinking habits, were of that cosmopolitan but fundamentally conservative elite. He never really changed in the course of his long service on the Supreme Court, although his political restitution after the war required a formal commitment to nationalism, a project in which he did seem to sincerely believe. He also grudgingly moved his court closer to an acceptance of some government intervention in the economy, and some advances in terms of racial justice. But he was never, and never would be, an adherent to the temperance program.

White's Louisiana political and cultural roots mandate a southern beverage as this era's totem. The age-old mint julep had held on as a plantation favorite, and was also enjoyed by White contemporary Teddy Roosevelt, but this drink's heyday was really the antebellum period. Alcoholic beverages with a Bayou State and/or Crescent City pedigree include the brandy milk punch—a Deep South holiday favorite—or the

Sazerac, but these two recipes are also somewhat antediluvian for a twentieth-century judicial era. With respect to the latter cocktail in particular, the New Orleans Online website offers this beverage history:

> Back in 1838, Antoine Peychaud created the drink in a French Quarter bar and named it for his favorite French brandy, Sazerac-de-Forge et fils. In 1873, the drink was changed when American Rye whiskey was substituted for cognac, and a dash of absinthe was added by bartender Leon Lamothe, and today he is now regarded as the Father of the Sazerac. In 1912, absinthe was banned, so Peychaud substituted his special bitters in its place.

Long after its creation, the Sazerac remained a popular fancy cocktail in its city of origin. But there was another contender for the true totemic cocktail of the White era, as this tidbit at the end of the above online entry hints: "In 1893 the Grunewald Hotel was built in the city, and at this time the hotel earned the rights to Ramos' Gin Fizz and the Sazerac."

And what was this *Ramos Gin Fizz*? New Orleans bartender Henry C. Ramos invented the frothy, egg white and orange-flower water gin fizz that bears his name in 1888 at his bar, the Imperial Cabinet Saloon on Gravier Street. It was originally called a "New Orleans fizz," and remains one of the city's most famous cocktails. Indeed, before Prohibition, the drink's popularity and exceptionally long twelve-minute mixing time had over twenty bartenders working at the Imperial at once making nothing but Ramos's gin fizz—and still struggling to keep up with demand.[8] *Imbibe!* notes that Ramos moved his operation in 1907 to the Stag Saloon, across the street from the well-known and well-appointed St. Charles Hotel, and it was here during Mardi Gras 1915 that he employed the legendary chain of thirty-five shaker men at once.[9] Both the Sazerac Bar (at the Grunewald) and the Ramos of New Orleans—and by this we must assume was meant Henry Ramos's Stag—are mentioned by lifestyle writers as among the eminent bars of the Gilded Age.[10]

There are other reasons to acclaim the **Ramos gin fizz** as the White era's cocktail. Fizzes were especially popular in the early decades of the new century, and other famous frothy concoctions also date from this period. For instance, 1918 saw the creation of the cream-based crème de menthe Grasshopper, the second-prize winning entry in a New York

City cocktail competition and hailing from another New Orleans establishment: Tujaque's Restaurant in the French Quarter. Its creator, Philip Guichet, went on to institutionalize the beverage at his restaurant's bar (still in operation). An exact date is less certain for the light and refreshingly foamy Clover Club cocktail, but its pedigree is undisputed: it was born as the house cocktail of the Clover Club of Philadelphia, a professional men's dining club founded in the late nineteenth century by a group of journalists who regularly hosted (and perhaps roasted) area politicians. The recipe ultimately emigrated to New York's Waldorf Astoria Hotel bar sometime around 1912 and from there acquired a sturdy pre-Prohibition popularity.[11] A cousin of the gin fizz family, the Clover Club contributes raspberry syrup to the egg white, citrus, and gin mixture and also entails a good bit of shaking. White Ladies and Pink Ladies—the latter allegedly named after the heroine in a 1911 light opera—belong to this oeuvre as well, with Cointreau and lemon, and grenadine and Applejack brandy, as the respective feature ingredients.

Ramos dictated a recipe for his New Orleans gin fizz to a reporter for the *New Orleans Item-Tribune* a few years before his death in 1928. Reproduced in *Imbibe!*,[12] it incorporates orange-flower water and milk or cream into the garden-variety silver (gin) fizz and is similarly served in a tall thin glass. The Ramos gin fizz was reportedly Louisiana governor Huey Long's drink, associated with him and his long-term stay at the Roosevelt Hotel in the late 1920s, which had by then succeeded the Grunewald in ownership.[13] New Orleans was notoriously "wet" during Prohibition, remaining well supplied with liquor imported from Mexico and the Caribbean. But even when the quality of spirits flagged, the milk and egg thickened gin fizzes and assorted Ladies disguised it well.

White would have patronized all the kinds of establishments serving up the tall Ramos fizz, both before and during his Supreme Court service. His city of New Orleans was a drinking town before and throughout Prohibition, with one sociologist of the time pronouncing, "Most of the men drink something every day."[14] There is no reason to doubt White's fortitude. Corpulent and thick-maned with a head of silver, wavy hair, he was almost a caricature of a nineteenth-century Southern senator. His especially hagiographic biographer Klinkhamer notes his "admitted ability as a raconteur."[15] So there is also no reason to question White's membership in and participation in the rituals of the political class of his time. Descended from a sugar plantation family from LaFourche Parish, White was part of the New Orleans political scene: his father had been governor as well as judge on the Louisiana Supreme Court. As a young man, he followed his state into secession but was exonerated after the Civil War and Reconstruction. He continued the education that had been interrupted by the war, studying law at the Tulane University of Louisiana—itself honored with its own signature cocktail during the White Court period.[16] After his own brief service on the Louisiana Supreme Court and before his term as a U.S. senator and then appointment to the U.S. Supreme Court in 1894 as associate justice, White was in private practice in Louisiana and living as a bachelor in the French Quarter. He spoke French fluently and was very much a part of the social scene: "His home," one biographer writes, "was associated with French cooking and fine dinners." Politician and gourmand, White was also clearly part of the city's social elite.[17] He was a member of the New Orleans Pickwick Club, a gentlemen's private social club that invited only blue-blooded business and professional elites as members.[18] Presumably, he was also a member of the old and equally elite men's carnival krewe of Comus, whose membership is still secret but was historically associated with membership in the Pickwick Club. For a time, the two organizations were one, with Pickwick being Comus's public front or face, but in 1884 the club and the Mistick Krewe of Comus severed all official ties; in the twentieth century, their memberships were not identical but there were members common to both groups. The Pickwick Club also included members who were part of the anti-Reconstruction Crescent City White League, a paramilitary organization composed of ex-Confederate officers and jilted planters and factors that was active during the 1870s.[19] The Pickwickians played a disturbingly recalcitrant role during the Reconstruction period in New Orleans, and the White League led violent protests/insurrections against Republican and black public officials and their racial enfranchisement policies.[20] In the full throes of the reactionary politics of the Jim Crow era, their activity was commemorated by the city's erection in 1891 of the Battle of Liberty Place Monument, which controversially stood in downtown New Orleans until late April 2017.

Throughout his life White was a member of some social, economic, political, or institutional elite, and there is no evidence that he ever questioned the dogma of that elite.[21] Or its privileges. The economics

Figure 6.1.   Pickwick Club Café and Card Room, at the 1028 Canal St. location, where the club was housed from 1896 to 1934. Chief Justice White was a member of the New Orleans Pickwick Club, an exclusive gentleman's social club. Private clubs such as this continued to provide alcoholic beverages to their elite member- ship throughout the Prohibition period, as well as being sites of the invention of a host of eponymous club cocktails. *Source: Original photographic plates, "The Pick- wick Club: Historical Summary, Act of Incorporation, By-Laws, Roster of Membership" (1929), Louisiana Research Collection, Tulane University, Augusto Miceli Papers 1813- 1975, Manuscripts Collection 924, Box 1, Folder 6)*

of Prohibition, and of the dry laws' operation even before that, meant that upper-class individuals had little problem obtaining and affording illicit alcohol.[22] Private clubs and their club cocktail preparations con- tinued with little interruption, and this would have been true at White's hometown Pickwick Club. Its closedness to outsiders precludes defini- tive research on its drinking activities, although archived ephemera held at the Louisiana Research Collection include an 1893 club financial statement with entries for "bar—gross receipts" and an undated Thanksgiving dinner menu that lists "Pickwick Club claret" among the offerings. "Club historian" Miceli casually referenced members enjoy- ing a cooling crème de menthe on the open summer gallery at one of the club's earlier, nineteenth-century locations. And invited guests to the club's current locale reported its service of the classic New Orleans gin fizz at its inner bar. A routine Internet search for "cocktails of the Pickwick Club" produces this contemporary hit:

> Drink: Pickwick Club
> From: The Westport Café, in "the Brooklyn of Kansas City"
> Description: Frothy
> The drink: light, citrusy, floral, bright. Off their House Cocktails list. With Citadelle gin, orgeat, orange blossom, lemon, and egg white, this refreshing and slightly tart cocktail is frothy from the egg whites and with a lightly floral and orange flavor. It finishes clean and bright and is a wonderful cocktail to sip.[23]

This eponymous cocktail bears more than a passing resemblance to the Ramos gin fizz, with a twenty-first-century mixology spin.

Whatever else he was, White was certainly clubbable. He was eminently "comfortable" on the court: White "had settled into Washington society . . . [and] even liked the Court's setting—the old Senate chamber, still close and clubby in its atmosphere."[24] One source even argues that White's gentlemanly affability made him—not Fuller—the one responsible for the custom of a formal greeting among the justices, each morning in the robing room. As the story goes, Chief Justice White would step to the center of the room and greet each colleague in order of seniority with a handshake and the words "Good Morning, Mr. Justice," with each justice in turn replying, "Good Morning, Mr. Chief Justice."[25]

Though the handshake formality is usually attributed to the equally genial Fuller, White was the more intensely sociable man. Finally married and once ensconced in the nation's capital, Chief Justice White's home was a hospitality center for Louisianans who found themselves in Washington for one purpose or another. "The meals, prepared and served in the tradition of New Orleans cooking, were famous."[26] Clearly, and as befitting that New Orleans style, cocktails were poured, for Mrs. White was also, like several of her predecessors, an accomplished hostess. Klinkhamer notes that as a justice "[White's] income was sufficient for him to preserve much of the southern life that he had enjoyed," and that he enjoyed engaging in "pleasant little courtesies" such as gifting his fellow justices (Lamar or McKenna) with a cigar.[27] Like his southern state predecessor Taney, White was a committed and life-long cigar smoker. By the end of his tenure as chief, he and John Marshall Harlan of Kentucky[28] were also the last of the old guard "tobacco chewing justices" left on the bench, with White "remain[ing] the same and continu[ing] to send a page boy out to buy a few cheap cigars for his use."[29]

White's old-timey personal style extended to the "maze of words" of his opinions, for his "writing embodied a number of the worst features of nineteenth century prose style."[30] This meant that his legal directives were somewhat obtuse and difficult to decipher. Happily, or unhappily, many of his court's alcohol-related pronouncements came from the pens of his judicial colleagues, so their import was less mistakable. Associate Justice Charles Evans Hughes, himself a future chief justice, applied his particularly crisp style to one of the White Court's earliest— and least mistakable—rulings on state restriction of liquor sales. "That the state, in the exercise of its police power, may prohibit the selling of intoxicating liquors, is undoubted," Hughes began in *Purity Extract and Tonic Co. v. Lynch* in 1912. The state's judgment as to how to proceed in protecting its people could legitimately include a prohibition on the sale of all malt liquors, "having regard to the artifices which are used to promote the sale of intoxicants under the guise of innocent beverages," Hughes then reasoned. The healthfulness and wholesomeness of the ingredients of the compound "Poinsetta" were thus no defense—nor was the fact that the malted cereal product was unfermented and contained no actual alcohol.

The White Court also upheld its predecessor's construction of the Wilson Act to allow states to regulate, tax, and even restrict the sale of imported liquor after its arrival in state, extending that rule to foreign as well as out-of-state imported liquor in a case that affected White's home state, *Frederick de Bary Co. v. Louisiana* (1913). But White's Court was also capable of carefully parsing the Wilson Act to prevent state taxation schemes from burdening the "right" to make interstate commerce shipments of alcohol—or, in White's own inimitable wordage:

> In the nature of things the protection against the imposition of direct burdens upon the right to do interstate commerce, as often pointed out by this court, is not a mere abstraction, affording no real protection, but is practical and substantial, and embraces those acts which are necessary to the complete enjoyment of the right protected.

(*Heyman v. Hays*, 1915; see also *Rosenberger v. Pacific Express Co.*, 1916)

The White Court continued to apply this principle and uphold even dubiously "inter"state practices of liquor sales—although by the time of *Rossi v. Pennsylvania* (1915), the opinion of the court did acknowledge that things might be changing. "The case arose before the passage of the act of March 1, 1913, known as the Webb-Kenyon act," Justice Pitney noted in *Rossi*, adding hastily, "and the effect of this legislation is therefore not now involved." He proceeded to reverse the conviction for violating the state's liquor license law by finding the business to be one in interstate commerce, as the court had similarly done in the decision of *Kirmeyer v. Kansas* (1915). Yet even when the White Court finally acknowledged the validity of the new antiliquor congressional statute, as it did in *Adams Express Co. v. Kentucky* (1915), its decisions found ways to circumvent the law. "The purpose of Congress in enacting the Webb-Kenyon Act was *not* to prohibit *all* interstate shipment or transportation of liquor into so-called dry territory" (emphasis added), Justice Day instructed, "but to render the prohibitory provisions of the statute operative whenever, and only when, the liquor is to be dealt with in violation of the law of the state into which it is shipped." As Day explained the purpose and the meaning of the new law:

> [It was] . . . to extend the prohibitions against the introduction of liquors into the states by means of interstate commerce. That the act did not assume to deal with all interstate commerce shipments of intoxicating liquors into prohibitory territory in the states is shown in its title, which expresses the purpose to divest intoxicating liquors of their interstate character *in certain cases. What such cases should be was left to the text of the act to develop.*
>
> It is elementary that the first resort, with a view to ascertaining the meaning of a statute, is to the language used. If that is plain there is an end to construction, and the statute is to be taken to mean what it says. (emphasis added)

The White Court's legal formulism, its mechanically literalist interpretation of legal statutes,[31] preserved some space for alcohol's use, in spite of the Webb-Kenyon directive. Because the Kentucky recipient of the liquor being shipped by Adams Express intended it only for his personal possession, not sale, he did not violate or intend to violate any law of the state for, as Day helpfully quoted the state supreme court, "there was never even the claim of a right on the part of the [state] legislature to interfere with the citizen using liquor for his own comfort, provided that in so doing he committed no offense against public decency by being intoxicated." *Adams Express* held that the Webb-Kenyon Act had "no application and no effect to change the general rule that the states may not regulate commerce wholly interstate," and since the conviction in this case was for an interstate transportation, *not* prohibited by the act, it had to be overturned.

The 1913 Webb-Kenyon Act, directed at overruling a doctrinal impediment put in place by the Fuller Court—and an impediment likewise sustained by White's Court, in the 1912 ruling in *Louisville N.R. Co. v. F.W. Cook Brewing*, which held that a carrier could not refuse to accept interstate shipments of intoxicating liquors consigned to local-option or "dry" points—seemed to have been stripped of all force by *Adams Express* in 1915. But appearances were deceiving. Once a state changed its alcohol prohibition law to include "bringing into the state intoxicating liquors intended for personal use and the receipt and possession of such liquors, when so introduced, for personal use" as West Virginia had by 1915, the congressional ban on interstate shipment to the dry state was fully consistent with the Constitution. As the White justices put it in *James Clark Distilling Co. v. Western Maryland R.R. Co.* (1917), a state could legitimately "restrict the means by which intoxicants for personal use could be obtained, even if such use was permitted." In *Clark*, the court's viewpoint was that "the exceptional nature" of intoxicating liquors justified "the enlarged right possessed by the government to regulate liquor." From here, it was a short step to what happened next. Preceding but presaging formal Prohibition, the White Court upheld in *Crane v. Campbell* (1917) state "bone-dry" laws that banned alcohol possession for personal use—although even the soon-to-pass Eighteenth Amendment did not do this. The *Crane* ruling thus allowed, as consistent with the Webb-Kenyon Act, confiscation of any alcohol shipped interstate, whether for commercial sale, gifting, or personal use, into states that had prohibited it or wished to block its entry.

How far the Supreme Court had traveled in a few short years is demonstrated by the spurt of purple prose from Justice McReynolds, writing for the court in *Crane*:

It must now be regarded as settled that, on account of their *well-known noxious qualities and the extraordinary evils shown by experience commonly to be consequent upon their use*, a state has power absolutely to prohibit manufacture, gift, purchase, sale, or transportation of intoxicating liquors within its borders without violating the guarantees of the Fourteenth Amendment. (emphasis added)

What measures "are reasonably appropriate or needful to render exercise of that power effective" were the state's to determine, McReynolds continued, and "an assured right of possession would necessarily imply some adequate method to obtain not subject to destruction at the will of the state." Since "the right to hold intoxicating liquors for personal use is not one of those fundamental privileges of a citizen of the United States which no state may abridge," there was no constitutional bar to what the state had done. There was only this small concession to liberty, and sanity, in McReynolds's opinion regarding the state law: "with its wisdom this Court is not directly concerned."

Webb-Kenyon had been the product of the efficacious lobbying by the Anti-Saloon League, which owed its success to operating as a nonpartisan pressure group. The ASL's tactic was classic special interest group politics:

Recognizing that whenever two political parties or two factions of the same party competed with approximate equality the support of a relatively small unattached group could be crucial, the league sought to demonstrate that it controlled enough votes to make the difference between election and defeat, thereby gaining candidates' acceptance of its programs in return for its endorsement.[32]

It successfully attached itself to Progressive reformers and their agenda, which for many included full-fledged national prohibition. But the success of prohibition laws was really a conflux of political and jurisprudential forces. White's Court did not so much assent to the former as support the latter: in other words, the justices upheld their visions of state sovereignty and individual liberty, not the policy attitudes of Progressives or prohibitionists. In the end, the outcome was the same, as is illustrated by the 1918 decision in *Eigner v. Garrity*, which held that "dram shop statutes"—assigning liability for harm caused by intoxicated persons to shop owners and liquor dispensers—were a legitimate exercise of the states' police powers.

Not only were state criminal statutes increasingly antialcohol, so was the official opinion of the American Medical Association. Its 1917 resolution opposed the use of alcohol as a beverage and urged that the use of alcohol as a therapeutic agent be discouraged.[33] World War I's wartime emergency further aided the antialcohol effort, spurring calls for temporary national prohibition as a measure to conserve grain for feeding the army, America's allies, and the domestic population. Acts of 1917 and 1918 banning production of distilled spirits and then the manufacture and sale of intoxicating beverages of more than 2.75 percent alcohol until demobilization reflected the belief that alcoholic beverages ought to be sacrificed under the circumstances.[34] The White Court upheld this extension of congressionally mandated prohibition in *Hamilton v. Kentucky Distilleries and Warehouse Co.* in 1919 as a legitimate exercise of congressional war powers. With Justice Louis Brandeis writing for a unanimous court, the decision allowed wartime prohibition to continue to function even after the armistice with Germany, as well as concurrently with the just-passed Eighteenth Amendment and National Prohibition Act—which President Wilson had of course vetoed. The court "may [not] pass upon the necessity for the exercise of a power possessed," Brandeis remarked stoically, perhaps thinking of the beverages he would soon forswear.

The White Court also upheld congressionally mandated prohibition legislation in *U.S. v. Hill* in 1919, but this time over the dissenting objections of Justices McReynolds and Clarke. The case's controversy predated the passage of the War-Time Prohibition Act of 1918 and the more all-encompassing and peacetime prohibition statute that was the National Prohibition Act of 1919; rather, it concerned an amendment to the interstate commerce regulations that the Supreme Court had previously upheld: the Wilson and the Webb-Kenyon Acts. *Hill* suggested that all would not be unanimous smooth sailing, when it came to judicial support for national prohibition policy: its majority's broad construction of congressional power to ban interstate commerce in alcohol, except for a limited set of sacramental, scientific, and medical purposes, was a bridge too far for McReynolds. The Reed Amendment of 1917 "as now construed," he fumed, "is a congressional fiat imposing more complete prohibition wherever the state has assumed to prevent manufacture or sale of intoxicants." Hill had been carrying a quart of liquor on his person as he rode a trolley from Kentucky into West Virginia, which at that point permitted possession of not more than one quart of alcohol for personal use but forbade its commercial manufacture or sale for beverage purposes. Congress's absolute ban on beverage alcohol was federal meddling in state affairs, pure and simple, for the *Hill* dissenters. "If Congress may deny liquor to those who live in a state simply because its manufacture is not permitted there, why may not this be done for any suggested reason—e. g., because the roads are bad or men are hanged for murder or coals are dug. Where is the limit?" McReynolds charged.

The limit appeared to be the Prohibition Amendment itself. In the midst of the wartime ascetic spirit, Congress had taken up the proposal for constitutional prohibition of alcohol. Ratification of an Eighteenth Amendment to the Bill of Rights was sure and swift. It read:

> **Section 1.** After one year from the ratification of this article the manufacture, sale, or transportation of intoxicating liquors within, the importation thereof into, or the exportation thereof from the United States and all the territory subject to the jurisdiction thereof for beverage purposes is hereby prohibited.
>
> **Section 2.** The Congress and the several States shall have concurrent power to enforce this article by appropriate legislation.
>
> **Section 3.** This article shall be inoperative unless it shall have been ratified as an amendment to the Constitution by the legislatures of the several States, as provided in the Constitution, within seven years from the date of the submission hereof to the States by the Congress.

With the amendment's passage in January of 1919, Congress duly passed the National Prohibition Act—also known as the Volstead Act, named after its chief sponsor, Rep. Andrew Volstead of Minnesota. The act had the effect of expanding the scope of wartime prohibition and extending the restrictions until the Eighteenth Amendment took effect. Significantly, Volstead also added a number of offenses to federal crimes, including the maintenance of any property where intoxicating liquor was manufactured, kept, or sold as a "common nuisance."[35] These criminal provisions—and their civil liberties' ramifications— would soon become the subject of much federal litigation.

Even before such scrutiny began, White's Court sat for the first constitutional challenge to the legitimacy of the Eighteenth Amendment itself, in a case brought in 1920 by the famed lawyer Elihu Root.[36] *Hawke v. Smith* challenged the procedures by which the amendment had been passed: the issue before the Supreme Court was whether a state had a right to reserve to its people the right to review its legislature's ratification of federal amendments. Ohio (and other states) had done so, in a state constitutional provision adopted in 1918, yet its legislature had voted to ratify the Prohibition Amendment and that ratification had been certified by the governor in 1919, without the benefit of a popular referendum. Root argued that the amendment was thus putatively invalid. The White Court held that the voters of the state could not overturn the state legislature's ratification of an amendment, as the Constitution says nothing about the people's right to review such legislative approval. Historian Kyvig argues that the Ohio referendum controversy "left an impression in some minds that national prohibition had been foisted on an unwilling American people by a crafty, well-organized minority using undemocratic means." The Supreme Court, nevertheless, "reflect[ed] the widespread support for national prohibition."[37]

There was more White Court complicity to come. A case from the 1919 term required the court to weigh in on whether 3.4 percent alcohol beer was considered "intoxicating" for the purposes of the Volstead Act. (It was.)[38] Consolidated into the *National Prohibition Cases* (1920), this decision permitting the act to define intoxicating [*sic*] beverages as containing as much or little as one-half of 1 percent of alcohol was joined with a decision that confirmed that the Eighteenth Amendment "had become part of the Constitution and must be respected and given effect the same as other provisions." The decision in *National Prohibition Cases* (also known as *Rhode Island v. Palmer*) "was an unusual one." The court "did not prepare a typical opinion. Rather, Justice Van Devanter announced the 'conclusions of the court.' These conclusions consisted of eleven numbered paragraphs that briefly summarized the majority's rejection of the arguments advanced by those challenging the prohibition amendment and the statute that enforced it."[39]

Both the form and the content of Van Devanter's opinion for the court sparked separate opinions from the other justices, both concurring and dissenting. Chief Justice White was among those who felt compelled to better explain and justify "that the amendment accomplishes and was intended to accomplish the purposes now attributed to it in the propositions concerning that subject which the court has just announced"—not that his turgid prose provided much in the way of clarification. But he, like dissenting Justices McKenna and Clarke, were troubled by the concept of a concurrent power of enforcement, "shared" between the federal government and the states. Their unease, however, reflected concern for the proper operation of states' prerogatives under dual federalism, and no justice questioned the legitimacy of the absolute ban on beverage alcohol. Still, at the same time as the White Court upheld Prohibition, it created a loophole. This was its "stockpiling" exception to the prohibition on "keeping" liquor found in the Volstead Act. The Eighteenth Amendment, Justice Clarke explained in *Street v. Lincoln Safe Deposit Co.* in 1920, "indicates no purpose to confiscate liquors lawfully owned when it became effective and which the owner intended to use in a lawful manner"—for his and his family's and his guests' personal consumption. Only liquor kept for the purpose of sale was illegal and could be confiscated. The vast wine cellars and liquor cabinets (and rented storehouses) of the elite would be safe.

The following year, the White Court justices' final year together, the White Court closed out the last of its procedural challenges to Prohibition. With Van Devanter writing, it affirmed in *Dillon v. Gloss* (1921) the power of Congress to limit the period for ratification of a constitutional amendment,[40] confirming the congressional Article V power to amend the Constitution and to choose the mode of exerting it. This was one of the "deathbed" decisions from the White Court, as White was nominally part of the unanimous court deciding it, even though the decision was announced within days of his demise following a bladder operation. The most sweeping of these interregnum cases came on June 1, 1921, when *U.S. v. Yuginovich* decided that Congress retained the power to tax the intoxicating liquors that the Volstead Act had made illegal to produce. The defendant distillers in the case argued that their indictment should be quashed on the grounds that the liquor revenue acts of Congress under which they were charged were repealed before the finding of the indictment, and that the acts of distilling charged to have been committed by them were after the date upon which the Eighteenth Amendment to the federal Constitution and the Volstead

Act became effective. This clever argument was to no avail, and some surreal reasoning was obtained for this decision, exemplified here in the words of Justice Day: "That Congress may under the broad authority of the taxing power tax intoxicating liquors notwithstanding their production is prohibited and punished we have no question. The fact that the statute in this aspect had a moral end in view as well as the raising of revenue, presents no valid constitutional objection to its enactment."

State discretionary choices, like those summarily rejected in *Hawke v. Smith* and defended only by dissenters in *National Prohibition Cases*, were also qualified by the White Court in a different context: that of regulating the Indian alcohol trade. *U.S. v. Nice* (1916) overruled the Fuller Court's 1905 decision in *Heff* that allowed states to regulate Indian drinking in their own laws; *Nice* upheld plenary congressional authority to deal with Native American citizens as if they were minors who needed protecting—meaning the sale of alcohol to them was subject to Congress's authority alone. Two rulings in 1914, *Perrin v. U.S.* and *Johnson v. Gearlds*, defended Indian Prohibition by enabling federal protections of Indians from alcohol trade to extend to buffer zones between reservations and state lands. *Hallowell v. U.S.* (1911) had been emphatic about the Indian's status: as Justice Day's opinion for a unanimous court declared "the mere fact that citizenship has been conferred upon Indians does not necessarily end the right or duty of the United States to pass laws in their interest as a dependent people." The decision upheld a conviction for introducing intoxicating liquor into Indian allotment land, despite the fact that "for many purposes the jurisdiction of the state of Nebraska had attached, and the Indian as a citizen was entitled to the rights, privileges, and immunities of citizenship." As previous Supreme Court decisions had made quite plain, of course, traffic in alcohol was not one of those "rights, privileges and immunities." But there was more. The U.S. government, *Hallowell* insisted, "within its own territory and in the interest of the Indians, had jurisdiction to pass laws protecting such Indians from the evil results of intoxicating liquors." Such paternalism toward the Native populations combined with White's Court upholding the value of a particularly sharp dual federalism; the result was the unstinting endorsement of a national Indian Prohibition.

The idea that the federal and state governments were sovereign in their separate jurisdictional spheres was applied across a range of issue contexts, including those involving alcohol restrictions. But the "dual federalism" system could also protect state prerogatives—once the state's jurisdiction was clearly established. This feature of the White era jurisprudence was evident in another Indian alcohol case decided just one year after *Hallowell*, *Clairmont v. U.S.* in 1912. With then associate justice and future chief justice Charles Evans Hughes writing, the White Court found that right-of-way land, ceded by treaty to a railroad construction project, ceased to be either Indian land or federal land, once the territory containing it became a state. Thus, an individual possessing a pint of whiskey while riding on the railroad and passing through reservation lands within Montana could not be charged with introducing intoxicating liquor into Indian country, since the right-of-way strip had had its Indian title extinguished. The effort the court made to prevent the alcohol prosecution in *Clairmont* dovetailed conveniently with dual federalism's notion of separate jurisdictional spheres. Still, the decision's victory for liquor was more anomaly than repudiation of Indian prohibition, for that same term in *Ex parte Webb,* the White justices held that neither admitting Oklahoma to statehood, nor the enabling act that did so, renounced Congress's control over the interstate liquor traffic in what had been the Indian territory of the state. (Reiterated in *U.S. v. Wright* (1913) and *Joplin Mercantile Co. v. U.S.* (1915); principle applied to Pueblo Indians in the new state of New Mexico in *U.S. v. Sandoval* in 1913.) Moreover, in 1918 in *U.S. v. Soldana*, the White Court construed yet another right-of-way treaty as creating an easement, not an extinction of Indian title, such that a train station platform in Crow Agency, Montana, was still Indian country subject to Indian prohibition statutes.

Despite all the drinking-related setbacks in its judicial record, it is worth noting that the White Court's criminal law jurisprudence in its final year and the first full year of existence of the Prohibition Amendment did not (yet) evidence the restrictive, law-and-order mentality it soon would on the High Court under the direction of the next chief justice, William Howard Taft. Instead, a sequence of White Court cases decided in 1921 (that did *not* involve enforcing Prohibition against its would-be violators) generally upheld a liberal interpretation of Fourth Amendment protections—those individual rights' protections against unreasonable searches and seizures of persons and their effects, and against warrantless searches without probable cause established. *Amos v. U.S.,* decided in February of 1921, was a liquor-related decision that was similarly (and unanimously) prodefendant.[41] But *Burdeau v. McDowell,* decided later that same year, inaugurated what would later become the full-throated "silver platter doctrine"—a disturbing expansion of the opportunity of federal government prosecutions to benefit from evidence obtained by forceful seizure at the hands of private, nonstate entities.[42] Still, *Burdeau* notwithstanding, these late White Court decisions overall illustrate the fairly proindividual defendant tenor of Fourth Amendment law just prior to Taft's ascension to the chief justice chair.[43]

Similarly, the very end of White's tenure also saw the beginning of the Supreme Court's struggle to consistently interpret the forfeiture device, found in both pre-Prohibition revenue statutes and the Volstead Act. The property seized was usually at this point an automobile, being used to transport intoxicating liquor (see *J.W. Goldsmith, Jr.-Grant Co. v. U.S.,* 1921). Conflicts between the penalties spelled out in the two bodies of law—as happened in *U.S. v. Yuginovich*—would not be ironed out until the Taft period.[44]

In this way, the White Court is the very last of the pre-Prohibition judicial eras, even though White's Court technically sat in judgment of the procedural regularity of the Prohibition Amendment itself. Yet despite deflection of the legal challenges to ratification, the law of the White era never fully embraced the Prohibition project as a nationally reformative and punitive operation. What White thought of it all personally we will never really know, but I like to picture him pouring over the sad irony of his historical fate while sipping on a Ramos gin fizz, Ojen frappe, or chilled Tulane cocktail. Or, perhaps, a succession of all three.

CONCLUSION

With the selection of the White era's honorary libation must come the acknowledgment of the elitist, racist politics that are likewise associated with his (and its) early twentieth-century New Orleans. Yet both "Progressive" and post-Reconstruction southern white elites shared a political affinity for racially supremacist ideas, just as they increasingly shared the public embrace of nationwide prohibition during White's time period. The White Court's jurisprudential commitment to the idea of separate spheres of autonomy for the federal and state governments led the justices to affirm all manner of antialcohol legislation, and thus became a useful prop for Prohibition's Eighteenth Amendment and Volstead Act.

7

THE TAFT ERA OF LAW, ORDER, AND BOOTLEGGING

The *Taft Court* (1921–1930) is headed by former president William Howard Taft—appointed, finally, by Republican president Warren G. Harding. Taft is the only former chief executive to so serve in both capacities, and by all accounts he endured his presidency but relished his chief justiceship. Dry though his era might have been, nothing is ever black and white—even the law. Neither was William Howard Taft, who both scathingly criticized and emphatically enforced Prohibition.

The interconnected politics of the presidency and the U.S. Supreme Court, and the court and Prohibition, were complex and multilayered during Taft's political lifetime. After losing his 1912 reelection to Democrat Woodrow Wilson thanks to Theodore Roosevelt's third-party candidacy and draining of Progressive Republican votes, Taft retired to the legal professoriate at Yale, where he wrote extensively in defense of local option laws—and local option only—forbidding the sale of liquor. For this, he was briefly advanced as a "wet" candidate for president in 1915. When President Wilson—with whom Taft had maintained cordial relations—was considering whom to appoint to the Supreme Court in early 1916,[1] the Anti-Saloon League vigorously campaigned against Taft as a potential nominee: he was labeled a "foe of Prohibition."[2] Yet once the situation changed, and the Eighteenth Amendment and the Volstead Act both passed, Taft altered his view—even "haranguing" his tippling colleagues and alumni at Yale for "violating their duty" and "ignoring their country."[3]

Notwithstanding liquor's "array of immoral and vicious effects" (as Taft would fulminate in a 1919 issue of the *Ladies Home Journal*), Taft reportedly celebrated the news of his appointment as chief justice—"the ambition of my life"[4]—with a glass of champagne in Montreal. This fact is confirmed by historian Ishbel Ross in *An American Family*: "[Taft] was dining with Sir Walter Cassels when news reached him {by telephone} that the Chief Justiceship was his. Sir Walter ordered a bottle of Pol Roget and Taft drank a glass with him to celebrate, the first he had had since {his daughter} Helen's wedding."[5] Taft's Montreal getaway would become one of a number of refuges for thirsty, well-heeled American tourists with the onset of Prohibition,[6] along with Cuba, Mexico, and various points of the compass beyond: from London, Paris, and the European continent to scattered colonial outposts of the British empire.

Likewise, "champagne had a good Prohibition," with a 300 percent increase in annual consumption when compared to the pre-Volstead years.[7] It is, therefore, the **champagne cocktail** that most appropriately commemorates that most enthusiastic of chief justices and his "dry" Supreme Court decade. The simple immersion of an Angostura bitters-soaked sugar cube in a glass of French bubbly would easily disguise that much of the "champagne" served during Prohibition was, in fact, just sparkling cider. Indeed, that unsettling truth calls to mind another Taft-related champagne-drinking incident. Taft family historian Ross provides the relevant tidbit that later in Taft's life when his heart condition required a protected diet, and when he was planning an Easter dinner with his sister-in-law, they stopped off at one Ambassador Jusserand's and drank to her health in "sparkling cider." The quotation marks are utilized by Ross . . . ironically? As a euphemism for champagne, or the presenting of it as such to the self-denying Taft?[8] We, like he, and like so many partakers during Prohibition, will never know. More certain was the vintage that figured in one additional episode from the period: Franklin Roosevelt, then assistant secretary of the Navy, reportedly spent the eve of Prohibition's effect (January 16, 1920) drinking champagne from the stores of Washington's Metropolitan Club.[9] To celebrate or commiserate: champagne serves.

It is nevertheless the case that Taft's appointing president, and the chief executive who greeted the Eighteenth Amendment, Warren G. Harding, favored Scotch and soda not wine as his drink of choice—even as his wetness took a backseat to his electoral debt to Wayne Wheeler's Anti-Saloon League and the cause of dry Republicanism.[10] That Harding (1921–1923) was the eager captive of the ASL's Wheeler is evident, first, in this sorry anecdote about his judicial staffing. Wheeler objected to the pending Supreme Court appointment of Senator John K. Shields of Tennessee, who had voted for the Eighteenth Amendment but against the Volstead Act, so Harding "capitulated instantly."[11] (Harding instead appointed railroad lawyer Pierce Butler who, while notably conservative, ultimately emerged as a vocal critic of the Prohibition enforcement regime. But a second Tennessean he subsequently named to the court, Edward Sanford, was a reliable if less than completely zealous prohibition supporter. So perhaps things were pretty much a wash for Wayne Wheeler.) On another occasion, constitutional law was the site of a Wheeler-Harding (non)contest. With the awareness of the prevalence and copiousness of liquor aboard the decks and parlors of British and French ocean liners and other passenger ships, Wheeler's interest was provoked, and he waved "a series of ancient Supreme Court decisions involving maritime law in front of Congress and the White House. . . . In 1922, Harding promptly declared American ships permanently dry and simultaneously announced that foreign ships coming into U.S. ports also had to be free of liquor."[12]

Political debts notwithstanding, Harding's and the early Taft era's Washington was one where, whatever one was drinking, one was drinking. A landmark of the Harding era was the previously mentioned Little Green House (and speakeasy) located on K Street, where his Ohio gang "cooked up the Tea Pot Dome scandal"[13]—an infamous corruption in an administration frankly rife with them. Famed bootlegger George Cassiday's operations supplying liquor to House members of Congress spanned 1920–1925, after which time (and an arrest) he shifted operations to the Senate, until he was closed down for good in 1930.[14] When Harding, after several years of setting a bad example (in several ways), died midterm in 1923, his successor Vice President Calvin Coolidge pursued a policy of "benign neglect" toward Prohibition.[15] Larz Anderson, a prominent and politically connected man of wealth, recalled that he had no problem obtaining high quality liquor during the months of "the season" that he and his wife spent in Washington. Still, he had this disheartened remark to make in his 1924 journal entry:

"Social life was more and more changed in Washington—prohibition cast its blight—there were fewer cocktail parties . . . but there was something to drink at all the dinners we went to . . . as official and semi-official and social dinners that are dry are not worth the while." [16]

Mostly nixed at official functions, cocktails spread from the public to the private sphere and the era of the home cocktail party was born. With far fewer servants than had staffed Victorian homes and their elaborate dinner parties, American households found the cocktail party a manageable—and increasingly necessary—alternative. "There are not many ladies in well-to-do houses now," a journalist commented in 1923, "who are not experts at mixing cocktails." [17] Prohibition and home cocktail parties so coincided that we find a New York State Supreme Court justice defending cocktail parties from the bench in 1925, asserting that his daughter and other "nice people" often "entertained in that fashion." [18] The mainstream press was decidedly wet, too, especially in Prohibition's later years: *Collier's* published a "Bartenders' Guide to Washington" in 1929, and a cocktail recipe printing from 1929–1930 listed a drink wittily named the Bridge Table (gin, brandy, apricot brandy, and lime juice) "because after a few of these your legs will fold up." [19]

As Taft's court tenure as chief is entirely encompassed by Prohibition, an honorable mention drink for this era must have some relationship to the notorious alcohol of the day: "bathtub" gin. It was so named not because it was batched up in bathtubs but because the height of the standard liquor bottles required that the home-distilled alcohol be topped off with water drawn from the bathtub tap. One of the most well known of these drinks developed to disguise the taste and lesser quality of such gin was the Orange Blossom. There is conflicting evidence that Taft ever drank one, just as conflicting evidence exists as to Taft's alcoholic consumption in general. He is, on the one hand, associated with moderation. Historian Gould says this about Taft and temperance: "Despite his own abstinence from alcohol, Taft had long been suspicious of prohibition as an answer to the nation's moral dilemmas. He did not believe that liquor control could be sustained." [20] Legal scholar Murchison confirms this reading of Taft, in part:

"A moderate drinker prior to the adoption of the 18th Amendment, Taft personally abstained from the consumption of alcoholic beverages once prohibition was established as federal law. In an article published in the *Ladies Home Journal* in 1919, he declared himself 'strongly in favor of the most practical laws to secure the rigid enforcement' of the 18th Amendment."

This campaign, Murchison continues, "was consistent with his general legal philosophy. He consistently advocated strict enforcement of all criminal law and emphasized the citizen's duty to follow the law."[21] So while opposed to the Prohibition amendment due to the feasibility of its enforcement, Taft was far from dismayed once it passed, saying this in a letter of 1918 to the *New Haven Journal Courier:* "I don't drink myself at all, and I don't oppose prohibition on the ground that it limits the liberty of people."[22] Taft would make his meaning more plain, with less equanimity, when he railed in that *LHJ* piece from 1919 that the "curtailment of personal liberty" was "small" in comparison with the benefits to society in prohibiting liquor's "vicious effects" upon the community.[23] Family biographer Ross notes that Taft and his wife, Nellie, had few disagreements, except over Prohibition. Ross also remarks that Taft surveyed the social scene of the "flaming 1920s" with some concern, even though he was a tolerant man. The speakeasies, and women puffing on cigarettes—he was accustomed to it, but he still didn't like it.[24]

On the other hand, Taft allegedly possessed proclivities toward the Bronx cocktail—a mixture of gin, sweet and dry vermouth, plus a splash of orange juice that is quite similar to the Orange Blossom, which omits the dry vermouth (and, when circumstances demanded, the vermouth altogether)—and the martini, as well as for serving Scotch and sodas to his White House political guests during his term in executive office. While as to this latter penchant there is little doubt, dubious sources like popular webpages are the ones that provide stories of (President) Taft quaffing Bronx and/or martini cocktails. To confound things further, the contemporary "presidential" menu at the Willard Hotel's Round Robin Bar lists a Manhattan with plenty of cherries as "Taft's" cocktail entry. A more reputable source, the webpage for the Smithsonian Associates' traveling lecture *Cheers to the Chief*, prepared by Museum of the American Cocktail cofounder Phil Greene, offered this explanation of the Taft cocktail connection:

> In September 1911, the *New York Times* chastened William Howard Taft for considering a cocktail made with orange juice to be a suitable morning beverage: "One annoying feature of President Taft's journey through the West has been the controversy caused by the

presence of Bronx cocktails at a breakfast party he attended. One
does not have to be a clergyman or a total abstainer to reprehend the
practice of drinking cocktails before breakfast."

Reprehending cocktails before breakfast was not much of a threshold.

Of the Bronx, *Imbibe!* says that in the first decades of the twentieth
century, it was the cocktail made safe for a nice middle-class person to
have before a meal, and was widely served at charity dinners and ban-
quets of state.[25] It was allegedly the alcoholic beverage that led to the
downfall of future founder of Alcoholics Anonymous Bill Wilson, when
the first one was served to him at a fancy cocktail party in 1917.[26] First
mixed at the end of the Fuller era, the Bronx cocktail—it seems safe to
say—is linked to Taft while president and does succeed to the lesser
quality Orange Blossom of the Taft judicial era. Nomenclature and
exact recipe aside, the gin and juice mix merits honorable mention as
the Taft totem.

But there was decidedly more to the mixology going on in the 1920s.
Two Washington Prohibition-era cocktails, developed by renowned DC
bartender Henry William Thomas, were the Major Bailey (gin with
sweet lemonade) and the Hong Kong (Scotch with sweet and dry vermouth plus a dash of Maraschino).[27] Prohibition's years of deprivation
tapped further inspirational creative juices. In 1922 the Blood and Sand
at London's Savoy Hotel Bar was introduced (although the recipe did
not appear in print until Harry Craddock's *The Savoy Cocktail Book* of
1930), another Scotch-based concoction that added Cherry Heering,
port wine or sweet vermouth, and orange juice to give it the appropriate
color and consistency; the drink commemorated a Rudolph Valentino
film of that same year in which the heartthrob of the silent screen
played a romantic and lusty bullfighter. In 1924, the coining of the
colloquial term "scofflaw" for one who frequented speakeasies and
flouted the National Prohibition Act was quickly followed by the creation of the honorary Scofflaw Cocktail at Harry's New York Bar in
Paris.[28] It married grenadine and lemon juice to rye (or Canadian whisky) and dry vermouth; grenadine itself did overtime duty as a flavor
masker and color enhancer in various Prohibition-era recipes. (See the
entry "Cocktails Suitable for a Prohibition Country" in the legendary
manual of 1930, *The Savoy Cocktail Book*. Barman Harry Craddock of

the Savoy Hotel in London crafted several making use of grenadine, in addition to strong-flavored syrups and juices.)

Of more orthodox cocktails that have soundly stood the test of time, several sources mention that the Sidecar was an invention of Prohibition. The deservedly successful and easy drinking Sidecar was the "son" of the more obscure Brandy Crusta. As cocktail historian David Wondrich tells it in *Imbibe!*, the Crusta was invented in New Orleans around 1850 by Joseph Santini at the Jewel of the South bar. Jerry Thomas, author of that famous first bartending guide, added it to his menu a few years later. While the Crusta itself never became hugely popular, it was an important step in the evolution of the cocktail per se, as it was the first spirits beverage, or among the first, to include fresh citrus juice as an ingredient. The Crusta's sugared rim was its signature; the Sidecar lost this decoration while gaining Cointreau orange liqueur as an ingredient. Most sources put the Sidecar's actual creation outside the United States on the European continent—specifically in Paris, where many American bartenders migrated after 1920 in search of quality work. Louis Beebe's 1946 *The Stork Club Bar Book,* reliable as to some Prohibition-era cocktail stories, says that barkeep Frank of the Paris Ritz bar built the first Sidecar in 1923 or so, in order to showcase a vintage 1865 cognac.[29] Once transported to the New World and remixed at the New York speakeasy nightclub The Stork Club, of course, the Sidecar was a less rarified and precious thing. A 1928 *Herald Tribune* cartoon, for example, depicted "the people's" presidential candidate, Wet Democrat Al Smith, shaking up a batch.[30]

Despite Prohibition, then, liquor flowed freely, over the border from Mexico and the Caribbean and across the international waters' Twelve Mile Limit[31] (itself the name given to a particularly lethal period cocktail that mixed up rum, rye, brandy, grenadine, and lemon juice)[32] to the ports and beaches of Florida, New Jersey, and Long Island, and into Detroit and points onward from the Canadian Club distillery across the river in Ontario.[33] Illegality created a sophisticated (black) market structure that heretofore had never existed.

Prohibition also birthed certain meaningful sociological innovations. First, the speakeasies that replaced the saloons of pre-Volstead times admitted both sexes, and women radically expanded their domain outside the home by drinking in public and otherwise displaying their political and social "liberation." (To Chief Justice Taft's consternation.)

Alcohol historian Gately goes so far as to say that "the removal of the prior taboo on women in saloons can be counted as one of the triumphs of Prohibition."[34] A second advance, to add to the novelty of the Flapper, was the change Prohibition occasioned in the reputation of spirituous liquor itself. "By forcing people to drink in the luxuriance of speakeasies or the comfort of their homes," one social history of alcohol writes, "Prohibition gave to alcoholic beverages a respectability they had never enjoyed during the heyday of the bumptious and unsanitary saloon."[35] Suddenly, to drink was to be both forward thinking and socially upright.

Some of this societal evolution played out in the attitudes of the justices during the Taft Court years. Some of it most emphatically did not. Urofsky has this to say about two of the Taft Court's most prominent associate justices and their attitudes toward drinking and Prohibition:

> [Oliver Wendall] Holmes and [Louis] Brandeis had bowed to the will of the people in accepting Prohibition, although in practice Holmes continued to enjoy his drink and to receive bottles from his friends. Brandeis had liked his beer and an occasional whiskey, and for many years at dinner he had served guests his good Kentucky bourbon that his brother, Alfred, regularly sent from Louisville. His views on democratic governance led him to support Prohibition after ratification, and in time he even came to be a fervent supporter of the ban on alcohol, believing it could improve the lives of working people.[36]

O, beware the convert! Indeed, one was more likely to encounter tea than tipples at the Brandeis home, as well as the company of the "Prohibition Portia" Mabel Walker Willebrandt, assistant attorney general from 1921 to 1929—who enjoyed the (presumably dry) intellectualism of the dinner party conversation.[37] Conversely, it is hardly surprising that Holmes, as befitted his general irreverence, took a more bemused and less rigid position. The latter was on full display in this famously recounted episode: "[W]hen presented with champagne at his eightieth birthday party in 1921, Justice Holmes offered the following defense of his decision to consume the champagne: 'The Eighteenth Amendment forbids the manufacture, transportation, and importation. It does not forbid the possession or use. If I send it back, I shall be guilty of transportation.'" Murchison goes on to remark that "this personal stance would seep into Holmes' Prohibition enforcement decisions, as they consistently employed a liberal construction."[38]

Still, Holmes was willing to allow the positive law of enacted prohibition regulation to be given a fair test, to see "whether it is a great social improvement or a mistake."[39] As he said in dissent in a theater ticket price regulation case in 1927, *Tyson v. Banton*,

> [T]he legislature may forbid or restrict any business when it has a sufficient force of public opinion behind it. . . . Wine has been thought good for man from the time of the Apostles until recent years. But when public opinion changed, it did not need the Eighteenth Amendment, notwithstanding the Fourteenth, to enable a State to say that the business should end.

Yet he was always a skeptic, commenting as much in his dissenting opinion in the otherwise unrelated maritime law case of *Knickerbocker Ice Co. v. Stewart* (1920). There, the White Court had analogized the legal question to sustaining the Webb-Kenyon Act in *James Clark Distilling Co. v. Western Maryland Railway Co.* (1917), observing that "because of the peculiar nature of intoxicants which gives enlarged power concerning them, Congress might go so far as entirely to prohibit their transportation in interstate commerce."[40] "I thought that [*Clark*] went pretty far in justifying the adoption of state legislation in advance," Holmes remarked somewhat sourly in his *Knickerbocker* dissent, "as I cannot for a moment believe that apart from the Eighteenth Amendment special constitutional principles exist against strong drink. The fathers of the Constitution so far as I know approved it."

As for less legendary justices of the Taft era, Justice Edward Sanford, a Tennessean appointed by Harding in 1923, had a background suggesting that he was strongly predisposed to favor Prohibition policy. He personally approved of home-state temperance efforts, the Knoxville newspaper in which his family owned an interest staunchly supported prohibition legislation, and as a justice Sanford wrote several of the Taft Court's pro-Prohibition decisions.[41] He was a loyal supporter of and regular vote for his chief justice, such that Taft made Sanford a part of the court's conservative "inner club" that regularly met at the chief justice's house on Sunday afternoons "for discussion and *libations*"[42] (emphasis added). Was something untoward and clandestine going on among these conservative, putative teetotalers? The entry on

Justice Sanford in the popular web-based information site *Wikipedia*, citing the respected online legal resource Oyez.org as its source, says the conversations included "libations and conviviality"; yet the Oyez website mentions nothing about "libations" (or "conviviality," for that matter). Ambiguity also surrounds the infamously cranky (and profoundly anti-Semitic) conservative Justice James C. McReynolds, inexplicably appointed by Wilson in 1914. Militantly antismoking, McReynolds—a lifelong bachelor but an incorrigible flirt—was known by all in the capital for his Sunday morning teas and brunches for his female society friends.[43] What he served the ladies, in those teacups—aside from his matchless charm—is not recorded.

Personal predilections and failings notwithstanding, Rooting Out Drink was the modus operandi of the Taft era. Yet from the beginning, Taft's Court was beset with controversy after controversy surrounding the enforcement of Prohibition and the prosecution of bootleggers. Its first constitutional ruling was also a federalism disquisition, finding that a state liquor license law continued to be valid after the passage of national prohibition. Pennsylvania's Brooks Law, as construed by the courts of the state, prohibited every sale of spirituous liquor without a license excepting only such sales that were made by druggists, and these were forbidden to sell intoxicating liquors except on the prescription of a regular physician. The defendant Vigliotti was found guilty of selling a preparation called Jamaica ginger, a patent medicine containing 88 percent alcohol and colloquially known as "Jake."[44] Taft's Court in the 1922 decision of *Vigliotti v. Pennsylvania* upheld the state law as "an additional instrument which the state supplies in the effort to make prohibition effective," and something fully consistent with the concurrent enforcement powers articulated in section 2 of the Eighteenth Amendment. Justice Brandeis's majority opinion for the court cited the White Court's *National Prohibition Cases* in support of the amendment's authority. Yet in an unusual action that is difficult to interpret, Justices Day and McReynolds—sometime critics of prohibition laws during the White era—dissented without opinion. Did the very states' rights federalism jurisprudence, that the White Court had used to uphold local prohibition laws, now engender some judicial misgivings regarding an unabashedly *national* prohibition system?

There seemed little sign of this in a subsequent decision in 1925, *Samuels v. McCurdy*, which recognized broad regulatory authority for states *and* the federal government under the respective prohibition statutes. The Taft Court affirmed a conviction under state law for mere possession of intoxicating liquor, but the case was complicated by an ex post facto consideration: the liquor in possession had been legally acquired and only later made illegal. Taft spoke out, both for state police powers and for nationwide prohibition law enforcement. The law was not an ex post facto or impermissibly retroactive law, he asserted, for "the penalty it imposes is for continuing to possess the liquor after the enactment of the law." The Chase era decision of *Bartemeyer v. Iowa* in 1873 and the Waite era follow-up in *Boston Beer v. Massachusetts* in 1877 had wrestled with similar dilemmas, but much less definitively. Taft also rejected any notion that the individual was due any compensation for deprivation of his property—in this case, the liquor he possessed at home for his personal use. Taft gave a veritable soliloquy on "demon rum," worth quoting at length for its sheer bluster:

> The ultimate legislative object of prohibition is to prevent the drinking of intoxicating liquor by any one because of the demoralizing effect of drunkenness upon society. The state has the power to subject those members of society who might indulge in the use of such liquor without injury to themselves to a deprivation of access to liquor in order to remove temptation from those whom its use would demoralize and to avoid the abuses which follow in its train. . . . The Legislature has this power whether it affects liquor lawfully acquired before the prohibition or not. Without compensation it may thus seek to reduce the drinking of liquor. It is obvious that if men are permitted to maintain liquor in their possession, though only for their own consumption, there is danger of its becoming accessible to others. Legislation making possession unlawful is therefore within the police power of the states as reasonable mode of reducing the evils of drunkenness. . . . The only question which arises is whether for the shrunken opportunity of the possessor of liquor who acquired it before the law, to use it only for his own consumption, the state must make compensation. By valid laws, his property rights have been so far reduced that it would be difficult to measure their value. That which had the qualities of property has, by successive provisions of law in the interest of all, been losing its qualities as property. For many years, every one who has made or stored liquor has known that it was a kind of property which because of its possible vicious uses might be denied by the state the character and attributes as such,

that legislation calculated to suppress its use in the interest of public health and morality was lawful and possible, and this without compensation. Why should compensation be made now for the mere remnant of the original right if nothing was paid for the loss of the right to sell it, give it away or transport it? The necessity for its destruction is claimed under the same police power to be for the public betterment as that which authorized its previous restrictions.

Taft's *Samuels* outburst occasioned one in dissent from Justice Butler. Butler objected to the cavalier dismissal of property and due process rights in the case, especially because the "plaintiff in error is a man of temperate habits, long accustomed to use alcoholic liquor as a beverage." Outraged, he continued,

[T]hat alcoholic liquors are capable of valuable uses is recognized by the whole mass of state and national regulatory and prohibitory laws, as well as by the state legislation in question. The liquors seized were valuable for such private use as was intended by the plaintiff. The insistence is that the state is without power to seize and destroy a private supply of intoxicating liquor lawfully acquired before the prohibitory legislation and kept in one's house for his own use. Such seizure and destruction can be supported only on the ground that the private possession and use would injure the public.

How? The justice charged. "Any suggestion," he proclaimed,

that the destruction of such private supply lawfully acquired and held for the use of the owner in his own home is necessary for or has any relation to the suppression of sales or to the regulation of the liquor traffic or to the protection of the public from injury would be fanciful and without foundation.

Speaking for all wets, closeted and out, and seemingly sputtering with disgust, Butler concluded,

any legislation which attempts directly to forbid the mere drinking or other private use of such liquors . . . would infringe constitutional provisions safeguarding liberty and property, [and] the power of the state to enact and enforce such legislation has not been established. . . . [T]he law is oppressive and arbitrary.

Harumph.

The Prohibition cases in general would mark one area in which the Taft Court's decision making was notably less harmonious than that court's decision making in general. Taft was known as his court's "social leader," for he was by and large a genial, happy-dispositioned person who disliked conflict of any kind; Taft worked very hard to mediate differences among the justices, and relieved tensions over case discussions with his sense of humor.[45] Things were indeed mostly cohesive on the Taft Court, and it was all very friendly—except in the contested area of Prohibition enforcement. There, a polarized bloc of opponents, made up of Butler, McReynolds, and conservative Westerner George Sutherland,[46] dissented fairly regularly from the core Taft majority. Such disunity—such "excited feelings," as he called them in a letter to his son—was notoriously distressing to the amiable Taft,[47] and he presumably coped with it all without the consoling aid of an evening cocktail.

The legal status of possession of liquor—in particular, liquor acquired before Prohibition went into effect—was a particularly fraught issue during the early Taft years. In a statutory ruling in 1922, the Taft Court evidenced its support for an expansive reach of the national prohibition statute. The *Coreli v. Moore* decision threw a worrisome monkey wrench into the 1921 *Street* precedent's creation of a stockpiling exception to the Volstead Act ban on "keeping" liquor. Justice McKenna's opinion for a unanimous court was forthright in its assertion that "the act declares that all of its provisions shall be liberally construed 'to the end,' to quote its words, 'that the use of intoxicating liquor as a beverage may be prevented.'" To that end, only liquor acquired before Prohibition's effect owned and possessed "in one's private dwelling" escaped the Volstead's clutches. "That character" of being privately possessed could not be assigned to liquor being stored a distance away in the bonded warehouses of the government, on which the plaintiff Coreli owed tax duties to be paid to the state of Missouri. Such fine-line drawing meant that many individuals had lost the ability to access the booze they thought safely squirreled away for a drier day. Their attention—and subsequently the court's—shifted to other methods of acquiring beverage alcohol: bootlegging.

Bootlegging—the making, distributing, or selling of illicit alcohol—was clearly trafficking in liquor, and so squarely raised the legal ques-

tion of not only governmental enforcement powers but also enforcement strategies. But trade in and transit of liquor could also implicate
international trade treaties, as did *Grogan v. Hiram Walker & Co.* in
1922. The case raised the question of whether the Eighteenth Amendment and the Volstead Act prohibited the transportation of intoxicating
liquors from a foreign port through a part of the United States to another foreign port. "Leakage" into the domestic market during such
transit was the ostensible concern. Holmes's majority opinion upheld
the letter of law forbidding transport and noted drily that "the Eighteenth Amendment meant a great revolution in the policy of this country, and presumably and obviously meant to upset a good many things
on as well as off the statute book." Justice McKenna, this time dissenting and joined by Day and Clarke, was unimpressed. In a passage drip-
ping with sarcasm, he rejected the broad sweep that the court was
giving to the Prohibition effort: "It presents," he mused sourly,

> the attractive spectacle of a people too animated for reform to hesi-
> tate to make it as broad as the universe of humanity. One feels
> almost ashamed to utter a doubt of such a noble and moral cosmo-
> politanism, but the facts of the world must be adduced, and what
> they dictate. They are the best answer to magnified sentiment. And
> the sentiment is magnified. The [Eighteenth] amendment and the
> Volstead Act were not intended to direct the practices of the world.

Ah, but by 1923, they were. A 1922 directive from the attorney
general made it unlawful for any ship, whether domestic or foreign, to
bring into U.S. territorial waters, or to carry while within those waters,
intoxicating liquors intended for beverage purposes, whether as sea
stores or cargo. Transatlantic and other passenger ships had, of course,
traditionally offered beverage alcohol and, with the beginning of Prohibition, had continued to store such alcohol while in port in the United
States. Now, even storing such wines and liquors in holds on board, for
the purpose of breaking them out after leaving the territorial United
States, was forbidden. Additionally, the attorney general's order prohibited any domestic ship to carry liquors for beverage purposes as cargo or
sea stores even when *outside* U.S. territorial waters. A collection of
steamship companies operating passenger ships between U.S. and
foreign ports brought suit in *Cunard SS Co. v. Mellon*, challenging this
enforcement policy pursuant to the National Prohibition Act. Justice

Van Devanter's opinion for the court explored dictionary definitions of the terms "transportation," "importation," and "territory" in upholding the drying out of cruise ships plying American waters. Or potentially plying American customers with booze. Van Devanter's reasoning was squarely in terms of national sovereignty, and its compulsion had a broad reach, for "when private individuals of one nation spread themselves through another as business or caprice may direct, mingling indiscriminately with the inhabitants of that other," such individuals "owe temporary and local allegiance"—in this case, to the national project of Prohibition. Anything else "would be obviously inconvenient and dangerous to society, and would subject the laws to continual infraction, and the government to degradation."

Dissenting Justices McReynolds and Sutherland could not abide this global reach of American Prohibition, and the ensuing violation of the general rule of international law that a foreign ship is identified with the country to which it belongs and that its internal affairs ordinarily are not subjected to interference. McReynolds's dissent expressed the resigned exasperation he seemed to have felt: "It would serve no useful purpose," he sniffed, "to give my reasons at any length for [my] conclusion."

The Taft Court's defense of concurrent national and state powers under the Eighteenth Amendment was as clear and marked as the Taft era's constitutional trend toward interpreting individual rights' provisions to favor the governmental interest in Prohibition enforcement. One of the earliest of the latter categories of cases was *Hester v. U.S.* in 1924, which created the so-called open fields exception to the Fourth Amendment protection against warrantless and unreasonable searches and seizures. Justice Holmes's exceedingly brief opinion for a unanimous court was untroubled by the revenue officers' recovery without a warrant of discarded and broken bottles, that they identified as containing moonshine, from the open land outside of the defendant's house. As Theodore Lacey asserts in his Princeton honor's thesis, "The Supreme Court's Fluctuating Reaction to National Prohibition in Fourth Amendment Decisions from 1920–1933," "the Court's decision in *Hester* is the first sign of divergence with the trend of liberal construction emphasized in the [search and seizure] cases" of the late White Court. But *Hester* was more than a dismissively narrow and literalist understanding of an individual's physical zone of privacy. Lacey himself goes further, stating the major judicial process claim of his thesis:

> Corresponding to the contention that the Court's Fourth Amendment decisions during the Prohibition era possessed a tenor congruent to the prevailing political sentiments of the time in which they were issued, the ideological fork in the road between *Hester* and previous opinions occurred concurrently with dry interest groups' advocacy for efficient enforcement of the Eighteenth Amendment and the period of time in which the anti-alcohol initiative possessed its most widespread support in the electorate and in Congress.[48]

The Supreme Court was following the election returns, in other words.

The pro-enforcement trend, coming at the expense of individual liberties, continued in *Steele v. U.S.* in 1925, which allowed a fairly elastic use of a warrant's description of the things to be seized to search a garage, and *Dumbra v. U.S.* that same year, which involved the search by federal Prohibition officers of a winery that possessed a permit for the production of "legal" sacramental wine. But the facts of *Byars v. U.S.* in 1927 caused the Taft Court to pull back: the defendant could not be prosecuted in federal court for possession of counterfeit strip stamps for liquor bottles, when that evidence had been seized through a state court–issued warrant for "intoxicating liquors and instruments and materials used in the manufacture of such liquors." A federal Prohibition agent had been invited along to join the search by local officers, and even though the warrant uncovered evidence of the violation of a federal statute, Sutherland's opinion for a unanimous court was adamant that the stamps found were not within the purview of the state search warrant and did not relate in any way to a violation of state law. But in an interesting act of hairsplitting, he closed the decision with this:

> We do not question the right of the federal government to avail itself of evidence improperly seized by state officers operating entirely upon their own account. But the rule is otherwise when the federal government itself, through its agents acting as such, participates in the wrongful search and seizure. To hold the contrary would be to disregard the plain spirit and purpose of the constitutional prohibitions intended to secure the people against unauthorized official action.

Sutherland was referring to the so-called silver platter doctrine, suggested by the Supreme Court in *Weeks v. U.S.* in 1914. *Weeks* established the exclusionary rule for the Fourth Amendment, such that evidence seized without a valid warrant by agents of the federal government was excluded from any federal indictment or prosecution. But it allowed an exception, for evidence obtained when state officers were acting alone, as these law enforcement personnel were not bound by the strict terms of the Fourth Amendment's protections against impermissible searches and seizures. Such potentially "tainted" evidence could be delivered to federal investigators and prosecutors for their use, no problem.[49] It was the participation of the federal Prohibition agent in the actual search in *Byars*, and the violation that thereby ensued, that crossed the constitutional line.

The enforcement strategies for Prohibition were many and varied. Some, like the operation in *Byars*, went beyond the limits of law. Others did not. *McGuire v. U.S.* (1927) like *Byars* involved an interesting technicality with respect to its search warrant, but this time the benefit of the doubt went to the government. Prohibition agents, conducting a search pursuant to a warrant, seized a large store of liquor but then proceeded to smash all but two bottles, which they retained as evidence of the Volstead violation. The question was whether their act of damage and putative criminal trespass invalidated the entire search as an illegal invasion. Justice Harlan Fiske Stone's[50] unanimous opinion held that it did not, nor did it require the government to sacrifice otherwise legitimate evidence for the enforcement of law, adding "a criminal prosecution is more than a game in which the government may be checkmated and the game lost merely because its officers have not played according to rule." *Tumey v. Ohio* (1927), on the other hand, saw the defendant's Fourteenth Amendment interest in due process of law vindicated, when the Taft opinion for the court found impermissible a state prohibition enforcement statute that authorized a town mayor to perform a judicial function and try a violator without the benefit of a jury or an appeal *and gave* that mayor a pecuniary interest in the conviction in the form of daily fines that accrued to the local treasury. (But cf. *Dugan v. Ohio*, 1928.) *Marron v. U.S.*, also in 1927, permitted a sweepingly broad search incident to a lawful arrest, where the items seized went well beyond what had been described in the warrant issued. Though "general searches have long been deemed to violate fundamental rights," the incremental logic of Butler's opinion for the court appeared to preserve little space that was protected from governmental action in pursuit of alcohol prohibition:

> When arrested, [the defendant] was actually engaged in a conspiracy to maintain, and was actually in charge of, the premises where intoxicating liquors were being unlawfully sold. Every such place is by the National Prohibition Act declared to be a common nuisance the maintenance of which is punishable by fine, imprisonment or both. The officers were authorized to arrest for crime being committed in their presence, and they lawfully arrested [the defendant]. They had a right without a warrant contemporaneously to search the place in order to find and seize the things used to carry on the criminal enterprise. The closet in which liquor and the ledger were found was used as a part of the saloon. And, if the ledger was not as essential to the maintenance of the establishment as were bottles, liquors and glasses, it was nonetheless a part of the outfit or equipment actually used to commit the offense. And, while it was not on [the defendant]'s person at the time of his arrest, it was in his immediate possession and control. The authority of officers to search and seize the things by which the nuisance was being maintained extended to all parts of the premises used for the unlawful purpose.

Marron interpreted that authority in an extremely generous way, to say the least.

Police work in the service of Prohibition enforcement also occasioned one of the Supreme Court's most famous Fourth Amendment cases—and, indeed, one of the few of our alcohol-related Supreme Court decisions to figure prominently in nearly every constitutional law textbook read by college undergraduates and first-year law students. That case and that decision is *Olmstead v. U.S.* (1928), in which the Supreme Court is first faced with Fourth Amendment search and seizure questions arising from "modern" electronic surveillance action by state law enforcement: wiretapping. That Olmstead the plaintiff was a bootlegger of some renown and "good" reputation (for the unadulterated quality of his liquor and his generally peaceable business practices), a sterling success in his Pacific Northwest–area business, and a former lieutenant in the Seattle police department to boot only adds to the luster of the case as an episode in the history of alcohol in American life and law.

Use of wiretapping in information gathering was spurred on by the need to fight the clever maneuvers of bootleggers against detection. The technology involved electronic tapping of phone wires physically outside the residence or office phone of interest; the idea was to listen in on conversations that planned and confirmed conspiracies to violate the Volstead Act, in order to allow Prohibition enforcement agents to set up dragnets to intercept incriminating liquor shipments and seize bookkeeping records. As the opinion of the court reprised the factual circumstances:

> Small wires were inserted along the ordinary telephone wires from the residences of four of the petitioners and those leading from the chief office. The insertions were made without trespass upon any property of the defendants. They were made in the basement of the large office building. The taps from house lines were made in the streets near the houses. The gathering of evidence continued for many months. Conversations of the conspirators, of which refreshing stenographic notes were currently made, were testified to by the government witnesses.

In the Olmstead wiretaps, the Prohibition Bureau "had a collection of transcripts that may have read like a bad film script,"[51] but melodramatic or no, the recorded conversations revealed large business transactions of a criminal nature. These conversations then became the basis for warrants issued to search for and seize the tangible evidence needed for criminal conviction. *Olmstead* and its companion cases raised a single question: whether the use of the evidence consisting of the records of private telephone conversations between the defendants and others— conversations intercepted by means of wiretapping—amounted to a violation of the Fourth and Fifth Amendments.

The 5–4 Taft-led court began by noting that there was no evidence of compulsion to induce the defendants to talk over their many telephones, so there was "no room in the present case for applying the Fifth Amendment unless the Fourth Amendment was first violated." On this question, Taft held that private telephone communication between two persons was no different than a casual conversation overheard in a public place. Because no trespass had occurred in the placing or using of the phone taps, there was no physical invasion amounting to a "search" of "material things"—persons, houses, papers, or effects. Taft explained the majority's reasoning in terms of a philosophy of the Constitution's original meaning or intent: "The Fourth Amendment is to be construed," he instructed, "in the light of what was deemed an unreasonable search and seizure when it was adopted." But Taft also added this addendum to his theory of constitutional interpretation: the amendment should also be construed "in a manner *which will conserve public interests* as well as the interests and rights of individual citizens" (emphasis added). Clearly, the "public interest" at issue was the enforcement of Prohibition.

Taft took up the charge of the four dissenters in the case, that the evidence had been obtained unethically and by a misdemeanor offense under state law, and so should be inadmissible. He rejected this application of the exclusionary rule in a tour through old English and early American legal cases. But the crux of the matter remained the need to enforce alcohol prohibition. "A standard which would forbid the reception of evidence if obtained by other than nice ethical conduct by government officials," he puffed, "would make society suffer and give criminals greater immunity than has been known heretofore." This familiar argument of end justifying the means would be reprised again and again, during later Supreme Courts' jousts with Fourth and Fifth Amendment rights—and those rights' public safety and public order exceptions. To posterity, the *Olmstead* case became less about policing the liquor trade and more about the Supreme Court's duty with respect to defending civil rights and liberties. Yet it is more than likely that the *Olmstead* majority saw things almost entirely through the lens of the whiskey bottle—even though both Taft and Van Devanter persistently resisted the effort to categorize the decision that way.[52] It was no matter and all in vain: the contemporary outcry against the decision was immense, it was likened to "A New Dred Scott Decision," and even the Anti-Saloon League refused to support it unequivocally—fearing the inevitable blowback should governmental "snooping" be thought favored for Prohibition enforcement.[53]

Justice Brandeis's dissenting opinion has come to be the most important legacy of the *Olmstead* case for American constitutional law. His arguments were focused on the privacy of persons in the modern age, for he saw wiretapping as a means of espionage against which general warrants were "puny instruments of tyranny and oppression" in comparison. Olmstead the bootlegging petitioner was, for Brandeis, a symbol of pernicious governmental invasion of personal liberty—an intrusion all the more insidious when undertaken "by men of zeal, well meaning but without understanding." There was no mistaking who those misbegotten men of zeal were. And there was more from the justice christened "the people's lawyer" for his career before being appointed to the Supreme Court. "The confirmed criminal"—the foul bootlegger, to put no fine point on it—"is as much entitled to redress as his most virtuous fellow citizen," Brandeis intoned, "no record of crime, however long, makes one an outlaw." Only the government had become outlaw, by the behavior that the court had sanctioned. As Justice Holmes wrote in his short, separate opinion: "I think it a less evil that some criminals should escape than that the Government should play an ignoble part." Prohibition, it seems, had made lawbreakers of everyone.

One member of the Taft Court had long rued the passage of the Eighteenth Amendment for just this reason, lamenting in particular the societal consequences of the widespread defiance of Prohibition. Speaking to the alumni of New York University School of Law back in 1923, by then former associate justice, John Clarke had charged that that disrespect "was metastasizing into disrespect for all laws, and that the end of this sorry and perhaps irreversible process was nowhere in sight."[54] Despite his serious misgivings, Clarke was not on the bench long enough to be one of the most appreciable critics of Prohibition—unlike McReynolds or Butler, who used what numerous occasions presented themselves to proffer legal arguments dissenting from overzealous Prohibition enforcement.

Such an occasion presented itself in the context of the Taft Court's carving out of the still-valid automobile exception to the Fourth Amendment search warrant requirement. This bending of the rules for government action had arisen in order to address bootleggers' trafficking practices—which utilized, to great effect, that American culture-changing invention, the Model T roadster. Cars functioned like "moving saloons," in some cases, and drunk driving skyrocketed in the 1920s. America's roadways were thus a frontline in the war on alcohol. In 1925 in *Carroll v. U.S.* a Taft-led coalition of the court declared that Prohibition agents did not need a warrant to stop and search a car they believed to be carrying contraband liquor. Then, as remains the case today, Taft's opinion reasoning was grounded, first, in the established recognition of

> a necessary difference between a search of a store, dwelling house, or other structure in respect of which a proper official warrant readily may be obtained and a search of a ship, motor boat, wagon, or automobile for contraband goods, where it is not practicable to secure a warrant, because the vehicle can be quickly moved out of the locality or jurisdiction in which the warrant must be sought.

Though a warrant was not required, a search of a mobile vehicle still could not be "unreasonable" within the terms of the Fourth Amendment. For Taft, the reasonableness of the search in the case turned on the fact that the automobile was proceeding from Detroit, an active and notorious center for illegally introducing and distributing spirituous liquors into the country.[55]

Taft's lengthy and somewhat torturous exposition inspired a separate opinion from Justice McReynolds, labeled as neither concurrence nor dissent. But a statement of profound dissatisfaction it clearly was. "The damnable character of the 'bootlegger's' business," he began, "should not close our eyes to the mischief which will surely follow any attempt to destroy it by unwarranted methods." Lacey interprets this as McReynolds's "theorizing that popular distaste for the bootlegging business had essentially led Taft to seek to destroy it by illegitimate means."[56] Whatever explained it, McReynolds could find no source in legal precedent or the Volstead Act that authorized what Taft had ruled. Further questioning the majority opinion's narrative construction of probable cause in the case, McReynolds exclaimed, "Has it come about that merely because a man once agreed to deliver whisky, but did not, he may be arrested whenever thereafter he ventures to drive an automobile on the road to Detroit!"

The same principle of presumed suspicion was applied to seafaring vessels in *Maul v. U.S.* and *U.S. v. Lee* both in 1927, which concerned Coast Guard actions of patrolling the so-called Rum Row of ships moored outside the twelve-mile limit of international waters in the Atlantic Ocean. From these cargo holds laden with liquor from Bermuda and the Caribbean, smaller boats ferried the goods to shore. Not only was such domestic navigation viewed with the same notoriety by the Taft Court as the traffic from Detroit had been, but the activities of those American vessels *beyond* the twelve-mile limit was also considered fair game. Justice Brandeis, writing for a unanimous court in *Lee*, upheld the Coast Guard boarding and incident search of the motorboat in the case, arguing that probable cause of a felony violation of revenue laws had been established through simple observation of the boat's proximity to a Rum Row vessel. No warrant was needed, the justice affirmed, because the boat was not being used as a residence; moreover, the search of the boat's deck was incident to a lawful arrest. And in any case, Brandeis added, the "search" only uncovered what was in plain view before the boat was even boarded: boxes of liquor that could be seen using a searchlight. "Such use of a searchlight is comparable to the use of a marine glass or a field glass," Brandeis commented. "It is not prohibited by the Constitution." A technological aid to ordinary observation did not change the Fourth Amendment calculus regarding an impermissibly invasive search, nor convert that search into one that required a warrant. This same reasoning was applied more extensively one year later, to another modern surveillance mechanism, in one of the Taft era's most famous civil liberties decisions—*Olmstead v. U.S.*—over the objection of four dissenters led by Justice Brandeis.

Prohibition enforcement was never given a total carte blanche; in *Gambino v. United States* (1927) for instance, the justices pulled back somewhat. State officers had stopped the defendants' automobile motoring near the Canadian border and, proceeding to conduct a warrantless search, seized alcohol from its interior. No federal officers participated in the police action. The liquor was admitted in evidence against the defendants in their subsequent federal trial for violation of the National Prohibition Act. The Taft Court, speaking through Justice Brandeis, reversed the judgments of conviction, holding that the evidence had been illegally seized without probable cause and should have been excluded. Pointing out that there was "no suggestion that the defendants were committing, at the time of the arrest, search and seizure, any state offense; or that they had done so in the past; or that the [state] troopers believed that they had," the court found that "[t]he wrongful arrest, search and seizure were made solely on behalf of the United States." In other words, the federal alcohol prosecution could not depend—or count on—the use of evidence illegally obtained by state law enforcement actors, when they were acting not to enforce their own laws but as federal surrogates. Brandeis's fine-tuning of what federalism in the Eighteenth Amendment context allowed, and his narrow application of the mandate from *Carroll*,[57] was a small victory for Fourth Amendment individual rights.

But *Gambino* was still more outlier than encouraging sign of a judicial respect for individual privacy. As one history of the period summarizes, in twenty separate cases between 1920 and 1933, the Taft and Hughes Courts engaged in "a broad strokes rewriting of a century's worth of Supreme Court jurisprudence." Even popular political culture of the time was making mention of the court's doings, for as historian Okrent continues, "In a *New York World* cartoon by Rollin Kirby, a figure representing the 18th Amendment was shown lynching a representation of the 4th, with a delighted member of the ASL looking on."[58]

Proceeding further afield, the Taft Court also closed the "medical use loophole" of Volstead and the Eighteenth Amendment by upholding supplemental congressional legislation prohibiting physicians from prescribing ordinary, intoxicating malt liquors for medicinal purposes. (This, unanimously, in *James Everard's Breweries v. Day* in 1924.) One Dr. Lambert also received his comeuppance in 1926 for "his acts as a physician in prescribing vinous or spirituous liquors to his patients for medicinal purposes in quantities exceeding the limits fixed by the National Prohibition Act." With Brandeis writing for the court, *Lambert v. Yellowly* held that "Whatever the belief of a physician in the medicinal value of alcoholic liquor, his right to administer it to patients is subordinate to the powers granted to Congress by the Eighteenth Amendment." The Taft majority justices were unpersuaded by the doctor's belief that

> the use of spirituous liquor internally as a medicine in an amount exceeding one pint in ten days is necessary for the proper treatment of patients in order to afford relief from human ailments, and that he does not intend to prescribe the use of liquor for beverage purposes. [He] alleged that, to treat the diseases of his patients and to promote their physical wellbeing, according to the untrammeled exercise of his best skill and scientifically trained judgment.

Dr. Lambert's was, of course, a long-standing theory about alcohol's medicinal use—albeit one that had been recently challenged by the Prohibition-era American Medical Association. It nevertheless found favor with Justice Sutherland, joined by McReynolds, Butler, and Stone, who dissented, in favor of the liberty of the medical profession's practice and—even more important—the interest in states' rights to control such local matters as the regulation of medical practice. Dual federalism could also be alcohol's friend and, in the hands of a vocally objecting minority, had become so.

That sizeable minority of states' rights objectors could not stop Taft's Court in its vigorous construal of forfeiture provisions under the Volstead Act—which the court did while *also* enforcing the criminal penalties of the alcohol revenue laws that were in effect when that act was passed (*U.S. v. Stafoff*, 1923).[59] Essentially, the Taft Court kept a dual set of diachronic punishments—forfeiture and fine—in effect. It also affirmed the constitutionality of forfeiting the property of an innocent owner when his vehicle or other property was used illegally in the liquor trade (*Van Oster v. Kansas*, 1926; *U.S. v. One Ford Coupe*, 1926—with Butler, McReynolds, and Sutherland dissenting on a technicality; *Dodge v. U.S.*, 1926; *Port Gardner Investment v. U.S.*, 1926—Butler and Stone concurring; *Commercial Credit Co. v. U.S.*, 1928). Liability was strict for the chief justice and his allies on the bench.

In other doctrinal developments in criminal law, Taft's Court put its constitutional imprimatur on the novel criminal procedure practice that would come to be known as plea bargaining. This began with two decisions in 1923 that held that Volstead Act violations did not require grand jury indictment because they were not "infamous" crimes under the Fifth Amendment (*Wyman v. U.S.* and *Brede v. Powers*).[60] The official recognition that the Sixth Amendment jury trial guarantee was a personal right that could be waived by the defendant did not come until *Patton v. U.S.* in 1930,[61] decided a few months after Taft had left the court and died. (Chief Justice Hughes was already presiding but not participating in the case.) Patton had been charged with conspiring to bribe a Prohibition agent; during his jury trial, one of the twelve jurors became incapacitated, and both sides agreed to continue with eleven. After a guilty verdict, the defendant challenged the right to waive the trial by jury as provided. Sutherland's opinion was a long disquisition on the history of the right to the jury; in it, he recognized that as the gravity of an offense increases, the caution about waiving a jury trial should also increase—with the implication being that Prohibition-related offenses were *not* of such gravity.

Plea bargaining was itself an effort to expedite the criminal justice system because of the load of Prohibition cases on the federal district court docket. Existing outside of the Constitution's procedural guarantees of due "processes" of law, it was invented by Manhattan federal prosecutor Emory Buckner. Concocting a docket-clearing opportunity called "Bargain Day," he invited Volstead offenders to plead guilty and waive trial in exchange for light sentences; with the cooperation of two federal judges, Buckner processed five hundred cases at a time.[62] An expedient for dealing with the rash of bootlegging prosecutions would forever change American criminal justice.

Another procedural "innovation" occurred in *U.S. v. Lanza* in 1922, in which the Taft Court exempted liquor law violators from the constitutional protections against double jeopardy due to the concurrent enforcement clause in the Eighteenth Amendment. To avoid the Fifth Amendment complication, Taft argued that the federal and state prohibition enforcement powers proceeded from different textual sources: Congress's was the Eighteenth Amendment's enforcement clause, but state prohibition laws derive their force, he argued "from power originally belonging to the states, preserved to them by the Tenth Amendment."[63] This forging of a novel doctrinal application of "dual sovereignty" meant that some violators could be (and were) prosecuted twice on the same evidence, in federal and then in state court, which further contributed to court clogging and uneven policing and enforcement.[64] The *Lanza* position was reaffirmed in *Hebert v. Louisiana* (1926), in a unanimous opinion authored by Justice Van Devanter. Agreeing that a pending federal charge for violating the Volstead Act did not preclude a prosecution for violating a state prohibition statute, even if both were relying on the same acts or offenses, the court found the twinned prosecutions an appropriate measure to "doubly denounce" the manufacture of intoxicating liquor.[65] *Albrecht v. U.S.* (1927), a case that also involved technical questions as to the validity of a warrant and the probable cause for indictment, added that no Fifth Amendment violation occurred if a defendant was prosecuted for the possessing and then the selling of the same cache of booze. This was not "imposition of double punishment," as the complaint creatively alleged; rather, and with the commonsense reasoning that Brandeis's unanimous opinion applied, "possessing and selling are distinct offenses" and so could be subject to separate convictions and separate penalties.

In what was almost an anticlimax to all else that was going on, the Taft Court also had one last cleanup decision on the matter of the procedural validity of the passage of the national prohibition laws. In 1925 in *Druggan v. Anderson* the justices ruled that Congress could constitutionally enact the Volstead Act before the date that the Eighteenth Amendment and presumably its enforcement clause became effective.[66] Justice Holmes wielded his venerable legal positivism in reasoning that the amendment became effective as a law upon its ratification, and thereby duly empowered Congress to legislate in anticipation for the enforcement of Prohibition when the year should expire, without necessarily awaiting that event. As he summarily concluded his brief unanimous opinion, "We think the case too clear for extended discussion."

Too clear it all was. Though Taft's personal and presidential objections to Prohibition were well known—as president he had vetoed the Webb-Kenyon Act and its restrictions on the interstate shipment of liquor—he assiduously served the cause of law and order once he became chief justice. As *Last Call* summarizes the jurisprudential trend, and then some:

> Taft led a fairly stable bloc of justices who rendered a series of decisions expanding the power of the federal government, over the generally consistent objections of McReynolds and his conservative allies . . . key decisions [that] weakened the 5th Amendment . . . [with] the justices [even finding] that requiring a bootlegger to file a tax return on his illegal earnings did not infringe on the 5th Amendment's protection against self-incrimination.[67]

This latter case, *U.S. v. Manly S. Sullivan* (1927), would become the foundation of the federal government's eventual conviction of gangster Al Capone for income tax evasion. Writing for a unanimous court in *Sullivan*, Justice Holmes found that gains from illicit traffic in liquor were subject to the income tax, and that the Fifth Amendment privilege did not protect the defendant from the requirement of filing a return.[68] The amendment's protection had been "pressed too far," said Holmes, speaking succinctly and concluding wryly: "It is urged that if a return were made the defendant would be entitled to deduct illegal expenses such as bribery. This by no means follows but it will be time enough to consider the question when a taxpayer has the temerity to raise it." A variant of such temerity would in fact mark the unsuccessful 1943 Supreme Court appeal of gangster Nucky Johnson—immortalized for many not as a Supreme Court litigant but as the character of Nucky Thompson in HBO's flamboyant period series *Boardwalk Empire*.

Legal scholar Murchison's assessment challenges somewhat the Prohibition history *Last Call*'s "stability and consistency" assessment of the
Taft years; instead, Murchison stresses that "despite the relative continuity in its personnel, Supreme Court doctrine regarding prohibition
issues was far from stable." Indeed, he argues that "the trend of the
Court's decisions parallels the political conflict over prohibition." The
ups-and-downs of that political conflict—or, more accurately, the down
and then up—shaped the court's own meandering legal policy making,
in Murchison's view. Yet even in the early and middle years of greater
public endorsement of enforcement, the Taft Court was willing to protect vested property interests over Prohibition zeal.[69] Still, its solicitude
for property rights, especially those of innocent property owners, also
coexisted with a relative lack of sympathy for those guilty of large-scale
or commercialized criminal violations[70]—but this latter sentiment generally continued all the way until repeal, when attitudes toward aggressive policing of bootlegging operations were generally on the wane.
Murchison also sees Chief Justice Taft (and his successor Hughes, for
that matter) as contributing relatively little to the development of the
criminal law during Prohibition, authoring no opinions in two key areas
(property forfeiture and jury trials), and making minor or only ancillary
contributions in Fourth Amendment, double jeopardy, and entrapment
rulings that shaped new doctrines. "The identity of the chief justice was
not the decisive factor in the developments of the prohibition era," he
concludes.[71]

Chief justice eras are not always the chief justice's, it is true. But Taft
put more of a mark on his court than some legal scholars are willing to
admit. Taft's mark, moreover, was larger and more all-encompassing
than singular decisions or particular doctrinal rules. Taft is perhaps best
remembered, in the popular imagination, as the chief justice who secured for the Supreme Court the budgetary authorization for its own
building. (When he is not being remembered, largely apocryphally, for
being the fattest chief executive who also got stuck in the White House
bathtub.) That accomplishment, which Taft would never see in real life,
reflected his staunch belief in the institutional independence and dignity of the judicial branch[72]—a belief that does much to explain Taft's
commitment to enforcing Prohibition as part of the judicial charge to
uphold the Constitution. Under Taft, the Supreme Court participated

in the state project of alcohol prohibition because of its commitment to law, and then became itself part of that state project.

The War on Alcohol thus renders this verdict on the Prohibition era: it was, quite simply, critical to the building of the modern American state, particularly the emergence of the twentieth-century federal penal state. Institution building, regulatory reforms, and constitutional activism—amendments and judicial decisions—were all part of this process.

As the Taft Court's decisions show, the "war on alcohol" radically expanded the surveillance arm of the police at the federal, state, and local levels. By 1929 and with the passage of the draconian Jones Act making first-time Volstead violations a felony, popular resentment toward the "Volstead army" spread beyond the immigrant ethnic working class—whose cultural drinking practices had long been a target of alcohol prohibition enforcement, as it also spread beyond their political allies—like Democratic presidential contender and fellow-Catholic ethnic Al Smith. Indeed, by the start of the new decade, resentment about Prohibition's heavy hand seethed within the largely Protestant middle class as well,[73] the group that had heretofore tacitly supported alcohol regulation. At the same time, that mainstream bloc of the American public was also questioning Prohibition's limited efficacy as well as recoiling from its unintended consequence of spawning a violent criminal syndicate organized around the booze trade.

But the Repeal of Prohibition was still years away. Moreover, the heady mixture of prohibitionist and punitive approaches toward illicit recreational substances, in which the federal government would play a leading role, was Prohibition's "most consequential harvest." It was also one that would carry over into future regulation of alcohol, and on into the coming "war on drugs" of the 1980s and its colossal penal state.[74]

In a letter to his son written in 1924, Taft noted ruefully, "It would seem as if more feeling could be engendered over the Prohibition Act than almost any other subject that we have in the Court." While the "feeling" to which the chief justice was referring was among the disputatious members of his Supreme Court,[75] there was plenty of outrage to go around. Some would argue that we are still feeling it: in the contemporary outcry against the "modern" American regime of law enforcement and criminal justice,[76] marked and deformed as it is by the statist legacy of the Taft years.

CONCLUSION

Taft's almost religious faith in the institutional role of the judiciary merged on his court with an unwavering law-and-order attitude toward the enforcement of Prohibition. Yet his era was also one of widespread public defiance of the law, which saw the invention of a host of cocktails to compensate for the varying quality of available liquor.

8

THE GIN COCKTAIL PARTY OF THE HUGHES ERA

The *Hughes Court* (1930–1941) has the unparalleled honor, in the history of alcohol in American life and law, of celebrating the repeal of Prohibition with the passage of the Twenty-First Amendment to the Constitution on December 5, 1933. Less heralded is that in April of that same year, the Cullen Act was passed, declaring beer up to 3.2 percent alcohol to be nonintoxicating and therefore not in violation of the Eighteenth Amendment. Thus the nation's brewers were allowed to resume operations—and employment, the real concern during the depths of the Great Depression, which had begun with the collapse of the stock market in 1929. Beer for sale was, of course, only the populist beginning. The politically upscale Mayflower Hotel on Connecticut Avenue, home to many an inaugural ball, was the first establishment in the capital to apply for a liquor license when Prohibition finally ended in Washington, DC, on March 1, 1934, with the expiration of the Sheppard Act.[1]

Charles Evan Hughes had been a man of Washington, on and off, for the many decades of his long career in politics and public service. He was appointed chief justice by Republican president Herbert Hoover, after having resigned as associate justice in 1916 to run unsuccessfully for president. In an odd coincidence, Hughes had been first appointed to the Supreme Court by President Taft in 1910, the president who had long promised Hughes the center chair and the chief justice whom Hughes would ultimately replace—allegedly, at Taft's urging from his sickbed. Hughes's stance on the political issues of his day, including on alcohol restrictions, was complicated, and his long career in and out of public life made (and makes) pigeonholing him difficult. With a political reputation as a party reformer, Hughes ran for president against incumbent Progressive Democrat Woodrow Wilson, both of whom stayed silent on the prohibition issue during the campaign, as each represented a party coalition composed of wets and drys. It was said that Hughes's aloofness and innate shyness was his undoing as a presidential candidate, yet he was apparently able to play the gadabout when the circumstances were right: in his biography, there is a famous story of Hughes the lawyer charming a barroom full of Westerners in the small-town hotel at which he was staying on business, by introducing himself and buying drinks all around.[2]

Hughes's attitudes on alcohol were never part of his public persona, although he participated in the early legal wrangling over the Eighteenth Amendment, declining an invitation to join with Rhode Island's challenge[3] and instead filing a friend of the court brief on behalf of twenty-one state attorneys general arguing the validity of the amendment. Other legal work was proreformist of a different nature, including representing United Mine Workers' officials and defending the rights of Socialist assemblymen in New York State to retain their legislative seats.[4] In December of 1920 Hughes was once again drafted into public life with a stint as President Harding's secretary of state, during which he freely availed himself of the numerous and well-catered celebrations at Washington's embassies and legations.[5] But he was no simple diplomatic gadfly, and nor was he part of Harding's hijinks at the little Green House or his drinking and poker parties on the second floor of the White House;[6] Hughes, rather, was known at the time as "the best mind in Washington."[7] Among his accomplishments as secretary was his negotiation of liquor treaties with Great Britain, based on his awareness that the enforcement of the Volstead Act "ran contrary to principles of international comity and . . . the law of the high seas."[8] Public service was followed by a return to his lucrative law practice representing large corporate business interests such as Standard Oil— ties that would (only) slightly complicate his confirmation by the Senate to be the Supreme Court's chief in February of 1930.

Chief Justice Hughes is probably best known for leading the court through its famous constitutional contretemps with President Franklin

Roosevelt over the New Deal and, later, the president's court-packing plan. That heady Roosevelt association produces a very particular cocktail connection, in that FDR is forever associated with the classic gin martini.[9] *Courtwatchers* recounts the story of FDR's famous poker parties, at which the president mixed dry martinis—the story coming from an attendee, the future associate justice William O. Douglas, whom FDR regularly invited, even after appointing him to the court in 1939.[10] Forever and always associated with the **Dry Martini** is President Roosevelt (1933–1945), and so must be the Hughes era.

Hughes's consumption of spirits is uncontested: as Murchison expresses it, "Hughes did not embrace the Eighteenth Amendment after its passage and continued 'to satisfy his personal fondness for good liquor when the occasion presented itself.'"[11] Indeed, early in his career, during the time of the late Fuller era, he had become accustomed to "a highball before bedtime." A letter of 1916 finds William Howard Taft recalling Hughes "sit[ting] up late into the night drinking Scotch whiskey and soda" while the two discussed campaigning for votes.[12] Nevertheless, soon after Hughes's appointment as associate justice, "he decided it would be best to get along under his own steam" and "confined his indulgence to an occasional, *light* social drink"[13] (emphasis added).

The martini is many things, but few would describe it as a "light" drink. Thus, Hughes's own personal connection to London dry gin is somewhat more indirect than that of his era's chief executive. Hughes's home state of New York, which he also served as governor from 1907 to 1910, is the indisputable state of origin of his era's totemic cocktail. *Dry Manhattan* identifies "the glamorous Hotel Knickerbocker" in New York City's Times Square as the reputed birthplace of the dry martini.[14] That specific point of origin is, of course, disputed, but undeniable is that once created—whether at the Turf Club, the Plaza Hotel, or elsewhere—the dry martini epitomized New York at night: the cocktail was one of the highlights of the pre-Prohibition bar service at the Waldorf Astoria, as well as one of the "famous cocktails" served by bartender William Mulhall at the Holland House.[15] In addition to Hughes's geographic link to the drink, his appointing president, Hoover, was known to enjoy a dry martini—daily, after Prohibition ended.[16] But it was "the martini rituals of President Franklin Roosevelt," with whose career Chief Justice Hughes's term so dramatically intersected, that "attracted national attention, and one could indeed argue that [Roosevelt] gave official sanction to the cocktail hour."[17] FDR is also credited with publicly mixing "the first legal Martini," and gave "the Martini rite" official cultural sanction.[18]

"The destiny of the Martini is easier to grasp than its early history," says cocktail enthusiast Lowell Edmunds in his *Martini, Straight Up*.[19] The martini almost certainly dates from the end of the Waite era, and came to early favor in its dry gin–dry vermouth form during the Fuller era. But it was really the 1910s leading up to Prohibition, and the 1920s themselves, that put the drink at the center of the mixology map. From Roosevelt's silver cocktail cups on display at the Hyde Park Library, to the cocktail set of glasses and shaker that had already become a typical wedding gift in the 1920s, the tools of the martini rite had become common in American households[20] and entrenched in American popular culture. Period cultural references to the cocktail abound—one being comedian W. C. Fields's quip that his favorite drink was the martini, by which he meant that "he had a bottle of gin in one hand and a bottle of vermouth in the other, and he took alternate pulls, favoring the gin."[21] Movies of the era were a spirited source of martini references. Actor Charles Butterworth, in the 1937 *Every Day's a Holiday* (starring and written by Mae West), delivers the immortal line, "You ought to get out of those wet clothes and into a dry martini." *The Thin Man* movies were redolent with drinking, and William Powell's on-screen persona, Nick Charles, could be relied upon to mix a batch of martinis in every film, starting in 1934. Attributed or misattributed to Manhattan writer and satirist Dorothy Parker is also the unforgettable quatrain of the age:

> I like to have a martini,
> Two at the very most.
> After three I'm under the table,
> After four I'm under my host.

The martini of the 1930s was chic, urbane, and so, so very modern. Even the iconic V-shaped cone glass—for the martini is one of the few bar drinks to be honored with its own distinctive glassware for its enjoyment—reeks of art deco modernism, the same aesthetic that shaped the art moderne design of FDR's Works Progress Administration (WPA) structures and projects. Why the martini is linked to the V-shaped angled glass is because "the cocktail too was perceived as au courant" in the late 1920s and early 1930s, "even though it had been around for forty or fifty years." As Edmunds explains it: "Prohibition made gin the favorite distilled spirit. Gin makes the Martini a favorite cocktail."[22] Gin was certainly featuring in cocktails before Prohibition, but after 1920, gin's strong and relatively easy to mimic taste made it a popular recipe for both home distillers and bootleggers, who often stretched their supplies of bona fide spirits by diluting them with grain alcohol and flavorings. Even so, such gin was best paired with ingredients that could mask its likely deficiencies. Ergo, the martini, with olives. But there was also the new social context of the new class and customs of drinkers in the 1920s–1930s, which was metropolitan and young and stylishly outré. For these "the Martini is perceived as new and is at home in the new glass."[23]

Much change, and not only constitutional, would take place during the Hughes Court years of 1930–1941. The martini symbolizes this new age but in a richly complex way, given its long pedigree—not unlike the way that the "new" in constitutional law edged into this judicial era. Some explanation is required, to put both Hughes and the martini in their proper context.

Hughes himself was hardly a denizen of a new modernity, as at the time of his appointment he was the oldest chief justice ever to begin service. He really came of age in the martini's first epoch of popularity, and prior to the Prohibition project which, privately, he never accepted.[24] Those private beliefs had little effect on the decisions of his court during the final years of Prohibition. By the time Hughes took over in 1930, his predecessor Chief Justice Taft had laid in a hefty body of proenforcement decisions. Hughes, as we shall see, authored only one of the "liberal" construction opinions on search and seizure issues and exerted little influence on Justices Butler and McReynolds, who led the revival of individual rights under the Fourth Amendment. They— not the chief—authored five of the seven Fourth Amendment opinions issued between 1930 and 1933 that reversed convictions and began the constitutional march back to pre-Prohibition sanity. Hughes's Court did preside during the Repeal campaign, and over an even more dramatic revolution in the constitutional order, but to call Hughes a force for the cutting edge, in law or fashion, would be inaccurate.

Hughes, rather, was a force for what was *classic*. As a jurist, he certainly projected this. With his distinguished white beard and commanding visage, he looked like a chief justice straight out of central casting—or God, as many remarked. (This included his colleague and mentee, Justice William Douglas.) His photographic memory, intellectual command of the law, efficient businesslike manner, and confident political savvy made him one of the most effective leaders in court history, during one of the Supreme Court's most difficult periods in history. Not only was Hughes saddled with a disagreeing and at times disagreeable court, he was also faced with a direct challenge from the president of the United States to his institution's very integrity. Indeed, at the height of the struggle between the justices and President Roosevelt over the constitutionality of the New Deal programs, Hughes's martini-drinking presidential adversary called him his "most dangerous, implacable enemy."[25] It took a leader of Hughes's stature and maturity to steer the court through the political maelstrom both it and the republic faced during his tenure.

Much of that political maelstrom swirled over the role of government in the economy, the role of the federal government in American life, and the role of the Supreme Court in constitutional government. Changes would occur to all three—but not before an antagonistic contest between FDR and the chief justice over the former's plan to "pack" the court with additional members. Those presumably compliant appointees would outvote and thus override the obstruction of the "Nine Old Men" from the "horse and buggy era," who were objecting to the New Deal's intervention in the American economy and invalidating its statutes and programs using the power of judicial review. FDR presented his judicial opponents as out of step with the times and was himself responsible for the unflatteringly antiquarian metaphor horse and buggy-ism—a reference which, of course, also calls to mind the generation of the martini's birth. Cocktail episodes likewise littered the field of battle. Simon's *FDR and Chief Justice Hughes* illustrates one, while capturing the political atmosphere after Roosevelt's reelection in 1936 and just in advance of his announcing of his plan to "reorganize" the federal judiciary:

> When the president hosted his annual dinner in honor of the justices on February 2 [1937], he was in noticeably high spirits. Before the guests of honor arrived at the White House, Roosevelt had mischievously considered whether he should have one cocktail, and not mention his Court-packing plan, or lay out mimeographed copies of

the Court bill beside each justice's place, in which case he would fortify himself with three cocktails.[26]

Of course, in the end, the conflict was defused: revised New Deal legislation lost its initial administrative and constitutionally suspect rough edges; Hughes led a narrow court majority to uphold a series of New Deal laws and policies thereby obviating the presidential need to circumvent the judiciary; and political opposition to the high-handedness of FDR's plan, combined with Hughes's own strategic lobbying against it, doomed the bill in Congress. Chief Justice Hughes was in many ways the victor in the larger war: he "astutely steered the Court away from outmoded constitutional interpretation that had obstructed progressive social and economic legislation," successfully defended his institution's independence "with dignity," and supervised the Supreme Court's transition to an enlarged new role in articulating the rights of individuals and persecuted minorities.[27]

Embodying the great change that was occurring—occurring but still grounded in respect for American tradition—was the court's new home. Completed and opened in 1935, the new Supreme Court building was a landmark advance, the third branch's first dedicated institutional space. Yet this modern pronouncement of an administratively fully realized judiciary was sheathed in a sumptuously neo-Classical architectural shell that matched the turn-of-the-nineteenth-century Capitol it faced. It is fitting, then, that the totemic cocktail of the same era be both classic and modern at the same time, as its Chief Justice Hughes was and had to be, and as the martini continues to be—in all of its many twenty-first-century permutations, "Choco-tini" and otherwise.

The very outset of Hughes's tenure, however, seemed somewhat more *plus ça change* than anything else, for his Supreme Court began by addressing yet another constitutional challenge to the procedural adoption of the Eighteenth Amendment. Hughes himself did not participate in the court's decision in *U.S. v. Sprague* in 1931, which declined to rise to the challenge, instead deferring to congressional judgment as to the use of ratification procedures. While popular opinion was turning against the Prohibition regime by the time of *Sprague*, wet forces were despairing of the practical political prospects of repeal. Yet even before the ultimate passage of the Twenty-First Amendment, the Hughes Court was signaling an end to judicial toleration of the feverish

federal enforcement power of years past: there were seven cases decided between 1930 and 1933 that involved violations of the alcohol
ban, and the defendants in all of these cases won at least partial victories.

An early high-water mark of the trend was *Taylor v. U.S.* in 1932,
where the Hughes Court declared a warrantless search of a distiller's
garage constitutionally unacceptable.[28] Writing with his typical and
somewhat artless succinctness, Justice McReynolds chastised the law
enforcement personnel in question:

> Although over a considerable period numerous complaints concern-
> ing the use of these premises had been received, the agents had
> made no effort to obtain a warrant for making a search. They had
> abundant opportunity so to do and to proceed in an orderly way even
> after the [whiskey] odor had emphasized their suspicions; there was
> no probability of material change in the situation during the time
> necessary to secure such warrant. Moreover, a short period of watch-
> ing would have prevented any such possibility. . . . [T]he action of the
> agents was inexcusable and the seizure unreasonable.

The lowly bootlegger as civil libertarian patriot comes through in this
final salvo: "Prohibition officers may rely on a distinctive odor as a
physical fact indicative of possible crime; but its presence alone does
not strip the owner of a building of constitutional guaranties."

Important precedents had been set in 1931 and 1932 as well, especially as far as limiting the authority of searches incident to arrest, in the
decisions in *Go-Bart Importing Co. v. U.S.* and *U.S. v. Lefkowitz*, respectively. *Grau v. U.S.* (1932) continued the 1930s trend of expanding
the individual's right to be free from government intrusion on his or her
private property. But what is more interesting about the case is that
Justice Owen Roberts parsed the actual terminology of the Volstead Act
to reverse the petitioner's conviction, because evidence of manufacture
(what supported the warrant) did not constitute evidence of sale (what
the petitioner had been charged with). Similarly, the court grew skeptical of what were "good cause" sources of information about reported
bootleggers. *Nathanson v. United States* (1933) illustrated the limits
beyond which a magistrate could not venture in issuing a warrant. A
sworn statement of an affiant that "he has cause to suspect and does
believe" that liquor illegally brought into the United States was located

on certain premises would not do, said Justice McReynolds for a unanimous court. An affidavit must provide the magistrate with a substantial
basis for determining the existence of probable cause, and the wholly
conclusionary statement at issue in *Nathanson* failed to meet this requirement. (*Sgro v. U.S.* in 1932, with Hughes writing for the majority,
also invalidated a reissued warrant as technically invalid because it was
based on an outdated or expired conception of probable cause.) Even
when a petitioner lost on a Fourth Amendment claim, the Hughes
Court would intervene on his behalf on the question of sentencing—an
occurrence that characterized the 1931 decision in *Husty v. U.S.* As one
student of the period put it: "The *Husty* Court's *words* appeared to
convey a growing disapproval of Prohibition. Essentially, the ruling was
as friendly to wets as was possible given the obvious limitations provided by the facts of the case"[29] (emphasis added). That emphasis on
"words" was the court giving full effect to what the otherwise draconian
Jones Act of 1929 authorized: that while increasing penalties for violations of the Volstead Act, the Jones Act did so "Provided, That it is the
intent of Congress that *the court*, in imposing sentencing hereunder,
should discriminate between casual or slight violations and habitual
sales of intoxicating liquor, or attempts to commercialize violations of
the law"[30] (emphasis added). With gusto, the Hughes Court did so
discriminate.

Legal scholar Murchison argues that dissatisfaction with national
prohibition significantly influenced the development of the doctrine of
entrapment in criminal law, as evidenced by the court's 1932 decision in
Sorrells v. U.S. and its recognition of the "gross abuse of authority" by
prohibition agents.[31] (Reversed and remanded, the charges against Sor-
rell were ultimately dropped.) Murchison also sees the Hughes Court
period of the early 1930s as particularly striking in its lax application of
the Volstead Act, with "the contrast with the sympathetic construction
in the opinions of the 1920s [being] vivid."[32] Purchasing liquor was not
a crime under the act as a result of *U.S. v. Farrar* in 1930, judges could
reduce sentences imposed by the act as a result of *U.S. v. Benz* in 1931,
and governmental ability to forfeit the interests of innocent owners of
property used to transport alcohol was severely restricted in *Richbourg
Motor Co. v. U.S.* in 1930. Still, *U.S. v. Ryan* in 1931 allowed the use of
general, broader forfeiture statutes to seize saloon furnishings used in
establishments selling intoxicating liquor, and *General Motors Accep-*

tance Corp. v. U.S., U.S. v. Commercial Credit, and *U.S. v. The Ruth Mildred* in 1932 all allowed those statutes' use to seize vehicles and vessels that had violated customs and navigation laws, that is, ones that were transporting liquor across international borders like that with Mexico.[33] As Murchison reads and attempts to explain these anomalously strict rulings, "Smuggling, like operating a saloon but unlike carrying liquor in an automobile, was not an activity in which ordinary citizens engaged."[34] Similarly, *Danovitz v. U.S.* (1930) read the Volstead Act broadly to permit destruction of property used in the illegal *manufacture* of bootleg whiskey—another activity outside the bounds of the average Prohibition violator.[35] But *U.S. v. Lafranca* in 1931 barred the collection of (federal) civil tax penalties from an individual who had previously been convicted of violating the Volstead Act with respect to "the same unlawful sales" now being taxed (he sold alcohol in his restaurant, and so became a "retail liquor dealer")—thus refusing to continue to honor exceptions to the double jeopardy protection. Lastly, the 1933 case of *Cook v. U.S.* construed a treaty with Great Britain to deny customs officials authority to board British vessels, undercutting somewhat the Harding era decision of *Cunard SS Co.* (And, no doubt, freeing scores of happy passengers to enjoy a good London Dry Gin.)

Hughes could finally call a halt to it all, speaking for his court in the 1934 case of *U.S. v. Chambers*: "Prosecutions for violations of the National Prohibition Act in a state, pending when the Eighteenth Amendment was repealed, cannot be continued." The court went even further in *Massey v. U.S.* (1934), holding that the repealing amendment abated not only pending prosecutions but cases in which convictions were being appealed: those convictions would be vacated on remand.[36]

There were also various Prohibition era alcohol taxation issues to resolve, some raising the larger issues of governmental power with which the Hughes Court was wrestling in the New Deal context. *U.S. v. Constantine* in 1935 found the Revenue Act of 1926, and the $1,000.00 excise tax it imposed on illegal liquor business, to be an invalid exercise of federal power. This excise tax, Justice Roberts's majority opinion held, was part of the enforcement apparatus of Prohibition: both its amount and the nature of its operation made clear that its purpose was punitive, not revenue generating. With the repeal of the Eighteenth Amendment, Congress no longer had the power to impose such a penalty for the violation of state law. So although retail in alcohol remained illegal in Alabama in 1934, its retail liquor dealers were lawfully subject only to the ordinary internal revenue tax of $25.00. Recently appointed Justice Benjamin Cardozo, joined by Justices Brandeis and Stone, dissented from this reasoning. The dissenters saw the higher, excise tax as "an appropriate instrument of the fiscal policy of the nation." Reasoning that "a business that is a nuisance, like any other *business that is socially undesirable*, may be taxed at a higher rate than one legitimate and useful," they concluded that Congress was well within its discretionary taxation powers (emphasis added). Cardozo went on: "By classifying in such a mode Congress is not punishing for a crime. . . . It is not punishing at all. It is laying an excise upon a business conducted in a particular way with notice to the taxpayer that if he embarks upon that business he will be subjected to a special burden. What he pays, if he chooses to go on, is a tax and not a penalty."

That the court's dispute in *Constantine* was not really about the Prohibition Amendment, or even about alcohol at all, but about the emerging question of the scope of federal governmental power was made obvious in Cardozo's final paragraph. "The judgment of the court," he began, "rests upon the ruling that another purpose, not professed, may be read beneath the surface, and by the purpose so imputed the statute is destroyed. Thus the process of psychoanalysis has spread to unaccustomed fields." If Congress called something a tax, then a tax it was, and the court had no business second-guessing its legitimacy. "There is a wise and ancient doctrine," Cardozo ended with a final flourish, "that a court will not inquire into the motives of a legislative body or assume them to be wrongful. There is another wise and ancient doctrine that a court will not adjudge the invalidity of a statute except for manifest necessity. Every reasonable doubt must have been explored and extinguished before moving to that grave conclusion."

The judicial debate in *Constantine* was part of a larger, unfolding battle on the bench: the battle among the justices over the New Deal programs' reliance on expanded notions of congressional power over commerce and of taxation. That a humble alcohol revenue provision engendered such lofty dissenting language signaled that momentous matters were indeed in play—on the docket, and in interbranch relations.

The Hughes Court's New Deal "switch in time to save nine"—its jurisprudential change of heart that protected its existing membership of nine justices—begat a new constitutional era, significantly altering existing judicial doctrine and expanding congressional power. Among Congress's Article I powers are to regulate commerce "among the several states" and to tax and spend "for the general welfare." Those broad grants of power had been whittled down by judicial reading of competing parts of the Constitution: the Tenth Amendment's reservation of powers not listed for Congress as belonging to the states, and the Fourteenth Amendment's protection of personal "liberty" from deprivation without due process of law—which the Fuller, White, and Taft Courts had generously constructed to protect contract and property rights from any encroachment by governmental regulation. (Some of those doctrinal innovations had, of course, also protected alcohol consumers and dealers.) With the Hughes Court's realignment with a new way of thinking about the relationship between the government and the economy, the court "broadly interpreted congressional commerce power, generously construed government's authority to tax and spend for the general welfare, and firmly rejected the once potent doctrine of 'substantive' due process that protected laissez-faire economic values."[37] This change occurred in decisions from 1937 to 1938. Prohibition, and the Eighteenth Amendment's granting of a federal police power to enforce it, had ended in 1933. What remained, and what was enhanced after the court's own shift, was a "plenary" congressional power to legislate on all aspects of interstate commerce—as well as on matters of intrastate or local commerce that affected the larger, national market or interest. It was the full and complete national power over commerce that had been Chief Justice John Marshall's understanding. What it allowed was a wide swath of congressional action on *anything* of a remotely commercial nature.

At least that was the way the Hughes Court's unreconstructed conservative justices, and FDR's New Deal opponents, saw it. A federal power potentially without limit.

The many clearly commercial facets of the alcoholic beverage trade obviously fit within this enlarged commerce power framework. But the politics of the new political economy of the New Deal had little to do with Repeal, per se, and vice versa—at least at the beginning. What would become clear, however, was that opposition to the federal overreach that characterized the enforcement of Prohibition was—for some—part and parcel of a likeminded opposition to Roosevelt's expansion of the federal regulatory state.

This helps to explain how a thoroughly retrograde conservative (and probably pretty dry) justice like James McReynolds could lead a civil libertarian charge against the abuses of Prohibition enforcement. His position seems downright strange, until one pauses to consider the ideological roots of the opposition to the Eighteenth Amendment and how it afterward morphed into a generalized opposition to FDR's New Deal. That states' rights advocacy could coincide with antiprohibitionism made perfect sense, as many "wets" diverged from Prohibition's supporters

> principally in their unwillingness to accept *the progressive notion of using federal power* to reshape social patterns and individual behavior. They would accept strict regulation and even governmental operation of the liquor industry, providing it were carried out at the state or local level where the people directly affected, or at least people of standing in the community like themselves, could determine policies to be followed.[38] (emphasis added)

Individual liberty to have a cocktail, in other words, stopped with the state's absolute right to legislate on behalf of the health, welfare, and morals of its people. It was *Congress's* meddling in drinking—and its concomitant as well as general purpose meddling in affairs that were the states' to direct—that upset conservative justices like McReynolds and Butler.

Plenty of constitutional and political liberals also wanted an end to Prohibition as well. Repeal itself—the passage of the Twenty-First Amendment rescinding the Eighteenth—took place through the unusual process of state ratifying conventions. Antiprohibitionists, who feared that dry pressure and recalcitrance in the state legislatures of only a few small, rural states could thwart majority desire to end Prohibition, insisted on its use. So each state set up its own convention, with delegate elections offering a clear choice between wets and drys.[39] The failed *Sprague* litigation had put the idea of state ratifying conventions on the political map, by suggesting that legislative ratification of constitutional amendments was essentially undemocratic and tainted.[40] The idea of submitting repeal to the people of the states directly appealed to the uncommitted members of Congress, who preferred a popular election on the issue so that they could avoid having to vote on its merits, and the idea of setting up conventions also relieved state legislators of having to vote on the merits of alcohol, an attractive option for many.[41] But the stampede for repeal was actually from the states to Congress, as bills in various states to set up ratifying conventions were rapidly passing by January of 1933. By the time Congress proposed the Repeal Amendment in February 1933, with its section 3 requiring convention approval, its accomplishment was well under way.[42] Indeed, in April of that year, Congress would amend the Volstead Act to permit sale of "non-intoxicating" light wines and beers of no more than 3.2 percent alcohol. The end of the drought was in sight.

Yet even as repeal of Prohibition was speeding to ratification in 1933, federal policy makers were forging a new system of national regulation for alcohol. That system was based on the new vision of congressional power over commerce. The Federal Alcohol Control Administration, created in October 1933, subjected the relegalized liquor trade to the New Deal National Recovery Administration's codes of fair competition.[43] These were the same industry codes that were struck down by the Supreme Court as going beyond congressional constitutional powers in the famous "sick chickens" *Schechter Poultry Co. v. U.S.* case in 1935. With this decision, government liquor control reverted to the states, where it had largely resided prior to Prohibition.[44] At the same time, the 1933 study "Toward Liquor Control" by lawyer Raymond Fosdick and engineer Albert Scott was commissioned by lifelong teetotaler John J. Rockefeller to provide a careful plan of alcohol control for state legislatures.

Two basic options were laid out: public monopoly of distribution, and licensing of private distribution. Whichever scheme was chosen, however, it was central to regulation that the "tied-house, and every device calculated to place the retail establishment [or bar] under obligation to a particular distiller or brewer, should be prevented."[45] Many of the alleged evils of the pre-Prohibition saloon era were said to involve

> excessive promotion of alcoholic indulgence by the suppliers and retailers of alcohol, who were often one and the same entity. . . . [T]he perception was that such "tied house" arrangements encouraged the promotion of alcohol consumption beyond acceptable limits: "Besides pressuring retailers to handle only their brands [of beer

or spirits], suppliers pushed retailers to increase sales whatever the social cost."[46]

No one wished to return to this awful system. After the failure and repeal of the Eighteenth Amendment regime, a desire thus remained for some kind of regulatory effort. What resulted were rules like minimum markup price for wholesale and retail tiers of the alcohol distribution chain. And those state laws—whether thwarting the vertical relationship between supplier and wholesaler, or ensuring minimum markup, brand representation, and exclusive sales territories—should be understood utterly unambiguously as intending one thing and one thing alone: to maintain alcohol at a certain price level so that it could not become too cheap and therefore too easily accessible.[47] Post-Repeal was a reaffirmation of temperance, through price fixing.

"Monopoly protection" or "monopoly franchise laws" essentially limit competition between wholesalers, by shielding wholesalers or distributors from competition by raising barriers to the termination of their contracts by suppliers—the brewers, vintners, distillers, or importers.[48] The monopoly franchise system frequently included an exclusive territory system, whereby a state granted to a wholesaler a geographic area in which it was the sole wholesaler for a given supplier.[49] While a three-tiered licensing system was set up in the "License States," where suppliers make or import the products, wholesalers distribute them, and retailers (wine, liquor, grocery, and package stores, and bars and restaurants) sell them to consumers, in the "Control States," the state itself buys the alcohol from the wholesalers (or, in some instances, is the wholesaler or distributor) and then sells directly to the public (in state-run liquor stores) after a markup. Again, state licensing and high taxation of alcohol were the price of repeal of a system of national prohibition.

All the states created versions of a three-tiered distribution system,[50] as well as regulatory commissions for alcohol beverage control—ABCs. (Control states' liquor stores are colloquially known as "ABC stores.") States also established an official drinking age (twenty-one to purchase in most) and drafted laws forbidding driving while intoxicated. Future solutions to the problems of alcohol, too, would come not from the failed experiment of strict prohibition, but from the realm of scientific inquiry and scientifically informed regulation.[51] Prohibition thus "succeeded in one thing: it created greater governmental regulation of alcohol, where almost none had existed before."[52]

The implications of this new regulatory regime were clear where the Hughes Court was concerned. In spite of its defense of citizen liberty against alcohol law enforcement efforts at the twilight of Prohibition,[53] and despite its ultimate "switch in time" that aligned the Supreme Court with a new national political order on the economic powers of Congress and the federal government, Hughes's was also the court that upheld the authority of *states* to *control the sale of alcohol* in their jurisdictions, "*unfettered* by the Commerce Clause" (*Ziffrin Inc. v. Reeves*, 1939; emphasis added). States, in other words, had broad authority over the marketing of alcohol and over what went on in places that served alcohol.[54] The Twenty-First Amendment had made that plain: in addition to a first section straightforwardly repealing "the Eighteenth article of amendment to the Constitution," the text of the second section read: "The transportation or importation into any State, Territory, or possession of the United States for delivery or use therein of intoxicating liquors, in violation of the laws thereof, is hereby prohibited."

The Hughes Court rulings of the mid to late 1930s embraced what is known as the "originalist" and "maximalist" interpretation of the amendment, which holds that its section 2 "was intended to return absolute control of liquor traffic to the states, free of all restrictions which the Commerce Clause might before that time have imposed."[55] Even the newly enlarged power of Congress over interstate commerce could not trump the state's authority over the alcohol trade.

This maximalist reading of section 2 happened in a series of decisions in the mid to late 1930s, beginning with *State Board of Equalization v. Young's Market Co.* (1936). The case was a challenge to the California statute imposing a license fee of $500 for the privilege of importing beer to any place within its borders, but with the license *not* conferring the privilege of also *selling* beer. For a wholesaler's license, which entitled the holder to sell to licensed dealers beer lawfully possessed, whether it be imported or of domestic make, the fee was $50. The plaintiff wholesalers refused to apply for an importer's license, claiming that the requirement discriminated against wholesalers of imported beer and that, hence, the statute violated both the commerce clause and the equal protection clause. Brandeis's majority opinion in

Figure 8.1. "Impossible Interview No. 11: Al Capone vs. Chief Justice Charles Evans Hughes, 1932," from Miguel Covarrubias's illustrated series of fictional conversations between two famous personalities of opposite character, commissioned by *Vanity Fair*. Hughes apparently tore the picture from the print issue of the magazine, and saved it with his papers. A halftone reprint of the original gouache was displayed as part of the exhibit "The Power of Image: Charles Evans Hughes in Prints, Photographs, and Drawings from the Supreme Court's Collection," at the U.S. Supreme Court, prepared by the Supreme Court Collection Curator's Office. *Source: Nickolas Muray Collection of Mexican Art, Harry Ransom Center, The University of Texas at Austin. Copyright: Maria Elena Rico Covarrubias*

Young's Market conceded that "[p]rior to the Twenty-First Amendment it would obviously have been unconstitutional to have imposed any fee for the privilege [of importing]." But no longer. "The amendment which 'prohibited' the 'transportation or importation' of intoxicating liquors into any state 'in violation of the laws thereof,' abrogated the right to import free, so far as concerns intoxicating liquors," Brandeis patiently explained. "The words used are apt to confer upon the state the power to forbid all importations which do not comply with the conditions which it prescribes. The plaintiffs ask us to limit this broad command." Brandeis would not do so, for the amendment plainly allowed states to choose any aid in policing the liquor traffic—from monopolistic control of all sales to less restrictive licensing schemes. As for any claim of discrimination against wholesalers by the state's liquor laws, Brandeis was clear: "A classification recognized by the Twenty-First Amendment cannot be deemed forbidden by the Fourteenth." (Reaffirmed in *Mahoney v. Joseph Triner Corp.,* 1938; *Indianapolis Brewing Co.* v. *Liquor Control Comm'n.,* 1939; and *Finch and Co. v. McKittrick,* 1939.)

Ziffrin Inc. v. Reeves (1939) illustrates the variety of factual contexts in which the Hughes Court's empowerment of states over alcohol occurred. The case involved Kentucky's efforts to regulate all aspects of its alcohol traffic, including placing conditions on its export from domestic distillers. The complainant's argument was that alcohol was a legitimate article of interstate commerce, and the Twenty-First Amendment had done nothing to change that. As McReynolds's unanimous opinion stated the proposition: "Although a state may prohibit the manufacture of liquor, if a state permits distillation, sale, and transportation—as Kentucky does—the rule of law is that the state may not annex to its consent to manufacture and sell the unconstitutional ban upon carriage of interstate exports of liquors by contract carriers." He then went on to reject it, providing this reasoning:

> Kentucky has seen fit to permit manufacture of whiskey only upon condition that it be sold to an indicated class of customers and transported in definitely specified ways. These conditions are not unreasonable, and are clearly appropriate for effectuating the policy of limiting traffic in order to minimize well-known evils, and secure payment of revenue. The statute declares whiskey removed from permitted channels contraband subject to immediate seizure. This is within the police power of the state, and property so circumstanced cannot be regarded as a proper article of commerce.

As justification, McReynolds returned to a pre-Prohibition understanding of state power over alcohol, rhetorically resembling a pre–New Deal description of the breadth of state powers in the federal system: "the State may decline to consider certain noxious things legitimate articles of commerce, and inhibit their transportation. Property rights in intoxicants depend on state laws, and cease if the liquor becomes contraband."

No justices ruling in these cases contemporaneous with the ratification of the Twenty-First Amendment questioned that its "words used" were "apt to confer upon the state" a very large power: to forbid that "which do[es] not comply with the conditions which it prescribes" for alcohol in the state. Was there more to the Hughes Court's vigorous empowerment of states when it came to alcohol? One study argues that both a popular majority post Prohibition and the post-Prohibition Supreme Court believed alcohol—and especially the alcohol trade—to be "a monstrous evil," and that this "vehemence" led the court to approve almost any state-level restriction.[56] Even if so, there were limits. In *Collins v. Yosemite Park & Curry Co.* (1938), a concessionaire that operated hotels, camps, and stores selling alcohol in Yosemite National Park, under a contract with the secretary of the interior, sought to prevent California authorities from enforcing the state's Alcoholic Beverage Control Act within the limits of the park. That state liquor law required the concessionaire to apply for permits for the importation and sale of liquor and to pay related taxes and fees. The Hughes Court found that the state had ceded to the United States, and that the United States had accepted, exclusive jurisdiction over Yosemite National Park, except insofar as the state had expressly reserved the right to tax persons and corporations within the park. In light of this, the court held that "[a]s there is no reservation of the right to control the sale or use of alcoholic beverages, such regulatory provisions as are found in the Act"—namely, the provisions concerning importation and sales permits and fees—"are unenforceable in the Park." Yet it was not so much that alcohol was free from state strictures; rather, federal lands were outside of the state's purview. *Collins* freed the camp store operator from observing state liquor regulations (but not from paying state taxes), but it did so out of national supremacy interests—well established in the court's new, New Deal era jurisprudence—and not because of any special solicitude for drinkers.[57]

The federal government was hardly powerless over alcohol, post-Repeal, especially when it came to established federal arenas of authority, such as over foreign imports and exports. An otherwise incidental per curiam decision of 1939, in *William Jameson & Co. v. Morganthau*, upheld federal control of truth-in-labeling for imported liquor. The appellant importer and distributor of alcoholic beverages had been denied the right to import its Jameson Whiskey into the United States under the label of "blended Scotch whisky" on the ground that—as an Irish distilling product—it was improperly labeled. Jameson brought suit against the secretary of the treasury and other officials to enjoin them from refusing to release the product from customs custody upon payment of the required customs duties, and also asked for a declaratory judgment that the Federal Alcohol Administration Act was unconstitutional and void. Rather dismissively, the Hughes Court would have none of it. "There was no substance to the contention" that the Twenty-First Amendment "gives to the States complete and exclusive control over commerce in intoxicating liquors, unlimited by the commerce clause, and hence that Congress has no longer authority to control the importation of these commodities into the United States," the justices scolded. "So far as the Federal Alcohol Administration Act itself is concerned, no substantial question of constitutional validity was raised," *Jameson* concluded, affirming the federal role in setting quality standards for liquor imports. Irish whiskey would have to (and of course ultimately would) make a name for itself on its own merits.

The Hughes Court's last alcohol case was one of its most interesting, for contemporary bar brand aficionados, at least: this was the 1940 trademark case of *Bacardi Corp. v. Domenech*. *Bacardi* presented the overwrought question of

> the validity of legislation of Puerto Rico prohibiting the use of trade marks, brands, or trade names, on distilled spirits manufactured in Puerto Rico if the marks, brands, or names had previously been used anywhere outside Puerto Rico, unless they had been used on spirits manufactured in Puerto Rico on or before February 1, 1936, or in the case of trade marks they had been used exclusively in continental United States prior to that date.

Chief Justice Hughes's opinion for the unanimous court went into great if not loving detail as to the history of Bacardi's rum production. "Bacardi rum," he explained,

> has always been made according to definite secret processes, has been extensively advertised and enjoys an excellent reputation. Under [Bacardi Corporation of America]'s agreement with its Cuban [sire] corporation, all rum designated by the described trade marks and labels was to be manufactured under the supervision of representatives of the Cuban corporation and to be the same kind and quality as the rum that the latter manufactured and sold. . . . For more than twenty years, save for the period during national prohibition, the Cuban corporation and its predecessors had sold rum in Puerto Rico and throughout the United States under trade marks which included the word "Bacardi," "Bacardi y Cia," the representation of a bat in a circular frame, and certain distinctive labels.

Hughes also carefully detailed the facts of the dispute. "The trademarks had been duly registered in the U.S. Patent Office," he began. "In March of 1936, Bacardi Corp. arranged for the installation of a plant in Puerto Rico and since then has been duly licensed to do business in Puerto Rico under its laws relating to foreign corporations." But the Puerto Rico legislature was also seeking to "protect the renascent liquor industry of Puerto Rico from all competition by foreign capital." Its statutory restriction was not on doing business or manufacturing of rum per se; rather, it was on using Bacardi's familiar trademarks and labels to designate *its* rum product, when that product was one being made in Puerto Rico. Presumably, the legislature's purpose was to build up and then protect the name and reputation of truly "domestic" brands of Puerto Rican rum.

Upholding both patent law and international treaties respecting it, Hughes ruled that "the United States in exercising its treaty-making power"—in this case, with Cuba, regarding uniform protection of trademarks—"dominates local policy." Thus was voided Puerto Rico's effort to prohibit the use of an international trademark on spirits being newly produced on the island. That rum was such a vital subject in the lingering aftermath of the Prohibition years, and on the eve of World War II and the cusp of the change from the Hughes to the Stone era, says much about its important place in the American market. Rum had been one of the foreign liquors to which a dry nation had turned, and a taste for the Caribbean product had definitely been acquired. When the industrial demands of World War II made domestic distilling difficult, rum would (again) fill the breach . . . and fill up the daiquiri pitchers. As the next chapter will show, there would be much to recommend it as the spirit of the coming (judicial) age.

So what of the "gin cocktail party of the Hughes era"? *Domesticating Drink* has this to say about the latter part of Hughes's tenure:

> After repeal in 1933, state regulatory agencies encouraged the "privatization of drinking," and by 1941 most alcohol in the country was sold for off-premises consumption. State package stores legitimized domestic drinking and undercut the public drinking rituals of historically male spaces. The new state alcohol regulations built upon and facilitated new cultural practices.[58]

But, of course, the cultural practice of drinking at home and the house-based cocktail party had already been established during the deprivations of Prohibition. Post-Prohibition's altered alcohol market—its incentivizing of "take-out" purchase of alcoholic beverage products—merely reinforced what had already been occurring. Alcohol was back as a legitimate part of American life, but domesticated.

There would be one last stand of the temperance forces, to stop mass-market alcohol advertising. A concession was won in 1936 when the distilled beverage industry promised to refrain on a voluntary basis from running radio commercials (and television commercials, in 1948). The beer industry, however, refused.[59] Home drinking of beer was already being simplified by the successful commercial production of beer in easily portable stainless-steel cans, which began in 1935.[60] Beer manufacturers recognized that brand loyalty was essential to market share, and attractively memorable packaging for its cans—made more memorable through melodious advertising—became an important part of cementing that loyalty with consumers and shoppers. For liquor, that memorable association between attractive packaging and the beverage it contained would be made through print advertising. Placement in particular glossy magazines would soon target specific markets, through the creation of liquor and lifestyle links.

Constitutional questions about the regulation of various kinds of promotional alcohol advertising were still decades away. But a last gasp of truly antialcohol feeling, united with a wish for sweeping constitutional action, did occur late in the Hughes era. It took the form of House Joint Resolution 661 to Propose a Constitutional Amendment to Prohibit Drunkenness. Introduced by Representative Smith of Oklahoma on April 21, 1938, its text was included in the recent National Archives exhibit "Amending America" (an exhibit dedicated to "highlight[ing] the remarkably American story of how we have amended, or attempted to amend, the Constitution"). The exhibit catalogue offered this commentary on the unsuccessful proposal:

"Instead of prohibiting alcohol sales, this amendment proposed to regulate personal behavior by prohibiting drunkenness. The absurdity of this was pointed out in a handwritten note at the bottom [of the document], which proposed adding on an equally far-fetched effort to abolish Saturday nights," and this additional deadpan addendum, "Congress and the several states shall have concurrent power to change human nature from time to time in its or their discretion."

CONCLUSION

The failed experiment of Prohibition succeeded in one thing: it normalized greater governmental regulation of alcohol than had ever existed before, and the Hughes Court docket was jam-packed with cases that showcase the justices' cooperation with those post-Repeal efforts. The restrictions on alcohol's public presence before and after the Twenty-First Amendment ushered in a new institution, one that would flower into an American cultural tradition: the at-home cocktail hour.

9

THE STONE ERA

Rumbustion

The *Stone Court* (1941–1946) is so brief a time period that assigning it a distinctive, specific alcoholic beverage may be difficult, or difficult to defend.[1] Harlan Fiske Stone, a law professor and long-serving associate justice (since 1925), first appointed to the court by his college classmate Calvin Coolidge and elevated by FDR, is remembered by most judicial scholars as a divisive chief and a poor court leader. He inherited a fractious group of justices with big personalities, many of whom had been his peers as associates and who either relentlessly compared him unfavorably with his predecessor Charles Evans Hughes, or had coveted the chief justiceship for themselves. The retiring chief Hughes was reportedly one of those who urged Roosevelt to nominate the Republican-appointed Stone in his place, arguing that the bipartisan gesture would bolster national unity and patriotic feeling during wartime. Stone's was indeed the "World War II patriotism" court, issuing the notorious Japanese internment and Jehovah's Witness compulsory flag salute decisions.[2] World War II not only influenced much of the Supreme Court's docket for the time period, it defined and shaped much of American drinking culture as well.

The Pacific theater of war was a prominent part of the American World War II experience. For many American soldiers, service in the South Pacific or Southeast Asia was their first encounter with the "exotic," with a part of the world with which most Americans were quite unfamiliar. Shipping out from California or Hawaii, these servicemen created and carried home "stories and snapshots of exotic Pacific lands and people they met in transit and on leave."[3] One element with which those stories and that experience combined was *rum*. Following Prohibition, rum was the least expensive of the legal spirits—one factor in its becoming central to the cocktails that would define the earliest iteration of the aesthetic phenomenon of "tiki." A fantasy sensibility that was the invention of a Southern California travel vagabond who christened himself "Don the Beachcomber," tiki was a tropical-themed decorated space—paradise brought to you—with rum-based fruit cocktails as its focal point. The first tiki bar was Donn Beach's Hollywood outpost, opened in late 1933 and named after his own invented persona (which was said to be based on a pseudonym he had once used while he was bootlegging).[4] Trader Vic's, the Oakland, California, tiki lounge born in 1937, would build upon its competing creation of an imaginary Polynesian experience, with a more defined set of fancifully named tiki drinks. What was common to both enterprises, beyond an indeterminate sultry locale, was the inspiration found in the rum drinks of the Caribbean tropics: the Hurricane of New Orleans, the rum punches of Trinidad and Jamaica, and the daiquiris of La Floridita in Havana.[5] Although tiki culture would only truly explode after the war,[6] and with the development of the tourist industry in Waikiki Beach (to where Donn Beach himself relocated) and the jungle mania it inspired, fruity potions were already familiar to an American public that had journeyed to far parts in search of a cocktail between 1920 and 1933.

Does the early history and temporal location of tiki justify the Mai Tai,[7] or similar tropical rum cocktail, as totemic for this judicial era? *And a Bottle of Rum* reports its date of origin as 1944, at Trader Vic's Oakland;[8] this story is confirmed by tiki history *Smuggler's Cove*.[9] Well documented about Stone was that he was "an avid traveler who had a great appreciation for Asian art."[10] It almost mocks his sincere and intellectual interest in things Asian to assign his era a tiki drink like the Mai Tai—a fake mash-up of the "oriental," using Jamaican rum, Dutch curaçao, and French orgeat.

A further complication is that Stone was known—and had been known, since his days at Columbia Law—as a wine connoisseur and collector. Indeed, he was "such a wine aficionado that he banned smoking at his dinners and *refused to serve cocktails* so as not to dull taste buds"[11] (emphasis added). Perhaps, but among the paper ephemera found among the many folders of the Harlan F. Stone Papers is a typescript list of cocktail recipes for a Clover Club, an Angostura bitters-laced dry martini from the bartender at the Union Club in New York, and something called a "Mme. Laboulaye's Cocktail" made with rum, pineapple and lemon juices, and egg white.[12] Appearing on the letterhead of one George B. McClellan of California Street in Washington, DC, the undated recipe list reads as a "who's who" of fashionable and tasty concoctions of the pre-Prohibition period—that Stone kept it (along with other drink lists and manuals) does not suggest a person who *hated* cocktails.

What is clear about the Stone period is that the decimation of the California wine industry during Prohibition, combined with the importation and production privations of the war period, induced the consumption of highballs or tall drinks to stretch what liquor was available. As cocktail historians David Wondrich and Jeff "Beachbum" Berry remarked in their 2015 Tales of the Cocktail seminar on wartime drinking: "World War II . . . changed how people drank on the home front. Many of those changes linger until today. American whiskey distilleries were needed by the military. Alcohol was used for torpedo fuel and other industrial purposes."[13] Wondrich showed a wartime menu from the tiki bar Trader Vic's that, above the list of liquors, noted: "The following are sold when available, which isn't very often these days." Unlike an earlier world war period, the 1940s were decidedly not a time of self-denial,[14] but they could be a time for economizing, as Wondrich and Berry elaborated:

> Everybody drank during World War II. The drinks at Trader Vic's that were "always on sale" included "imitation whiskey and imitation rum." When whiskey could be found, it was often watered down. That is when people started adding a big splash of club soda to Old Fashioned's, which some bartenders still do today. Rum was still distilled in the Caribbean, and Americans started drinking more of it.[15]

In general, Caribbean rum—and shaken drinks that used it—became popular during World War II when other spirits were in short supply.[16] Rum was thus as thoroughly Americanized and as central to American drinking culture in the war era as it had been in the time of colonial

America. Peck adds this boogie-woogie footnote to the general state of affairs in his *Prohibition Hangover*: "To make up for the shortage of whiskey, the country imported rum from the Caribbean. Rum and Coke became a popular drink during the war, not least because of the Andrews Sisters' smash hit song 'Rum and Coca-Cola.'"[17] *And a Bottle of Rum* confirms the importance of rum in the World War II period and confirms that rum and Coca-Cola had attained iconic status by 1946, having become the de facto national drink of the troops during the war.[18] The same source continues, "[N]o spirit benefited from the long national drought as much as rum. With ample supplies in the islands and a newly developed taste for the stuff among everyday Americans," rum enjoyed a post-Prohibition, Depression, and war-era heyday.[19] Rum sidecars, rum sours, rum Collins—classic cocktails could all use rum as the spirit base. Two drink fads of the 1940s, the daiquiri (Cuba's offspring, Ernest Hemingway's favorite) and the rum swizzle (Bermuda's contribution; one of the older recipes was presented in the 1941 *Old Mr. Boston De Luxe Official Bartender Guide*) proved that rum went down easy and mixed well with everything. Pungent tropical juices made lesser booze slide down easier, no doubt. The 1941 *Here's How to Mix Drinks* offered a particularly lethal but liberally fruited recipe for the famous Zombie (five kinds of rum, apricot brandy, brown sugar, lime juice, pineapple juice), allegedly re-creating the original 1934 recipe from Don the Beachcomber.[20] Likely it was an imaginative imitation, as Donn Beach was notorious for concealing even the labels of his "secret ingredient" syrups and flavorings for his proprietary tiki drinks from his bartending staff so that recipes could not be leaked to competitors. (It was all very OSS spycraft, very period appropriate.)

That the encoded Zombie rum punch migrated into a celebrity category all its own is indicated by its presence, among a toney list of vintage champagne and select cocktails, on a special menu from a 1944 dinner at the equally toney Bohemian Club of San Francisco—a menu saved by Stone and included among his judicial papers held at the Library of Congress. Tongue-in-cheek drink names abound on the hand-lettered and illustrated menu card—including dry, "drei," and "try" martinis, with the Zombie listed last as *"mise en biere"*: meaning the action of putting the corpse in a coffin and burying it.[21] (Lethality being the Zombie's stock in trade; see the 1941 recipe listed above.) Interestingly, the wine-loving Stone also saved a commercial brochure for "Felton's

Old Rum," marking an X next to the distiller's recipe for Fish House Punch—a powerful preparation in its own right made with cognac, peach brandy, and Felton's Pilgrim Rum.[22]

But Bacardi remained the rum to beat—so much so that U.S. drinkers often used "Bacardi" interchangeably with "rum."[23] Its brand significance recalls the 1940 *Bacardi* decision that bridged the Hughes and Stone eras. The 1946 *Stork Club Bar Book* even referred to a Bacardi Cocktail, essentially a daiquiri made with a splash of grenadine instead of sugar.[24] The Bacardi Cocktail served en coupe was as refined as the rum and cola highball was not, as the Rum and Coke was as plebeian as the swanky Stork Club wasn't—for the latter was as swanky as a public place pretending to be a private club (or was it vice versa?) could muster.[25]

The New York City supper club, located in midtown Manhattan just off 5th Avenue, was a favorite destination for movie stars, government officials, and business moguls from 1929 to 1965. Celebrated more for its scene than its cuisine, the Stork Club did host wine tastings of the like that Chief Justice Stone might have appreciated.[26] As a great oenophile, Stone seems more deserving of stemware service than a humble highball, and at first blush appears suited for an evening at the Stork. It was a place of fashionable cocktails[27] for fashionable people: the Stork Club hosted celebrities, executives, and government officials, including Roosevelts, Kennedys, New York governor Thomas Dewey, presidential daughter Margaret Truman, FBI director J. Edgar Hoover, and future president Dwight D. Eisenhower—it was the café to see and be seen (in). Supreme Court Justices William O. Douglas and Tom Clark (the latter of the Vinson Court, the Stone Court's successor) each left documented thank you notes, written to Stork owner Sherman Billingsley on Supreme Court stationery.[28] During the war, servicemen and officers patronized it, when going out on the town was an almost patriotic act of defiance in defense of the free world. The Stork Club's famous owner "Sherm" was himself a great supporter of the USO, and his important link with national politics was solidified by his invitation to the Truman Inaugural Ball in 1949.

The Stork Club and its café culture clearly straddled the Stone era and its successor era of Chief Justice Fred Vinson (1946–1953), as the supper club's patronage by that Vinson-era and Truman-appointee justice Tom Clark attests.[29] Of Stone's Stork Club connection, there is no direct evidence, so we can say only this: Stone practiced corporate law in New York City, after attending Columbia University where he also later served as dean of law. He lived in Manhattan near the campus, at the apartment building the Colosseum. But he left the bright lights of the big city for government work in the nation's capital, beginning in 1924 with his service as President Calvin Coolidge's attorney general. His time as a New Yorker clearly did not coincide with the Stork's (legal) heyday. Moreover, his professional pedigree made it more likely he would find himself a guest at the truly exclusive, private Union Club of the City of New York—whose in-house "R.M.B. Cocktail" recipe he had retained with his other personal papers. Club cocktails and cocktailing, of course, continued unabated throughout Prohibition, as previous chapters have discussed.

Stone was said to have lamented the unkind destiny that had "inflicted public office and prohibition on me at the same time," and tried to move the contents of his New York cellar of fine wines to the District of Columbia when he was appointed attorney general.[30] In that office, he had enforced prohibition laws vigorously, even though he considered them bad laws and an undue infringement on individual freedom. Stone thought the prohibitionists of his day were "do-gooders" and referred to the Women's Christian Temperance Union as the "We see to you'ers." Yet he did not really care for hard liquor and rarely took any, according to remarks his son made for the 1978 *Yearbook of the Supreme Court Historical Society*; Stone instead enjoyed and saw no harm in table wines, sherry, and the like.[31] "First, last, and always a professor" in the words of Stone's judicial colleague William Douglas, his tastes clearly ran to the more connoisseur than his era's rather pedestrian Rum and Coke, and reports as to Stone himself suggest a gourmand but not an overindulger. In Washington, the fashionably elegant Raleigh Hotel seemed to be a Stone wining-and-dining favorite, after 1933, and he was also a member of the city's Literary Society where arts mixed with epicurean indulgence. His judicial office, particularly as chief justice of the United States, gained him entrée into the private Bohemian Club, a San Francisco–based men's club founded "to promote a fraternal connection among men who enjoyed the arts." Stone attended many wine dinners put on at the club's Owl Room—so regularly that his hosts inscribed the backs of a series of dinner menus as members of "the Stone Society of the Sons of the Vine."[32] Whether he was an honorary member or just a frequent celebrant at the Bohemians' "Wine and Food Society" gatherings, "Mr. Justice Stone" was clearly celebrated for his wine knowledge and appreciation.

Figure 9.1. 1941 Bohemian Club menu, for a wine "breakfast" attended by Harlan F. Stone and in honor of a fellow judge. *Source: Harlan F. Stone Papers, Boxes 85/ 87; Library of Congress*

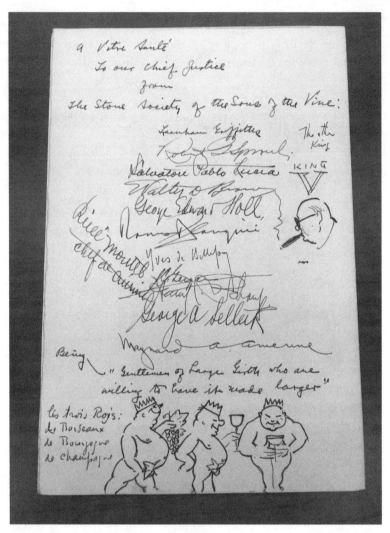

Figure 9.2. The backside of a similar 1942 Bohemian Club wine dinner menu, inscribed for the Chief Justice by its attendees as the "Stone Society of the Sons of the Vine." *Source: Harlan F. Stone Papers, Boxes 85/87; Library of Congress*

Many sources comment on this predilection of Stone's—including Alpheus Thomas Mason's seminal biography *Pillar of the Law*, which identifies him as "an avid and educated collector of fine wines."[33] Stone also liked to bring into work a collection of cheeses from home—one assumes, to accompany some of those wines. *Courtwatchers*, recounting a story from the notes of Justice Frank Murphy, has Justice Felix

Frankfurter good-naturedly taunting Chief Justice Stone during a lengthy conference discussion:

F: I suppose you know more than those who drafted the Constitution.

S: I know some things better than those who drafted the Constitution.

F: Yes, on wine and cheese. [*laughter*][34]

Not all of Frankfurter's taunting of his chief was so lighthearted.

Stone and his wife hosted a lavish dinner party for his clerks every five years, so reports former clerk Bennett Boskey.[35] It is easy to imagine those dinners, supplemented with fine vintages from the chief's personal cellar. It is also possible to imagine them concluding with the Stinger, a simple but elegant marriage of cognac and (white) crème de menthe. First mentioned in a cocktail book published 1917, the Stinger gained a 1940s following as an after-dinner drink; it appears in Beebe's *Stork Club Bar Book* under the category "Night at the Stork Club." Its French brandy base seems refined enough for the grape lover Stone and could be a totemic rival to the personally (sort of) referent, Asian-by-way-of-tiki-themed cocktail the Mai Tai, or the period dominant but otherwise personally unsuitable rum and Coca-Cola, or the delightfully dangerous and widely imitated potion the Zombie. Any—or none—of these elixirs are qualified to serve as emblem of the trends of the Stone years. Yet in the end, nothing is certain about the Stone era other than the prevailing presence of **rum**—except, of course, on the palate of its chief justice—just as nothing was certain about the Stone bench: not its conferences over cases, which were often overlong and inconclusive, nor its case outcomes, which were frequently divisive and occasionally nasty.

What conviviality existed on Stone's Court—and there surely was some—was largely a function of the social energies of Associate Justice James Byrnes, who regularly had the justices over to his house for dinner "and then led them in postprandial songs."[36] Contrast this bumptious but gentlemanly fellowship with the more prosaic reality that "beer consumption in the U.S. increased by 50% between 1940 and 1945, probably as a result of the reduced supply of liquor" being pro-

duced during World War II.[37] On the other hand, the religiously animated, antiaddiction group Alcoholics Anonymous was founded in
1935, "but really took off in the early 1940's."[38] The short Stone era was
thus a study in contrast, and of conflicting tendencies—about alcoholic
beverages and drinking, and within judicial decision making.

Some of those contrasts and conflicts played themselves out in the
justices' wrangling over alcohol and the Constitution. In terms of alcohol-related decisions from the Stone bench, the criminal procedure
case of *McNabb v. U.S.* in 1943 was a substantively important one,
particularly in the development of a constitutional jurisprudence of civil
rights and liberties. The defendants' long detention and dubious interrogation conditions had occurred after five members of the McNabb
family in rural Tennessee had been arrested for killing a federal alcohol
tax agent. With Justice Felix Frankfurter writing, the Stone Court held
that the confessions obtained were invalid, as lacking fundamental fairness under due process of law. Alabama-born Justice Hugo Black would
have gone further, arguing separately that the Fifth Amendment rights
of the "hillbilly mountaineers" had been violated.[39] Liquor was more
context than subject in *McNabb*, but the case showed the existence of
an alcohol subculture, whose members' behavior and treatment by law
enforcement suggested that bootleggery remained a target of governmental persecution.

Alleged persecution came in a more sensational Fifth Amendment
claim, in the 1943 appeal by famed bootleg operator and New Jersey
political boss Enoch "Nucky" Johnson of his federal income tax evasion
conviction. Johnson was challenging the state attorney's comments to
the jury in his trial, that his exercise of his Fifth Amendment right not to
testify and possibly incriminate himself, constituted an indication of his
guilt. At issue was his declining to speak about converting cash "dona-
tions" from a numbers syndicate for political protection favors, received
between 1935 and 1937, into funds for his own use without paying taxes
on them. As one source explained the dispute:

> When Johnson admitted on the stand that he had also received
> $1200 a week from gamblers in 1938, also in his view tax-free, he was
> accused of voluntarily admitting a new crime rather than being pro-
> tected by his earlier 5th Amendment claim. The question for the
> court was whether a defendant's assertion of his constitutional privi-

lege on one charge could fairly be used to test his credibility on another one.[40]

The Stone Court, with Justice Douglas writing, upheld his conviction on the grounds that he had waived his objection. The case is interesting in that it involved a colorful figure from the Prohibition era, and also because of the interjustice political wrangling that ensued over how to approach it—wrangling that was testimony to the interjustice acrimony that existed and inflamed normal judicial relations.[41]

Even in less high-profile alcohol-related cases, intracourt sparks could fly. *Duckworth v. Arkansas* in 1941 took an otherwise unremarkable, judicially deferential position as to what kind of alcohol transit-related regulations were reasonable under the Twenty-First Amendment. Yet the case nevertheless engendered a clash of judicial minds and pens. The Arkansas statute required a permit for the transportation of intoxicating liquor through the state, obtained for a nominal fee—the object of which was to identify those who engage in such transportation, and their routes and points of destination, thus enabling local officials to ensure transportation without diversion, in conformity with the permit. The Stone Court held that the regulation did not violate the commerce clause or trod on the federal power over interstate commerce. Still, the Stone opinion for the court was careful not to rule too expansively for state efforts to control liquor traffic. "The efforts at effective regulation, state and national, of intoxicating liquor," he observed, "evidenced by the long course of litigation in this Court, have not left us unaware of the peculiar difficulties of controlling it, or of its tendency to get out of legal bounds." The present requirement was a reasonably constructed local rule was all Stone would say on the matter.

That limited position was not sufficient for concurring Justice Jackson, who wryly commented, "I do not suppose the skies will fall if the Court does allow Arkansas to rig up this handy device for policing liquor on the ground that it is not forbidden by the commerce clause, but, in doing so, it adds another to the already too numerous and burdensome state restraints of national commerce and pursues a trend with which I would have no part." Good New Dealer he, Jackson argued that the Supreme Court should adjudicate this liquor controversy as "properly determined by guidance from the liquor clauses of the Constitution." He worried about jurisprudentially slippery slopes slicked by booze that

might lead to the court's justifying further, non-booze-related state intrusions into national commerce. "These clauses of the Twenty-first
Amendment," he complained,

> create an important distinction between state power over the liquor
> traffic and state power over commerce in general. The people of the
> United States knew that liquor is a lawlessness unto itself. They
> determined that it should be governed by a specific and particular
> constitutional provision. They did not leave it to the courts to devise
> special distortions of the general rules as to interstate commerce to
> curb liquor's "tendency to get out of legal bounds." It was their
> unsatisfactory experience with that method that resulted in giving
> liquor an exclusive place in constitutional law as a commodity whose
> transportation is governed by a special constitutional provision.

The majority, Jackson felt, cavalierly "brushe[d] aside the liquor provisions of the Twenty-first Amendment."

This would not happen, at least in the way Jackson feared, for in a
case not three years later, the Stone Court defined—*and narrowed*—
the parameters of state regulatory power under the Twenty-First
Amendment. The court noted that the mere "shipment [of liquor]
through a state is not transportation or importation into the state within
the meaning of the Amendment," so states could not go beyond the
limits of reasonable necessity in their regulatory efforts. Although the
specific regulation of liquor transit was sustained in *Carter v. Virginia*
(1944), the rhetoric of Justice Stanley Reed's opinion for the court was
in keeping with its—and Jackson's—national supremacist constitutional
vision in general.

The same general vision guided the majority decision in *Johnson v.
Yellow Cab Transit* (1944). This case asked the Stone Court to adjudicate between the jurisdictions of federal enclaves like military posts
within states and the states themselves, for the purposes of alcohol
possession. Officers at Fort Sill, Oklahoma, at that point a dry state, had
contracted with a supplier in Illinois to deliver through the bordering
state of Missouri a quantity of liquor and wine for the officers' mess.
That liquor was seized in transit by Oklahoma enforcement officers,
and the supplier sued to recover the liquors so that they could be duly
delivered. Applying the *Carter* principle, the Black majority found the
seizure invalid. But the opinion demurred on another matter, that being

that military reservations adopt the penal laws of their respective states, according to the federal Assimilative Crimes statute. Stipulating that the laws of Congress (including those on the legality of alcohol) control federal enclaves in states, Black posited this:

> Should we decide the [federal] statute outlaws the shipment, such a decision would be equivalent to a holding that more than 200 Army Officers, sworn to support the Constitution, had participated in a conspiracy to violate federal law. Not only that, it would, for practical purposes, be accepted as an authoritative determination that all army reservations in the State of Oklahoma must conduct their activities in accordance with numerous Oklahoma liquor regulations, some of which, at least, are of doubtful adaptability.

Justice Frankfurter, dissenting with Roberts, took a harder line on the matter. "Assuming that the military could assert [a liberal liquor] policy in the interest of Army morale," he hectored,

> there is wholly lacking any manifestation that the Army deems it necessary for the morale of its officers that at Fort Sill conduct should be permitted which, if committed in the surrounding territory of Oklahoma, would offend its penal laws. So far as the War Department has indicated a policy, its policy . . . is to adopt on military reservations the laws of their respective States.

The dissenters' argument fell on deaf ears, of course: federal interests—enhanced by military (recreational) needs—trumped state prohibition concerns.

Another judicial set-to occurred in *U.S. v. Frankfort Distilleries* in 1945, which concerned an effort by a group of out-of-state liquor producers and importers to combine to sustain artificially high in-state retail prices for their products; certain types of "Fair Trade" price maintenance contracts were lawful in the state of Colorado. But also of relevance was that, at the time, liquor was in short supply due to the diversion of distillery resources to the production of industrial alcohol serving the war effort. The companies' combination affecting Colorado sales in effect made a scarce commodity more dear. Justice Black's opinion for the court left no doubt where the Stone Court stood on the plenary national power to regulate the economy, including interstate liquor commerce: "The sole ultimate object of respondents' combination in the instant case was price fixing or price maintenance. And with reference to commercial trade restraints such as these, Congress, in passing the Sherman Anti-Trust Act, left no area of its constitutional power unoccupied; it 'exercised' all the power it possessed." Though Justice Frankfurter concurred, he had this to say about the commerce power and the states' authority under the Twenty-First Amendment:

> The Twenty-first Amendment made a fundamental change, as to control of the liquor traffic, in the constitutional relations between the States and national authority. Before that Amendment—disregarding the interlude of the Eighteenth Amendment—alcohol was for constitutional purposes treated in the abstract as an article of commerce just like peanuts and potatoes. As a result, the power of the States to control the liquor traffic was subordinated to the right of free trade across state lines as embodied in the Commerce Clause. The Twenty-first Amendment *reversed this legal situation by subordinating rights under the Commerce Clause to the power of a State to control, and to control effectively, the traffic in liquor* within its borders. The course of legal history . . . made necessary the Twenty-first Amendment in order to permit the States to control the liquor traffic, according to their notions of policy *freed from the restrictions upon state power which the Commerce Clause implies as to ordinary articles of commerce.* (emphasis added)

As he had intimated in *Johnson v. Yellow Cab,* Frankfurter was articulating for the liquor context an entirely different version of federalism than what the "Roosevelt Court" had been upholding since 1937. It was grounded in the power that the Twenty-First Amendment gave to states, over a commodity that was *not* simply one among many in the stream of commerce. Alcohol was different, and alcohol was also at the center of a major philosophical dispute within the Stone Court, over the theory and practice of federalism—a dispute that would carry over into the next judicial era. And while cases such as *Levers v. Anderson* (1945)—dealing with the question of what kind of review procedure was statutorily required for annulment of a permit to operate a wholesale liquor business under the Federal Alcohol Administration Act—might suggest that little in the way of major constitutional law with regard to alcohol came the Stone Court's way, the reality of *Carter* and *Frankfort Distillers* is rather different.

One of the Stone Court's last alcohol-related rulings was also one of the most salient for the post-Prohibition constitutional policy on alcohol. The decision in *New York v. U.S.* in 1946 rejected a state's claim for tax immunity for its business of bottling state mineral water, so the case's alcohol relatedness was tangential. But as Justice Frankfurter analogized the situation in his judgment for the court: "When States sought to control the liquor traffic by going into the liquor business, they were denied immunity from federal taxes upon the liquor business. We certainly see no reason for putting soft drinks in a different constitutional category from hard drinks."

Frankfurter further relied on two liquor-centric precedents for his decision in the New York case: the 1905 *State of South Carolina v. United States*, in which the 6–3 Fuller Court held that license taxes charged by the federal government on persons selling liquor were not invalidated by the fact that those sellers were the agents of the state, which had itself engaged in the liquor business by establishing dispensaries for the wholesale and retail sale of spirituous liquor, and then prohibited sale by other than the dispensers; and the 1934 *State of Ohio v. Helvering*, where the Hughes Court held that the state itself, when it becomes a dealer in intoxicating liquors, by creation of a state monopoly, falls within the reach of the federal internal revenue tax either as a "person" under the statutory extension of that word to include a corporation, or as a "person" without regard to such extension.

There were several votes concurring in the result in *New York v. U.S.*, including one voiced in a concurrence by the chief justice, and a dissenting opinion from Justices Douglas and Black. The dissenters took direct aim at the *South Carolina* precedent, arguing the more general point that it did not state

> the correct rule. A State's project is as much a legitimate governmental activity whether it is traditional, or akin to private enterprise, or conducted for profit. . . . [A]s Mr. Justice White said in his dissent in *State of South Carolina v. United States*, any activity in which a State engages within the limits of its police power is a legitimate governmental activity.[42]

Including vending liquor, or running a bottled water emporium. But it was the final sentence of then-Associate Justice White's *South Carolina* dissent, which the Stone Court dissenters did not quote, that revealed just why those earlier dissenting justices had similarly objected to a federal tax on a state instrument: "the state of South Carolina had complete and absolute power over the liquor traffic and could exert, in dealing with that subject, such methods and instrumentalities as were deemed best," White lamented, "and the United States was without authority to tax the agencies which the state called into being for the purpose of dealing with the liquor traffic." The federal tax threatened to undermine that sovereign state effort with respect to *liquor*. It was alcohol, and the utterly legitimate state project of regulating alcohol, that made all the difference to the *South Carolina* dissenters.

Oddly, Frankfurter, who had defended state efforts to control liquor in *Johnson v. Yellow Cab* and *Frankfort Distillers*, was not receptive to a related claim applied to the *New York* case. Perhaps it was the importance of the federal tax power in the latter case, perhaps it was the explicit presence of a bolstering Twenty-First Amendment claim in the former cases. Still, he and Wiley Rutledge—the only justice to join his plurality opinion—had no answer for the *New York* dissenters' question: Must the state pay the federal government for the privilege of exercising its inherent sovereign power? And—more to the point, for our purposes—pay for its inherent sovereign power over "demon rum"?

The Stone Court's uneasy navigation of the federalism thicket that sprung up post-Repeal was on full display in 1946. The Stone justices' corrosive disagreements went well beyond alcohol and the law, affecting and infecting their disposition of the range of issues that came before them. The high rate of legal dissensus on the disputatious Stone Court recommends a totemic (and a therapeutic!) beverage where the ingredients do not combine, and intermingle into a new composite, but remain distinctive and distinguishable . . . and even at odds or in opposition to one another.

No *good* cocktail fits this description. Moreover, more than any other era, the Stone era is one of marked divergence between the tastes of its chief and the tendencies of the time. A disconnect in beverages, and so in the law: the chief justice who so infrequently led the pronouncements of the court that bears his name was utterly at odds with his era's patterns and preferences when it came to drink.

CONCLUSION

The tension between the national supremacist vision of the federal commerce power and the recognition of the states' special power over alcohol under the Twenty-First Amendment was never really resolved in the Stone era. It is also an era for which a defining cocktail is difficult to pinpoint (beyond rum being the defining spirit), due to the many conflicting personal, cultural, and politicoeconomic tendencies of the time period. For the Stone era, this tension and this conflict would seem to go hand in glove.

10

THE OLD-FASHIONED VINSON ERA

The *Vinson Court* (1946–1953) was almost as brief an era as its predecessor's, and equally as discordant a court. But unlike the Stone era, the choice of its totemic cocktail is an easy one: the **Bourbon Old-Fashioned**. This was Harry (and Bess) Truman's drink; Fred Vinson was Harry Truman's man, a political and poker buddy, a loyal supporter of the New Deal, the Fair Deal, and presidential power under his appointing president.[1] Vinson was also a Kentuckian.

Possibly at no time since the Waite justices had plied one another with good whiskey was bourbon such a big part of court life as it apparently was under Vinson. Fellow Kentuckian and Associate Justice Stanley Reed was certainly known to patronize his state's official liquor. A Stanley Reed clerk from the 1953 term reports being entertained at the justice and his wife's apartment at the Mayflower Hotel, for cocktails and dinner that included "an offering of Kentucky bourbon and water."[2] Additionally, Vinson Court member Hugo Black, who began his public life in Alabama not only as a member of the KKK but as "personally and politically dry,"[3] was not adverse to a bourbon to help with sleepless nights pondering difficult cases, according to the memoir of his wife, Elizabeth, as recounted in *Courtwatchers*. "Why don't you take a little bourbon," she would suggest, "and so he pours a splash of bourbon on ice, fills the glass with water, and soon is sound asleep."[4] Not all drinking by Vinson era justices was so therapeutic. Fellow Truman-appointee on Vinson's Court, Harold Burton, was an inveterate Washington partygoer whose "meager" opinion output was blamed on his enjoyment of "a continued round of parties."[5] Finally, bourbon would also be there to help smooth the troubled waters that roiled the Vinson bench. After the particularly contentious case involving the court's 1952 repudiation of President Truman's seizure of steel mills to avert a strike interrupting production during the Korean War, Justice Black invited the president and the justices to his home as a peace gesture. As Justice William Douglas reported, "at the start, Truman was polite but seemed 'a bit testy,' but after the bourbon and canapés were passed, he turned to Hugo and said, 'Hugo, I don't much care for your law, but, by golly, this bourbon is good.'"[6]

Harry Truman had appointed Vinson because he was "one of the boys": well liked, easy to get along with, sociable, and friendly—Vinson had been part of the golf and poker-and-whiskey games of his congressional colleagues, which had included Truman, then a senator. Well versed in the ways of informal, personalistic politics, Vinson had also had long and successful experience directing a large federal bureaucracy, "perhaps leading him to think that he could boss the Supreme Court in the same firm and gentle way."[7] The president clearly hoped his appointee as chief could transfer his personable, political qualities to the judicial setting and unite and lead the disputatious Supreme Court of his time. But although the sitting justices "personally liked Vinson," they were no more amenable to following his direction than they had been to following Chief Justice Stone, "whom they respected far more."[8] Vinson's lack of distinction as a jurist and his relative laxity in assigning himself opinions to write earned his judicial colleagues' professional disdain, and Vinson was in fact much more comfortable chumming around with Truman and his friends in Congress than with the brethren.[9] They, likewise, never saw him "as one of their own."[10] Interestingly enough, Vinson also did not socialize with his law clerks—their relations were "uniformly proper" and "lacked any personal component."[11] His discomfort with the environment of the court seems to have carried over into his relations with the young JDs working for him. One can conclude that it is unlikely he poured anything for any of them, at any time, just as he did little in the way of kicking back recreationally with his fellow justices. Yet specific confirmation is hard to come by. "There has been relatively little written about Vinson," says Brandeis biographer Melvin Urofsky, almost as if his career did not warrant a biography.

Yet insight into Fred Vinson the man provides valuable insights into midcentury American mores. Vinson's was the easy camaraderie of the old-boys-club Congress of his day. His métier would have been the Cub Room at the Stork Club: that manly, dark-paneled inner sanctum for VIPs and high-level operators.[12] The Stork Club, and its public café culture, clearly segued into the Vinson era from the preceding era of Chief Justice Stone, and we have documentary evidence of its patronage by Vinson-era and Truman-appointee Justice Tom Clark. Both Vinson and Clark would have been acculturated into the (largely male) cocktail rituals of the time period: those quintessential power lunches and dinners that defined the intersecting worlds of government, business and finance, and the entertainment industry.

One thinks of the Bourbon Old-Fashioned on the rocks as the iconic drink of the Man in the Gray Flannel Suit, the cultural standard-bearer of 1950s corporate America—even though the fictional character actually drank mostly martinis and Manhattans, and highballs as the night wore on at the suburban cocktail parties that surrounded him and his ilk. The novel of the same title, published in 1955, confirms the practice in this passage:

> On Greentree Avenue, cocktail parties started at seven-thirty, when the men came home from New York, and they usually continued without any dinner until three or four o'clock in the morning. Somewhere around nine-thirty in the evening, Martinis and Manhattans would give way to highballs, but the formality of eating anything but hors d'oeuvres in-between had been entirely omitted.

Retro cultural artifacts are equally specific as to iconic beverages of the Vinson era. One of the first-season episodes of the hit cable-television series *Mad Men*, set early in the midcentury decade it would profile, depicts the main character, Don Draper, seated in a dimly lit cocktail lounge, drinking the Old-Fashioned whiskey cocktail in its telltale "lowball" glass. We the viewer assume the time period to be the mid-1950s—likely a year or two after the close of the Vinson era but still very much part of its sensibility.

Called the cocktail of "suburban sociability,"[13] the Old-Fashioned is identifiable by the distinctive class of "rocks" barware glasses that bear its name. In this, it is like its younger sibling the martini. Unlike the martini, however, the *Old*-Fashioned harkens back to the origins of the whiskey cocktail, at the dawn of the age of cocktails. Thus its name, which quite explicitly evokes its inherent and overt conservatism: it is a drink that predates the other, "fancy" cocktails that followed in its wake. It is associated with going back to a simpler, better time—a time of unfussy classics and clear rules of order in cocktail preparation. This is ironic, of course, because in the post–World War II, post–Repeal of Prohibition years of the 1940s and early 1950s, the Old-Fashioned was gussied up with elaborate fruit garnishes, sweetened, and even splashed with seltzer. As Ted Saucier's 1951 *Bottoms Up* gushed, "Today, all types of old fashioneds [*sic*] are popular."[14] David A. Embry's *The Fine Art of Mixing Drinks* is more forthright as to the deleterious effects of the Prohibition era on mixology, noting that the need for various sweet emollients to make drinkable the "vile" bootleg liquor of the day led to all manner of "pernicious recipes" and "ridiculous formulas"—including tinkering with the classic, "truly magnificent" Old-Fashioned cocktail.[15] Embry's utterly delightful cocktail manual, first published in 1948 and in subsequent editions throughout the 1950s, notes sourly that "most of the present generation learned to drink and most of the present-day bartenders learned their profession" during a period that encompassed Prohibition, "and the remaining years have not yet been sufficient to erase wholly the ignoble effects of that era."[16]

Variation in recipe notwithstanding, the classic drink's "old-fash-ioned-ness" evokes the postwar project of suburbanization in America, which while bringing about a radical reformatting of American life, was ostensibly a return to a society based on and organized around the traditional nuclear family. Conscious public policy choices were aimed at restoring the U.S. economy to peacetime stability and U.S. society to its prewar "normalcy": the use of the GI Bill for (largely male) college education and the Federal Housing Administration for (largely white) single-family housing loans, the federal-aid highway program (and, lat-er, the Federal Aid Highway Act of 1956 that enabled the creation of the interstate highway system) that buoyed the American automobile and construction trades industries, and the structuring of the industrial and corporate labor markets around male single-income earners and unpaid female wives and homemakers.

If normalcy included a return to traditional gender roles, then that meant the end of the use of women as workers in the traditionally male-dominated industrial trades that had been decimated by the wartime draft. Women's economic emancipation was at least a generation away; their postwar economic role was as domestic consumers of products. (Or as domestic servants, depending on their race and social class.) The domestic realm was also where women served drinks, as home hostesses in high heels pushing bar carts. Hence, "old-fashioned" also clearly describes one of the Vinson Court's most (in)famous decisions, liquor-related or otherwise: the sex discrimination case of *Goesaert v. Cleary* in 1948, which upheld a Michigan law banning a woman from obtaining a state bartender's license unless she was the wife or daughter of the male owner of a licensed liquor establishment.

The state law in the case can be understood in terms of the female-protectionist and antisaloon legislation of the late nineteenth century, which distinguished between family and non-family-oriented alcohol establishments: beer gardens and bowling alleys versus bars and pool halls. Family activity spaces lacked the worrisome connotations of (masculine) saloons and so were not subject to the same regulatory strictures as to women's presence.[17] But the decision in the case is best understood through another reading, that of postwar America's return to traditional family values. Women had filled the ranks of factory workers, truckers, and laborers during World War II, and had also picked up the towel to serve as barkeeps when men vacated these jobs to join the war effort. But with wartime's end, male privilege and union pressure "which preyed on people's concerns for the family unit and female virtue" drove states concerned with employment issues to pass new laws prohibiting women bartenders in the period following the war's temporary socioeconomic changes. Michigan's 1945 statute was one such effort. "Who wants the hand the rocks the cradle mixing whisky sours?" one local editorial opined.[18]

Frankfurter's opinion for the court unwittingly(?) echoed this sentiment, saying that "the Constitution does not require legislatures to reflect sociological insight, or shifting social standards." Ah, but in *Goesaert v. Cleary*, that is exactly what the Vinson Court's decision *did* require of the Constitution: that it confirm the postwar social thinking about gender roles. "The oversight assured through ownership of a bar by a barmaid's husband or father," Justice Frankfurter nattered in his majority opinion, "minimizes [moral and social] hazards that may confront a barmaid without such protecting oversight. This Court is certainly not in a position to gainsay such belief by the Michigan legislature."[19] Three dissenters saw the law as nothing more than discrimination against women owners of liquor establishments, who could neither bartend themselves nor employ their daughters—even if a man were present "to keep order."

Orderly dispensation of liquor was also a theme in several Vinson era cases involving illegal distilleries. *Bozza v. U.S.* (1947) upheld a conviction for operating an illegal still with this gem of a narrative from Justice Black's majority opinion:

> [I]t is argued, there was no evidence that the petitioner acted with knowledge that the distillery business was carried on with an intent to defraud the Government of its taxes. . . . Petitioner assisted in the manufacture of alcohol in Chirichillo's still which was operated under conditions of secretiveness in an apparently abandoned farmhouse. The finished alcohol was carried to Newark in a car which followed another car, sometimes the petitioner's.
>
> The members of the jury could properly draw on their own experience and observations that lawful stills, unlike the still in which petitioner worked, usually are not operated clandestinely and do not deliver their products in the fashion employed here. The members of the jury were not precluded from drawing inferences as to fraudulent purposes from these circumstances, nor were they compelled to believe that this petitioner was oblivious of the purposes of what went on around him. Men in the jury box, like men on the street, can conclude that a person who actively helps to operate a secret distillery knows that he is helping to violate Government revenue laws. That is a well-known object of an illicit distillery. Doubtless few who ever worked in such a place, or even heard about one, would fail to understand the cry: "The Revenuers are coming!"

While three dissenters did not find sufficient evidence of aiding and abetting to defraud the government of revenue, the case illustrated that supervising the control of bootlegged alcohol remained a task for the Vinson Court—more than a decade after the end of Prohibition.

This was likewise the task in *Trupiano v. United States*, decided in 1948. A search of an illegal distillery was made without a warrant, even though the agents who conducted the search had ample information and time within which to secure one. Since there was no reason but the convenience of the police that could justify the warrantless search, Justice Frank Murphy's opinion for the court found it unreasonable. By contrast, in *Brinegar v. U.S.* in 1949, Justice Wiley Rutledge's opinion for the court denied a Fourth Amendment challenge to a warrantless search of an automobile that had revealed illegal liquor. The *Brinegar* decision likened the situation to the Taft era ruling of *Carroll v. U.S.*, which Rutledge sketched painstakingly:

> From the facts of record, we know, as the [federal] agents knew, that Oklahoma was a 'dry' state. At the time of the search, its law forbade the importation of intoxicating liquors from other states except under a permit . . . which there is no pretense Brinegar had secured or attempted to secure. This fact, taken in connection with the known 'wet' status of Missouri and the location of Joplin close to the Oklahoma line, affords a very natural situation for persons inclined to violate the Oklahoma and federal statutes to ply their trade. The proof therefore concerning the source of supply, the place of probable destination and illegal market, and hence the probability that Brinegar was using the highway for the forbidden transportation, was certainly no less strong than the showing in these respects in the *Carroll* case.

The emotive *Brinegar* dissent from Justice Jackson, joined by Frankfurter and Murphy, opined thusly in response:

> [I]f we are to make judicial exceptions to the Fourth Amendment . . . it seems to me they should depend somewhat upon the gravity of the offense. If we assume, for example, that a child is kidnaped and the officers throw a roadblock about the neighborhood and search every outgoing car, it would be a drastic and undiscriminating use of the search. The officers might be unable to show probable cause for searching any particular car. However, I should candidly strive hard to sustain such an action, executed fairly and in good faith, because it might be reasonable to subject travelers to that indignity if it was the only way to save a threatened life and detect a vicious crime. *But I should not strain to sustain such a roadblock and universal search to salvage a few bottles of bourbon and catch a bootlegger.* (emphasis added)

One can almost hear the justice's grunt of disgust.

The Vinson Court case record on alcohol included few blockbusters, as it was by and large a time of standing pat. The Vinson justices presided over a series of statutory cases in the early 1950s about alcohol price fixing by liquor companies such as Seagram and Calvert, in the wake of the new state alcohol beverage control laws and with Sherman Act antitrust considerations. Another decision that likewise illustrates the context of the times was *Blumenthal v. U.S.* in 1947, which concerned a conviction for conspiring to sell whiskey—Old Mr. Boston Rocking Chair Whiskey was the brand in question—at prices above the ceiling set by regulations of the Office of Price Administration, in violation of the Emergency Price Control Act of 1942. The federal rule was set to prevent profiteering during wartime shortages of booze; the court supported it with little comment. The Vinson Court's final alcohol case was a per curiam decision in *U.S. v. Lane Motor Co.* decided in February 1953; Vinson would die in September. *Lane* cleared up the relatively minor matter of whether a vehicle used solely for commuting to an illegal distillery was being used in violating the revenue laws of the Internal Revenue Code and was thus forfeitable. The court concluded it was not.

The War on Alcohol summarizes the post-Repeal culture of alcohol use in this way: new state liquor authorities established the appropriate parameters of relegalized recreational liquor use with their own moralistic assumptions, reigning in the transgressive, experimental, and un-regulated world of Prohibition era nightlife.[20] In subsequent decades, the policing of leisure—including remaining segments of alcoholic leisure—would continue to be undertaken, deploying societal conventions of suitable behavior. The *Goesaert* case certainly fits this description. But the Vinson era case law—concerning bars, illegal backwoods still setups, and such "public" liquor dispensaries—belies one dominant trait of the times: drinking in the 1950s was increasingly done at home and integrated into new postwar patterns of middle-class recreational leisure. The cocktail parties of *The Man in the Gray Flannel Suit* may have been outsized libertine affairs, but they aptly characterized the era's principal site of liquor consumption. The fleeting urban age of the Stork Club café society—of the gleeful public ritual of cocktailing and entertaining freely and openly—was moving into the suburban living room and backyard.

Historians writing in the 1950s generally denigrated Prohibition as "not merely an aversion to drunkenness and to the evils that accompanied it, but to the immigrant drinking masses, to the pleasures and amenities of city life, and to the well-to-do classes and cultivated men."[21] Yet such smug conceit disguises the fact that the Vinson era was guilty of aversions of its own: to "daring" or unconventional political views and lifestyles, to social changes that threatened to upset existing racial and gender hierarchies. At times, the Vinson Court participated in these period aversions—acceding, for instance, to abuses of individual rights in the face of Cold War anticommunist hysteria, or enforcing laws that restricted "a woman's place." At other times, Vinson Court majorities inched toward progress—beginning, for example, the slow, incremental march to dismantling the legal system of racial segregation in the United States. Its mixed legacy reveals a court that was reluctant to lead public opinion and more comfortable deferring to it.

CONCLUSION

A conservative court and a conservative drink for a conservative time.

I I

THE WARREN ERA
Swanky Swilling

The *Warren Court* (1954–1969) spans the *Mad Men* midcentury period and the Swinging Sixties, a time of real change in American society and in alcohol consumption habits. Earl Warren's era begins in the time of the Little Black Cocktail Dress: as Genevieve Antoine Dariaux of *Elegance* would say, "the dress worn by a guest at a cocktail party should be scarcely décolleté at all, and should always be accompanied by a hat."[1] Stylish, proper, precise—as was the setting for the enjoyment of cocktails through the early 1960s. Warren's era closes with the onset of the Sixties countercultural revolution, which brought about among other things a serious hiatus in the smart formality of the cocktail hour— and all that it included, from dress to drinks. Formality ended too on the capital hospitality front on Warren's watch, for the 1960s saw the end of the annual ritual of the justices paying a collective call on the president, and of his giving of a state dinner (replete with wine pairings, presumably) in the court's honor.[2]

In terms of liquor, at this point in the history of alcohol in American life, the grain spirit vodka joins the American bar. Vodka had made limited inroads during Prohibition, joining its clear cousins white rum and tequila as exotic or "ethnic" spirits that could be substituted in traditional cocktail recipes such as sours and highballs, or doctored to resemble gin or whiskey. (One shudders to think.) Vodka is especially interesting, however, in that it was a marketing executive's invented "classic" cocktail that popularized the liquor with the general American public. That cocktail was the Moscow Mule, created at a Hollywood tavern in 1941 as a vodka version of the Scotch and ginger ale–based Mamie Taylor and served "'by tradition' (wholly fabricated) in a 5-oz. copper cup."[3] Heublein, a company that had become famous for its bottled Club Cocktails, had acquired the brand rights for an old Russian vodka that had been renamed Smirnoff (from the more redolently Slavic "Smirnov") by its expatriate White Russian owners before they sold it off. John Martin of Heublein concocted the Moscow Mule to sell the new spirit in his company's portfolio. What happened, of course, was that the drink, and vodka, was a hit. Soon, Smirnoff was promoting other "easy to guzzle" drinks like the Screwdriver (the return of the Orange Blossom), the Bloody Mary, and the Vodka Collins. As Embury's *The Fine Art of Mixing Drinks* adds, the "magnificent advertising and sales promotion tactics" were such that between 1950 and 1955, vodka bottled in the United States jumped from 387,000 gallons to almost 7 million. Of that latter amount, well over one-third was sold in Earl Warren's native state of California.[4]

Even more significantly for American vodka sales, the vodka martini enters the cocktail lexicon. The fictional character James Bond popularizes it; like the suave spy and international man of mystery, the vodka martini is cool, calm, and collected. (It was allegedly the favorite of snappy crime writer Dashiell Hammett as well.) By the late 1950s, lighter flavors in liquor were in, and the dry vodka martini—well chilled—fit this bill to perfection. Vodka would also

> go perfectly with the austere outlook of modernism. The drive was to get rid of the clutter of the past and welcome the clean lines of modern architecture. Vodka was as invisible as the glass walls now cladding the new skyscrapers, as light as the clean lines of the Scandinavian furniture now in homes. The brown spirits—bourbon, rye, and rum—were part of the old regime, the spirituous version of an overblown Victorian home. The future belonged to the transparent.[5]

The period of the late 1950s to early 1960s was also the height of Cold War tensions with Soviet Russia and vodka was a decidedly "Russky" product. Yet worsening relations did little to interrupt the vodka craze in the United States during that same time period. By the 1970s and after the end of the Warren era, vodka overtook whiskey as the nation's most popular distilled spirit.[6] Vodka's inauguration into the spirits pantheon would ultimately produce the popular fruity and sweet mixed drinks of the same time period, the nadir of American mixology. The 1970s also firmly ended the classy cocktail rituals so associated with American midcentury glamour. The once-swanky cocktail lounge would succeed to the throbbing discotheque and to even more casually banal "happy hour" watering holes. Informal drinking and rapidly and inexpertly slung together (vodka) drinks became the rule, and what was "in."

But before this sad state of affairs took hold, before the reign of the "Vodkatini" (a term that never caught on) yielded to that of frightening successors like the vanilla-forward Harvey Wallbanger and the adult milkshake White Russian, there was the vodka version of the classic gimlet. Originally a simple jigger of gin, smidge of simple syrup, and the juice of half a lime over cracked ice, the Gimlet took to vodka like members of the Warren Court took to vodka gimlets.

Some background is in order. California governor Earl Warren was appointed by moderate Republican president and decorated commanding general Dwight D. Eisenhower ("Ike"), who was not a noted drinker as chief executive, for his heart condition forced him to cut back his alcohol intake by the time he took office. Other presidents of Warren's time period made more substantive cocktail contributions. John F. Kennedy, whose brief but stylish "Camelot" presidency is a cultural landmark of this era, favored the still relatively obscure and glamorous upstart, the daiquiri. His Democratic Party's liberal progressivism on civil rights[7] was favored by the liberal activist Warren majority in decisions such as *Brown v. Board of Education* (1954), *Heart of Atlanta Motel v. U.S.* (1964), and *South Carolina v. Katzenbach* (1966). Lyndon Baines Johnson, whose appointments to the court had something to do with that liberal activism, was a (blended) Scotch drinker—reputedly, Cutty Sark and soda. This is confirmed by alcohol trade journalist Garrett Peck in *Prohibition Hangover*, who reports that Johnson even took it with him golfing; and confirmed once again in an anecdote from *Of Courtiers and Kings* regarding President Johnson's appearance at a black-tie dinner in honor of Chief Justice Warren where he "chug-a-lugged" a Scotch.[8] The Scotch highball was certainly the iconic drink of men of power and men in power, and long had been. A relative newcomer to the period, however, was the Scotch-based Rusty Nail, a

Drambuie cocktail allegedly patronized (enthusiastically) by the Rat Pack—Sinatra[9] and friends—providing another JFK connection. The Warren era would seem to present a difficult choice at the bar. WWWD? That is, what would the chief himself drink?

Former clerks provide some needed information. Earl Warren certainly entertained and liked to regale his companions over a long lunch (at the University Club, the restaurant in Union Station) or at his annual black-tie dinner for his entire office staff and their spouses.[10] Plenty of drinking went on. At a clerks' reunion held at the Metropolitan Club in 1961, for instance, JFK was a surprise guest, who further surprised by requesting a beer to drink, which the small private bar did not have on hand but hustled out to acquire.[11] A more valuable and less quirky account of the Warren Court imbibing again mentions Warren's Saturday lunches at the University Club (or the Federal City Club) and, even more significant, says "the chief justice liked to relax with a drink or two before lunch on Saturday (*vodka gimlets* on the rocks)"[12] (emphasis added). The law clerk–sourced Supreme Court exposé *The Brethren* corroborates the place (University Club), the occasion (Saturday lunch ritual), and the cocktail (the gimlet).[13] This confirmatory information certainly fits the period, the ascendance of vodka, and the specific popularity of the **Vodka Gimlet** cocktail. It is the appropriate totem for the Warren era, no question. Indeed, Raymond Chandler's iconic fictional creation, detective Philip Marlowe, had himself switched from whiskey to gimlets by 1953, with the publication of Chandler's penultimate crime novel *The Long Goodbye*.

The vodka gimlet was also William Douglas's drink during the 1950s and 1960s. Warren's tenure as chief witnesses the beginning of the long and embarrassing decline and legendary (mostly vodka-fueled) boozing of Associate Justice William O. Douglas. Douglas, one of FDR's first appointees, served on the Supreme Court a long time; by most accounts, he was too smart for the job, became quickly bored, and preferred the pursuit of other extracurricular interests. Nature and environmentalism was one, drinking and womanizing was another. Douglas's marital problems and alleged moral turpitude were the subject of both gossip and threatened congressional resolutions for investigation into his character throughout the 1960s. Behind-the-scenes tell-all *The Brethren* gives little suggestion that Douglas was a heavy drinker—for by the time of its writing in 1975, he wasn't. Bruce Allen Murphy's 2003 biography *Wild Bill* confirms as much with a story of Douglas breaking out the Scotch bottles with his clerks to celebrate the Supreme Court's 1974 decision against President Richard Nixon's claim for "executive privilege." The justice "poured a Dubonnet for himself," Murphy reports, with Douglas "saying that *by now* any other kind of liquor made him sneeze"[14] (emphasis added). Murphy provides many, more scurrilous details about Douglas,[15] but only one should concern us here: by 1953 and after the divorce from his first wife, "Douglas, who was always a heavy drinker . . . now began drinking to even greater excess. Now allergic to the gin he once preferred, Douglas consumed massive quantities of *vodka gimlets* (always with an onion instead of an olive). . . . [I]t was not uncommon for him to drink his lunch of three or four gimlets."[16]

One wonders if author Murphy is mixing up his nomenclature and confusing the gimlet, which seldom if ever takes either garnish, with a Vodka Gibson, which would by definition take a pickled onion accent. In any case, the Murphy passage illustrates that Douglas, like many American drinkers of the time period, made the transition from gin and gin-based cocktails to vodka as the preferred base spirit. Douglas's own former fondness for the Hughes era (gin) martini cocktail was more or less coincident with his judicial tenure during that same Hughes era—with Supreme Court Historical Society's cookbook of the justices, *Table for 9*, providing indirect corroboration by providing a martini recipe straight from the jigger of William O. himself.[17]

Mixology contributions aside, Douglas's philandering and drinking continued throughout the 1960s and his second marriage, with Douglas oftentimes staying overnight at the same University Club where Warren was inclined to hold his Saturday lunches. Douglas married his fourth (and final) wife, Cathy, in 1966 when she was still a twenty-two-year-old college student—he was sixty-eight—and, fittingly enough, working as a cocktail waitress at the Three-Star Restaurant in Portland, Oregon.[18] A photo taken after their Encino, California, civil ceremony captured the two of them drinking a wedding toast from a shared, V-shaped martini glass. One assumes that glass was filled with vodka.

Although his pattern of excessive consumption was impressive, Douglas was certainly not unique in his avid pursuit of the liquid high life. This was, after all, the era of the three-martini business lunch. Yet a growing disfavor toward unrestrained drunken behavior signaled the

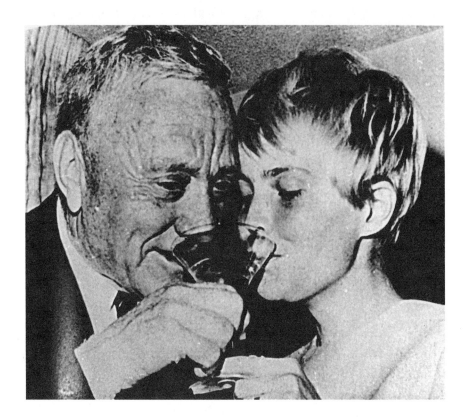

Figure 11.1. Justice William O. Douglas toasting his new bride Cathy, Encino, CA, July 15, 1966. *Source: Courtesy of the William O. Douglas Collection, Yakima Valley Museum*

beginning of a shift in American attitudes about drinking. Disapproval of booze swilling had existed before, of course, but now the clinical term "alcohol abuse" began to be used. Of specific relevance to the Warren period is that in 1956, the American Medical Association for the first time designated alcoholism as a major medical problem and urged that alcoholics be admitted to general hospitals for care. Some would argue that this significant development marked the acceptance among the medical profession of the "disease concept of alcoholism."[19] Also of note during the Warren era was the work of the Research Council on Problems of Alcohol, later the Yale Center of Alcohol Studies (relocated to Rutgers University in 1962), and its medical research on alcoholism that extended to the prevention of alcoholism through

education, investigations of drinking-related traffic problems, and studies of other health complications of alcohol use. One of the center's
most important contributions was its own popular dissemination of "the
modern disease conception of alcoholism," promoted by Dr. E. M.
Jellinek.[20] Neither did popular films of the time period shrink from
painting an unflattering portrait of the out-of-control drinker who had
lost his (and her) way: midcentury cinematic bookends *The Lost Week-
end* (1945) and *Days of Wine and Roses* (1962) were a far cry from the
debonair debauchery depicted in the Thin Man movies or the ribald
characterizations of W. C. Fields.

A new cultural icon was being created: the "problem" drinker.[21]

Not coincidentally, the Warren Court ruled on one of the first constitutional law cases about the medicalization of alcohol abuse. *Powell v.
Texas* in 1968 raised the Eighth Amendment question of "cruel and
unusual punishment" in asking whether chronic alcoholism is a disease
that should mitigate guilt for the offense of public drunkenness. Seriously divided, the justices were not persuaded that the disease concept
of alcoholism had a clear meaning or a ready treatment. The plurality
judgment in the case reflected the complexity of the opinion of the
times toward alcoholics and their "cure."

A direct correlate to *Powell* was the 1962 decision in *Robinson v.
California,* where another divided bench had invalidated under Eighth
Amendment grounds a statute that made the "status" of narcotic addiction a criminal offense, for which the offender may be prosecuted "at
any time before he reforms." California had said that a person could be
continuously guilty of this offense—whether or not he had ever used or
possessed any narcotics within the State, and whether or not he had
been guilty of any antisocial behavior there. The *Robinson* opinion
noted in a footnote that "in its brief the appellee stated: 'Of course it is
generally conceded that a narcotic addict, particularly one addicted to
the use of heroin, is in a state of mental and physical illness. So is an
alcoholic.'"

The analogy was clearly in the Warren Court's mind in 1968. LBJ-
appointee Justice Thurgood Marshall's plurality opinion for the court
acknowledged that the late 1960s were still a time of condemnation—of
"the harsh moral attitude which our society has traditionally taken toward intoxication and the shame which we have associated with alcoholism" as Marshall put it. Yet the plurality's real concern was that accept-

ing the Eighth Amendment argument, and branding alcoholism a psychological illness that required therapy not incarceration, would ultimately be a worse outcome than the current—albeit ugly and unjust— state of affairs for habitual drunkards like Leroy Powell. As Marshall explained:

> It would be tragic to return large numbers of helpless, sometimes dangerous and frequently unsanitary inebriates to the streets of our cities without even the opportunity to sober up adequately which a brief jail term provides. . . . The picture of the penniless drunk propelled aimlessly and endlessly through the law's "revolving door" of arrest, incarceration, release and re-arrest is not a pretty one. But before we condemn the present practice across the board, perhaps we ought to be able to point to some clear promise of a better world for these unfortunate people.

Marshall's opinion attracted only four votes total, one being the chief's. "The chief was clearly troubled by the case," said a Warren clerk of the time who worked on the case, recounting his recollection of it. It was Warren who allegedly shaped the plurality opinion, reflecting his own view that the inevitable result of decriminalizing public drunkenness by alcoholics would be involuntary and, likely, lengthy and ineffective "civil commitment." At least under the present legal system, Warren apparently mused, the chronic alcoholic convicted of public intoxication got a few days in jail to sober up, some solid food, "and, most important of all, his or her liberty back once he or she had served his or her brief sentence." "It was vintage Earl Warren," this clerk concluded, for it was an argument "at bottom intensely empathetic and humane," while also focusing on the practical impact of legal rules and governmental actions on real people.[22] Still, the deciding vote in the *Powell* case belonged to concurring Justice Byron White, a Kennedy appointee. White distinguished *Powell* from the situation in *Robinson*. Though both kinds of addicts are, presumably, diseased, Powell (the drunk) was guilty not of his affliction or status—what for Robinson (the junkie) had been the criminal "act." Powell was instead guilty of the action of displaying his drunkenness *in public*, something over which he allegedly did have control. Drinking and public decorum was a cultural value of the time, of course, but there was also class bias at work in the *Powell* case, regarding acceptable and accessible "social drinking." Alcoholics who were itinerants or poor did not have private clubs or living rooms to contain their drunken episodes, as middle-class boozers did. What could be hidden was not censored, at least not by the town policeman.

Broad cultural effects of a growing disapproval of heavy drinking would not be felt for decades. Thus, the cocktail flow did not cease during Warren's tenure. This meant that the opportunity to purchase liquor for home consumption remained a central concern and a recurring legal topic. Both states and state-regulated liquor wholesalers attempted to influence the liquor market—sometimes successfully, sometimes not. A relatively insignificant Federal Alcohol Administration Act statutory construction case, *Black v. Magnolia Liquor Co.* in 1957, is useful for what it tells us about what types of liquor were being purchased and drunk in the Warren period.[23] The opinion includes this factually descriptive paragraph:

> [D]uring the period in question Johnny Walker Scotch and Sea-gram's V. O. Whiskey were in short supply, while Seagram's Ancient Bottle Gin and Seagram's 7-Crown Whiskey were plentiful, Ancient Bottle being a poor seller. Respondent, in order to increase its sales of Ancient Bottle Gin and 7-Crown Whiskey, compelled retailers to buy them, which they did not desire, in order to obtain the other two whiskeys which they did desire.

While this wholesaler's stratagem did not fly with the Warren justices, they readily upheld a state law regulating alcohol prices in *Joseph F. Seagram and Sons v. Hostetter* in 1966. The New York State Liquor Authority had fixed mandatory minimum retail prices for spirits, applying these to spirit brand owners. All contentions—that the provisions placed an illegal burden upon interstate commerce conflicted with federal antitrust legislation and thus fell under the Supremacy Clause and violated both the Due Process Clause and the Equal Protection Clause of the Fourteenth Amendment—were found to be without merit. With respect to liquor destined for use, distribution, or consumption in the state, the unanimous court held that the Twenty-First Amendment "demands wide latitude for regulation by the State." And "nothing in [that] Amendment or any other part of the Constitution," the court continued significantly, "requires that state laws regulating the liquor business be motivated exclusively by a desire to promote temperance." The announced purpose of the legislature was "to eliminate 'discrimination against and disadvantage of consumers,'" as a result of monopolistic pricing practices by dominant distillers and their wholesalers. This, the justices felt, was entirely appropriate state action.[24]

But the national supremacy or "cooperative" federalism oriented Warren Court was *not* prepared to let state alcohol policy utterly trump interstate commerce clause concerns, as it had made clear in *Hostetter v. Idlewild Bon Voyage Liquor Corp.* in 1964. *Idlewild* concerned the now-familiar practice of purchasing "duty free" liquor upon embarking on international airline travel. The appellee business, under Federal Bureau of Customs supervision and beginning in 1960, "purchase[d] bottled intoxicants at wholesale outside New York, br[ought] them into the State and at an airport there s[old] them at retail for delivery abroad to international airline travelers." The state liquor authority sought to forbid the practice as sale of alcohol unregulated by the state. Rejecting the state claim, the court first acknowledged that "a State is totally unconfined by traditional Commerce Clause limitations when it restricts the importation of intoxicants destined for use, distribution, or consumption within its borders," but then added, "both the Twenty-first Amendment and the Commerce Clause are parts of the same Constitution. Like other provisions of the Constitution, each must be considered in the light of the other, and in the context of the issues and interests at stake in any concrete case." Congress, the unanimous court reminded, regulates commerce with foreign nations.

Dept. of Revenue v. James Beam Distilling Co. in 1964 similarly upheld federal power as superior to state regulatory authority, even under the Twenty-First Amendment. The Warren Court held that the Export-Import Clause, a constitutional provision that flatly prohibits any state from imposing a tax upon imports from abroad, prevented the state of Kentucky from slapping a tax on Scotch whiskey that Jim Beam was importing for sale in the state. The ruling was unequivocal regarding the federal–state powers balance:

> To sustain the tax which Kentucky has imposed in this case would require nothing short of squarely holding that the Twenty-first Amendment has completely repealed the Export-Import Clause so far as intoxicants are concerned. Nothing in the language of the Amendment nor in its history leads to such an extraordinary conclusion. This Court has never intimated such a view, and now that the claim for the first time is squarely presented, we expressly reject it.

Still, the decision in *James Beam* also left no doubt as to the state's plenary authority within its legitimate Twenty-First Amendment realm:

> We have no doubt that under the Twenty-first Amendment Kentucky could not only regulate, but could completely prohibit the importation of some intoxicants, or of all intoxicants, destined for distribution, use, or consumption within its borders. There can surely be no doubt, either, of Kentucky's plenary power to regulate and control, by taxation or otherwise, the distribution, use, or consumption of intoxicants within her territory after they have been imported.

Despite this caveat, Justice Black joined by Justice Goldberg nonetheless dissented, arguing that the decision "deprives the States of a large part of the power which I think the Twenty-first Amendment gives them to regulate the liquor business by taxation or otherwise." The seriousness of the constitutional issue did not prevent Black from injecting a little liquor-related levity into his dissenting opinion, when he remarked:

> Although I was brought up to believe that Scotch whisky would need a tax preference to survive in competition with Kentucky bourbon, I never understood the Constitution to require a State to give such preference. (My dissenting Brother asks me to say that this statement does not necessarily represent his views on the respective merits of Scotch and bourbon.)

In concluding, Black provided this history lesson on the Twenty-First Amendment and on alcohol-related jurisprudence in general:

> Whatever may have been the virtue or the constitutional soundness of the fiction that articles imported from abroad are "imports" so long as they remain "in their original packages," that doctrine was expressly attacked in the Senate debate on the Twenty-first Amendment as rendering the States "powerless to protect themselves against the importation of liquor into the States." The Amendment was meant to bury that obstacle to state power over liquor, and the doctrine of "original package," which the Senate consciously rejected, should not be revived after 30 years' interment, once again to be used to deprive States of power the Senate so clearly wanted them to have and the people so clearly granted them. Section 2 of

the Amendment, born of long and bitter experiences in the field of liquor regulation, should not be frustrated by us.

Black's soliloquy in *James Beam* suggests that Warren Court efforts to balance federal and state interests in alcohol regulation were still unsteady, at best.

The Warren Court also begins the long judicial disquisition on the constitutional parameters of policing drunk driving. In *Breithaupt v. Abram* in 1957, the majority ruled that blood samples, taken involuntarily by a skilled technician to determine a driver's state of intoxication, do not violate substantive due process guarantees under the Fourteenth Amendment. Such rights guarantees protect individuals from deprivations of liberty that violate the notion of "fundamental fairness." Writing for a 6–3 majority, Justice Tom Clark (he of Stork Club lore) argued that blood alcohol tests were necessary as a matter of public policy to ensure traffic safety on roads and highways, and that "modern community living requires modern scientific methods of crime detection." Chief Justice Warren and Justice Douglas both wrote dissenting opinions in which they argued that the involuntary blood sample taken in the case was "repulsive" and an obvious violation of individual liberty by the state.[25]

The *Breithaupt* decision did little to settle the issue, particularly once the Warren Court incorporated Fourth Amendment unreasonable search and seizure and Fifth Amendment self-incrimination protections against the states and their treatment of individuals. Such "incorporation" meant that the court was defining the liberty interest guaranteed by Fourteenth Amendment due process of law with greater precision, saying that states could not take actions that deprived individuals of certain rights enumerated in the first eight amendments of the Bill of Rights. With this, and with the dissenting position of Warren and Douglas ostensibly enhanced by several subsequent, more liberal appointees, the court moved to revisit its *Breithaupt* holding. Almost a decade from its first foray into the subject of policing drunk driving, the Warren justices took the 1966 case of *Schmerber v. California* for the distinct purpose of clarifying whether admitting involuntary blood samples into evidence in a state criminal prosecution violated newly applicable Fourth or Fifth Amendment rights. It was a 5–4 decision. Justice William Brennan's majority opinion first held that blood samples do not implicate the Fifth Amendment right against self-incrimination because the extraction and chemical analysis of blood samples do not involve "even a shadow of testimonial compulsion." He followed this distinction between words and physical evidence with a somewhat wobbly Fourth Amendment stance. "Ordinarily," Brennan observed leadingly, search warrants are required "where intrusions into the human body are concerned." Yet *Schmerber*, it seemed, was not one of those ordinary situations.

The Brennan majority found the attempt to secure blood without a warrant but incident to the arrest of Schmerber to be appropriate, for the simple biochemical reason that blood alcohol begins to diminish shortly after a person stops drinking. The arrest had been supported by probable cause in the form of behavioral and physiological evidence of impairment of faculties, but the driver Schmerber had refused a breathalyzer test and, on advice of his counsel, had also refused the blood extraction. Blood was taken anyway, in the course of his hospitalization for injuries resulting from his roadway accident. Schmerber's primary refusal of the breathalyzer was admitted into evidence during his criminal trial, over his objection that drawing inference from it was compulsory self-incrimination. Brennan was unmoved.

> "The same facts as established probable cause [for the arrest]," he argued, "justified the police in requiring petitioner to submit to a test of his blood-alcohol content. In view of the time required to bring petitioner to a hospital, the consequences of delay in making a blood test for alcohol, and the time needed to investigate the accident scene, there was no time to secure a warrant, and the clear indication that in fact evidence of intoxication would be found rendered the search an appropriate incident of petitioner's arrest."

Nevertheless, at the close of the majority opinion, Brennan added this tempering caveat:

> We reach this judgment only on the facts of the present record. The integrity of an individual's person is a cherished value of our society. That we today hold that the Constitution does not forbid the States minor intrusions into an individual's body under stringently limited conditions in no way indicates that it permits more substantial intrusions, or intrusions under other conditions.

Four dissenting justices wrote separate dissenting opinions in *Schmerber*. In a brief statement Chief Justice Warren reiterated his dissenting position in *Breithaupt v. Abram*, where he had argued that involuntary blood samples violate substantive notions of due process of law. Justice Douglas also reiterated his dissenting opinion in *Breithaupt* but added that physical invasions into the human body violate the right to privacy enumerated in *Griswold v. Connecticut* (1965) and that "[n]o clearer invasion of this right of privacy can be imagined than forcible bloodletting of the kind involved here." Justice Hugo Black authored an impassioned dissent in which he argued that officers had violated Schmerber's privilege against self-incrimination. "I deeply regret the Court's holding," he wrote, "[b]elieving with the Framers that these constitutional safeguards broadly construed by independent tribunals of justice provide our best hope for keeping our people free from governmental oppression." Finally, Justice Abe Fortas wrote that the involuntary blood sample was an act of violence that violated substantive due process liberty, and that states may not resort to acts of violence when prosecuting crimes. Despite these strenuous objections, *Schmerber*'s position on blood alcohol dissipation as an automatic exigency exception to the warrant requirement would stand, and would not receive a more (liberty) encouraging follow-up until the 2013 Roberts Court case of *Missouri v. McNeely*.

Other liquor-related behaviors adjudged by the Warren Court seem more vintage than contemporary, although these cases about old-fashioned bootlegging operations did generate some progressive individual rights results. A minor Fifth Amendment victory was scored for moonshining in *U.S. v. Romano* in 1965, where the court affirmed overturning the convictions because "presence at an illegal still carries no reasonable inference of the crime of possession, custody, or control of the still proscribed by [federal law]." Yet *U.S. v. Gainey* in 1965 found the Warren Court rejecting a due process challenge to a similar conviction that resulted from the trial judge's instructions informing the jury of statutory provisions that authorized it to infer guilt from the respondent's unexplained presence at the still site. Perhaps the southern gothic factual scenario convinced the justices, as it was recounted in a footnote to the court's opinion:

The evidence for the prosecution showed that an old Dodge truck with darkened headlights drove up to the site of a secluded still, hidden in a swamp in Dooly County, Georgia. The respondent, Jackie Gainey, left the truck, turned on a flashlight, and walked toward the still. There he was confronted by state and federal revenue agents. The respondent attempted to flee, but, after a short chase, he and his waiting colleagues were apprehended.

The court construed the statute in *Gainey*, and its instruction for juries, as a rule of evidence only—not an inexorable command. But that was not enough for Justice Black, who wrote a strong dissent, nor Justice Douglas, who filed a partial dissent. Still another 1965 decision involving illegal distilling, *U.S. v. Ventresca*, found that probable cause for a warrant to search had been established by the following federal investigators' observations:

The affidavit described different occasions when a car was driven to the rear of respondent's house with loads of sugar or empty tins; the loading at the house of apparently full five-gallon cans; the smelling by Investigators as they walked in front of the house of fermenting mash; and their hearing the sound of a motor pump and metallic noises from the direction of the house. . . . [A] search warrant [was issued] on the basis of the affidavit, pursuant to which a still was found for the illegal possession and operation of which respondent was convicted.

Douglas, joined by the chief, dissented in *Ventresca*, finding the aforementioned facts inadequate to support the warrant and hearsay to boot. *Romano*, *Gainey*, and *Ventresca*, while otherwise fairly minor cases, are interesting in that they show both the prevalent operation of illegal stills (the latter one in Massachusetts!) and persistent federal efforts to shut them down continuing throughout the 1960s.[26]

Another such case, *Chapman v. U.S.* in 1961, fits squarely within the Warren reputation as a court protective of civil liberties—no matter who the criminal defendant might be, including a moonshiner.[27] State police officers, acting without a warrant but with the consent of petitioner Chapman's landlord, who had summoned them after detecting the odor of whiskey mash on the premises, entered the petitioner's rented house in his absence through an unlocked window. They found an unregistered still and a quantity of mash. When the petitioner Chapman returned and entered the house, he was arrested by a state officer. Federal officers, also without warrants, arrived soon thereafter and took custody of the petitioner, samples of the mash, and the still. The evidence seized was admitted over the petitioner's objection at his trial and he was convicted of violating the federal liquor laws. The Warren justices held the search and seizure to be unlawful, with even the so-called conservative members of the early Warren Court joining the majority. (Only Justice Clark dissented fully, apparently persuaded by the fact that "under Georgia law, the use of premises for the manufacture or the keeping of liquor for disposition works 'a forfeiture of the rights of any lessee or tenant under any lease or contract for rent.'") Moreover, even in 1957, the Warren Court appeared to be chipping away at state resistance to the federal exclusionary rule, as the facts and holding in *Benanti v. U.S.* indicate. The question the case presented was whether evidence of bootlegging obtained as the result of wiretapping by state law-enforcement officers, without participation by federal authorities, was admissible in a federal court. Police in New York state, suspecting that the petitioner and others were dealing in narcotics in violation of state law, obtained a warrant in accordance with state law authorizing them to tap the phone wires of a bar the petitioner Benanti was known to frequent. The police then overheard a conversation between Benanti and another person in which it was said that "eleven pieces" were to be transported that night at a certain time and to a certain place in New York City. Acting on this information, the police followed and stopped a car driven by the petitioner's brother. No narcotics were found but hidden in the car were eleven 5-gallon cans of alcohol without the tax stamps required by federal law. The alcohol was turned over to federal authorities and Benanti was convicted of the illegal possession and transportation of distilled spirits. Warren's opinion for the unanimous court excluded the use of the evidence for the federal alcohol conviction, because it had been obtained through an impermissibly broad use of a state warrant.

Other important Fourth Amendment victories had alcohol-related subtexts, such as *Berger v. N.Y.* in 1967. The Warren Court invalidated New York's eavesdrop law as too broad, and "a trespassory intrusion into a constitutionally protected area." The case's colorful facts paint a florid picture of state-level corruption:

Berger, the petitioner, was convicted on two counts of conspiracy to bribe the Chairman of the New York State Liquor Authority. The case arose out of the complaint of one Ralph Pansini to the District Attorney's office that agents of the State Liquor Authority had entered his bar and grill and without cause seized his books and records. Pansini asserted that the raid was in reprisal for his failure to pay a bribe for a liquor license. Numerous complaints had been filed with the District Attorney's office charging the payment of bribes by applicants for liquor licenses. On the direction of that office, Pansini, while equipped with a "minifon" recording device, interviewed an employee of the Authority. The employee advised Pansini that the price for a license was $10,000, and suggested that he contact attorney Harry Neyer. Neyer subsequently told Pansini that he worked with the Authority employee before and that the latter was aware of the going rate on liquor licenses downtown.

The eavesdrop order was applied to Neyer's law office, and recordings made implicated the petitioner Berger as a go-between involving the issuance of liquor licenses for the Playboy and Tenement Clubs, both of New York City. Justice Douglas, in concurrence, had this to say about the decision: "it overrules *sub silentio Olmstead v. United States,* and its offspring, and brings wiretapping and other electronic eavesdropping fully within the purview of the Fourth Amendment." The Warren Court would officially overrule the Taft era *Olmstead* decision, and extend Fourth Amendment protection to all areas where a person has a "reasonable expectation of privacy," later that same term in *Katz v. U.S.* (1967).

An interesting footnote to the long-term impact of Prohibition on constitutional law involve the compulsory Bible reading and school prayer cases that the Warren Court addressed in the early 1960s. *Abington v. Schempp* (1963) and *Engle v. Vitale* (1962) were decisions in which Warren majorities would break new ground in defining and enforcing the separation of church and state under First Amendment prohibition of the establishment of religion. The Bible reading and school prayer statutes themselves were the legislative fruit of "an increasing embrace of militant Protestant religiosity during the 1920s," when such compulsory religious practices were first enacted into law.[28] That "militant Protestant religiosity" was, of course, also responsible for the temperance movement and its ultimate goal, the illegalization of alcohol.

The Warren Court period is usually thought of as the most progressive era of judicial policy making in the history of the Supreme Court, and decisions like the above church–state cases are often included in that assessment. Yet many judicial scholars speak of the "two" Warren Courts, jurisprudentially speaking. It is personnel differences that define them. From 1953 until Felix Frankfurter's retirement in 1962, liberal tendencies were held in check by a conservative, judicially restrained coalition. From 1962 and with the replacement of Frankfurter by Arthur Goldberg, liberals had a working majority and the activist decisions so closely identified with the Warren era begin to occur. Do these two Warren Courts map onto the liquor decisions as well? Perhaps, but not perfectly. For instance, *Jones v. United States*, decided in 1958, provides an instance of the early Warren Court's recognition of the importance of scrupulous adherence to procedural fairness—even when a moonshiner was the beneficiary. Federal alcohol agents had secured a warrant to search a home during the daytime, having observed substantial evidence that illegal liquor was being produced. Rather than executing the warrant, they waited until the evening, when they entered and searched the home. The court held, with Justice Harlan writing, that probable cause to believe that the house contained contraband was not sufficient to legitimize a warrantless search. "Were federal officers free to search without a warrant merely upon probable cause to believe that certain articles were within a home, the provisions of the Fourth Amendment would become empty phrases, and the protection it affords largely nullified," he lectured in *Jones*. A practitioner of judicial restraint not noted for his ringing rhetoric on behalf of civil libertarianism, Harlan drew the line at slipshod police work and an overly casual attitude toward the niceties of due process of law.

Even moonshiners had rights, said that Warren Court of 1958. So echoed and reaffirmed the court in *Chapman* of 1961. Unlike the Taft bench, these Warren justices did not place a great premium on enforcement against illegal alcohol production—certainly not so great a premium as to justify warping constitutional understandings of privacy or due process. The "second," liberal Warren Court affirmed this perspective. But narrow majorities of *its* justices also drew the line at broadly read Fourth Amendment rights that protected the dermal integrity of drunk drivers like Schmerber, and at broadly construed notions of "cruel and unusual punishment" that absolved habitual drunks like Powell of criminal liability for their actions.

Which, then, was the more "conservative" Warren bench on matters of alcohol?

CONCLUSION

Running the historical gamut from policing moonshining to blood-alcohol testing in drunk driving cases, Warren era decisions with respect to alcohol begin an undoing of the Taft era's most stringent criminal law rulings. The Warren period is also the sociocultural highpoint of swanky cocktailing, a custom that would die a slow but decisive death through the next judicial era, as cultural mores and mixology tastes radically changed.

12

THE BURGER ERA

Twilight of the Cocktail Lounge

The *Burger Court* (1969–1986) is the era during which Americans (re)discovered wine as a beverage, particularly white wine and especially the chardonnay grape, or—as white wine became generically and almost universally (and often incorrectly) known in this time period—"Chablis." But there was more than just plonk being drunk. The rebirth of the California wine industry, its recovery from the doldrums induced by Prohibition, was marked by a truly mind-boggling occurrence in 1976: the historic upset at a blind wine-tasting competition, organized by a British wine merchant, between the great French growers and the upstarts of the then-relatively unknown and lightly regarded Napa Valley. As the *Time* magazine journalist covering the tasting pronounced: "the unthinkable happened: California defeated all Gaul." At this so-called Judgment of Paris, the "top soaring" red was not from Bordeaux but from Stag's Leap Cellars, and American Chardonnays took four of the five prizes among the white wines, facing off against the best white Burgundies.[1] Chief Justice Warren Burger, something of a gourmet snob, was himself a collector of fine wines. Like his precursor Chief Justice Stone, he was reported to have kept a cellar in the basement of the Supreme Court building.[2]

This trait and the era's general demographic trend in terms of alcohol consumption would seem to demark the Burger era's signature drink. There are, nevertheless, complications. Burger was appointed by

President Richard Nixon—who was as affiliated with the Palo Alto Trader Vic's Navy Grog as he was with a sleight of hand in disguising the cheapish wine being served at his various executive gatherings, while at the same time assuring he was poured the fine vintage.[3] Adhering to Nixon, moreover, is more than a faint tinge of alcoholism. Cheever's study, *Drinking in America: Our Secret History*, discusses some of the hair-raising details.[4] Raised a Quaker in Yorba Linda, California, Nixon only learned to drink as a naval officer, during his deployment to the South Pacific in 1943. But he had a notoriously low capacity for alcohol, and a few drinks—a cocktail and wine with dinner—would render him drunk and slurring. He was not a quantity alcoholic but physiologically he had a disability; his inability to handle more than one drink was well known to his intimates. As Nixon's presidency faltered in 1973 in the wake of the Watergate scandal (the resounding defeat of his executive privilege argument before the Supreme Court in 1974 cannot have helped matters either), his drinking got worse and at times interfered with his dispatch of foreign and even military policy, including his prosecution of the war in Vietnam.

Richard Nixon as a president is of course associated with major events in American politics, not the least of which was the threat of impeachment that led to his ultimate resignation—the first and to-date only U.S. president to do so. He was also the presidential candidate who successfully ran on behalf of the interests of the so-called silent majority of mainstream Americans who opposed the most extreme and destabilizing activities of the antiwar and civil rights movements. Nixon was quite critical of the Warren Court as well; his campaign rhetoric promised the appointment of "strict constructionists" who would adhere to the Constitution as written and not attempt to broaden constitutional rights understandings to adapt to contemporary social problems. Nixon's appeal to social conservatism found its expression in his Supreme Court appointments. The four justices he named, including Chief Justice Burger, remade the "Nixon Court" in his image—at least on some issues, particularly those concerning law and order. Criminal law, of course, often intersects with the use and abuse, or the effort at wholesale enjoyment, of alcohol.

Nixon's own alcoholic intake apparently included highballs and martinis[5] as well as wine, even as the twilight of tiki time and his beloved Trader Vic's Navy Grog certainly coincide with the Burger era. Yet it is not Nixon who defines the iconic beverage for the Burger era, even though Nixon the chief executive shaped the personnel of the Burger Court. Rather, Chief Justice Burger's tenure is so long—his chief justiceship spans more than a decade and a half of American imbibing— and his own disposition is so well known, that the *white wine craze* must be his era's defining feature. Rebecca Hurley, his law clerk toward the end of the chief's term, confirms Burger's appreciation of wine and states that "German whites" were a particular favorite.[6] Blue Nun liebfraumilch, anyone? Unfortunate but true, at the beginning of the Burger era, Mateus rosé and other light, insipidly sweet wines (Riunite, Lancers, and the aforementioned Blue Nun) were marketed to a youthful generation of novice drinkers, and a more freewheeling generation of drinkers than had existed before. A contemporary favorite became the wine cooler or wine spritzer, a soda-pop-like confection that prevailed in the popular culture annals of 1970s drinking and in such period handbooks as *Playboy's Host and Bar Book* of 1971. Although Burger himself would never have desecrated his vintages in this way, his era's **white wine spritzer** is and must be his court's totemic beverage.

Overall, the Burger period is something of a nadir in cocktail mixology—the era of the proverbial and minimally palatable "mixed drink." How did it all happen?

The long cultural moment of the cocktail party, begun as an act of defiance (and survival) during Prohibition and reigning supreme as an entertainment for decades after, was being replaced in a cultural milieu no longer defined by dressing up and cocktailing. People still drank, of course, but style setters were now identified by their rejection of all that was rule- or recipe-governed. "Uptight" was the worst of insults, and a free-and-easy, macramé and jug wine kind of spirit prevailed. Thus was born, in the late 1970s, the American "fern bar," identifiable says the website Punchdrink.com by its "ignoble catalog of overly sweet drinks with tacky names and shelf-stable ingredients." Vodka was pressed into service big time; giving life to such syrupy creations as the Harvey Wallbanger[7] and Long Island Iced Tea,[8] downed along with various frothy concoctions like the coconut rum-based Piña Colada, the colorful California tall drink the Tequila Sunrise, and the ever popular and sweetly fizzy wine spritzer. A singles' scene staple, the brightly kitschy fern bar was an aesthetic fashioned to appeal to young people—newly "liberated" young women especially—and the drinking and dating rituals of the opening onslaught of the sexual revolution of the 1970s. The actual quality of the alcoholic drinks was unimportant, because people *did things* in the bars of the Burger era: disco dancing, pickups, lines of coke. The precision cocktail of yesteryear and the posh cocktail lounge of yore could not survive the onslaught. Drinking in bars took on a *Looking for Mr. Goodbar* kind of vibe, even as cocktail *lounges*—when they still existed, that is, as sad and lonely adjutants to bowling alleys, Holiday Inns, and hopelessly fussy restaurants, or scarily dark outposts along derelict stretches of highway or dilapidated city blocks—acquired the uncool and vaguely disreputable patina of stale cigarette smoke, seedy upholstery, and dissipated old people.

The classic cocktail had lost its cachet, and with it its social protection. As if to signal as much, the organization Mothers Against Drunk Driving (MADD) was also founded during Burger's tenure, in 1980. Some backstory is pertinent: In 1970, the federal government created the National Institute on Alcohol Abuse and Alcoholism, in response to the heavy use of alcohol in the decades of the postwar economic boom and the related public health concerns of that heavy use. The years 1980 and 1981 marked the peak of American alcohol consumption in the twentieth century, and American drinking has been on a downward slide ever since.[9] Part of that decline can be explained by spirits being outpaced by wine, bottled wine coolers, and beer. And, in fact, home brewing of beer was legalized under the presidency of Jimmy Carter in 1979,[10] ultimately leading to a microbrewers' renaissance in the late 1980s and 1990s. What happened, then, was that a lighter style of alcoholic beverage was gaining ground in American tastes, even as a more circumscribed tolerance for "drinking and . . ." was developing, society-wide. Even in terms of gross intake of alcohol, the American thirst was gradually drying over the course of the Burger era. For perspective, we can note that per capita consumption of alcohol was about 2 1/2 gallons in 1860, edging up slightly in the first two decades of the twentieth century. As states began passing state-level prohibition laws, national consumption of alcohol started to drop and was just under 2 gallons per capita on the eve of Prohibition. Since Repeal, consumption increased from just under 1 gallon per capita in 1934 to the all-time high of 2 3/4 gallons of 1980–1981. Yet by 2000, consumption was down to 2.18 gallons, and still dropping.[11] Consumers and their tastes were changing.

The watershed year of 1981 was well into the Burger period and marked its later stages. (Burger resigned in 1986.) The 1970s, the years that came before, were by no means abstemious times. Moreover, *Courtwatchers* comments that almost all the modern justices have found a way to socialize with their clerks outside of chambers, "if only by inviting them for cocktails with their spouses."[12] So the prim cocktail hour did persist on the Burger Court. Still, not all time spent with alcohol during the Burger era was so decorous. *The Brethren* recounts an incident in which Justice William Douglas invited his new clerks for drinks in his chambers in summer of 1974—something that might well appear rather scandalous if it happened today.[13] By early 1975, Douglas had had the massive stroke that would incapacitate him, though this did not stop him from "le[ading] the way to the hotel bar" after a rambling fifteen-minute speech at a Sierra Club awards ceremony later that year.[14] Noted raconteur Justice Thurgood Marshall, whose tenure spanned the Warren and Burger periods, was also at this point in time in ill health brought on by "lifestyle choices": he smoked heavily and "at times drank too much."[15]

Overindulgences aside, the casual but by no means meager partake of wine figures most prominently in chronicles of the Burger era. It was even part of a wager between the chief and his colleagues at one of the justices' weekly conferences in 1973. The wager concerned their opinion workload at the time, which was much, much heavier than it is on the current Supreme Court. As Burger recounted the episode to the court press officer, "I said 'I'll buy you a bottle of wine if I am wrong [about the annual workload], and you can get me one if I'm not.'"[16] As early as 1970, Chief Justice Burger was playfully urging his colleagues to celebrate Justice John Marshall Harlan's birthday luncheon "by breaking out a bottle of chilled German grape juice."[17] *The Brethren* also recalled an episode when then-Associate Justice William Rehnquist and his clerks were eating an informal brown bag lunch in one of the court's interior courtyards—only to be joined by the chief justice's more pretentious lunch outing: "Burger's messenger set up a small table with silver service and a white linen tablecloth. Moments later, Burger came out with his clerks. Burger, his jacket on, poured the wine."[18] At the chief's annual reunion with his former clerks, Burger typically began with a glass of sherry followed by a glass of white wine. For the "WEB Fete Society" dinner of 1973, an elaborate meal was planned and six wines were carefully chosen, "all in consultation with the Chief, a life-long member of an international wine tasting society." In an echo of the elaborate repasts of the Waite era, the menu listed the following wines and brandies: Zellinger Riesling 1970, Dry Sack Sherry, Muscadet 1970 Sevre et Marne Beau Soleil, Chateauneuf-du-Pape 1971 B&G, Margaux 1966 B&G, Courvoisier VSOP.[19] *Wild Bill* further recounts that after Douglas's (somewhat forced) retirement, Chief Justice Burger would stop by his emeritus justice's office to chat, "often bringing a favorite wine or a jar of homemade preserves."[20] What nonvinous anecdotes exist relate to holdovers from earlier court eras—such as John Marshall Harlan's rebellious intake of Rebel Yell Bourbon (and Lark cigarettes) while dying in his hospital bed in 1971,[21] or Hugo Black's inspiration for his ringing opinion in the 1971 *Pentagon Papers Case* found in the words of an old southern (whiskey) drinking song, "I'm a Good Old Rebel."[22]

The upshot of all this Burger era merriment is that wine, not hard liquor, was the greater part of it. Yet even with the declining use of

Figure 12.1. Artist Betty Wells captured a casual moment at the annual dinner of the Supreme Court Historical Society in 1977; Chief Justice Warren Burger is on the far left. The sketch appeared as the cover illustration for the 2015 issue of the Supreme Court Historical Society Quarterly, celebrating the Society's 40th anniversary. *Source: Courtesy of Betty Wells, artist's personal collection*

spirits during this period, there was plenty of room for intemperance—as well as railing against it, in the form of new types of state and federal regulations. A seeming epidemic of alcohol-induced highway fatalities in particular spurred various actions: the aforementioned formation of the pressure group MADD and the creation of its youth-analogue Students Against Drunk Driving (SADD) in 1981;[23] an investigative commission initiated by President Ronald Reagan in 1982 and the 1983 "Drinking and Driving Can Kill a Friendship" ad campaign by the U.S. Department of Transportation; and the passage of the National Minimum Drinking Age Act of 1984, which required all states to raise the minimum age for the purchase and "public possession" of alcohol to twenty-one. This act was a concerted federal effort to roll back some states' lowering of the minimum drinking age (MDA) to eighteen during the Vietnam War, when the ongoing military draft and passage of the Twenty-Sixth Amendment in 1971 spurred a general enfranchisement of eighteen-year-olds as adults. In the realm of imbibing, however, the lowered MDA created a state of affairs known as "blood borders," as young drinkers drove across state lines to get a drink on, and then weaved back home—or into head-on collisions.[24]

Whether as a result of the many new antidrink regulations, or a Nixon-shaped court's emerging spirit of social conservatism, the Burger era was a veritable open bar of alcohol-related cases. In its decisions, the Burger Court confronted many and myriad new constitutional questions that were alcohol inflected, directly or indirectly. And while its decisions can hardly be described as a "conservative counterrevolution" to the Warren era of liberal legal progressivism,[25] its decisions on alcohol and the law did drift over time toward a less cavalier attitude toward drinking in American life. Still, just as during the Warren era, the Burger record was mixed, with some rulings censorious and others decidedly libertarian.

To begin, more or less, at the chronological beginning of the court era, two cases decided in 1971 pitted individual procedural rights concerns against state authority to regulate alcohol-related subjects. The 1971 case of *Wisconsin v. Constantineau* was by far the more important of the two. It concerned a state statute, pursuant to which the plaintiff's name was posted by the chief of police in local retail liquor outlets, as someone to whom intoxicating beverages should not be sold. The statute's scheme was challenged as abridging fundamental notice and hear-

ing requirements of the due process clause of the Fourteenth Amendment. The questionable constitutionality of the public posting of names
of persons who had allegedly engaged in "excessive" drinking is easy to
understand; harder is any rationalization for such state paternalism. The
statute was a relic of the immediate post-Prohibition era and had been
on the books for some forty years: the posting, without notice or hearing, applied to any person who by excessive drinking produced certain
conditions or exhibited specified traits, such as exposing himself or family "to want" or becoming "dangerous to the peace" of the community.
The 6–3 court invalidated it, but the justices' split was no doubt influenced by the perspective expressed—as an admission but decidedly not
a justification—in Justice Douglas's majority opinion. As he acknowledged, "We have no doubt as to the power of a State to deal with the
evils described in the [statute]. The police power of the States over
intoxicating liquors was extremely broad even prior to the 21st Amendment."

To be sure, the dissenters, led by the new chief justice, did appear to
be more motivated by states' rights concerns than by any neotemperance ideology. But whether or not the former or the latter was the issue
on which the decision really turned, Douglas's *Constantineau* opinion
gained a larger stature, beyond its original context. That stature was as a
precedential holding that "reputation" was a protected liberty interest
under the Fourteenth Amendment. Yet as narrated in *The Brethren*,
the ruling's meaning was subsequently twisted and ultimately confined
by its original, access-to-alcohol facts. Faced with deciding the defama-
tion case of *Paul v. Davis* in the 1975–1976 term,

> [Justice] Rehnquist believed he saw a way to circumvent the Wiscon-
> sin decision. The posting of the woman's name, he argued, not only
> harmed her reputation but deprived her of a right created by the
> state—the right to purchase and obtain liquor. . . . She had lost
> reputation *plus* the right to buy liquor. The latter was a right estab-
> lished by state law; reputation was not. (emphasis added)

Justice Brennan, however, objected when he reviewed the Rehnquist
majority opinion draft for the 1976 case, arguing that "in the *Wisconsin
v. Constantineau* opinion, Douglas had made it clear that the reputation
issue was 'the *only* issue present.'"[26] In the end, qualifying the earlier
ruling, Rehnquist's *Davis* decision seemingly enshrined a "right to buy

liquor" as an interest or privilege of which a state could not deprive someone without due process of law. Brennan dissented vigorously, saying this about Rehnquist's construction of the precedent in his *Davis* dissenting opinion:

> *Wisconsin v. Constantineau*, which was relied on by the Court of Appeals in this case, did not rely at all on the fact asserted by the Court today as controlling—namely, upon the fact that "posting" denied Ms. Constantineau the right to purchase alcohol for a year. Rather, *Constantineau* stated: "The only issue present here is whether the label or characterization given a person by 'posting,' though a mark of serious illness to some, is to others such a stigma or badge of disgrace that procedural due process requires notice and an opportunity to be heard."

So was it the shame of being branded as somebody socially unacceptable, or the shame (and inconvenience) of being "cut off" that constituted the harm? Rehnquist's interpretation of *Constantineau* made it sound as if the liberty interest in a good drink rather than in one's good name was what was at stake—a holding oddly pregnant with proalcohol implications, if there ever was one.

The idea of a constitutionally protected "reputational right" (that cannot be deprived without due process) becomes relevant in examining the other alcohol-related Burger Court case of 1971. Alcohol—moonshining, to be exact—was the context for a Fourth Amendment challenge to a federal tax investigation in *U.S. v. Harris*. The question in the case was whether the investigator's affidavit supporting the search warrant, the execution of which resulted in the discovery of illicit liquor, was sufficient to establish probable cause. That affidavit had been based on "a *reputation* with the investigator for over four years as being a trafficker in non-tax paid distilled spirits" (emphasis added), as well as on information provided by a confidential informant. As in *Constantineau*, a plaintiff's reputation regarding alcohol was critical to the state's law enforcement action—although Harris was not exactly being punished without due process for his supposed reputation regarding liquor, as Constantineau had been. Yet the thin reed of a purportedly nefarious reputation with a federal investigator, as the principal support for the long arm of the law (i.e., the search and seizure), may explain why upholding the validity of the warrant in *Harris* commanded only a judgment of the court, in a plurality opinion authored by Chief Justice Burger.

Conversely, the plurality's law-and-order mentality in *Harris* might simply have been a feature of the attitude present in another search and seizure decision from 1970, which had upheld federal government regulation of the liquor industry. That decision, *Colonnade Catering Corp. v. U.S.*, put it thusly:

> We deal here with the liquor industry long subject to close supervision and inspection. As respects that industry, and its various branches including retailers, Congress has broad authority to fashion standards of reasonableness for searches and seizures. Under the existing statutes, Congress selected a standard that does not include forcible entries without a warrant. It resolved the issue, not by authorizing forcible, warrantless entries, but by making it an offense for a licensee to refuse admission to the inspector.

The liquor industry and liquor commerce had traditionally been under the government's watchful regulatory eye—and the dodgier branches of that industry and commerce, all the more so. Douglas's majority opinion in *Colonnade Catering* offered this further history lesson:

> In 1791, the year in which the Fourth Amendment was ratified, Congress imposed an excise tax on imported distilled spirits and on liquor distilled here, under which law federal officers had broad powers to inspect distilling premises and the premises of the importer without a warrant. From these and later laws and regulations governing the liquor industry, it is argued that Congress has been most solicitous in protecting the revenue against various types of fraud and to that end has repeatedly granted federal agents power to make warrantless searches and seizures of articles under the liquor laws.

Acquire the reputation of being a shady trader in distilled spirits at your own risk, in other words, because the law of alcohol regulation is not on your side.

Alcohol was also part of the backstory in a major Fourth Amendment privacy ruling from 1976, *U.S. v. Miller*. Miller, a Georgia moonshiner, had been charged with having alcohol distilling equipment and whiskey on which liquor tax had not been paid. The Bureau of Alcohol, Tobacco, and Firearms (ATF) issued subpoenas to two of Miller's banks, requesting records of Miller's accounts. The banks complied with the subpoenas, and the evidence was used at Miller's trial where he was convicted of possessing an unregistered still, carrying on the business of a distiller without giving bond and with intent to defraud the government of whiskey tax, possessing whiskey upon which no taxes had been paid, and conspiring to defraud the U.S. government. The convicted moonshiner challenged the inclusion of the evidence from his bank accounts. A 7–2 Burger Court held that Miller had no right to privacy that protected his bank records. Writing for the majority, Justice Lewis Powell asserted that the "documents subpoenaed are not [Miller's] 'private papers'" but are, instead, part of the bank's business records. Miller's rights were not violated when a third party—his bank—transmitted information to the government that he had voluntarily disclosed (and entrusted) to that third party.

Constitutional ripples from the *Miller* doctrine are still being felt in contemporary discussions about the investigatory power of the War-on-Terror "surveillance state," and in related cultural handwringing over personal digital data collection and dissemination by social media providers like Facebook.[27] A more immediate implication of the decision—one suggested by its notable contrast to the holding in *Constantineau*—was that the Burger Court was honing its law-and-order profile as it gained more Nixon appointees, such as Powell and Rehnquist. President Nixon was, of course, an avowed opponent of the Warren Court's expansive protection of the rights of the accused, which included its generous construction of the Fourth Amendment's prevention of governmental prying into individual affairs.

Other Burger era alcohol-related cases raised nation-state inter-governmental relations questions—structural rather than individual rights' concerns. The Burger Court was in general much more solicitous of states' rights in the federal system than its predecessor courts had been: Nixon's was an era of "new federalism." In a series of rulings in the early 1970s, Burger's Court applied its emerging concern for federalism to the subject of liquor sales. A seemingly mundane state taxation case of the early Burger Court period, *Heublein Inc. v. South Carolina Tax Commission* in 1972, nevertheless required careful dissection of the federal and state interests involved, because of South Carolina's horrifically complex state alcohol beverage control (ABC) system. "This Court made clear in the early years following the adoption of the Twenty-first Amendment," the *Heublein* court argued, quoting the 1964 *Hostetter* decision, "that by virtue of its provisions a State is totally unconfined by traditional Commerce Clause limitations when it restricts the importation of intoxicants destined for use, distribution, or consumption within its borders." The requirement that, before engaging in the liquor business in South Carolina, a manufacturer do more (in actuality: pay more) than merely solicit sales, was held to be an appropriate element in the state's system of regulating the sale of liquor. The tax regulation in question was therefore valid.

Another seemingly mundane Mississippi liquor taxation issue evolved into a question of Marshallian proportions in the case of *U.S. v. Mississippi Tax Commission*—so much so that it was litigated two separate times, in 1973 and again in 1975. Like *Heublein, Mississippi Tax Commission* was woefully complex; unlike *Heublein,* the Mississippi ABC cases provoked two dissenters, who saw the federalism implications of the decisions as fairly broad and important. State law required out-of-state liquor distillers and suppliers to collect from military installations within Mississippi and to remit to the state tax commission a tax in the form of a wholesale markup on liquor sold to the installations. Because before 1966 Mississippi had prohibited the sale or possession of alcoholic beverages within its borders, the state had created the State Tax Commission as the sole in-state importer and wholesaler of alcoholic beverages, not including malt liquor. The statute authorized the Tax Commission to purchase intoxicating liquors and sell them "to authorized retailers within the state including, at the discretion of the commission, any retail distributors operating within any military post . . . within the boundaries of the state, . . . exercising such control over the distribution of alcoholic beverages as seem[s] right and proper." The commission was also authorized to "add to the cost of all alcoholic beverages a price markup designed to cover the cost of operation of the wholesale liquor business, yield a reasonable profit, and keep Mississippi's liquor prices competitive." It was a fairly typical arrangement for a "control" state, save the application of the markup to instrumentalities of the United States—liquor stores on base—as the purchasers of the liquor. An earlier stage of the litigation, *Mississippi Tax Commission* I, had been before the Burger Court in 1973 and had held, in a majority opinion written by Justice Thurgood Marshall, that the Twenty-First

Amendment did not empower a state to tax or otherwise regulate the importation of distilled spirits into a territory over which the United States exercises exclusive jurisdiction. Subsequently viewing the mark-up as, in fact, a sales tax, Justice William Brennan's seven-member majority in *Mississippi Tax Commission* II found it to be unconstitutional as a state tax imposed upon the United States.

Brennan cited with authority Chief Justice John Marshall's seminal ruling in *McCulloch v. Maryland*. The Mississippi liquor revenue was thus converted into a fundamental principle of constitutional federalism and the supremacy clause of Article I, for "the power to tax" was as much "the power to destroy" in the 1970s as it had been in 1819. Or in the 1930s, for that matter: however powerful a grant of authority to states, the Twenty-First Amendment had not abolished federal immunity. The grandiose implication of the contest in *Mississippi Tax Commission* found indirect confirmation in the opinions of its dissenters. Dissenting in both I and II, Justice Douglas, joined by Justice Rehnquist, called the ruling(s) "an amazing decision doing irreparable harm to the cause of States' rights under the Twenty-first Amendment."

A "near beer" case decided in 1976 would even more profoundly influence state efforts to exert control over access to alcoholic beverages than had previous judicial tinkerings with the ABC system. *Craig v. Boren* (1976) was also a major ruling on the equal protection clause of the Fourteenth Amendment, enshrining the doctrine of heightened scrutiny for gender-based legal classifications. This one was an Oklahoma law using a gender-differentiated legal age for the purchase of low-alcohol 3.2 percent beer, with males legal to purchase at age twenty-one, but females able to buy it at age eighteen. *Craig* appeared on the Burger Court docket at a time when sex discrimination and the role of women in American society were hot topics, socially and legally; it likewise came to the court during the period of the pending ratification of the ultimately unsuccessful Equal Rights Amendment (ERA).

Craig posed several gender equality and alcohol regulation questions quite starkly. Could a state really make distinctions between men and women in the way Oklahoma had, when it justified them in terms of gender-based stereotypes about male and female roles in courtship, alcohol consumption, and driving under the influence? The state's statute assumed that young men took a custodial responsibility for the young women they dated, in terms of driving them on dates as well as

generally dating women younger than themselves. Therefore, an eighteen-year-old female could be trusted to drink legally, as she was more
than likely in the company of an older male who was also shepherding
her to and from each beery assignation. Never mind that by the terms
of the statute, it was only the purchasing not the drinking of 3.2 percent
beer by eighteen- to twenty-year-old males that was prohibited at law,
and there was nothing to prevent an eighteen-year-old female from
buying beer for her still underage (driving) escort. Oklahoma stubborn-
ly presumed that male standards of maturity determined that twenty-
one should be his age for purchase, "loose-fitting generalities concerning the drinking tendencies of aggregate groups" be damned.

Patently irrational though the state's scheme seemed, it raised important questions about gender, society, and of course, alcohol. Was
classifying people, and apportioning their rights and responsibilities,
according to their sex and conventional sex roles basically reasonable
and therefore constitutional? Or did a state need to prove more about
the link between gender and drinking behavior in order to satisfy the
concern for equal protection of law? The statistics on drunk driving
arrests supplied by the state were consistent with its legal position, but
less than overwhelmingly convincing. It mattered little to the debate
that the legal classification in the case attached to the opportunity to
obtain beer for recreational drinking, or that the gender basis of it
actually disadvantaged men and not women—even though "sex discrimination" was ordinarily thought to be a problem for women's equal
rights and opportunities. In the grand scheme of things, the case was a
constitutional showdown on several fronts, only one of which was the
state law of alcohol.

Oklahoma, like Mississippi, had initially been a dry state immediately following the repeal of the Prohibition Amendment. Fundamentalist
religious interests were strong in the state, which remained "bone-dry"
until 1959. Intoxicating beverages were thus viewed with suspicion, if
not the taint of sinfulness. The empirical connection between the Oklahoma statute's "non-intoxicating 3.2% beer" and the asserted "important governmental objective in the traffic safety" seems to have been
presumed by all involved, although how a "non-intoxicating" beverage
could affect anyone, whatever their age or sex, seems a question that
needed to be asked. (It was asked, somewhat mockingly, by Justice
Stevens in his concurring opinion.) The answer, it turned out, was a

historical relic. The Oklahoma beer law reflected the initial, staged repeal of Prohibition, which began with FDR's modification to the Volstead Act regarding what beverages were considered "intoxicating." Beer of certain lesser potency was not, and was therefore legal even while the Eighteenth Amendment was still in effect. This was the first installment of relegalizing alcohol in the United States; later, most states would give free rein to a broader range of intoxicants for those aged twenty-one and older. Yet teetotaling Oklahoma still cast a wary eye at low-alcohol "near" beer and its slippery slope to rampant drunkenness. When the wave of state laws lowering the age of legal adulthood to eighteen were passed in the early 1970s, Oklahoma followed suit—except with respect to beer-buying under the age of twenty-one. Thus the age- and gender-based purchasing restriction—which the Burger Court invalidated, by a 7–2 vote, arguing that sex-based legal classifications had to pass a more intensive, "intermediate" level of scrutiny than a deferential, reasonableness test. Both the chief and fellow Nixon-appointee Rehnquist dissented.

The upshot was that 3.2 percent beer would henceforth be off limits to all drinkers in Oklahoma under the age of twenty-one. The developmental significance of the *Craig* decision for equal protection law aside, also noteworthy was the Brennan majority opinion's historical synopsis of alcohol and the American state. It is worth quoting at length—both as a review of the alcohol case law covered in previous chapters, and for the skeptical perspective it reflects:

> The Twenty-first Amendment repealed the Eighteenth Amendment in 1933. . . . This Court's decisions since have confirmed that the Amendment primarily created an exception to the normal operation of the Commerce Clause. . . . Once passing beyond consideration of the Commerce Clause, the relevance of the Twenty-first Amendment to other constitutional provisions becomes increasingly doubtful. As one commentator has remarked:
>
> Neither the text nor the history of the Twenty-first Amendment suggests that it qualifies individual rights protected by the Bill of Rights and the Fourteenth Amendment where the sale or use of liquor is concerned. Any departures from this historical view have been limited and sporadic . . . [and c]ases involving individual rights protected by the Due Process Clause have been treated in sharp contrast. For example, when an individual objected to the mandatory

"posting" of her name in retail liquor establishments and her characterization as an "excessive drink[er]," the Twenty-first Amendment was held not to qualify the scope of her due process rights. *Wisconsin v. Constantineau* (1971).

It is true that *California v. LaRue* (1972), relied upon the Twenty-first Amendment to "strengthen" the State's authority to regulate live entertainment at establishments licensed to dispense liquor, at least when the performances "partake more of gross sexuality than of communication." *Nevertheless, the Court has never recognized sufficient "strength" in the Amendment to defeat an otherwise established claim of invidious discrimination in violation of the Equal Protection Clause. Rather,* Moose Lodge No. 107 v. Irvis (1972), *establishes that state liquor regulatory schemes cannot work invidious discriminations that violate the Equal Protection Clause.* (emphasis added)

Brennan's review of alcohol case law in his *Craig* opinion was directed toward qualifying state power over Americans' drinking. The 1972 *Moose Lodge* was indeed an important ruling for the principle that the state's conceded power to license the distribution of intoxicating beverages did *not* justify use of that power in a manner that conflicted with the equal protection clause. Still, the actual holding was not really a victory for racial equality: the Rehnquist majority (which Burger joined) did not find that the private club in the case, practicing racial exclusion in service, was guilty of state action violating civil rights just by virtue of possessing a state liquor license. Dissenting Justices Douglas and Marshall were irritated by the sophistry, offering this observation:

This state-enforced scarcity of licenses restricts the ability of blacks to obtain liquor, for liquor is commercially available only at private clubs for a significant portion of each week. Access by blacks to places that serve liquor is further limited by the fact that the state quota is filled. A group desiring to form a nondiscriminatory club which would serve blacks must purchase a license held by an existing club, which can exact a monopoly price for the transfer. The availability of such a license is speculative at best, however, for, as Moose Lodge itself concedes, without a liquor license a fraternal organization would be hard pressed to survive.

Thus, *the State* of Pennsylvania *is putting the weight of its liquor license,* concededly a valued and important adjunct to a private club, *behind racial discrimination.* (emphasis added)

Moose Lodge, it is fair to say, upheld the *principle* that discriminatory access to the state-created right to purchase alcohol was a violation of the Fourteenth Amendment's provision that "no state shall deny to any person the equal protection of laws." Its majority opinion simply did not see this principle as applicable to the practice at issue in the case.

Moose Lodge's ambiguity as a precedent was perhaps one of the reasons that Chief Justice Burger dissented from the ruling in *Craig*, and "was in general agreement with" Justice Rehnquist's dissenting opinion in the case. The dissenters disagreed with the finding of gender-based discrimination in the access to near beer, as well as with the holding that gender-based classifications had to survive more than just a rational-basis scrutiny to pass muster. Rehnquist—seemingly channeling Justice Field in *Crowley v. Christensen*—also observed this: "The Court does not discuss the nature of the right involved, and there is no reason to believe that it sees the purchase of 3.2% beer as implicating any important interest, let alone one that is 'fundamental' in the constitutional sense of invoking strict scrutiny. . . . The personal interest harmed here," he sourly concluded, "is very minor." This, from the man who that same year would (disingenuously) read into the *Constantineau* precedent a due process liberty interest in the state-created right to purchase liquor.

The changing fortunes of eighteen-year-old drinkers notwithstanding, what to do about drinking by juvenile-aged persons also became a judicial matter in the 1975 case of *Wood v. Strickland*. Arkansas high school students, expelled from school for violating a school regulation prohibiting the use or possession of intoxicating beverages at school or school activities, brought suit against school officials, claiming that the expulsions infringed their rights to due process of law. Absence of evidence was alleged, and a lower federal court weighed in on the matter—entailing that it parse whether the school rule forbade beverages containing in excess of a certain alcoholic content, or beverages containing any alcohol. This technicality arose because the students were charged for their "spiking" of the punch served at a meeting of an extracurricular school organization attended by parents and students. Heeding such details, a loving recitation of the facts of the dispute began the Burger Court's opinion in the case:

Respondents drove across the state border into Oklahoma and purchased two 12-ounce bottles of "Right Time," a malt liquor. They
then bought six 10-ounce bottles of a soft drink, and, after having
mixed the contents of the eight bottles in an empty milk carton,
returned to school. Prior to the meeting, the girls experienced second thoughts about the wisdom of their prank, but by then they were
caught up in the force of events and the intervention of other girls
prevented them from disposing of the illicit punch. The punch was
served at the meeting, without apparent effect.

A convoluted series of events then transpired, culminating in the expul-
sion.

In reviewing the federal claims, the court of appeals had interpreted
the school regulation prohibiting the use or possession of intoxicating
beverages as being linked to the definition of "intoxicating liquor"
under Arkansas statutes. This, in the Burger Court's eyes, was where
things went awry. "It is not the role of the federal courts," the Byron
White majority warned, "to set aside decisions of school administrators
which the court may view as lacking a basis in wisdom or compassion
[even though] public high school students do have substantive and procedural rights while at school." The Burger Court vacated and remanded the case without a dispositive answer to the due process question, but it did remark that federal civil rights laws did "not extend the
right to relitigate in federal court evidentiary questions arising in school
disciplinary proceedings or the proper construction of school regulations," and were "not intended to be a vehicle for federal court correction of errors in the exercise of school officials' discretion that do not
rise to the level of violations of specific constitutional guarantees."

A partial concurrence/partial dissent commanded four votes, including that of the chief. The somewhat inconclusive ruling in *Wood v.
Strickland* came in the wake of the path-breaking *Tinker v. Des Moines
Independent Community School District* decision of 1969. Over two
limiting concurrences and two dissents, that Fortas-led Warren Court
majority had upheld the First Amendment speech rights of a group of
minor school children who had worn black armbands to class in protest
of the Vietnam War and had been sent home by their school principal.
"It can hardly be argued," the *Tinker* majority opinion famously cried,
"that either students or teachers shed their constitutional rights . . . at
the schoolhouse gate." Yet *Tinker*'s "uncritical assumption," in the

words of concurring Justice Potter Stewart, that the constitutional rights of children are "coextensive with those of adults," found itself narrowed by the Burger Court in matters of school discipline involving alcohol.

Not too surprisingly, then, juveniles and the fairness of school alcohol policy were again at issue in the 1982 decision in *Board of Education of Rogers, Arkansas v. McCluskey*. A tenth-grade student suspended for being intoxicated on school grounds sought injunctive relief, alleging that the manner in which school board regulations were enforced denied him due process. Rejecting the claim, and smoothing out whatever unclarities remained after *Wood*, the per curiam court noted firmly that "federal courts are not authorized to construe school regulations"—on alcohol, discipline, or any other matter. Deference to the judgment and discretion of school officials was the Burger Court's approach, extricating itself from the morass of second judgment it associated with the *Tinker* holding. Yet dissenting justices Stevens, Brennan, and Marshall saw more afoot in the court's very taking of the *McCluskey* case. As Justice Stevens mused, "Today we exercise our majestic power to enforce a School Board's suspension of a 10th-grade student who consumed too much alcohol on October 21, 1980. If the student had been unjustly suspended, I wonder if the Court would consider the matter of sufficient national importance to require summary reversal. I doubt it." For the dissenters, the insignificant case was exhibit A in the Burger majority's campaign to willingly intervene to enforce a law-and-order mentality in society at large. A tipsy juvenile was simply the convenient vehicle.

As Brennan had intimated in his decisional synopsis in *Craig*, the Burger Court also presided over a decade-plus-long (1972–1986) series of cases about state regulation of nude dancing in establishments where alcohol was served. As with the cases about disciplining underage drinking, the chief concern for the court seemed to be social order. But it was not so much liquor's potential destabilizing force per se that prompted the Burger justices in these decisions about strip clubs as it was the convenient presence of the regulatory leeway that the Twenty-First Amendment gave to states: the heady conflict between the latter and the First Amendment freedom of expression in "dance" constituted a golden opportunity to rein in social and sexual licentiousness. The Burger Court thus drew upon the states' Twenty-First Amendment powers to affirm states' legitimate interest in maintaining public morals and the normative order—essentially convinced that "common sense indicates that any form of nudity coupled with alcohol in a public place begets undesirable behavior." This language was from one of the last rulings on the subject, *New York State Liquor Authority v. Bellanca* in 1981, in which the per curiam decision argued rather conclusively, "The State's [broad] power to ban the sale of alcoholic beverages entirely includes the lesser power to ban the sale of liquor on premises where topless dancing occurs." Earlier decisions, such as *California v. LaRue* (1972), had held that the broad powers of the states to regulate the sale of liquor, conferred by the Twenty-First Amendment, outweighed any First Amendment interest in nude dancing—which involves, the court reproved, "only the barest minimum of protected expression." (A pun was intended, surely.) *LaRue*'s reasoning, that a state could therefore ban such dancing as part of its liquor license control program,[28] motivated Justice Marshall to decry in dissent that "the framers of the [Twenty-First] Amendment would be astonished to discover that they had inadvertently enacted a *protanto repealer* of the rest of the Constitution." Hyperbole though this might have been, the Burger-led majorities in these cases were more than willing to see things from the states' perspectives. The reason for the multiple cases on the nude dancing and drinking topic was not any social conservative lack of conviction, but the Burger Court's own uncertain doctrine regarding obscenity—defining it ("I know it when I see it"), and thereby determining the outer limits of First Amendment protection for sexually explicit communications.

Despite this trend of permitting state regulation of alcohol-dispensing establishments, the Burger Court was less comfortable with state strangleholds on the operation of the broader liquor marketplace. Wading deeply into the technicalities of regulating the competitiveness of the alcohol market were the 1980 case *California Retail Liquor Dealers Assoc. v. Midcal Aluminum* and the 1982 case *Rice v. Norman Williams Co.* The first decision unanimously found California's wine-pricing system to constitute resale price maintenance in violation of the Sherman Act. The second decision upheld against the Sherman Act, Federal Alcohol Administration Act (which prohibits a distiller or wholesaler from establishing exclusive retail outlets), and due process challenges a provision of California's alcoholic beverage laws that stated that a "licensed importer shall not purchase or accept delivery of any brand of distilled spirits unless he is designated as an authorized importer of such brand by the brand owner or his authorized agent." The *Rice* case sustained and therefore maintained the franchise system that was part of states' three-tiered distribution system for alcohol. Yet the earlier *California Retail Liquor* case had *not* found that the Twenty-First Amendment protected the state's wine-pricing system, noting that "recent cases have emphasized federal interests to a greater degree than had earlier cases." The court's analysis in *California Retail* went further, too:

> There is no basis for disagreeing with the view of the California courts that the asserted state interests behind the re-sale price maintenance system of promoting temperance and protecting small retailers are less substantial than the national policy in favor of competition. Such view is reasonable and is supported by the evidence, there being nothing to indicate that the wine-pricing system helps sustain small retailers or inhibits the consumption of alcohol by Californians.

One of the justifications for the franchise or licensing system that states adopted subsequent to Prohibition was its furtherance of state goals like temperance. The two California cases of 1980 and 1982 suggested that the Burger Court would not automatically defer to states' characterization of the interests allegedly served by an alcohol regulation.

Nor did it. Subsequently, the court struck down in 1984 in *Bacchus Imports, Ltd. v. Dias* a Hawaii liquor excise sales tax that exempted indigenously produced products. Those included pineapple wine manufactured in the state and *okolehao*, a brandy distilled from the root of an indigenous shrub of the Hawaii islands. The state's unabashed purpose was to encourage the development of the Hawaiian liquor industry, which it argued posed no competitive threat to America's major distillers. The Hawaii Supreme Court had held that the tax did not illegally discriminate against interstate commerce because the 20 percent excise was on wholesalers, and the ultimate burden was borne by retail consumers in Hawaii. The 5–3 ruling made short shrift of the state's economic protectionism justification, chastising that "the central purpose of the [Twenty-First] Amendment was not to empower States to favor local liquor industry by erecting barriers to competition." The White-led majority went further. Implementing one of the balancing tests for which the Burger Court was notorious, the *Bacchus* majority argued that the constitutional test for the evaluation of state liquor regulations was that any regulation with discriminatory effects must be "supported by [a] clear concern of [the Twenty-First] Amendment in combating the evils of an unrestricted traffic in liquor." What were these clear or core concerns that went into the balance? "Promoting temperance" and "combatting the perceived evils of an unrestricted traffic in liquor" were mentioned but not elaborated upon in *Bacchus* as two possibilities.[29] The whole *Bacchus* exercise of constructing meaning for section 2 the Twenty-First Amendment was somewhat ironic, in that Justice White began his exposition by noting "the obscurity of [its] legislative history." If so, why was he so confident in the correctness of "recent Twenty-first Amendment cases emphasiz[ing] federal interests to a greater degree than had earlier cases"?

That confidence did not convince the three dissenting justices who, led by Justice Stevens, reminded that "only 11 days ago, we stated that a direct regulation on 'the sale or use of liquor' within a State's borders is the 'core sec. 2 power' conferred upon a State." Stevens was referring to *Capital Cities Cable v. Crisp*, a unanimous statement on behalf of federal power over state interests, albeit in a different alcohol regulation context. Stevens and his codissenters, future Chief Justice William Rehnquist and fellow states-rights stalwart Sandra Day O'Connor, distinguished the rulings by noting that difference in context—and by noting the *Capital Cities* decision's acknowledgment of it. In addition, in a final, further defense of state power over alcohol, Stevens's *Bacchus* dissent conjectured that,

> Hawaii may surely prohibit the importation of all intoxicating liquors. It seems clear to me that it may do so without prohibiting the local sale of liquors that are produced within the State. In other words, even though it seems unlikely that the okolehao lobby could persuade it to do so, the Hawaii Legislature surely has the power to create a local monopoly by prohibiting the sale of any other alcoholic beverage.

Potentially worrisome, surely, for prospective future tourists to the Pacific island paradise!

Lost in the verbiage of the Hawaii case was that the Burger justices were striking a new balance between a maximalist and a minimalist reading of state power under the Twenty-First Amendment. As the

Bacchus majority put it, the court was now engaged in a "pragmatic effort to harmonize state and federal powers" over liquor in American life and the American marketplace.

This jurisprudential trend toward such pragmatic balancing had been foreshadowed by *Larkin v. Grendl's Den,* an odd little case from 1982. "Circumstances," the court intoned there, did permit deference to local alcohol zoning ordinance—even though the specific alcohol ordinance under review in fact violated the establishment clause of the First Amendment. (It was a principle-practice ruling, not unlike what the Burger Court had done in *Moose Lodge.*) Chief Justice Burger's opinion for a 7–1 *Larkin* court employed his infamously intricate "*Lemon* test," outlined in his majority opinion for his court's seminal ruling on church–state separation (*Lemon v. Kurtzman*, 1971). In *Larkin,* Burger first recognized that the ordinance—which vested power in and permitted churches and schools to veto liquor licenses for nearby establishments—had a valid secular purpose, the first prong of the *Lemon* test. "Plainly schools and churches have a valid interest in being insulated from certain kinds of commercial establishments, including those dispensing liquor," Burger nattered reasonably. "Zoning laws have long been employed to this end, and there can be little doubt about the power of a state to regulate the environment in the vicinity of schools, churches, hospitals, and the like by exercise of reasonable zoning laws," he puffed more huffily.

But it was the delegation to private, religious entities "the repository of the State's power under the Twenty-first Amendment" that was the problem: it violated the second "primary effect of advancing religion" prong of the *Lemon* test. Dissenting Justice Rehnquist was unconvinced—moving him to utter that "silly cases make bad law," in a riff on Oliver Wendell Holmes's noted aphorism (that "hard cases make bad law," which Holmes uttered in a 1904 dissent regarding the application of the Sherman Anti-Trust Act to a securities company). Rehnquist's reasoning was simple: "a quite sensible Massachusetts liquor zoning law," he posited, had been converted by the court into "some sort of sinister religious attack on secular government reminiscent of St. Bartholomew's Night." Noting that houses of worship would have mostly secular, commonsense reasons for opposing a barroom as a next-door neighbor, he reserved for another time and a future case a situation in which a church was attempting to impermissibly impose a theological dogma involving alcohol through vetoing a liquor license. (Yet he was unable to resist commenting in a footnote, "I doubt whether there exists a denomination that considers supporting the liquor license applications of its members to be a part of its theology. However else a church's goal in objecting to issuance of a liquor license on such a basis might be characterized, it would certainly be strictly temporal.") Arguably, Rehnquist was understating the religious doctrine underpinning the prohibition movement, and the prohibition of the use of alcohol or "strong drink," generally.

No "core" concerns, temporal or otherwise, could be evoked to permit states to object to liquor ads carried on cable television channels, however; carriage of which was exclusively a federal regulatory matter. So said the aforementioned *Capital Cities Cable v. Crisp* of 1984. *Capital Cities* offered a (not so) crisp balancing test of its own, one that also found its way into the *Bacchus* majority opinion of the same term: the court would henceforth look for "whether the interests implicated by a state regulation are so closely related to the powers reserved by the Twenty-first Amendment that the regulation may prevail, notwithstanding that its requirements directly conflict with express federal policies."

This major federal preemption ruling came about because of Oklahoma's ban on the advertising of alcoholic beverages. Twenty-First Amendment considerations did not rescue the ban, but in true Burger Court ad hoc balancing fashion, "require a pragmatic effort to harmonize state and federal powers within the context of the issues and interests at stake." That judicial pragmatism was painstakingly rendered. "Here," the *Capital Cities* court continued,

> Oklahoma's interest in discouraging consumption of intoxicating liquor is limited, since the State's ban is directed only at occasional wine commercials appearing on out-of-state signals carried by cable operators, while the State permits advertisements for all alcoholic beverages carried in newspapers and other publications printed outside Oklahoma but sold in the State.

Oklahoma's own flabby inconsistency was its downfall. Not only that, its squeamishness with respect to demon rum was a rather minor matter in the grand scheme of things. "The State's interest," the unanimous court harrumphed, "is not of the same stature as the FCC's interest in ensuring widespread availability of diverse cable services throughout the United States."

The Burger Court's chronologically final alcohol-related decision nevertheless continued to struggle with the state's role in the regulation of the alcohol marketplace. In *Brown-Forman Distillers v. N.Y. State Liquor Authority* in 1986, a 5–3 court invalidated the state's liquor price controls as violating the commerce clause by directly regulating interstate commerce. Nor could the Twenty-First Amendment save the Alcohol Beverage Control Law, for "The Commerce Clause operates with full force whenever one State attempts to regulate the sale of alcoholic beverages in another State. Moreover, New York's affirmation provision may interfere with the ability of other States to exercise their own authority under the Twenty-first Amendment." *Brown-Forman* would be an important statement against local protectionism and a free market precedent to which the Burger Court's successor would return, again and again. Along with *Bacchus* and *Capital Cities,* it was a strong statement on behalf of national power and national economic interests from a supposedly pro "new federalism" court.

Arriving at the appropriate degree of regulation of liquor commerce was one thing. Major individual rights issues—such as the fundamental fairness of sentencing procedures in capital punishment cases—could also find themselves importantly inflected with alcohol-related concerns on the Burger Court docket. Such was the case in *Gardner v. Florida* in 1977. In an attempted mitigation of his death sentence, the petitioner testified that "he had consumed a vast quantity of alcohol during a day-long drinking spree which preceded the crime, and professed to have almost no recollection of the assault itself." His testimony, if credited, was "sufficient to support a finding of at least one of the statutory mitigating circumstances." Yet critical information in a presentencing investigation report, upon which the trial judge based his capital sentence, had not been made available to defense counsel; on the basis of this, the plurality judgment invalidated the sentence on due process considerations. The chief concurred in the judgment without opinion. The anticlimactic nature of the *Gardner* ruling should not disguise the importance of the issue it raised: whether being drunk diminished responsibility for one's actions, including heinous actions. No definitive resolution meant that the issue ultimately passed to the Burger Court's successors: it would be almost twenty years before the Supreme Court under Chief Justice Rehnquist would address a similar question before again arriving at only a plurality in judgment (see *Montana v. Egelhoff* in 1996).

In criminal law more generally, the technology of detecting and the procedures for policing drunk driving produced a host of constitutional questions to answer. (Or, alternatively, produced the same constitutional question to be answered again and again, in a host of successive cases.) The subtext for all of them was just how heinous a crime drunk driving was, and the verdict on *this* question definitely hardened as time went on. Even in 1979, with the Burger Court's first such case, the justices recognized and affirmed the acute safety hazard posed by drunk drivers. *Mackey v. Montrym* became something of a foregone conclusion after that, with the court rejecting a due process challenge to the state's hearing procedures for arrested drivers who refused a breath-analysis test. The 5–4 majority found "the compelling interest in highway safety" to justify Massachusetts in making a summary suspension effective, pending the outcome of the available and prompt postsuspension hearing. That interest was substantially served by the summary suspension for several reasons:

1. it acts as a deterrent to drunk driving;
2. it provides an inducement to take the breath-analysis test, permitting the state to obtain a reliable form of evidence for use in subsequent criminal proceedings; and
3. it "summarily removes from the road licensees arrested for drunk driving who refuse to take the test."

The four dissenters, led by Potter Stewart, saw the matter differently. "The question in this case, simply put," he began,

> is whether a person who is subject to losing his driver's license for three months as a penalty for allegedly refusing a demand to take a breath-analysis test is constitutionally entitled to some sort of hearing before his license is taken away. . . . The suspension penalty itself is concededly imposed not as an emergency measure to remove unsafe drivers from the roads, but as a sanction to induce drivers to submit to breath-analysis tests. In short, *the critical fact that triggers the suspension is noncooperation with the police*, not drunken driving. (emphasis added)

The law-and-order mentality for which Burger's Court would become known overrode this civil libertarian concern. And even Justice Stewart seemed a bit sheepish about expressing it, closing his dissent as he did with the words: "I do not mean to minimize the importance of breath-analysis testing as part of a state effort to identify, prosecute, and rehabilitate the alcohol-ridden motorist."

With the creation of MADD in 1980 and on the cusp of other societal changes with respect to attitudes toward driving under the influence, the Burger Court more aggressively and consistently shaped the law in a punitive fashion. Refusal to submit to blood alcohol testing upon being detained for suspected drunk driving, and the evidentiary consequences of such refusal, were examined in the 1983 case of *South Dakota v. Neville*. The Burger Court reaffirmed what the Warren Court had intimated back in 1966 in *Schmerber*: that no privilege against self-incrimination is violated by such evidence being admitted at trial, nor is due process violated by such refusal being considered putative evidence of guilt. The newfangled "Intoxilyzer" or breath-analysis test to register a blood-alcohol concentration was at the center of a due process challenge in *California v. Trombetta* in 1984, and the court rejected the notion that preservation of defendant breath samples was necessary for the opportunity to impeach the incriminating test results. "The evidence," the unanimous opinion reasoned, "must possess an exculpatory value that was apparent before it was destroyed, and must also be of such a nature that the defendant would be unable to obtain comparable evidence by other reasonably available means. Neither of these conditions was met on the facts of this case."[30] What is most interesting about the *Trombetta* opinion, historically speaking, is the scrupulous attention it paid to describing "The Omicron Intoxilyzer (Intoxilyzer) . . . a device used in California to measure the concentration of alcohol in the blood of motorists suspected of driving while under the influence of intoxicating liquor."

The colorful facts and constitutional challenges of the drunk driving arrest in *Welsh v. Wisconsin* in 1984 proved more troublesome and sharply divided the deciding justices. Those facts and challenges are worthy to reproduce in the full case headnote:

> On the night of April 24, 1978, a witness observed a car that was being driven erratically and that eventually swerved off the road,

coming to a stop in a field without causing damage to any person or property. Ignoring the witness' suggestion that he wait for assistance in removing his car, the driver walked away from the scene. The police arrived a few minutes later and were told by the witness that the driver was either very inebriated or very sick. After checking the car's registration, the police, without obtaining a warrant, proceeded to the petitioner's nearby home, arriving at about 9 p. m. They gained entry when petitioner's stepdaughter answered the door, and found petitioner lying naked in bed. Petitioner was then arrested for driving a motor vehicle while under the influence of an intoxicant in violation of a Wisconsin statute which provided that a first offense was a noncriminal violation subject to a civil forfeiture proceeding for a maximum fine of $200. Petitioner was taken to the police station, where he refused to submit to a breath-analysis test. Pursuant to Wisconsin statutes, which subjected an arrestee who refused to take the test to the risk of a 60-day revocation of driving privileges, petitioner requested a court hearing to determine whether his refusal was reasonable. Under Wisconsin law, a refusal to take a breath test was reasonable if the underlying arrest was not lawful. The trial court, ultimately concluding that petitioner's arrest was lawful and that his refusal to take the breath test was therefore unreasonable, issued an order suspending petitioner's license. The Wisconsin Court of Appeals vacated the order, concluding that the warrantless arrest of petitioner in his home violated the Fourth Amendment because the State, although demonstrating probable cause to arrest, had not established the existence of exigent circumstances. The Wisconsin Supreme Court reversed.

Held:

The warrantless, nighttime entry of petitioner's home to arrest him for a civil, non-jailable traffic offense, was prohibited by the special protection afforded the individual in his home by the Fourth Amendment.

The Brennan-led majority had this final, somewhat tart verdict on the whole affair:

Petitioner's warrantless arrest in the privacy of his own bedroom for a noncriminal traffic offense cannot be justified on the basis of the "hot pursuit" doctrine, because there was no immediate or continuous pursuit of the petitioner from the scene of a crime, or on the basis of a threat to public safety, because petitioner had already arrived home and had abandoned his car at the scene of the accident.

Arrived home and passed out, to be more precise.

Burger found *Welsh* an inapposite vehicle for constitutional law making, noting only this in his separate statement: "THE CHIEF JUS-TICE would dismiss the writ as having been improvidently granted and defer resolution of the question presented to a more appropriate case." But a concurring Justice Blackmun had this more substantive, sermon-like statement to make:

> I join the Court's opinion but add a personal observation.
>
> I yield to no one in my profound personal concern about the unwillingness of our national consciousness to face up to—and to do something about—the continuing slaughter upon our Nation's high-ways, a good percentage of which is due to drivers who are drunk or semi-incapacitated because of alcohol or drug ingestion.
>
> And it is amazing to me that one of our great States—one which, by its highway signs, proclaims to be diligent and emphatic in its prosecution of the drunken driver—still classifies driving while intox-icated as a civil violation that allows only a money forfeiture of not more than $300 so long as it is a first offense. The State, like the indulgent parent, hesitates to discipline the spoiled child very much, even though the child is engaging in an act that is dangerous to others who are law abiding and helpless in the face of the child's act. Our personal convenience still weighs heavily in the balance, and the highway deaths and injuries continue. But if Wisconsin and other States choose by legislation thus to regulate their penalty structure, there is, unfortunately, nothing in the United States Constitution that says they may not do so.

Blackmun's moral harangue seemed very much a sign of the times, the clearly changing times with respect to the casual use of alcohol in American life.

Corroboration of such can be found in this comment from the other-wise unrelated freedom of speech decision in *City Council v. Taxpayers for Vincent*, also in 1984 and authored by Justice Stevens:

> For example, even though political speech is entitled to the fullest possible measure of constitutional protection, there are a host of

other communications that command the same respect. An assertion that "Jesus Saves," that "Abortion Is Murder," that every woman has the "Right to Choose," or that *"Alcohol Kills"* may have a claim to a constitutional exemption from the [billboard] ordinance that is just as strong as "Roland Vincent–City Council." (emphasis added)

Stevens's throwaway analogy reveals that, for him and his colleagues, the content of the antialcohol message was obviously on a par with the words of democratic debate, in terms of First Amendment validity and importance.

Judicial disapprobation of drunken driving mirrored ever more serious social disapprobation. But in the judicial context, that sentiment had to be balanced against constitutional values, as Blackmun was very much conceding in *Welsh*. One such value was the Fifth Amendment protection against compelled self-incrimination, and the "*Miranda* warnings" that the Warren Court had established to guarantee it (*Miranda v. Arizona*, 1966). It was likely personally distasteful to the Burger justices that impaired driving and an ensuing misdemeanor arrest was the occasion for an extension of *Miranda* guarantees in the 1984 case of *Berkemer v. McCarty*. The court held that a person subjected to custodial interrogation is entitled to the benefit of the procedural safeguards enunciated in *Miranda*, regardless of the nature or severity of the offense of which he is suspected or for which he is arrested.[31] Civil liberties protection notwithstanding, it is the facts that gave rise to the dispute that really pique a somewhat morbid interest:

> After observing respondent's car weaving in and out of a highway lane, an officer of the Ohio State Highway Patrol forced respondent to stop and asked him to get out of the car. Upon noticing that respondent was having difficulty standing, the officer concluded that respondent would be charged with a traffic offense and would not be allowed to leave the scene, but respondent was not told that he would be taken into custody. When respondent could not perform a field sobriety test without falling, the officer asked him if he had been using intoxicants, and he replied that he had consumed two beers and had smoked marijuana a short time before. The officer then formally arrested respondent and drove him to a county jail, where a blood test failed to detect any alcohol in respondent's blood. Questioning was then resumed, and respondent again made incrimi-

nating statements, including an admission that he was "barely" under the influence of alcohol.

Such an egregious display of impairment was, unfortunately, not unique to the *Berkemer* case.

Los Angeles v. Heller in 1986 concerned another extreme case of DWI (the nomenclature generally used in state laws in cases from this period). The arrest was the context for a per curiam statement by the Burger Court about probable cause, the excessive force used by arresting officers, and jury instructions to ascertain the officers' liability for damages resulting from such. But again, it was the facts that produced the dispute—positively picaresque facts—that command attention, and indicate that the Supreme Court is often treated to the worst examples of alcohol's place in American life:

> The officers administered a series of field sobriety tests. Apparently dissatisfied with the results, the officers decided to take Heller to the station to undergo a breath test. When notified that he was under arrest, however, Heller became belligerent. One of the defendants, Officer Bushey, attempted to handcuff him. An altercation ensued. In the course of the struggle, Heller fell through a plate glass window.

One can visualize.

Alcohol in American life and law had long colored relations between the United States government and Native Americans. Alcohol in Indian law had been a topic absent from the Supreme Court docket for many years before the Burger Court rendered a pair of new decisions. In *U.S. v. Mazurie* in 1975, it approved congressional delegation of control over alcohol on reservation (delegating, specifically, the federal power to regulate commerce [in alcohol] with the Indian tribes) to tribes and tribal governments—even when the "Indian" land was held in fee by non-Indians and the persons regulated were non-Indians: in this instance, the bar owner seeking a liquor license for an establishment (The Blue Bull) on the outskirts of an unincorporated village within the reservation. Later, in 1983, and informed by "historical notions" and "tradition," the Burger Court allowed states to tax liquor (in the form of requiring a state license to sell liquor) on reservation lands. *Rice v. Rehner* (1983), it is true, upheld a tradition of concurrent state and federal jurisdiction over the use and distribution of alcoholic beverages in Indian country. But the decision also contained this patronizingly dismissive statement from Justice O'Connor, its author: "There is no tradition of tribal sovereign immunity or inherent self-government in favor of liquor regulation by Indians." Justice Blackmun had this retort to it, in dissent:

> It is hardly surprising, given the once-prevalent view of Indians as a dependent people in need of constant federal protection and supervision, that tribal authority until recent times has not extended to areas such as education, cigarette retailing, and development of resorts. . . . And "[c]ontrol of liquor has historically been one of the most comprehensive federal activities in Indian affairs."

The self-government principle ostensibly endorsed in *Mazurie* was snatched back in *Rice*, seemingly in the interest of protecting state revenue from alcohol sales.

If one compares *Rice* to *Mississippi Tax Commission* and its less states-friendly view of the federal–state division of authority over alcohol, one might well ask whether the Burger Court was consistent with respect to its theory of federalism, in the Indian liquor law versus the state ABC tax cases. A similar question might be raised about its relative (lack of) solicitude for state interests in the commerce clause and state economic protectionism rulings on the alcohol marketplace. In the area of Indian law and alcohol, state regulatory interests were supported by the Burger justices—though perhaps not as strongly as the justices supported a state's interest in restricting drinking in strip clubs. But, of course, no competing, federal power claim buttressed the freedom interests of a nudie club's owners, employees, and customers. Yet no very potent federal claim, it also seemed, really reinforced the Indian nations' autonomy with respect to decisions about alcohol taxation policies on Indian land.

Perhaps consistency of this kind, a consistent judicial vision of federalism, is too much to ask for. Perhaps the Burger Court is best thought of as an internally divided and transitional court, struggling to articulate a coherent constitutional vision. Assessing the Burger years has spawned a cottage industry of inquiry into whether it indeed was the counterrevolution that began the march toward our modern-day judicial conservatism, or whether it wasn't at all. With respect to alcohol and the law, the Burger era was a messy pottage of moralism and free market messaging. Yet it seems a much more modern era of alcohol, the Constitution, and the court than the Warren period only a few years before it. Perhaps that is because its judgments, and judgmentalisms, resemble our own. We like (to) drink, but not the drinker. The Burger Court was the same, and that curious combination of guilt and pleasure in all things alcohol that so marks today's America finds its most direct precedents in that court's decisions—decisions that laid the constitutional groundwork for better quality drinking, for sure, as well as better policing of drinking's disruptive effects.

CONCLUSION

The Burger era rivals and arguably surpasses the Fuller era in the volume, variety, and doctrinal complexity of its alcohol-related docket of cases. In adjudicating the balance between individuals' rights and the power of states to control where alcohol is used and sold, the Burger Court displayed the same jurisprudential qualities it demonstrated overall: the construction of multifactor balancing tests that produced somewhat inconsistent but generally moderate rulings. The Burger era also marks the ascent of the cult of moderation in drinking—although the full force of this mentality would not be felt for at least a decade.

13

THE REHNQUIST ERA OF NEOTEMPERANCE

The Rehnquist Court (1986–2005) was a time of heightened alcohol-related litigation and some very prominent alcohol-oriented decisions in constitutional law. The roughly twenty-year period has also been called, by several commentators, an era of "neotemperance," booze-wise. "Neo" denotes a return—of sorts—to an altered but still recognizable form of an established viewpoint or practice. By the time of the Rehnquist era, for instance, one could speak without irony about *neo*conservatives, or simply "neocons" for short.[1] These were the former progressives and left intellectuals who had bandwagoned onto the "Reagan Revolution," that New Right movement for social and fiscal conservatism that came to national political preeminence beginning with the election of Republican president Ronald Reagan.

"Neo" seldom demarcates the renewed adoption of an unchanged or cryogenically preserved viewpoint, for the simple reason that ideologies always exist in a historical context and ideas grow and change with time. Thus, Reagan's and the Bushes' neoconservatives were, strictly speaking, not very "conserving" at all. Likewise, "temperance" had originally referred to a *tempered* or moderate consumption of alcohol; only later in the movement's lifespan did it signify a complete abstinence and prohibition position. Post-Repeal of Prohibition, late twentieth-century temperance is a bit fuzzy in its contours but no less judgmental in its attitude than earlier versions.

The "neo"temperance of the Rehnquist era coexisted rather awkwardly with an appreciable emphasis on restoring the enjoyment of good quality beer, wine, and spirits—after the relative dearth of taste that defined 1970s and early 1980s drinking, Chief Justice Burger's German wine cellar notwithstanding. That said, William Rehnquist, elevated from associate to chief by the aforementioned Republican President Reagan, was a noted beer drinker who favored "Miller's Light," as he called it. He was famous also for his one beer, one cigarette every day at lunch for much of his long Supreme Court service. A former Burger law clerk from the early 1980s remembered Rehnquist lunching with the court clerks at the Capitol Hill Hawk 'n' Dove over a cheeseburger and a draft beer.[2] Two clerks from the late 1990s confirmed the meal and occasion (a cheeseburger lunch) but at a different location (the Monocle, also on Capitol Hill), and included a cigarette smoked afterward.[3] The smoking aside, Chief Justice Rehnquist was in good company: beer has been the dominant alcoholic beverage in the United States since the late 1970s, when distilled spirits peaked, then declined. Also significant—and originally introduced by the beer brewers industry—was the "drink responsibly" alcohol advertising campaign that distinguished Rehnquist's era of alcohol in American life. Thus, **light beer**, that relatively innocuous, low-calorie innovation of the diet-conscious "Me decade," deserves pride of place as the iconic alcoholic beverage of the Rehnquist era.

Still, light beer is not much of a "drink," per se. Fortunately, there is a potential honorable mention and truly classic cocktail for the Rehnquist period: the **Margarita**. Not only was it a recreational drinking staple across the decades of the 1980s and 1990s, its Mexican provenance also honors native-Arizonan Justice Sandra Day O'Connor, herself also a Reagan appointee (in 1981), and the first woman on the High Bench. Buried among the files of the Harry S. Blackmun Papers, the judicial papers of the late associate justice and member of the Burger and Rehnquist Courts (through 1994), is a 1992 party invitation from John and Sandra O'Connor for a barbeque gathering at their home. Her use of a formal, officious invitation card to advertise the gathering for "Fajitas and Frivolity" was charmingly irreverent—and promised a lively and, possibly, well-lubricated time.[4] The agave-based spirit tequila (originating in the Mexican state of Jalisco) and its principal delivery system the "marg" had risen to popular prominence by the early years of the Rehnquist period, which O'Connor's Southwestern party theme indirectly confirms. The margarita also became, like the martini, a vessel for such infinite variation in ingredients and preparation (strawberry, watermelon, or Midori, fancied up with Grand Marnier, salt-rimmed, no salt, "top shelf," frozen) as to depart from the classic in all but name (and signature stepped-diameter glass).[5]

The margarita, of course, had a long history, dating back to its roots in the Daisy, a late nineteenth/early twentieth-century cocktail that used gin, lemon juice, and the bar syrup grenadine as a sweetener. *Imbibe!* gives an interesting account of the drink before mentioning that it was likely the antecedent of the margarita, with tequila, lime juice, and triple sec (or other orange liqueur) substituted in.[6] "Margarita" means "daisy" in Spanish; Mexico, and other points South of the Border, became favorite drinking destinations during the years of Prohibition, and Americans' favorite cocktails migrated along with them to

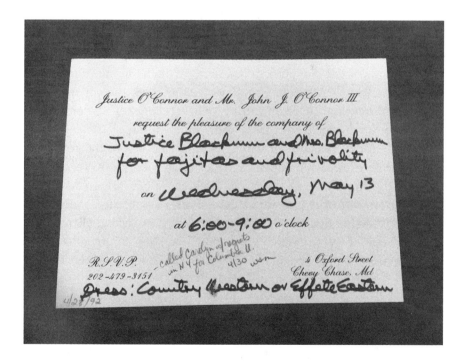

Figure 13.1. Justice Sandra Day O'Connor's May 1992 party invitation card, promising "Fajitas and Frivolity." *Source: Harry S. Blackmun Papers, Box 1406, folder 10; Library of Congress*

those Latin American cantinas. Relatedly, but contrastingly, some cock-tail historians alternatively locate the roots of today's margarita in a 1920s–1930s period adaptation of the Parisian-born, Prohibition-era Sidecar cocktail to Mexican ingredients.[7] Whatever its story and many variations in preparation, one imagines that O'Connor served the classic on-the-rocks, "old school" version at her fete.

The margarita—frozen and otherwise—was not the only "fun" cock-tail that regained a foothold with American drinkers during the Rehn-quist era. Its close cousin, the frozen blender machine daiquiri, was a friendly competitor on many a TGIF drink list from the early 1980s onward. The simple and elegant daiquiri, a midcentury classic, gained with its slushy-machine preparation a myriad of flavor options (some synthetic) and food coloring shades (always synthetic). Purveyors known as "daiquiri shops" could even be counted on to offer a "frozen-daiquiri 'margarita'"—attesting, at the very least, to the widespread popularity of both drinks. The rainbow hues of these frosty beverages were equaled only by the 1990s later but no-less-ubiquitous mixology contribution, the radiantly pink *Cosmopolitan*. Vodka based and cranberry juice suf-fused, the "cosmo" rode the popularity wave of the contemporaneous introduction of various variants of flavored "martinis," served straight up and jumbo sized. Supposedly invented by the bartender/manager at "fern bar" Henry's Africa in San Francisco in 1988, the cosmopolitan went on to become the "ladies drink" par excellence of the *Sex in the City* set of fin de siècle XX Manhattan and its aspirant locales. It came to define an era: not only of women's imbibing, but of the revival of mixed drinks over wine and beer in American alcoholic beverage tastes. Yet like the sweetly easygoing Bronx cocktail before it, the cosmopoli-tan soon crossed over into vapid mass-market popularity—becoming, by the post-Rehnquist period, a somewhat gauche cocktail cliché. Still, in its heyday, its go-to availability—combined with its precious jewel-like glow—emblematized the go-go economic boom of Ronald Rea-gan's no-less-rosy Morning in America.

The Reagan Revolution effected many changes in American politics and policy—most especially, an anti–big government crusade and cele-bration of the virtues of tax cuts, deregulation, and the free market. Although the Reagan period is synonymous with the greed-fueled, con-spicuous consumption, and Courvoisier-quaffing period of the stock market boom in the 1980s, its remaking of the America state also coincided with a distinctly "Godly" sort of politics: that being the emergence of the Christian Right as a social force in American life and public policy. Folded into the Reagan agenda and Reagan-Bush electoral coalition, its social force was expended on moral disapproval and legal action against many things that threatened "family values"—among them, boozing it up. Hence the inspiration for this chapter's title, reiterating others' explicit branding of the 1990s to 2000s as "the new temperance movement."[8] Yet clearly, in spite of the changing tenor of the times regarding alcohol use over the course of the Rehnquist era, socializing with alcohol did continue on the modern Supreme Court—as both the chief's daily draft beers and O'Connor's festive fiesta clearly establish. (To say nothing of all those cosmos being quaffed after hours.)

One of the social drinking traditions on the court was a formal welcoming cocktail party for new clerks. But clerks in the increasingly ideologically polarized Rehnquist era did not find it to be much of an icebreaker between clerks and justices, for "the clerks from each Chambers tended to congregate among themselves, diplomats from nine separate nation-states, wine cups in hand, appraising their counterparts around the chandeliered room."[9] The détente was uneasy, and opportunities for jollity were vanishingly scarce. As time went on, and the distance between the political and legal visions of the American Right and Left increased, so did the voting distance between the court's right and left blocs of justices and the personal distance between their clerks. Even liquor could not bridge the gap.

The reportedly tense nature of Rehnquist-era court cocktail parties had little to do with the chief justice himself. Indeed, court insiders report several amusing anecdotes about Rehnquist's own personal unstuffiness and sense of humor. He once approved a ribald and irreverent skit for the 1976 court Christmas party, performed by his clerks and satirizing the politics of President Ford's appointing of a successor to Douglas,[10] and presented himself to the Burger conference another day in a way that defied tradition: attending "in a court softball team t-shirt. He also did little to dispel the impression that he was drinking straight Scotch or bourbon at his desk, even though the amber liquid in the glass was really his favorite beverage, apple juice."[11] During his long tenure on the bench (1972–2005), Rehnquist was known for orchestrating the annual Christmas party and organizing the incoming "party for law clerks" each fall. Punch spiked with vodka was served at the former;

sherry among other libations had also been ordered for one of these, in 1976, of which there were a few bottles left over that later went into the mix. [12] So despite his associate justice reputation as a staunch conservative and the "Lone Ranger" author of uncompromising solo dissents, Rehnquist was a fun-loving fellow and, more important, a well-liked and fair-minded chief justice who generally fostered a convivial atmosphere among his colleagues on his court. Not *so* convivial that his other favorite beverage, "Miller's Lite," was downed in the Rehnquist chambers (or secreted in his desk drawer, a la Justice Douglas)—that would have been beyond the pale for his court era and time period. But his own personal habits and behaviors generally suggest a healthy work-life balance: "Miller Time" in moderation. [13]

Some of his court's docket concerned beer as well. The most significant such case was *South Dakota v. Dole* in 1987, which permitted the federal government to condition states' receipt of federal highway funds on their compliance with a national minimum drinking age of twenty-one for all alcoholic beverages. South Dakota was permitting nineteen-year-olds to buy low-alcohol or "near beer," in defiance of the federal mandate of the National Minimum Drinking Age Act of 1984. Near beer, of course, had figured in the annals of constitutional law before: in the Burger era decision in *Craig v. Boren* (1976), which invalidated a gender-based scheme for regulating sales of low-alcohol 3.2 percent beer. With the passage of the NMDA act, most states fell in line to reduce highway fatalities caused by young drinkers driving, and driving across state lines to obtain legal alcohol. Some states, like Louisiana (home to that 24-hour party city, New Orleans) tried not-so-subtle subterfuges to keep its liquor sales revenue up, such as the presence of adult "guardians" to legitimize and legalize underage drinking—fine in principle but positively ludicrous when interpreted to mean that one twenty-one-year-old collegian "accompanied" a barroom full of eighteen-year-olds downing Jaeger shots. *Dole* tested the principle, less ridiculously, of whether constitutional federalism allowed states to deviate from the federal government's moral message and social policy on alcohol. Chief Justice Rehnquist led the seven-justice majority that held that indirect encouragement of state action, to obtain uniformity in the states' drinking ages, was a valid use of the congressional spending power.

Some might well wonder how the erstwhile "new federalism" advocate from the Burger years could so readily support national muscle as against states' rights and putative reserved powers. It is well known that chief justices sometimes moderate their personal, judicial views in the interest of making majorities and speaking for the institution of the court. Rehnquist's position in *Dole* might also have reflected his basic agreement with the similarly flexible viewpoint expressed by his appointing president, on the latter's policy of a uniform federal MDA of twenty-one:

> Now, some might feel that my decision is at odds with my philosophical viewpoint that state problems should involve state solutions and it isn't up to a big and overwhelming government in Washington to tell the states what to do. And you're partly right. But the thing is, this problem is much more than a state problem. It's a national tragedy. . . . And in a case like this, . . . I have no misgivings about a judicious use of federal inducements to encourage the states to . . . save precious lives. [14]

Ronald Reagan himself was a deliberately austere drinker, having been profoundly and negatively impacted by the rampant alcoholism of his father. First Lady Nancy, too, was notorious for her own "Just Say No" antidrug campaign—its rhetorical harshness but dubious efficacy proving, once again, that prohibitionism dies a hard death in the U.S. mindset.

Decidedly not decided in *Dole* was the question of whether Congress might in fact lack the power to directly impose a national minimum drinking age. There was that pesky problem of the Twenty-First Amendment—"the bounds of which have escaped precise definition," Rehnquist noted almost breezily. Dissenting justices William Brennan and Sandra Day O'Connor were less sure that the amendment was not an "independent constitutional bar." Justice O'Connor's extensive dissenting opinion summed itself up with the conclusion that Congress lacked the power, under the commerce clause or any other constitutional provision, to "displace" state regulation of this kind. "The regulation of the age of the purchasers of liquor," she urged, "just as the regulation of the price at which liquor may be sold, falls squarely within the scope of those powers reserved to the States by the Twenty-first Amendment."

When it came to selling suds to legal adults, the Rehnquist Court was more solicitous of the free and open opportunity to crack a cold one. And it did so by squarely maintaining a minimalist reading of the Twenty-First Amendment in the commercial context. *Healy v. The Beer Institute* in 1989 invalidated a Connecticut beer price affirmation statute as violating the commerce clause because of its impermissible practical effect of controlling commercial activity wholly outside the state. The statute required out-of-state shippers to take account of their Connecticut prices in setting border-state prices, restricting their ability to offer promotional and volume discounts in the border states and thereby depriving them of whatever competitive advantages they might possess based on the local market conditions in those states. A majority took exception to such hamstringing of the regional beer market. The court's opinion reaffirmed that the Twenty-First Amendment does not immunize state laws from commerce clause attack where their practical effect is to regulate liquor sales in other states—following almost to the letter the late Burger Court ruling in *Brown-Forman Distillers v. N. Y. Liquor Authority* (1986). This time, Chief Justice Rehnquist dissented, along with Stevens and O'Connor—just as he had also dissented in *Brown-Forman* as an associate justice. Observing with vexation in *Healy* that there were no in-state brewers and so no local industry was being impermissibly protected, the chief justice complained that "even the most restrictive view of the Twenty-first Amendment should validate Connecticut's efforts to obtain from interstate brewers prices for its beer drinkers which are as favorable as the prices which those brewers charge in neighboring States."

Who exactly benefited from the Connecticut law seemed very much in question in *Healy*. But beer drinkers had more to unambiguously cheer in *Rubin v. Coors Brewing Co.* (1995), where the Rehnquist Court invalidated a federal ban on beer labels indicating the brew's alcohol percentage, deeming it a violation of the First Amendment protection of commercial, informational speech. The government's claim to power under the Federal Alcohol Administration Act, and its claimed interest in preventing a "strength war" between beer brewers, were both substantial, said the Clarence Thomas opinion for eight justices and one concurring justice. Yet all agreed that the regulation itself was too extensive and did not directly advance the state interest or objective, especially when beer strength was a legitimate and accepted part of beer advertisements, and when the permitted labeling of a product as "malt liquor" clearly went after the strength market. With the decision in *Rubin,* beer drinkers would henceforth know exactly how much alcohol was in their drink of choice—whether they chose it on this basis or not.

The Rehnquist Court's alcohol docket extended well beyond the chief justice's favorite brew. Yet compared to the bloated docket of its predecessor the Burger Court, the Rehnquist Court's was relatively streamlined. Rehnquist as chief began the process of shrinking the Supreme Court's overall docket of cases accepted for full review and decision. So in addition to a reduction in the total number of cases decided each term, from a Burger era high of about 150 to a Rehnquist era average well under 100, the Rehnquist justices heard fewer factual variations on different constitutional questions. [15] They waited, in other words, for issues to sharpen and legal conflicts in courts below to mature before electing to decide legal questions. Instead of hearing myriad cases on nude dancing and service of alcohol, or on blood-alcohol testing parameters in drunk driving incidents, then, Rehnquist's Court heard fewer cases, but provided more conclusive rulings.

Those more conclusive rulings suggest a greater sense of policy focus when it came to alcohol in American life. A 1988 statutory decision is an interesting window into the judicial mind-set of the early Rehnquist era, and the alcohol-related constitutional decisions that occurred during it. *Traynor v. Turnage* concerned the validity of extending Veterans Administration disability benefits. The case was the occasion for the Rehnquist Court to rule that disabling alcoholism was properly understood as "the result of [a person's] own willful misconduct," and so, was not a disorder that merited extension of the statutory benefits eligibility period. Primary alcoholism, that is, excessive drinking not attributable to an underlying psychiatric disorder, was, in other words, a "willfully caused handicap." Alcoholics were not, then, equivalent to persons with disabilities, against whom VA benefits' extension could not discriminate. Still the opinion cautiously concluded this: "This litigation does not require the Court to decide whether alcoholism is a disease whose course its victims cannot control. It is not our role to resolve this medical issue on which the authorities remain sharply divided. Our task is to decide [what] Congress intended."

A narrowly textualist form of statutory construction and a formalist default to legislative intent prevailed in this judicial disquisition on alcohol and its freely willed use and abuse. The Rehnquist Court's generally conservative constitutionalism—the original-meaning-of-the-words approach to interpreting the Constitution that animated its Republican-appointed justices—dovetailed with many of its decisions' somewhat hard-heartedly judgmental view of drinking in American life.

This attitude seemed to be in evidence from Rehnquist's very first term as chief, with the decision in *Newport v. Iacobucci* in 1986. The case was a continuation of the Burger Court's immersion in the nude dancing and service of alcohol question. A per curiam opinion found that the state's broad regulatory authority, conferred by the Twenty-First Amendment in the context of liquor licensing, indisputably included the power to *ban* nude dancing in bars and outweighed any First Amendment interest *in* nude dancing. Even if, under the Kentucky Constitution, a city could not ban the sale of alcohol without approval by local election, it did not follow that a city could not go ahead and legislate against nude dancing in venues where alcohol was sold. Generally, the Rehnquist Court stated, states may delegate their power under the Twenty-First Amendment as they see fit. Justice Stevens had a different reading of what was going on, saying this in his *Iacobucci* dissent:

> In recent years, the Court has completely distorted the Twenty-first Amendment. It now has a barely discernible effect in Commerce Clause cases, see, *e. g., Brown-Forman Distillers Corp v. New York State Liquor Authority*, (1986); *Bacchus Imports, Ltd. v. Dias*, (1984), but, under *Bellanca* and the Court's decision today, it may be dispositive in First Amendment cases. This paradox cannot be overstated: reading *Bellanca* one would have thought that the Court was prepared to recognize some bite in the Twenty-first Amendment. The intervening decisions in *Brown-Forman* and *Bacchus* demonstrate, however, that it is toothless except when freedom of speech is involved.

"The Court is quite wrong," Stevens concluded with a flourish, "in proceeding as if the Twenty-first Amendment repealed not only the Eighteenth Amendment, but some undefined portion of the First Amendment as well."

Stevens was making an important and, what would turn out to be, a very prescient point. He was arguing that the Supreme Court's vindication of regulated drinking was misplaced: strong only where it cabined personal lifestyle liberties, but tepid where it interfered with commercial liberties.

Complications with the latter kind of Twenty-First Amendment latitudinarianism arose later that same term, in the New York liquor pricing case of *324 Liquor Corp. v. Duffy* in 1987. *Duffy* set the tone for the beer case of *Healy* and, indeed, for the rest of the Rehnquist era decisions on the free market of alcohol. The New York scheme was invalidated under a Sherman antitrust challenge and rejected as a valid exercise of a state's Twenty-First Amendment power. The majority noted— over the objection of the new chief justice in dissent—that although § 2 of the amendment qualifies the federal commerce power, the amendment does not operate to "repeal" the Commerce Clause wherever state regulation of intoxicating liquors is concerned. The question in each case, the majority continued, is "whether the interests implicated by a state regulation are so closely related to the powers preserved by the Twenty-First Amendment that the regulation may prevail, notwithstanding that its requirements directly conflict with express federal policies." The decision closed with this observation on the alleged "interests"—such as incentivizing temperate use of alcohol—"closely related" to state powers under the amendment:

> It is not necessary to consider whether New York's pricing system can be upheld as an exercise of the State's power to promote temperance. The [NY] Court of Appeals did not find that the statute was intended to promote temperance, or that it does so. This Court accords great weight to the views of the State's highest court on state law matters, and customarily accepts the factual findings of state courts in the absence of exceptional circumstances.

"No such exceptional circumstances appear in this case," *Duffy* concluded. In other words, game on, 324 Liquor, and the offering of liquor price reductions at retail.[16]

Duffy's dissenters—the lonely voices of O'Connor and Rehnquist— stressed that the point was not whether New York's ABC law was "'effective' in preserving small retail establishments or in decreasing alcohol consumption"; the point was whether the state had the authority to make that policy choice—"exceptional circumstances" be damned.

As if on cue, pace Stevens in *Iacobucci*, circumstances negating a Supreme Court check on state overreach were still easy to come by in one type of case. In a narrowly decided, plurality judgment in *Barnes v. Glen Theatre* in 1991—a case, by the way, that was clearly cleaning up stray matters from *Iacobucci*—the court found that a state has the constitutional authority to ban public nudity, even as part of expressive conduct such as dancing, because it furthers a substantial government interest in protecting the morality and order of society. The relevance of the case for our study here is that one of the appellees was the Kitty Kat Lounge, which sold alcoholic beverages to accompany its nude exotic dancing performances. That liquor businesses were traditionally subject to greater state regulation obviously did not work in favor of the Kitty Kat's case. But as with the Burger era, one is never quite sure whether the Rehnquist era's strip club decisions were driven more by the law of alcohol regulation or a judicial distaste for tawdry sexuality.

It is certainly true that outside the men's club bar service context, the Rehnquist justices freed the liquor industry from many kinds of state regulation: of pricing in *Duffy* and *Healy*, on price advertising as a form of protected, commercial speech in *44 Liquormart v. Rhode Island* (1996), and of distribution in the form of direct sale, out-of-state wine shipments in *Granholm v. Heald* (2005). But the path to that free market deregulation was not always straight. A confusing and splintered decision in 1991 had found the Rehnquist Court cautiously ordering retrospective application of the *Bacchus Imports* rule outlawing state protectionist excise taxes on liquor. In this case, *James Beam Distillers v. Georgia* (1991), the petitioner was seeking a refund of taxes it paid under Georgia's law for 1982, 1983, and 1984; the lower court had declared the discriminatory excise tax statute unconstitutional, but refused to apply its ruling retroactively. By contrast, a similar case decided one year earlier, involving a refund for taxes paid as a result of an invalidated, locally preferential tax on alcoholic products made from Florida citrus and bottled in state, had been decided unanimously (*McKesson Corp. v. Florida Alcohol & Tobacco Division*, in 1990). Yet state regulatory interests could still survive, albeit by narrow margins. The supremacy clause, federalism, and the regulation of sales of alcohol on military bases were the issues in *North Dakota v. U.S.* in 1990.

Among the concerns raised by the case was the provision of alcohol for sale at the best price, with Defense Department package stores pitted against the state liquor importation and distribution system put in place under the Twenty-First Amendment. A plurality concluded somewhat weakly that the state regulations were not invalid under the Supremacy Clause.

The context of alcohol use seemed to make all the difference, with ordinary consumers of liquor to be distinguished from unseemly drinkers, along with each group's respective rights. Habitués of strip clubs and drunken drivers fell into the latter, unseemly category, and protection of their liberties suffered accordingly. Indeed, the Rehnquist Court could be fairly uncompromising in enforcing state regulation of personal consumption as well as of its deleterious social effects or harm to public safety.

Case in point was the court's vigorous upholding of the use of drunk driving sobriety checkpoints. The breakthrough ruling allowing a checkpoint system without individualized suspicion came in 1990 in *Michigan v. Sitz*. *Sitz* did admit that such checkpoints are "seizures" under the Fourth Amendment, and so must pass a "reasonableness" inquiry, by the amendment's own terms. But interestingly, the 5–4 decision, with a majority opinion written by the chief justice, rejected the lower court's finding that the checkpoint system failed an "effectiveness" test. In harmony with what he and fellow *Sitz* majority member O'Connor had stressed in *Duffy*—that the court should not sit in judgment of whether state actions in pursuit of their Twenty-First Amendment regulatory powers over alcohol were "effective" or not—Rehnquist defended the state's choice of means in *Sitz*. Judging "the degree to which the seizure advances the public interest," he argued, was not meant to "transfer from politically accountable officials to the courts the choice as to which *among reasonable* alternative law enforcement *techniques* should be employed" (emphasis added). States were dealing with "a serious public danger" and should be accorded the discretion to select their own conceptions of effective programs to address it—once the Supreme Court had given its imprimatur of a program's general reasonableness. Which it did to the idea of the sobriety checkpoint.

The spirit of the age was clearly that of state scrutiny of individual drinking—as was made crystal clear by Justice Blackmun's rather self-satisfied puffery in his brief concurrence. "In 1971," he reminded his colleagues, "I noted that the 'slaughter on the highways of this Nation exceeds the death toll of all our wars,' and that I detected 'little genuine public concern about what takes place in our very midst and on our daily travel routes.' . . . I am pleased, of course, that the Court is now stressing this tragic aspect of American life."

Brennan's *Sitz* dissent was less charitable regarding the "minimal intrusion" posed by the sobriety checkpoint stops—or about the need for it. "In the face of the 'momentary evil' of drunken driving," he cautioned, "the Court today abdicates its role as the protector of [the] fundamental right" of individual privacy. Stevens also objected in his dissenting opinion to the "suspicionless, surprise seizures" that would invariably unfold in the dead of night. Their potential for menace, and misuse, was obvious to him:

> A check for a driver's license . . . is far more easily standardized than is a search for evidence of intoxication. A Michigan officer who questions a motorist at a sobriety checkpoint has virtually unlimited discretion to detain the driver on the basis of the slightest suspicion. A ruddy complexion, an unbuttoned shirt, bloodshot eyes or a speech impediment may suffice to prolong the detention. Any driver who had just consumed a glass of beer, or even a sip of wine, would almost certainly have the burden of demonstrating to the officer that her driving ability was not impaired.

The indignity—not to mention the potentially abusive hazards—of such discretion-laden invasion of persons' integrity fell on largely deaf ears by this time, with the Rehnquist Court also upholding mandatory breath, blood, and drug testing of public employees (in "safety sensitive" positions) without individualized suspicion. The ruling in *Skinner v. Railway Labor Executives' Association* in 1989 followed a series of major train accidents, but the case record produced no conclusive evidence of widespread intoxicant use by engineers and railroad operators. As Stevens's *Sitz* dissent rhetorically asked, quoting an earlier dissent by Justice Scalia from another random drug-testing procedure case: "What better way to show that the Government is serious about its 'war on drugs' than to subject its employees on the front line of that war to this invasion of their privacy and affront to their dignity?"

And what better way to illustrate the court's commitment to (neo)temperance in American life than its assent to the drunk driving crackdown of the 1990s. A per curiam decision in *Pennsylvania v. Bruder* in 1988 had set the MADD-era tone. After his vehicle was stopped by a police officer, the respondent Bruder took field sobriety tests and, in answer to questions, stated that he had been drinking. He failed the tests and was then arrested and given *Miranda* warnings of his Fifth Amendment privilege against self-incrimination. At his trial, his statements and conduct before arrest were admitted into evidence, and he was convicted of driving while under the influence of alcohol. The lower court reversed the conviction on the ground that the statements that Bruder uttered during the roadside questioning were elicited through custodial interrogation and should have been suppressed for lack of *Miranda* warnings. But the Rehnquist Court held that Bruder was not entitled to a recitation of his constitutional rights prior to arrest, and his roadside responses to questioning were admissible. Although unquestionably a seizure, the court viewed the stop as having the same noncoercive aspects as an ordinary traffic stop detention: a single police officer asking Bruder a modest number of questions and requesting him to perform simple tests in a location visible to passing motorists. Years later, in the 2004 decisional bookend of *Illinois v. Lidster,* the Rehnquist Court upheld another drunk driving conviction, for a motorist snagged in a roadblock set up to inquire about a recent fatal accident, because the roadblock itself did not violate the Fourth Amendment. The constitutionality of the information-seeking stop was what was at issue, with the arrest for drunk driving as merely an incidental— but clearly beneficial—by-product.

Indeed, such arrests seemed presumptively valid during the Rehnquist era—in spite of the fact that *Leocal v. Ashcroft* in 2004 qualified the gravity of the drunk driving offense, ruling that an alien's state conviction for DUI was not a "crime of violence" and thus not an "aggravated felony" warranting deportation. Yet *this* ruling seemed to contradict what the Rehnquist Court had ruled in 1994: that an uncounseled (without benefit of attorney representation) misdemeanor conviction for DUI was valid when used to enhance punishment at subsequent conviction (*Nichols v. U.S.*, a Rehnquist opinion for the court). The Rehnquist Court had previously opined on the nature of the DUI offense, ruling in 1993 that driving under influence in a national park was a petty offense, for jury trial purposes (*U.S. v. Nachtigal*, a per curiam opinion); and, in 1989 in *Blanton v. City of North Las Vegas,* that there is no Sixth Amendment right to a trial by jury for persons charged (under Nevada law) with DUI—with the criterion for determining the seriousness of an offense being the severity of the maximum authorized penalty fixed by the legislature. The unanimous opinion in *Blanton* elaborated that "this Court has long held that *petty* crimes or offenses are not subject to the Sixth Amendment jury trial provision" (emphasis added).

So was drunken behavior behind the wheel deserving of special opprobrium, or not?

In a 1996 ruling on criminal sentencing law more generally, the Rehnquist Court seemingly left little doubt—rhetorically, anyway—as to where it stood in its opinion of drunkenness as a human condition. The court held in *Montana v. Egelhoff*—narrowly but dramatically—that barring evidence of a defendant's voluntary intoxication from being taken into consideration in determining the existence of a mental state elemental to committing a criminal offense did *not* violate the due process clause.[17] The plurality judgment authored by Justice Scalia and joined by the chief justice noted "the stern rejection of inebriation as a defense" as "a fixture of early American law."[18] Scalia's opinion also cited this passage from a Marshall era legal source:

> Justice Story rejected an objection to the exclusion of evidence of intoxication as follows:
> "This is the first time, that I ever remember it to have been contended, that the commission of one crime was an excuse for another. Drunkenness is a *gross vice*, and in the contemplation of some of our laws is a crime; and I learned in my earlier studies, that so far from its being in law an excuse for murder, it is rather an aggravation of its malignity." (*United States* v. *Cornell*, CC R. I. 1820) (emphasis added)

Continuing in *Egelhoff*, Scalia noted that "by the end of the 19th century, in most American jurisdictions, intoxication could be considered in determining whether a defendant was capable of forming the specific intent necessary to commit the crime charged." But then, in a burst of historical legalese, his plurality opinion concluded thusly:

> The burden remains upon respondent to show that the "new common law" rule—that intoxication may be considered on the question

of intent—was so deeply rooted at the time of the Fourteenth
Amendment (or perhaps has become so deeply rooted since) as to be
a fundamental principle which that Amendment enshrined. That
showing has not been made.

After all, the *Egelhoff* Court reasoned,

> A large number of crimes, especially violent crimes, are committed
> by intoxicated offenders; modern studies put the numbers as high as
> half of all homicides, for example. . . . Disallowing consideration of
> voluntary intoxication has the effect of increasing the punishment for
> all unlawful acts committed in that state, and thereby deters drunk-
> enness or irresponsible behavior while drunk. The rule also serves as
> a specific deterrent, ensuring that those who prove incapable of con-
> trolling violent impulses while voluntarily intoxicated go to prison.
> And finally, the rule comports with and implements society's moral
> perception that one who has voluntarily impaired his own faculties
> should be responsible for the consequences.

"Deter[ing] . . . irresponsible behavior while drunk" is an entirely legitimate state objective, in other words, as a reflection of society's moral
stance regarding the "vice" of voluntary "drunkenness." Judicial ruling
as social disapprobation does not come any clearer than this.

Technical law enforcement questions nevertheless persisted, in
terms of policing the safety of America's roadways. *Pennsylvania v.
Muniz* in 1990, decided the same year as the checkpoint case of *Sitz*,
proffered another severely split decision. A follow-up to and, to some
degree, an elaboration of *Bruder, Muniz* ruled on whether various incriminating utterances of a drunken-driving suspect, made while per-
forming a series of sobriety tests, constituted testimonial responses to
custodial interrogation for purposes of the self-incrimination clause of
the Fifth Amendment. (Some did, some didn't.) The facts of the controversy add to our appreciation of drunk driving law enforcement practices during the Rehnquist Court era. Muniz had been arrested for
driving while under the influence of alcohol on a Pennsylvania highway.
Without being advised of his rights to remain silent and request and
await the advice of legal counsel, he was taken to a booking center
where, as was the routine practice, he was told that his actions and voice
would be videotaped. He then answered seven questions regarding his
name, address, height, weight, eye color, date of birth, and current age,

stumbling over two responses. He was also asked, and was unable to give, the date of his sixth birthday. In addition, he made several incriminating statements while he performed physical sobriety tests and when he was asked to submit to a breathalyzer test. He refused to take the breathalyzer test and was advised, for the first time, of his *Miranda* rights. Both the video and audio portions of the tape were admitted at trial, and he was convicted.

Muniz's innovation—and its limited extension of the rights' protections offered to suspects, compared with *Bruder*—came in the decision's somewhat specious parsing of the case facts. While finding that the videotape of the questioning and sobriety testing generally exhibited physical rather than testimonial evidence within the meaning of the Fifth Amendment, the Brennan majority narrowly concluded that Muniz's answers to the birthday question were testimonial and should have been suppressed. Only Justice Marshall, in his separate partial dissent and partial concurrence, disagreed entirely with the court's creation of a "routine booking question" exception to the Miranda requirement. Marshall also maintained that the sobriety tests themselves were the "functional equivalent" of express questioning and that, therefore, Muniz's incriminating statements in connection with the sobriety tests and the attempted breathalyzer test were the products of custodial interrogation.

But drunk driving, and its procedural prosecution, could also be the occasion for more uncompromised protection of Fifth Amendment rights, as happened in *Grady v. Corbin* in 1990. A 5–4 decision held that the double jeopardy clause barred a subsequent prosecution for vehicular homicide because, in order to establish an essential element of the offense charged in that prosecution—that is, criminal recklessness or negligence—the government proved conduct for an offense for which the defendant Corbin had already been prosecuted. The defendant had already pled guilty to two misdemeanor traffic citations for driving while intoxicated; the presiding judge in this case was not informed that his actions had caused a fatality and that a homicide investigation was pending. Once Corbin was indicted, the government prosecutor, in order to prove the defendant's reckless or negligent disregard for his dangerously drunken state as an ultimately lethal driver, essentially prosecuted him a second time for the same DUI offenses.

The majority's most telling remark on the rather sad state of affairs that the case presented was this: "that drunken driving is a national tragedy and that prosecutors are overworked and may not always have the time to monitor seemingly minor cases as they wind through the judicial system do not excuse the need for scrupulous adherence to constitutional principles." In other words, according to the Brennan majority opinion, "with adequate preparation and foresight, the State could have prosecuted Corbin for the offenses charged in the traffic tickets and the subsequent indictment in a single proceeding." The "national tragedy" of drunk driving was therefore not a license for abuse of defendants' rights—even reprehensible, repeat-offending defendants. Interestingly, the four *Grady* dissenters did not take this rhetorical bait in opposing the decision. They rather maintained that Corbin was being prosecuted twice for the same conduct but not the same offense, and that only the latter was forbidden by the Fifth Amendment. Indeed, it barely registered with dissenting Justice Scalia, who spoke at greatest length for all of them, that the case concerned drunk driving at all.

The sheer frequency of drunk driving arrests and convictions meant that such cases could be the pretext for constitutional rights challenges unrelated to DUI enforcement itself. The previously discussed roadblock case of *Illinois v. Lidster* comes to mind, but a better example is *Florida v. Wells* in 1990, which presented a drunk driving arrest as the occasion for a more general Fourth Amendment doctrinal clarification. The *Wells* Court invalidated the opening of closed containers (in this instance, a suitcase in the car's trunk containing marijuana, for which the defendant was subsequently prosecuted) encountered during an inventory search of the trunk of the arrestee's impounded car, as "insufficiently regulated to satisfy the Fourth Amendment." The Rehnquist-authored decision essentially approved the state policy—one that allowed a police officer latitude to determine whether a particular container should be opened in light of the nature of the search and characteristics of the container itself—as not per se violating the Fourth Amendment, even though the court did *not* approve the instant search in *Wells* itself. The ruling stands for the principle that drunk driving—however prevalent—cannot be a gateway to any and all police intrusions into personal privacy.

Still, other cases in the Rehnquist Court record show a judicial intolerance for—or, at least, a judicial impatience with—certain drinking behaviors. The landmark religious free exercise ruling of *Employment Division v. Smith* (1990)[19] was tangentially but still materially alcohol related, in that the individuals fired from their jobs for religiously affiliated use of a controlled narcotic substance (peyote) were drug and alcohol abuse counselors at a private addiction rehabilitation treatment organization. That irony was probably not lost on the *Smith* majority, for the respondents' First Amendment freedom of religion claim challenging their denial of unemployment benefits subsequent to their termination was ultimately denied. A puritanical streak also ran through the decision in *Dallas v. Stanglin* of 1989, where the Rehnquist Court rejected a First Amendment freedom of association and equal protection challenge to a city ordinance licensing "Class E" dance halls, which included age and hour restrictions. Such dance halls restricted admission to persons between the ages of fourteen and eighteen and limited their hours of operation; the challenge in the case came from an operator of an adjacent adult roller rink who wanted to offer free access between the spaces. Holding that "the Constitution does not recognize a generalized right of 'social association' that includes chance encounters in dance halls," the Rehnquist majority went on to argue that the age-based distinction was justified under the equal protection clause because

> the city could reasonably conclude that teenagers might be more susceptible to *corrupting influences* if permitted to frequent dance halls with older persons, or that limiting dance-hall contacts between adults and teenagers would make less likely illicit or undesirable juvenile involvement *with alcohol*, illegal drugs, or promiscuous sex. (emphasis added)

Some liberties were clearly not respectable enough to protect at law. Or were *Smith* and *Dallas* simply reflecting the era's censorious attitude toward intoxication?

What we can say is that the Rehnquist Court's decisions were generally mirrored by structural adjustments made legislatively to the regulation of alcohol, during the Rehnquist era. For example, in October 2000, the Twenty-First Amendment Enforcement Act was passed, which gave federal courts the power to intervene in cases involving interstate wine shipping, especially from sales over the Internet. The act also induced states, through federal highway matching funds, to lower their drunk driving threshold for blood-alcohol concentration from 0.10 to 0.08; by 2004 every state had acceded.[20] MADD's activism also furthered other regulatory legislation: the Zero Tolerance Law of 1995, forbidding minors from driving with any alcohol in their bloodstream; and states' passage of laws suspending the driver's license of an adult who knowingly provides alcohol to a minor—the so-called social host liability laws.[21] The Homeland Security Act of 2001 split responsibility for the regulation of alcohol between two agencies, essentially honing and specializing it. The Justice Department picked up the Bureau of Alcohol, Tobacco and Firearms (ATF), which solely handles enforcement and fights alcohol and tobacco smuggling. A second bureau, the Treasury Department's Alcohol and Tobacco Tax and Trade Bureau (TTB), was tasked with upholding federal regulations and collecting alcohol excise taxes.[22] Alcohol and its use were back under a comprehensive scheme of national governmental scrutiny—as thoroughgoing (if less absolute) as that under Volstead and the Eighteenth Amendment.

Yet when their own (generally elite) class interests aligned with freer access to alcohol, the Rehnquist justices demonstrated a decidedly less condemnatory stance—and one that confirmed many of the justices' already evident, anticommercial regulation stance. The relevant decision, of course, is *Granholm v. Heald* in 2005, the decision that "freed the vine." *Granholm* tested the constitutionality of state blockage of interstate direct wine sales, or Internet and mail-order transactions between in-state customers and out-of-state vineyards and wineries. Dating from the Repeal era, sending wine through the mail or via a common carrier direct to a drinker was illegal in twenty-three states and a felony in some, including Florida, Kentucky, and Utah.[23] Neither Michigan nor New York, the states involved in the Supreme Court case, prohibited direct sales to consumers by in-state wineries—setting up a classic Twenty-First Amendment versus commerce clause contest. Were the states' laws impermissible economic protectionism or legitimate state control of alcohol trafficking?

As the 5–4 decision headnotes remarked, direct sales have been "influenced by an increasing number of small wineries and a decreasing number of wine wholesalers, [and] have grown because small wineries may not produce enough wine or have sufficient consumer demand for their wine to make it economical for wholesalers to carry their products." Among the materials that are part of the National Archives file on the case is a July 2003 report from the Federal Trade Commission, "Possible Anticompetitive Barriers to E-Commerce: Wine." An internal court memorandum to the chief deputy clerk itemizes several additional "research articles": a journal article from *Regulation* on "Regulating Wine by Mail," a BATF (Bureau of Alcohol, Tobacco, and Firearms) industry circular, and the National Association of American Wineries' "Wine Facts 2004." As these supplemental documents suggest, and a legal scholar at the time observed, whether they were speaking as wine enthusiasts or free market proponents, "the Justices' questions in oral arguments seemed to point toward a ruling favorable to the wineries."[24]

A favorable ruling was indeed what ensued, but it was hardly a universal acclamation of viniculture. First of all, the vote was close: only a narrow majority of five justices supported the position that the state wine laws discriminated against interstate commerce and that the protectionist discrimination was neither authorized nor permitted by the Twenty-First Amendment. The beer-drinking chief was not one of them. Justice Anthony Kennedy's majority opinion in *Granholm* sternly held that the amendment "did not give States the authority to pass nonuniform laws in order to discriminate against out-of-state goods, a privilege they never enjoyed" under the Constitution. He was joined in his admonition by what can only be described as a core group of fellow wine-drinking justices: Antonin Scalia, Ruth Bader Ginsburg, Stephen Breyer . . . and New Hampshire native David Souter, the lone Spartan-living jurist of the bunch. Nevertheless, and despite the majority's strongly worded affirmation of a free market for wine consumers, there were four dissenters who vehemently defended the states' position. Justice Clarence Thomas's longer and major dissent, a mechanically textualist rendering of the 1913 Webb-Kenyon Act, might initially be dismissed as simply odd. But Thomas went to the real crux of the matter at the close of his opinion:

> The Court begins its opinion by detailing the evils of state laws that restrict the direct shipment of wine. It stresses, for example, the Federal Trade Commission's opinion that allowing the direct shipment of wine would enhance consumer welfare. The Court's *focus*

on these effects suggests that it believes that its decision serves this Nation well. (emphasis added)

In other words, Thomas and his three fellow dissenters were intimating that the majority justices were voting their own personal, rosé-colored opinions of good public policy.

Were they? Justice Stevens's relatively brief dissent, joined only by Justice O'Connor, stressed that "our Constitution has placed commerce in alcoholic beverages in a special category." Then, more pointedly, Stevens observed that,

> Today many Americans, particularly those members of the younger generations who make policy decisions, regard alcohol as an ordinary article of commerce, subject to substantially the same market and legal controls as other consumer products. That was definitely not the view of the generations that made policy in 1919 . . . or in 1933.

The years, in other words, of the enactment of the Eighteenth and the Twenty-First Amendments, respectively. From this latter view, Stevens continued, came an "understanding of a State's right to discriminate in its regulation of out-of-state alcohol"—an understanding he explicitly associated with the great jurist (and Prohibition enforcer) Louis Brandeis. Like Thomas, Stevens ultimately saw the majority's opinion as reflecting contemporary preferences:

> The notion that discriminatory state laws violated the unwritten prohibition against balkanizing the American economy—while persuasive in contemporary times when alcohol is viewed as an ordinary article of commerce—would have seemed strange indeed to the millions of Americans who condemned the use of the "demon rum" in the 1920s and 1930s. Indeed, they expressly authorized the "balkanization" that today's decision condemns.

Stevens concluded with this final, choice flourish:

> Today's decision may represent sound economic policy and *may be consistent with the policy choices of the contemporaries of Adam Smith who drafted our original Constitution*; it is not, however, consistent with the policy choices made by those who amended our Constitution in 1919 and 1933. (emphasis added)

By "the policy choices" of Smith's contemporaries and the Constitution's framers, we must assume that Stevens meant the free market and not a John Marshall–esque affinity for the grape.

Public policy analysts concur that the *Granholm* majority was "in tune with the current popular attitude toward beverage alcohol": that far from being the demon rum of yore, it is a commodity like any other in the market economy. An "ordinary article of commerce" was the phrasing Stevens's dissenting opinion used somewhat mockingly—but nonetheless echoing decades of judicial opinions on alcohol up through the early decades of the twentieth century. *Granholm* by and large returned to that pretemperance movement understanding, at least with respect to alcohol in the marketplace. As such, and according to the overwhelmingly supportive Rehnquist Court majority but minus its chief, beverage alcohol should be subject to wide choices and competitive prices for consumers.[25] Another policy scholar continues in this vein and expands on the decision's inherent cultural meaning:

> Since Prohibition there has been a dramatic role reversal in terms of the meaning of drinking in this country and this change is exemplified by the direct shipment debate. The direct shipment controversy reveals the continuing desire of middle and upper middle class Americans [read: the Supreme Court "elite"] to assert their views regarding drinking on the lower classes. This desire is apparent in the many newspaper articles concerning direct shipment, which heap condescension and ridicule on those who might support direct shipment bans.[26]

The "dramatic role reversal in terms of the meaning of drinking" to which this author refers concerns abstinence and who practices it. Once fashionably middle class, abstaining from alcohol was a clear statement that one was non-immigrant/non-ethnic/non–working class with regard to one's alcohol use—one was, in other words, "refined." Today, abstinence of the soft-drinking-only variety is derided by "the better sort" as a lack of sophisticated appreciation for the finer things in life, or as motivated by the kind of antique religiosity that only bullyingly uneducated or pitiably narrow-minded people embrace.[27]

In terms of its impact, it is important to note that the *Granholm* decision only barred discriminatory treatment of out-of-state wineries, and that the dissents provided a vigorous states' rights defense of the state power to regulate interstate wine shipments. States simply had to do so even-handedly. Michigan, in follow-up legislation to the 2005 decision, mandated that out-of-state wineries were only allowed to ship directly to consumers—they could not ship directly to retailers or restaurants, a privilege that in-state wineries maintained.[28] So a patchwork of producer direct shipment regulations remains—including for small-batch distillers, the liquor equivalent of boutique wineries whose production is too small to attract the economies-of-scale attention of major, licensed distributors and wholesalers. While thirty-seven states currently permit some form of direct shipment of wine to consumers, a 2010 Wine Institute report found that many of the conditions in these regulations were either so complex or so expensive as to discourage wineries from complying.

Regardless of its erratic effect, certain analysts read *Granholm* as signaling something fundamental in terms of the American political economy of alcohol. One in particular says, "In rejecting the 'demon rum' model as a basis for determining the scope of the 21st Amendment, the Court has made a 'paradigm shift,' in which . . . 'one conceptual world view is replaced by another.'" That new worldview is "an intoxicating blend of Adam Smith's 18th century economic theory and today's e-commerce . . . to conclude that impediments to the direct shipment of wine disrupts the flow of commerce between the states and unnecessarily burdens consumers."[29]

Would that the blend of Adam Smith included his eighteenth-century's balanced yet bon vivant sensibility toward drinking—as Justice Stevens archly accused.

While *Granholm* may or may not laud a major turning point in the American regime of drink, it certainly vindicates the contemporary American passion for wine, including a passion for the quality and desirability of domestically produced wine. Does it—should it—bestow on California cabernet sauvignon the distinction as another Rehnquist era honorable mention beverage? Perhaps. But the true benefits of the "free the vine" decision would accrue to the Rehnquist Court's successor, staffed as it has been by several real red wine enthusiasts. (Most, to be sure, holdovers from the Rehnquist era.)

Even so, *Granholm,* itself, was a curious close to an era of neotemperance and "Remember to drink responsibly." The Rehnquist Court's rulings widened opportunities to obtain choice, quality, and well-priced

278 CHAPTER 13

beverage alcohol in the marketplace, while affirming the community's responsibility and authority to curtail "irresponsible" boozing. Americans of the era largely accepted the neoliberal contradiction.

CONCLUSION

State price controls, protectionism, and price advertising bans gave way to a free market of alcohol sales by the end of the Rehnquist era. Still, a social opprobrium had attached to inebriation—particularly behind the wheel—which the Rehnquist justices consistently and firmly supported. The contrast between the two jurisprudential trends is echoed in the contest between the era's two signature drinks: Rehnquist's light beer, and the 1980s contribution to American popular culture: the frozen blender margarita. The rainbow-hued frozen margaritas of the Rehnquist era were the last hurrah of drinking as unexamined fun. Cocktails were about to become serious business, in more ways than one.

14

THE RETRO ROBERTS ERA

Running a Tab

We arrive at last at Last Call, and our own era of alcohol in American life and law. The current *Roberts Court* (2005–) has been concurrent with the reemergence of the cocktail culture, the rise of the craft and artisanal cocktail, and a nostalgia for "a legendary past"[1] of the authentic period cocktail, the 1920s speakeasy, and the midcentury cocktail lounge. While enthusiasts would date the rebirth of pre-Prohibition cocktail artistry in the United States with the opening in 1994 of Angel's Share in Manhattan's East Village, it took the next decade or so for the past to be fully resurrected and dispersed across the American beverage landscape.[2]

One of the signal features of today's cocktail movement is the rediscovery of the cocktail by the *young*. Among these newest aficionados, that rediscovery extends to a veritable worship of all things cocktail, from the obsession with historically accurate spirits and drink recipes, to the reverence for vintage barware and barkeep haberdashery. Such youthful enthusiasm converts what could have been an exercise in fusty antiquarianism into the height of hip. The Roberts era, too, has been a time of young, vigorous justices—the result of contemporary presidents' preference for appointing relatively young jurists, to extend their own legacies into the law for a good long time. John Roberts was himself one of the youngest chief justices ever appointed, and at fifty was the youngest member of the Supreme Court at the time of his nomination and confirmation. He was something of an accidental chief, in that President George W. Bush initially named him for the seat of retiring Associate Justice Sandra Day O'Connor. Chief Justice Rehnquist's intervening sudden death in September of 2005 squashed both plans: O'Connor agreed to stay on the bench until successors could be placed, to prevent the court's short staffing, and Bush quickly renominated Roberts for the chief's chair. Fittingly, Roberts had once served as Rehnquist's law clerk, back when Rehnquist had been an associate. Despite his relative youth as a judge, Roberts had had a long career in Republican Party politics and was something of a "movement conservative." He nevertheless successfully and famously presented his judicial self at his confirmation hearing before the U.S. Senate as merely "an umpire, calling balls and strikes."

America's favorite pastime references notwithstanding, Roberts is not known as a beer man, as was his predecessor. Neither does the still-youthful Roberts have a reputation as a wild, carousing youngster akin to that of William O. Douglas, who began his court service at the tender age of forty. Instead, the mild-mannered Indianan is rather moderate when it comes to bellying up to the bar and demonstrates no particular or signature alcoholic beverage preference. That his era is one of the rediscovery of the art of mixology is therefore rather ironic, and also a bit befuddling. We must, it seems, search beyond the chief's own predilections for his era's totemic cocktail.

With respect to drinks and their preparation, an especially pertinent (and, appropriately, nonalcoholic) Roberts era decision is *POM Wonderful LLC v. Coca-Cola Co.* from 2014. The court heard the case about truth-in-labeling with respect to Coca-Cola's pomegranate juice products, ostensibly without realizing the true stakes of the contest for a future of meticulous mixology.

The dispute concerned pomegranate juices made by Coca-Cola's Minute Maid division, and was between the parent company and POM Wonderful, a small producer of various pomegranate juices and teas. POM Wonderful claimed a Lanham Act trademark violation by Coca-Cola, based on the premise that its highlighting of what was a fairly small amount of real pomegranate juice in its Minute Maid product was misleading and presented unfair competition for POM's better, and more expensive, juice product. In response, Coca-Cola cited the Food and Drug Administration's power over food and beverage labeling as the controlling legal factor, and one that blocked private suits under the Lanham Act to allege unfair competition arising from false or misleading product descriptions. The Anthony Kennedy opinion for a unanimous court held that POM could go ahead and challenge Coca-Cola's presentation of its blended juice product, clearing the fruit product company to take on the soft drink giant.

But the ramifications of the technically complex case went so much further than that. Pomegranate juice and syrup—the latter known commercially as grenadine—have been mainstays of contemporary craft cocktail mixology; recipes using the original fruit-based ingredient (or "artisanal" grenadine) abound on current, high quality bar menus.[3] Whether or not Chief Justice Roberts's own taste preferences are coincident, his court's *POM* decision has profound implications for quality control and verisimilitude aspects of current bartending practices.[4] Indeed, several of the "hippest," retro period cocktails are made with grenadine, which was all the rage in the 1900s. One such ingredient-appropriate cocktail—and loosely eponymous for the Roberts era—is the Jack Rose (i.e., for John "Jack" Roberts). A barroom staple of the golden age of the American saloon that relies on Applejack brandy as its base spirit and grenadine as its sweetener, this tasty recipe is only now beginning to enjoy the restoration to the cocktail pantheon already possessed by classic if stolid formulas such as the Manhattan—the Roberts Court's decision "freeing the pomegranate" making no small contribution to this contemporary consumer trend.

POM Wonderful aside, a more fanciful cocktail homage to the Roberts era might be the mid-1990s to early 2000s' favorite of the ladies of the hit HBO show *Sex in the City*, the cosmopolitan.[5] This, in light of the markedly high number of women justices serving (three at once, four in total) on the Roberts bench, makes the "cosmo" at least worth mentioning—although few now laud the drink as an especially exalted achievement in mixology. Its gendered resonance notwithstanding, we must be mindful of the ruby-hued cocktail's ignoble status as one made safe for a nice middle-class person to have before (or, in the case of the *Sex in the City* characters, instead of) a meal, a la the Bronx Cocktail a century earlier.[6] Cosmos are "common," and not in a good or appropriate way in relation to the current cocktail renaissance. A much more *suitably rarified* cocktail homage to the all-time high number of women serving on the Roberts Court would be the Mary Pickford Cocktail: a

Prohibition era, forgotten gem made with white rum, fresh pineapple juice, *grenadine*, and Maraschino liqueur. Named for silent-screen film actress Mary Pickford, it is said (according to *Imbibe* magazine) to have been created for her in the 1920s at the Hotel Nacional de Cuba, on a booze cruise she took to Havana with Charlie Chaplin and Douglas Fairbanks. And speaking of Hispano-America, the first Latina justice, Puerto Rican Sonia Sotomayor appointed in 2009, could also merit the more or less authentically Caribbean mojito for honorable mention as the era's totem—particularly as it also fits with what cocktail writer Peck has to say about current alcohol market trends: "Today's cocktail culture is all about customization . . . even so-called standard cocktails, like *the nation's favorite the Margarita,*[7] allow for considerable variation. . . . [M]any cultural preferences have [similarly] shifted away from mass-market goods and toward customization or niche products"[8] (emphasis added).

Just as the Rehnquist-era margarita became a platform for the mingling of ever more precious tequilas and obscure orange liqueurs, there is now a muddled-mint and lime mojito for every taste and every new artisanal variety of sugar cane–based spirits, the mojito's basic base spirit. (Which was originally, of course, Cuban white rum.) Fancying up very ordinary and even very simple working-class cocktail recipes marks the contemporary cocktail scene, and it is difficult to think of more of a "cocktail of the *campo*" than a mojito, aka the Ti Punch of the islands of the French Caribbean, aka the Caipirinha, which is Brazil's national drink and folk remedy for the common cold. Only the sugar cane–based spirits change in the prototypes; it is the prices that follow suit, for their more glamorous, craft bar progeny.

Upmarket and uncommon is all, in this Roberts era age. And just as the Fuller era (1888–1910) was a golden age of many cocktails, the Roberts Court is presiding over the revival of a plethora of vintage spirits and bar recipes—indeed, in many cases, it is Fuller era spirits and recipes that are being revived. What was once unimaginably rare and overly scrupulous is now a norm of authenticity and connoisseurship for the craft cocktail set.[9] Cocktail choices are limitless—as is the need for studious preparation in ordering one, lest one be thought an alcohol philistine or a liquor neophyte. (Pity the poor soul who still prefers a pedestrian cosmo.)

But in spite of all this, it is wine, and particularly **red wine**, that recurs again and again in personal lore of the Roberts period. "Tinto"— as Sonia Sotomayor would likely say it—is, in so many ways, the totem of this judicial time. Perhaps the most famous (or infamous) "red wine incident" involved Ruth Bader Ginsburg and her impaired, rather dozy appearance at President Obama's 2015 State of the Union address. It was a celebrated—if not the most celebrated—popular culture episode involving alcohol and the justices during the Roberts era, and was partly responsible for turning "the Notorious RBG" into something of a folk hero. Recounted in the book of the same title,[10] Justice Ginsburg "blamed" her colleague Anthony Kennedy for overserving her a delectable vintage at the justices' annual pre-SOTU dinner.

"RBG" is herself strongly associated with the most gourmand of tendencies among the justices, through the person of her late husband, Martin, who was an accomplished amateur chef. Indeed, he was the subject of a tribute cookbook honoring his recipes, *Chef Supreme*, published with the justice's blessing in 2015 by the Supreme Court Historical Society. Ginsburg also put her own good taste on public display, teaming up with Justice Sotomayor for an unusual program on culinary traditions at the court, sponsored by the Smithsonian in June 2016. National Public Radio's captioning of the event was "For a Cordial Supreme Court, Keep the Food and Wine Coming."

Among the topics the two justices discussed in the program, *Legal Eats: Food and Culture at the U.S. Supreme Court*, were the contemporary occasions in which wine drinking is part of court custom. Among those mentioned were the justices' toasting each other on their birthdays at lunchtime, and the chief bringing the wine. A pre-State of the Union Address formal dinner, complete with wine, has also become a tradition for at least some of the justices. "One year, Justice [Anthony] Kennedy came with a couple of bottles of Opus One from California," Ginsburg recounted at the Smithsonian event, confirming the rumors. "That was the first time I fell asleep during the State of the Union," she deadpanned for the bemused audience. The two female justices also explained the tradition that when a new justice joins the court, the most junior justice throws a welcoming feast. As Maria Godoy for NPR reported the *Legal Eats* disclosures, "The conservative Justice Samuel Alito threw the liberal Sotomayor's fete—complete with a Spanish guitar player (in honor of her Hispano-Iberian heritage) and a bottle of wine with a picture of the Supreme Court and her name printed on the label." One presumes it was a Rioja.

Justice Antonin Scalia, who passed away in February 2016 during Roberts's tenure, was likewise strongly associated with red wine, as in this reminiscence:

> The Thursday conferences with his Supreme Court clerks were thrilling, but it was the lunches at AV Ristorante Italiano on Capitol Hill in Washington that best brought out the true nature of Supreme Court Justice Antonin Scalia.
>
> Stephen Miller, then a white-collar defense lawyer at a Philadelphia law firm who clerked for Scalia in 1998 and 1999, remembers fondly those lunches of pizza with anchovies and glasses of red wine, when Scalia and his clerks would relax and take on topics large and small.[11]

And this one:

> [O]ne of my fondest memories is an afternoon spent drinking two bottles of red wine and eating pizza at A.V. Ristorante, a now-defunct Italian spot in Washington, with Scalia and my fellow clerks for Justice David Souter, liberals all. Scalia was relaxed, warm and witty—charm itself, trading ideas and arguments and treating us with complete equality. I remember thinking that if this was the devil, he certainly assumed a most pleasing form.[12]

The passing of Scalia, and the long vacancy that ensued on the Roberts Court before a nominee was confirmed to replace him, constitutes the end of the Roberts era for the purposes of this study of the Supreme Court bar. Not only was the extended post-Scalia period of an eight-justice court a historical landmark of sorts—bracketing, as it did, the surprising and equally landmark November 2016 election of unconventional and outsider presidential-candidate Donald Trump—but the death of "Nino" Scalia meant the loss of a red wine–drinking fixture on the high bench. His demise was the passing of an era in more ways than one.

What happened post-Scalia, moreover, and during a Trump presidency, takes the narrative to a new place, both judicially and in American history. That place is the Roberts Court II, and is beyond the scope of the present inquiry. Significantly, though, the forty-fifth

American president is an avowed teetotaler—a quality not seen in the chief executive since the single term of Jimmy Carter, 1976–1980. While it is true that John Roberts's appointing president, George W. Bush, also did not drink, he had given up alcohol after a somewhat dissolute youth. Whether a difference in degree or kind, it is nevertheless the case that Carter—not unlike Rutherford B. Hayes before him—removed liquor from the White House altogether, while reformed alcoholic George W. condoned the official service and enjoyment of spirituous beverages. He just did not partake himself . . . any more. By all accounts, Donald Trump also happily pours for others at White House functions—indeed, among the businesses in his family portfolio is a Virginia winery, managed by his son Eric.[13]

Current chief executive abstention from alcohol notwithstanding, the Roberts bench demonstrates a wide variety of predilections when it comes to drink—although going totally dry does not appear to be one of them. In addition to all the red wine flowing, a confidential source reports that Justice "Opus One" Ginsburg enjoys Campari; this Italian amaro is typically taken with club soda over ice as an aperitif. It also finds use in cocktails. A Sanguinea might be an interesting—if obscure and seldom drunk—honorable mention homage to the RBG-Roberts era, made as it is with:

> 1 ounce Campari
> 2 ounces *pomegranate* juice
> 2 ounces grapefruit juice (preferably fresh-squeezed)
> grapefruit twist
> serve over ice

Of course, the classic cocktail that utilizes Ginsburg's Campari is the *Negroni*, which is very possibly the comeback kid of contemporary fashion cocktails. Once a solidly B-list specialty, this inspired marriage of gin, sweet Italian vermouth, and Campari was first mixed in 1919 at a Florence café at the request of its first imbiber and namesake Count Camillo Negroni.[14] Its spread to the United States was halted by Prohibition, and was halting thereafter—perhaps initially induced through its consumption by Hollywood actors filming on location in Italy after World War II, who talked up its unlikely but entrancing twinning of the bitter and the sweet. But not until the recent cocktail renaissance did the Negroni really surface in American mixology, and the reasons are still something of a mystery. The attraction of bitters in contemporary cocktail culture may in part explain the breakout success of the elegantly balanced drink. (*Bitterly* appropriate for the Roberts era, some would say.)

Whatever the story, Negronis have become so trendy in this second decade of the twenty-first century that they, like martinis and margaritas before them, inspire ever-novel reimaginings: up versus rocks, barrel-aged gin versus whiskey as base spirit (the latter converting the Negroni into the Boulevardier), Campari versus Cynar, infinitely new and improved sweet vermouths, "white" Negronis made with tequila and Suze, frozen summertime variants—the list goes on. As the *Food and Wine* website explains, "Capitalizing on the bittersweet Negroni spell that the country was under, Gruppo Campari and *Imbibe* magazine joined forces to introduce National Negroni Week [in 2013]. The annual June celebration encourages bars across the country to serve their take on Negronis." The commercial viability of the Negroni is not entirely the result of distiller promotion but has certainly benefited from such recent bursts of corporatization of American consumer culture. However it became so firmly ensconced on both contemporary bar lists and the contemporary cocktail palate, the justly popular **Negroni** is the best candidate for honorable mention totemic drink of the Roberts Court I period . . . grenadine-laced cocktail exotica notwithstanding.

There remains, however, this bracing Robertsian chaser: the same confidential source who spills the Campari with respect to RBG reminds us that Chief Justice Roberts hardly drinks—"just a glass of wine, from time to time," this source remarks. He is also known to arrive to work early—7:30 a.m.—likely setting a rather different tone than in previous, more bilious court eras. The 2015 law clerks' memoir *Of Courtiers and Kings* contains multiple references to drinking, cocktail parties, and such with respect to clerks and their justices, and to the general culture of alcohol in and around the Supreme Court over the course of the mid-to-late twentieth century. Reading it, one gets the distinct feeling that the hard liquor swilling of earlier days has been firmly replaced with a glass or two of wine as the social drink of choice. There is, moreover, clear indication that legalized social disapprobation of drunk driving reaches a cultural apogee under Roberts. Heavy (if more or less controlled) alcohol use, to say nothing of reckless behaviors with alcohol that might have been tolerated in the past, find no such space in today's workplace or community life.[15]

The contemporary, critical attitude is apparent in Roberts era alcohol case law, which has been dominated by the Rehnquist era topic of drunk driving and search-and-seizure related constitutional questions. The 2016 decision in *Birchfield v. North Dakota,* the most complete Robertsian statement to date, is telling in its tone, let alone its content. That Justice Samuel Alito opened his majority opinion with this sentence, "Drunk drivers take a grisly toll on the Nation's roads, claiming thousands of lives, injuring many more victims, and inflicting billions of dollars in property damage every year," left little doubt that the blood-alcohol testing at issue would be upheld as a public safety measure/ legitimate governmental interest outweighing individual privacy concerns.

Decided with the companion cases of *Bernard v. Minnesota* and *Beylund v. Levi, Birchfield* clarified an issue dating from the Warren era: the scope of permissible warrantless blood-alcohol testing of suspected drunk drivers. An earlier Roberts Court case, *Missouri v. McNeely* in 2013, had tried, and failed, to definitively settle the matter, with the justices being too divided to agree on anything more than a one-case-at-a-time compromise rule. The 5–4 partial plurality judgment held rather limitedly that in drunk driving investigations subsequent to arrest, the natural dissipation of alcohol in the bloodstream does not constitute an exigency *in every case* sufficient to justify conducting a blood test without a warrant. Rather, exigency in drunk driving cases "must be determined case by case based on the totality of the circumstances." While the ruling affirmed the basic principle from *Schmerber* that, absent "an emergency that justifie[s] acting without a warrant," police may not conduct warrantless blood testing on suspects, *McNeely*'s narrow coalition and negotiated agreement made some kind of follow-up decision inevitable.

Birchfield tightened up that sort of flabby flexibility. The combined 2016 cases asked whether, in the absence of an authorizing warrant, a state could make it a crime to refuse to take a chemical test to detect the presence of alcohol in the person's blood. In the effort to combat drunk driving accidents and deaths on their roadways, several states had passed "informed consent" laws that stipulated, as a condition to the privilege of a state driver's license, submitting to blood-alcohol testing when stopped under suspicion. Penalties for refusal to comply with such testing had typically been civil in nature, usually the suspension of the driving license. But as the fine and incarceration penalties rose for conviction on second and third offenses of DUI, drivers who were stopped and failed field sobriety tests would routinely refuse a chemical blood-alcohol test since the penalty for doing so was far less severe than the alternative of certain conviction with the blood-alcohol evidence. Criminal penalties for refusal were thus an effort to add "teeth" to informed consent laws and to target repeat DUI offenders.

However, once blood-alcohol testing included breath *and* blood samples, and *both* were taken without a warrant, the defendants in the *Birchfield* cases argued that the states had gone too far. North Dakota and Minnesota were, in essence, conditioning drivers' licenses on a person's willingness to surrender his Fourth Amendment right to be free from unreasonable and, at times, invasive, warrantless searches.

As *SCOTUSblog* presciently commented on the oral arguments: "After today's argument, blood tests without a warrant may be a lost cause. The only real question may be whether enough Justices are convinced that, even if a breath test is only minimally invasive, warrants are easy enough to obtain that they should be required anyway." The answer, of course, as we now know, was no. The court held that while both breath tests and blood tests constitute searches under the Fourth Amendment, requiring breath tests under the search-incident-to-arrest doctrine is constitutional. Requiring blood tests, however, is not—not without a warrant. Justice Alito's majority opinion proceeded to analyze both types of tests, weighing on the one hand "the degree to which [the test] intrudes upon an individual's privacy," and on the other hand "the degree to which it is needed for the promotion of legitimate governmental interests." Breath tests, he concluded, do not implicate significant privacy concerns; blood tests, by contrast, are significantly more intrusive. With respect to the government's interest, the Roberts Court concluded in *Birchfield* that the mandated refusal penalties serve the very important function of providing an incentive to cooperate in alcohol testing. Requiring breath tests, then, legitimately serves the state's goal of policing drunk driving and providing traffic safety and is the least invasive means of doing so.[16]

Like *Schmerber* fifty years before, the *Birchfield* cases raised the question of a practical solution to the problem of prosecuting and deterring the drinking motorist. The recidivist drunk driver is clearly more of a public safety threat than the habitual public drunk in another Warren era case of *Powell v. Texas*, but both became figures of social opprobrium for *the way* they exhibit their drinking: offensively, publicly. Neither lawmakers, judges, nor juries of "respectable" people could envision themselves behaving—or having to behave[17]—as Birchfield or Powell did. These irredeemable "drunks" thus elicit little sympathetic consideration for their rights' interests, when those rights' interests arise in the course of state enforcement against their behavior. While the legal implication of *Birchfield* for all of us is, as Justice Sotomayor closed her partial dissent, that the warrant requirement "become[s] nothing more than a suggestion," the decision's cultural message is that driving while impaired/driving under the influence is so lowdown and loathsome as to justify a personal privacy invasion during custodial arrest—"minimal" though that personal privacy invasion might be.

Earlier Roberts Court cases had offered a mixed bag of individual rights' protections in the alcohol use context. In addition to the aforementioned *McNeely*, a 2011 case, *Bullcoming v. New Mexico,* held that the introduction of a blood-alcohol analysis report through the testimony of a nontesting, noncertifying analyst violated the right of a defendant to confront a witness against him, protected by the confrontation clause of the Sixth Amendment. Yet in the 2006 case of *Brigham City, Utah v. Stuart* the court held that regardless of their subjective motives, police officers were justified in entering a home without a warrant, when what they observed included outdoor juvenile beer drinking and loud noises and crashes inside the house. The three pre-*Birchfield* decisions of *McNeely, Bullcoming,* and *Brigham City* led in no clear direction with respect to alcohol and civil liberties, but *Birchfield* itself was immediately preceded by the unsettling 5–4 ruling in *Navarette v. California* (2014). This decision found that an anonymous 911 tip, on its own, constituted reasonable suspicion to stop a vehicle for suspected driving under the influence. A conviction for drug possession ultimately resulted in the case, because as the police officers approached the stopped motorist, they smelled not alcohol but marijuana emanating from the passenger compartment. The subsequent vehicle search revealed an illegal truck-bed load of the Schedule I narcotic substance, being transported without the requisite state permit for medical distribution.

For the *Navarette* majority, the 911 caller's report of being run off the road created "the reasonable suspicion of an ongoing crime such as drunk driving," replete with all the ensuing urgency that that crime elicits. For the dissent, though, the call was of questionable reliability and credibility and was supported by no corroborating behavior observed by the patrolmen as they began following the tipped vehicle. Scalia's dissenting opinion challenged the majority's empirical argument that drunk drivers will of course drive more carefully once they see a police car. "That is not how I understand the influence of alcohol," he noted drily, continuing that "the dangers of intoxicated driving are the intoxicant's impairing effects on the body—effects that no mere act of will can resist." Corroborating behavioral evidence thus should have been evident and, therefore, could reasonably be required to confirm the validity of the anonymous 911 tip. Not doing so categorically violated the Fourth Amendment's protection against *un*reasonable searches and seizures, unjustified by probable cause. Concluding his dissent with one of his infamous bon mots, Scalia found the court's *Navarette* opinion "serves up a freedom-destroying *cocktail*" (emphasis added).

Criminal law rulings about sentencing were also affected by alcohol-related concerns, as in *Porter v. McCollum*'s 2010 holding that counsel's failure to uncover and present mitigating evidence of a defendant's alcohol abuse, during the penalty phase of his murder trial, was ineffective assistance that violated the Sixth Amendment right to legal representation.[18] Despite its general recognition of alcohol abuse's debilitating effect on criminal defendants' mental capacities, the Roberts bench was somewhat inconsistent regarding the law's sensitivity to the relevance of alcohol-related problems for personal, legal culpability. The statutory ruling in *Begay v. U.S.* (2008) was that driving under the influence was not a "violent felony" within the meaning of the Armed Career Criminal Act—despite DUI's well-known likelihood of visiting serious vehicular violence on innocent persons. *Clark v. Arizona* (2006), on the other hand, took a hard line on "alcohol as an excuse." There, the first-term Roberts Court found that Arizona could narrow its insanity test for excusing defendants from criminal responsibility for their acts and in so doing could exclude from the definition of "incapacity" disorders resulting from severe but voluntary intoxication or withdrawal from the use of alcohol. In the words of the statute that the decision upheld: "Mental disease or defect does not include disorders that result from acute voluntary intoxication or withdrawal from alcohol or drugs, character defects, psychosexual disorders or impulse control disorders."

Clark himself was a paranoid schizophrenic, and his condition also did not rise to the level of "moral incapacity" that defined exculpatory insanity, under Arizona law. As Justice David Souter's majority opinion explained in justification of the ruling, the state's "prohibition of 'diminished capacity' evidence" by criminal defendants did not violate due process of law because,

> mental disease and capacity evidence may be considered only for its bearing on the insanity defense, and it will avail a defendant only if it is persuasive enough to satisfy the defendant's burden as defined by the terms of that defense. The mental-disease and capacity evidence is thus being channeled or restricted to one issue and given effect only if the defendant carries the burden to convince the fact finder of insanity; the evidence is not being excluded entirely, and the question is whether reasons for requiring it to be channeled and restricted are good enough to satisfy the standard of fundamental fairness that due process requires.

"We think they are," Souter concluded, noting that Arizona's rule sought to avoid confusion and misunderstanding on the part of jurors. To be sure, disorders that resulted from alcohol abuse and addiction were a form of personal irresponsibility, but they were not in themselves mental impairment that diminished a defendant's understanding of the rightness or wrongness of his actions. (Or were not, in the majority's words, a "mental disease [that] rendered a particular defendant incapable of the cognition necessary for moral judgment or *mens rea* or otherwise incapable of understanding the wrongfulness of the conduct charged.") The highly technical nature of the court's inquiry and reasoning in *Clark* did not disguise its presumption—similar to that of the Rehnquist Court in its 1996 ruling in *Montana v. Egelhoff*—that law could "implement society's moral perception that one who has voluntarily impaired his own faculties should be responsible for the consequences." Indeed, the state relied in its argument on the *Egelhoff* decision as a precedent—although dissenting justice Kennedy chastised Arizona for doing so.

The decisional record of the Roberts Court I was almost exclusively concerned with the pathologies of alcohol use. That record in our survey of the Roberts period to date coincides with some juicy personal anecdotes about drinking, as well as with a cocktail-savoring and wine-tasting renaissance in America. How then should we conclude our final chapter in this Supreme Court saga of drink in American life and law?

. . . And then there were eight . . .

However it is remembered in terms of constitutional jurisprudence, the Roberts era will forever be known as a watershed in judicial appointment politics and executive–congressional relations.[19] After Justice Antonin Scalia's sudden death in early February 2016, with nine months of President Barack Obama's final term remaining, Senate Republicans led by Majority Leader Mitch McConnell refused to hold hearings on any Obama nominee to replace the conservative justice, arguing that the vacancy should be held for the next, freshly elected president. This recalcitrance continued even once Obama had named the eminently well qualified and ideologically moderate DC Court of Appeals chief judge Merrick Garland as Scalia's putative successor. In a spectacle without precedent, Garland dangled, and the U.S. Supreme Court remained an eight-member body for the November 2016 election, and on through the transition period leading up to the January 2017 inauguration of Republican president-elect Donald Trump. McConnell's gamble had paid off, with the Supreme Court vacancy going to the GOP. President Trump wasted little time nominating a replacement for Scalia—as he had very explicitly pledged to do on the campaign trail. Indeed, as a presidential candidate, he took the most unusual step of releasing a list (actually, two successive lists) of prospective candidates for the vacant Supreme Court seat. Trump vowed to appoint a justice in the mold of Scalia and his judicial vision of interpreting the Constitution according to its original meaning; he also pointedly promised to select his nominee from the names on the list. Trump made good on his word on January 31, 2017, almost one year to the date that Scalia shuffled off this mortal coil and vacated his seat on the Roberts Court.

Not surprisingly, in the interlude with an even number of justices evenly divided between conservative and liberal policy leanings, the Supreme Court accepted very few high profile or highly contentious cases for review and decision. It was less a practitioner of John Roberts's much vaunted philosophy of judicial restraint than an advertisement for purposive and defensive deferral of judgment. No alcohol-related cases penetrated its resolve to wait out the nation's biggest legal problems, until the tie-breaking number of nine votes could be restored.

Roberts's Court purported in its opinions to be merely maintaining the legal trend set in motion by the Rehnquist Court's drunk driving decisions. Perhaps this is what it did. The Roberts justices were clearly serious about cocktailing's social costs, and its consequences for the practice of a sober, healthy lifestyle. But during the Roberts period of 2005–2016 there was also a great deal of seriousness about and avid partaking in the preparation and appreciation of cocktails.

Contradictions between alcohol in American life and in American law had been present in previous court eras, to be sure, but the Roberts era found its own distinct symbol for the period's paradoxes: the pseudo-speakeasy. Re-creations of the scofflaw watering holes of the 1920s proliferated across the American barroom scene of the 2000s and early 2010s—complete with hidden, "secret" entrances, drinks served in coffee cups, and a general atmosphere of clandestine naughtiness. But seldom any real naughtiness: the period craft cocktails were much too expensive for true overindulgence and, anyway, we all have to get up and be productive the next morning nowadays.

Dress-up pretending at an earlier era's decadence was never more earnest, nor more charmingly self-delusional.

CONCLUSION

Whatever its credentials in the authenticity department, the still-unfolding Roberts era has certainly been a political time when a stiff drink was in order . . . just to get through things.

EPILOGUE

A Return to Normalcy Cocktail

As the previous chapter stated, this study closes with the Roberts Court's 2015–2016 term—a milestone in terms of the exercise of the senatorial advice and consent component of the federal judicial appointment power.[1] Our cocktail (book) of decisions thus ends with the rulings from this term that was "the end of political normalcy" with respect to judicial selection politics.

Whether this highly politicized and partisan polarized state of affairs is a temporary disruption or a new normal is beyond the purview of *Glass and Gavel*. But coincidentally, there have been prior, fervent calls for a "return to normalcy" in American politics. This refrain, calling for a return to the way of life before the turbulence of World War I, was presidential candidate Warren G. Harding's campaign slogan in the election of 1920. We have of course met President Harding already, as Chief Justice Taft's appointing president and flagrant flaunter of the strictures of Prohibition. Perhaps a "normalcy cocktail"—evoking both Harding's hallowed pre-Prohibition era, and that era's celebration in contemporary mixology—would be an appropriate yet lighthearted send-off for the Roberts era, as well as finale for this book on the judicial cocktail of decisions prepared at the Supreme Court bar.

The currently resurgent and previously mentioned *Jack Rose* would qualify, chronologically speaking.[2] It of course also uses pomegranate grenadine syrup—the signature bar ingredient of the Robertsian *POM*

Wonderful period as well as the trendy cocktail accent of the American *Belle Époque*. The recipe first appeared in print in 1899, according to *Imbibe!*, which also claims that the drink had been made famous at Fred Eberlin's eating house on Wall Street in the 1870s–1880s.[3] The wholesomely Americanness of its base ingredient, applejack brandy, lends the drink a special suitability for the era of "making America great again." The Jack Rose, moreover, is deeply rooted in the chemistry of American mixology for, as the *Fine Art of Mixing Drinks* reminds us, "just as the Side Car is essentially the same type of cocktail as the Daiquiri with different base liquors and sweetening agents, so is the Jack Rose essentially the same as the Side Car with apple brandy used in place of grape brandy and grenadine used in place of Cointreau."[4]

Or what about a *Ward 8*, which originated in 1898 in Boston at the bar of the Gilded Age restaurant Locke-Ober and *also* has the distinction of using grenadine? Its numerical name has the additional tongue-in-cheek charm of explicitly evoking the short-staffed Roberts Court of the Obama–Trump interregnum. The Ward 8 achieved such popularity in its day that a bottled version produced by the Santa Clara Company was awarded a trademark in 1915 for "Compounds of Whisky, Grenadine-Syrup, Rock-Candy Syrup, and Lime-Juice." Following the end of Prohibition, Locke-Ober reopened its bar using this recipe for the pre-war drink:

> 2 ounces rye whiskey (blended whisky may be substituted)
> 1/2 ounce fresh lemon juice
> 1/2 ounce fresh orange juice
> 1 teaspoon grenadine
> Maraschino cherry (optional)
>
> Shake the rye whiskey, lemon juice, orange juice, and grenadine with ice; then strain into a chilled cocktail glass. Garnish with a maraschino cherry, if desired.

A return to normalcy indeed. Oh, if only it were so!

There is some reason for hope. On the eve of the confirmation hearings for Trump Supreme Court nominee Judge Neil Gorsuch, a piece in the February 4, 2017, issue of the *New York Times* noted that Gorsuch was a college cocktailer at Columbia University in the mid-to late-1980s, drinking martinis and Manhattans. Not only that, his marathon, 30-plus hours Senate confirmation hearings featured a rare, explicit mention of alcohol. After eleven and a half hours of senatorial questioning of the nominee on the second day (March 21, 2017) of the committee hearing process, Louisiana Senator John Kennedy got what amounted to the Last Word. The jovial, freshman Republican senator was the final questioner, and he closed with this salutation to a clearly tired Judge Gorsuch and a nearly empty committee room: "I don't know if you're a drinking man, but go have a cocktail after this . . . just don't drink vodka!" (Whether that final salute was an oblique overture to President Trump's then still-unfolding entanglements with Russian operatives during his campaign and transition, or merely a disparaging of the consumption of Earl Warren's favorite liquor, we cannot truly know.)

Is Neil Gorsuch destined to be the honorary justice of the cocktail renaissance of the 2000s? Time will tell. In any event, the restoration of the Roberts bench to its full strength of nine justices—despite the labored path to that full strength—begins a new story of a "second" Roberts Court in a political era like no other in American history.

The Supreme Court's influence on the role of alcohol in American life and law would seem to be the least of our contemporary concerns.

I would argue not. What we have learned in our tour through the Supreme Court bar is that our Constitution and our justices are nothing if not resilient in times of trial and tribulation. If alcohol was occasionally the helpmeet to that resilience, it was also at times an inconvenient and unwelcome accessory in public life, accommodated to the law through truly judicious effort.

Yet the cocktail, that potent symbol of American ingenuity, has survived both eras of restriction and the age of Sour Mix. In this study of the Supreme Court's role in constructing the legal regimes of alcohol's regulation and enjoyment, one might ask: why fixate on the cocktail, per se, throughout these various legal eras? The answer—aside from the sheer nerdy pleasure of placing particular cocktails in their respective eras of American sociopolitical development—is that the cocktail has been a talisman of the most important moments of nexus between alcohol, law, and politics in the United States. When we think of the age of the political saloon and its rough-and-tumble American democracy, or the time of the speakeasy and its socially transgressive nightlife, or the postwar creation of suburban domesticity and its myths of a middle-class society, we can picture a cocktail—and, often, a very specific cocktail—at the center of things. Even our current, New Millennium finds the cocktail interwoven with contemporary debates over the social and economic impacts of urban gentrification—as upscale, hipster craft cocktail joints displace the local "dive" bars that served the also displaced racial and ethnic minorities priced out of their suddenly trendy neighborhoods. The cocktail in political and legal time has always been infused with issues of gender, class, and race—as have the Supreme Court's decisions on the use and restriction of alcohol, and as have eras of American sociopolitical development. Indeed, the very first epoch of mixed drinks—Chief John Marshall's great age of punch ("one strong one weak, one sour one sweet")—should not pass without remark for what *it* conveyed about the antebellum system of race. It was, after all, the white gentlemen's black servants who did much of the toiling behind the bar, mixing up those batches of punch, nogg, and julep.[5] Ephemera it may be, but the cocktail is also richly resonant of who we are and who we have been, as Americans.

The cocktail continues to serve as a talisman of our times. As we anticipate what lies in store for the Roberts Court II, I would argue that we contemplate a second "cocktail (book) of decisions." No simple sedative or solace, this volume can collect and analyze beverages from the age of the "Moscow Tool." This snarky variant on the Moscow Mule was being advertised on the blackboard outside one barroom in the New Orleans French Quarter on Inauguration Day, January 20, 2017. And it seems it was only one of many such sendups. The onset of the Trump era occasioned the creation of multiple lists of "tribute" cocktails— satirically composed and/or titled cocktails poking more than gentle fun at the new chief executive.[6] Archivists of our era must set to work in preserving these secretions of popular culture.

Joking aside, there is ample reason to think that the iconic cocktail for a Trump era should reach back to the golden age of mixology—as President Trump, for some conservative supporters, reaches back to the golden age of the Grand Old Party. Such times are eerily coincident with the vintage of Harding's "Return to Normalcy."

Conservative scholar Charles Kesler is one openly nostalgic fan of Trump's political agenda. As conservative commentator Andrew Sullivan noted in a column from May 2017,

"Kesler . . . saw in Trump's instincts on immigration and trade a return to 19th century Republicanism, which he believes is newly relevant in a post–Cold War world. The party of McKinley and Coolidge had, after all, been one that favored tariffs. The party platform of 1896 declared, 'We renew and emphasize our allegiance to the policy of protection, as the bulwark of American industrial independence, and the foundation of American development and prosperity.' In 1924, the GOP platform reiterated this: 'We believe in protection as a national policy.' Kesler saw Trump as tapping into this old Republicanism, noting that he was the first president in living memory to use the word *protection* favorably in his inaugural address."[7]

William McKinley, as attentive readers of the Fuller Court chapter will recall, is one of the few presidents to be honored with an eponymous cocktail: "McKinley's Delight," that lively variant of the Manhattan that supposedly christened his candidacy of 1896. Serving at the height of an unresolved "civil war" between wets and drys, McKinley was also laid low by the whiskey that was used in a vain attempt to keep him alive after he was shot by his anarchist and ex-bartender assassin.[8] A somewhat discomforting choice of president to seek to emulate, McKinley nevertheless presided over a grand time in American cocktailing. Calvin Coolidge, too—that beneficiary of another president's untimely but in his case natural death—oversaw the headiest years of Prohibition and "speaking easy" over a diverse mix of inspired concoctions. Coolidge's unhealthy predecessor, none other than President Harding, had already returned things to normalcy with the Scotch whiskey secreted in his executive golf bag.[9] Looking back at our history of alcohol in American life and law, then, it is plain to see that Republican eras were frequently good times for booziness.

If this is the Republicanism that Trump harkens back to, we can all raise a glass in unison.

NOTES

PREFACE AND INTRODUCTION

1. Mark Will-Weber, *Mint Juleps with Teddy Roosevelt: The Complete History of Presidential Drinking* (Washington, DC: Regnery Publishing, 2014).

2. Susan Cheever, *Drinking in America: Our Secret History* (New York: Twelve, Hachette Book Group, 2015), 1.

3. This institution proudly but likely incorrectly bills itself as the capital's oldest saloon; its "historic landmark" postcard purposefully re-creates many earlier such souvenir postcards of elegantly appointed nineteenth-century barrooms.

4. Judicial biography is one of the more academic strands of this line of work.

5. Intriguingly, one of the conference sponsors was distilled spirits purveyor Joseph E. Seagram and Sons. See David E. Kyvig, ed., *Law, Alcohol, and Order: Perspectives on National Prohibition* (Westport, CT: Greenwood Press, 1985).

6. Kenneth M. Murchison, *Federal Criminal Law Doctrines: The Forgotten Influence of National Prohibition* (Durham, NC: Duke University Press, 1994), 1.

7. A recent exception is the very fine *The War on Alcohol: Prohibition and the Rise of the American State*, by Lisa McGirr (2015). McGirr connects the expansion of the criminal enforcement and surveillance state under the regime of Prohibition to the creation of the modern regulatory state in the United States.

8. Melvin I. Urofsky, *Division and Discord: The Supreme Court under Stone and Vinson, 1941–1953* (Columbia: University of South Carolina Press, 1997), 7.

9. Credit for use of this metaphor in this way must go to Justice Antonin Scalia who, in a dissent toward the end of his judicial career, accused the majority in a highway sobriety checkpoint case of "serving up a freedom-destroying cocktail."

PROLOGUE

1. Joshua Glick, "On the Road: The Supreme Court and the History of Circuit Riding," *Cardozo Law Review* 24, no. 4 (2003): 1766.

2. Kenneth B. Umbreit, *Our 11 Chief Justices: A History of the Supreme Court in Terms of Their Personalities,* vols. 1 and 2 (Port Washington, NY: Kennikat Press, 1938), 31–32.

3. Eric Burns, *The Spirits of America: A Social History of Alcohol* (Philadelphia, PA: Temple University Press, 2004), 26.

4. David Wondrich, *Punch: The Delights (and Dangers) of the Flowing Bowl* (New York: Perigee Books, Penguin, 2010), 51.

5. Clare Cushman, *Table for 9: Supreme Court Food Traditions and Recipes* (Washington, DC: Supreme Court Historical Society Publication, 2017), 3.

6. Christine Sismondo, *America Walks into a Bar: A Spirited History of Taverns and Saloons, Speakeasies and Grog Shops* (New York: Oxford University Press, 2011), 54.

7. Sismondo, *America Walks,* 71.

8. Jack S. Blocker, "Tidy Pictures of Messy Behavior," review essay of Peter Thompson, *Rum Punch and Revolution* (1999), *Journal of Urban History* 29 (2003): 476.

9. Sismondo, *America Walks,* 82.

10. Blocker, "Tidy Pictures," 475.

11. Wayne Curtis, *And a Bottle of Rum: A History of the New World in Ten Cocktails* (New York: Three Rivers Press, 2006/2007), 80.

12. Sismondo, *America Walks,* 74; Burns, *The Spirits of America,* 7.

13. Quoted in Blocker, "Tidy Pictures," 478.

14. David Wondrich, *Imbibe!* (New York: Perigee Books, Penguin, 2007, 2015), 159.

15. Curtis, *And a Bottle of Rum,* 82–83.

16. The mint sling was identical to the pre-ice julep: alcohol with a little sugar and some water, with a scrape of nutmeg over the top or a sprig of mint in it, is how Wondrich (2015) characterizes it.

17. Wondrich, *Imbibe!*, 172.

18. Ibid., 217.

19. *And a Bottle of Rum* says it was principally utilized in antiabolitionist, Southern, and later alcohol prohibitionist propaganda (Curtis, 127–29).

20. Mark Edward Lender and James Kirby Martin, *Drinking in America: A History* (New York: The Free Press, 1987), 30.

21. W. J. Rorabaugh, *The Alcoholic Republic: An American Tradition* (New York: Oxford University Press, 1979), 9.

22. Sismondo, *America Walks*, 76; Burns, *The Spirits of America*, 9 .

23. Garrett Peck, *The Prohibition Hangover: Alcohol in America from De-mon Rum to Cult Cabernet* (Rutgers, NJ: Rutgers University Press, 2009), 56. In a recent act of clever branding by a nonprofit organization, "George Washington's Rye Whiskey" was secured as a registered trademark held by the Mt. Vernon Corporation, and subsequently adopted as the Official State Spirit of Virginia. "Made according to Washington's original recipe," avows the mount-vernon.org website, and further declares: "George Washington was once the largest whiskey producer in America. Today Mount Vernon continues the tradition of producing whiskey as well as other small batch distilled spirits at its historic Distillery & Gristmill site. *George Washington's Rye Whiskey*® is available for purchase in-person only at the Shops at Mount Vernon."

24. Burns, *The Spirits of America*, 39–40.

25. Curtis, *And a Bottle of Rum,* 138.

26. Ibid., 139.

27. Lender and Martin, *Drinking in America*, 31.

28. Ibid., 33.

29. Ibid., 51.

30. Burns, *The Spirits of America*, 45.

31. Rod Phillips, *Alcohol, a History* (Chapel Hill: University of North Carolina Press, 2014), 169.

32. Sismondo, *America Walks*, 85.

I. THE MARSHALL ERA OF PUNCH AND THE PUBLIC HOUSE

1. There is one earlier case, *Pesich v. Ware* from 1808, which concerned a suit about the recovery of cargo from a shipwreck—cargo that included kegs of wine, brandy, and cordials. But the decision turned less on alcoholic beverage per se and more on the law of salvage to be applied to the wreck and its contents' value. There was nevertheless some dispute about whether the goods were forfeited because they were found concealed and unmarked, with the

duties on them ostensibly not having been paid or secured. Case law about evading alcohol revenuers has a very long pedigree.

2. Duvall otherwise "made little—if any—significant impact during his tenure," according to Northwestern University website source oyez.org, which goes on to say that "none of [his opinions] were significant to anyone but the parties involved." Let that record now stand corrected.

3. David Wondrich, *Imbibe!* (New York: Perigee Books, Penguin, 2007, 2015), 82.

4. David Wondrich, *Punch: The Delights (and Dangers) of the Flowing Bowl* (New York: Perigee Books, Penguin, 2010), 243.

5. Punch was in fact the first alcoholic beverage served at English coffee-houses, as the service of wine or beer, but not liquor drinks, required a government license. David Wondrich and Jeff Berry, "Members Only: Club Cocktails in History," seminar presentation at the annual meeting of Tales of the Cocktail, New Orleans, LA, July 21, 2016.

6. Mary Newton Standard, *John Marshall and His Home* (avail. Collection of the Supreme Court Historical Society, 1913, 1st printing), 36.

7. Standard, *John Marshall*, 37, 39.

8. Clare Cushman, *Courtwatchers* (Lanham, MD: Rowman & Littlefield Publishers, 2011), 15.

9. H. H. Walker Lewis, *Without Fear or Favor: A Biography of Chief Justice Roger Brooke Taney* (New York: Houghton Mifflin, 1965), 241.

10. See also Clare Cushman, *Table for 9: Supreme Court Food Traditions and Recipes* (Washington, DC: Supreme Court Historical Society Publication, 2017).

11. Cushman, *Courtwatchers*, 38.

12. Garrett Peck, *Prohibition in Washington, D.C.: How Dry We Weren't* (Charleston, SC: The History Press, 2011), 23.

13. Interestingly, also not far from the current site of the Temperance Fountain. Donated in 1887 by a dentist-crusader in the temperance movement, "the Temperance Fountain was originally placed at a prominent location: Seventh and Pennsylvania Avenue, across from Center Market and near . . . the halfway point between the Capitol and White House. . . . The message was to drink water, not whiskey, as there were, by then, so many saloons along the Avenue to tempt passersby.

14. James Sterling Young, *The Washington Community, 1800–1828* (New York: Columbia University Press, 1966), 71.

15. Young, *The Washington Community*, 76–77.

16. Ibid., 76.

17. Ibid., 77.

18. Ibid., 78.

19. Ibid., 79.

20. G. Edward White, *The Marshall Court and Cultural Change, 1815–1835* (New York: Oxford University Press, 1991), 376.

21. White, *The Marshall Court,* 160–61.

22. Ibid., 158, 184.

23. Ibid., 186–88.

24. Ibid., 193.

25. Ibid., 191.

26. Cushman, *Table for 9,* 5.

27. White, *The Marshall Court,* 381.

28. Ibid., 382.

29. Young, *The Washington Community,* 94.

30. Ibid., 102.

31. Ibid., 214.

32. W. J. Rorabaugh, *The Alcoholic Republic: An American Tradition* (New York: Oxford University Press, 1979), 103.

33. Quoted in Lewis, *Without Fear or Favor,* 278.

34. Rorabaugh, *The Alcoholic Republic,* 19.

35. Evan T. Lawson, "The Future of the Three-Tiered System as a Control of Marketing Alcoholic Beverages," in *Social and Economic Control of Alcohol: The 21st Amendment in the 21st Century,* ed. Carole L. Jurkiewicz and Murphy J. Painter (Boca Raton, FL: CRC Press, 2008), 47.

36. Mark Edward Lender and James Kirby Martin, *Drinking in America: A History* (New York: The Free Press, 1987), 47.

37. Christine Sismondo, *America Walks into a Bar: A Spirited History of Taverns and Saloons, Speakeasies and Grog Shops* (New York: Oxford University Press, 2011), 95.

38. Wondrich, *Imbibe!,* 215; Wayne Curtis, *And a Bottle of Rum: A History of the New World in Ten Cocktails* (New York: Three Rivers Press, 2006/7), 195.

39. Wondrich, *Imbibe!,* 227.

40. Iain Gately, *Drink: A Cultural History of Alcohol* (New York: Gotham Books: New York, 2008), 149, 151.

41. Lender and Martin, *Drinking in America,* 56.

42. Ibid., 52–53.

43. Ibid., 68; Eric Burns, *The Spirits of America: A Social History of Alcohol* (Philadelphia, PA: Temple University Press, 2004), 80.

2. THE LONG TANEY ERA OF THE
MINT JULEP

1. The case raised no constitutional issues, and was part of the Supreme Court's ordinary appellate jurisdiction—a workload of routine appeals the High Court was saddled with until legislative reform of the federal judicial system at the close of the nineteenth century.

2. W. J. Rorabaugh, *The Alcoholic Republic: An American Tradition* (New York: Oxford University Press, 1979), 196.

3. David Wondrich, *Imbibe!* (New York: Perigee Books, Penguin, 2007, 2015), 192.

4. Gregory Priebe and Nicole Priebe, *Forgotten Maryland Cocktails: A History of Drinking in the Free State* (Charleston, SC: American Palate, The History Press, 2015), 95.

5. Andrew Barr, *Drink: A Social History of America* (New York: Carroll and Graf, Publishers, 1999), 46.

6. H. H. Walker Lewis, *Without Fear or Favor: A Biography of Chief Justice Roger Brooke Taney* (New York: Houghton Mifflin, 1965), 68.

7. Barr, *Drink*, 203.

8. Wondrich, *Imbibe!*, 195–96.

9. Mark Will-Weber, *Mint Juleps with Teddy Roosevelt: The Complete History of Presidential Drinking* (Washington, DC: Regnery Publishing, 2014), 113.

10. Christine Sismondo, *America Walks into a Bar: A Spirited History of Taverns and Saloons, Speakeasies and Grog Shops* (New York: Oxford University Press, 2011), 121.

11. An inventive and influential mixologist, Willard also set off the Peach Brandy Punch craze and defined the apple (brandy) toddy (Sismondo, *America Walks,* 109–110; Wondrich, *Imbibe!*, 52). Ted Saucier's *Bottoms Up* of 1951 (p. 254) shows the homage paid to bartender Willard, in that a peach and apricot brandy cocktail was still being offered by the hotel at that time and was being called the Willard Hotel cocktail (see also Wondrich, *Imbibe!*, 9, 12).

12. Wondrich, *Imbibe!*, 10–11.

13. Catherine Gilbert Murdock, *Domesticating Drink: Women, Men, and Alcohol in America, 1870–1940* (Baltimore, MD: The Johns Hopkins University Press, 1998), 106.

14. Wondrich, *Imbibe!*, 53.

15. Iain Gately, *Drink: A Cultural History of Alcohol* (New York: Gotham Books, 2008), 315.

16. Lewis, *Without Fear or Favor,* 263.

17. Lewis, *Without Fear or Favor,* 26; confirmed in Kenneth B. Umbreit, *Our 11 Chief Justices: A History of the Supreme Court in Terms of Their Personalities,* vols. 1 and 2 (Port Washington, NY: Kennikat Press, 1938), 203.

18. Priebe and Priebe, *Forgotten Maryland Cocktails,* 66.

19. Confirmed by Priebe and Priebe, *Forgotten Maryland Cocktails,* 68.

20. Wondrich, *Imbibe!,* 161.

21. Lewis, *Without Fear or Favor,* 258–59.

22. Ibid., 464.

23. Eric Burns, *The Spirits of America: A Social History of Alcohol* (Philadelphia, PA: Temple University Press, 2004), 65.

24. Burns, *The Spirits of America,* 82.

25. Lewis, *Without Fear or Favor,* 230.

26. Priebe and Priebe, *Forgotten Maryland Cocktails,* 41, 59.

27. Lewis, *Without Fear or Favor,* 233.

28. Ibid., 192.

29. Will-Weber, *Mint Juleps,* 84.

30. Garrett Peck, *The Prohibition Hangover: Alcohol in America from Demon Rum to Cult Cabernet* (Rutgers, NJ: Rutgers University Press, 2009), 61.

31. Carole L. Jurkiewicz and Murphy J. Painter, "Why We Control Alcohol the Way We Do," in *Social and Economic Control of Alcohol: the 21st Amendment in the 21st Century*, ed. Carole L. Jurkiewicz and Murphy J. Painter (Boca Raton, FL: CRC Press, 2008), 4.

32. Lewis, *Without Fear or Favor*, 83, 251.

33. John Niven, *Salmon P. Chase: a Biography* (New York: Oxford University Press, 1995), 82.

34. Lewis, *Without Fear or Favor*, 277–78.

35. Ibid., 278–79.

36. Ibid., 314.

37. Carl Brent Swisher, *Roger B. Taney* (New York: MacMillan, 1935), 353.

38. Lewis, *Without Fear or Favor*, 257.

39. Ibid., 269.

40. Ibid., 286.

41. Ibid., 279.

42. Ibid., 466.

43. This latter, according to Clare Cushman, in remarks during her moderation of the 2016 Smithsonian program "Legal Eats." See also *Courtwatchers* p. 123, 208.

44. Clare Cushman, *Courtwatchers* (Lanham, MD: Rowman & Littlefield Publishers, 2011), 143.

45. Quoted in Lewis, *Without Fear or Favor*, 318.

46. Ibid.

47. Peter Charles Hoffer, William James Hull Hoffer, and N. E. H. Hull, *The Supreme Court: An Essential History* (Lawrence: University Press of Kansas, 2007), 100.

48. See Lewis, *Without Fear or Favor*, 423ff, but cf. Melvin I. Urofsky, *Dissent and the U.S. Supreme Court* (New York: Pantheon Books, 2015).

49. Swisher, *Roger B. Taney*, 399–402.

50. Ibid., 359.

3. THE CHASE ERA

1. John Niven, *Salmon P. Chase: A Biography* (New York: Oxford University Press, 1995), 35, 43–44, 72, 205.

2. Niven, *Salmon P. Chase*, 399.

3. Peter Charles Hoffer, William James Hull Hoffer, and N. E. H. Hull, *The Supreme Court: An Essential History* (Lawrence: University Press of Kansas, 2007), 108.

4. Niven, *Salmon P. Chase*, 389.

5. Ibid., 377.

6. Ibid., 58–59.

7. Catherine Gilbert Murdock, *Domesticating Drink: Women, Men, and Alcohol in America, 1870–1940* (Baltimore, MD: The Johns Hopkins University Press, 1998), 19.

8. Niven, *Salmon P. Chase*, 110.

9. Ibid., 199–200.

10. Ibid., 372.

11. Christine Sismondo, *America Walks into a Bar: A Spirited History of Taverns and Saloons, Speakeasies and Grog Shops* (New York: Oxford University Press, 2011), 138.

12. Daniel Okrent, *Last Call: The Rise and Fall of Prohibition* (New York: Scribner, 2010), 9.

13. The temptations of that postwar Washington could be terminal, too. The "free and intemperate use of intoxicating liquors"—the undoing of one Federalist jurist back in the days of the early Republic—would claim the career of a second federal judge during the Chase era: Mark W. Delahay, appointed by Lincoln to the federal district court in 1864, and presented with articles of impeachment in 1873 for "intoxication off the bench as well as on the bench." Delahay resigned from office that same year before any trial could be held. Once again and as with Judge Pickering in 1803, drunkenness met the constitutional standard for impeachment—or, at least, confounded one's holding office "during good behavior."

14. Andrew Barr, *Drink: A Social History of America* (New York: Carroll and Graf, Publishers, 1999), 46. H. H. Walker Lewis, *Without Fear or Favor: a Biography of Chief Justice Roger Brooke Taney* (New York: Houghton Mifflin, 1965), ch. 2; Iain Gately, *Drink: A Cultural History of Alcohol* (New York: Gotham Books, 2008), 254–55.

15. Murdock, *Domesticating Drink*, 62.

16. Alice Hunt Sokoloff, *Kate Chase for the Defense: A Biography* (New York: Dodd Mead and Co., 1971), 50–51.

17. Niven, *Salmon P. Chase*, 202–3.

18. Field also earns the distinction of being the only other justice as political as Chase on the latter's court. As Hoffer et al. characterize him: "A brilliant small man with a large ego (he posed for his portraits with his hand inside his vest like Napoleon Bonaparte) . . . [Field] made the High Court a platform for his politics" (*The Supreme Court*, 111); Niven, *Salmon P. Chase*, 402.

19. Niven, *Salmon P. Chase*, 25, 141.

20. Ibid., 234; Sokoloff, *Kate Chase*, 50–51.

21. Niven, *Salmon P. Chase*, 340.

22. Ibid., 442.

23. Ibid., 444.

24. Sismondo, *America Walks*, 111–12.

25. Quoted in David Wondrich, *Imbibe!* (New York: Perigee Books, Penguin, 2007, 2015), 20.

26. Wondrich, *Imbibe!*, 141.

27. Ibid., 142–43.

28. Gately, *Drink*, 255.

29. Murdock, *Domesticating Drink*, 73.

30. Ibid., 107.

31. Gately, *Drink*, 315.

32. Ibid., 317.

33. Eric Burns, *The Spirits of America: A Social History of Alcohol* (Philadelphia, PA: Temple University Press, 2004), 94.

34. This one also applied to beer; Gately, *Drink*, 316.

35. Burns, *The Spirits of America*, 94.

36. Carole L. Jurkiewicz and Murphy J. Painter, "Why We Control Alcohol the Way We Do," in *Social and Economic Control of Alcohol: The 21st Amendment in the 21st Century*, ed. Carole L. Jurkiewicz and Murphy J. Painter (Boca Raton, FL: CRC Press, 2008), 4.

37. Robert J. Miller and Maril Hazlett, "The 'Drunken Indian': Myth Distilled into Reality Through Federal Indian Alcohol Policy," *Arizona State Law Journal* 28 (1996): 248.

38. *In re Henderson's Distilled Spirits* (1871).

39. The case facts had involved imported dry goods, but the statute in question also applied to "wine, rum, brandy, whiskey and other distilled spiritous liquors, &c." and to "persons selling the same by wholesale, bale or package, hogshead, barrel, or tierce." Interestingly, it is one of the few nonunanimous Marshall Court rulings, occurring later in the Marshall era.

40. Melvin I. Urofsky, *Dissent and the U.S. Supreme Court* (New York: Pantheon Books, 2015), 97.

41. Field provides a fuller explanation for the legitimacy of state "health" measures with respect to alcohol—and their lack of constitutional abrogation—in his Fuller era testimonial of 1890, in *Crowley v. Christensen.*

4. THE WAITE ERA OF THE GRAND POLITICAL SALOON

1. See Christine Sismondo, *America Walks into a Bar: A Spirited History of Taverns and Saloons, Speakeasies and Grog Shops* (New York: Oxford University Press, 2011), 181. While other sources find the etymological account to be apocryphal at best, there is no doubt that Grant was a fixture at the Willard, as he was at the Ebbitt, which functioned as a boardinghouse saloon near the White House. Its current iteration, the Old Ebbitt Grill, commemorates the association with its period-replicate Grant's Bar, off the main Atrium.

2. C. Peter Magrath, *Morrison Waite: The Triumph of Character* (New York: Macmillan, 1963), 306.

3. Ibid., 306.

4. Ibid., 257.

5. Clare Cushman, *Courtwatchers* (Lanham, MD: Rowman & Littlefield Publishers, 2011), 122.

6. David Wondrich and Jeff Berry, "Members Only: Club Cocktails in History," seminar presentation at the annual meeting of Tales of the Cocktail, New Orleans, LA, July 21, 2016; but cf. Philip Greene, *The Manhattan: The Story of the First American Cocktail* (New York: Sterling Epicure, 2016), which disputes both accounts.

7. David Wondrich, *Imbibe!* (New York: Perigee Books, Penguin, 2007, 2015), 233.

8. Garrett Peck, *Prohibition in Washington, D.C.: How Dry We Weren't* (Charleston, SC: The History Press, 2011), 25, 110 [recipe].

9. Wondrich, *Imbibe!*, 147.

10. Ibid., 148.

11. Daniel Okrent, *Last Call: The Rise and Fall of Prohibition* (New York: Scribner, 2010), 194.

12. Wondrich, *Imbibe!*, 57.

13. Ibid., 115–18.

14. Eric Burns, *The Spirits of America: A Social History of Alcohol* (Philadelphia, PA: Temple University Press, 2004), 179.

15. Catherine Gilbert Murdock, *Domesticating Drink: Women, Men, and Alcohol in America, 1870–1940* (Baltimore, MD: The Johns Hopkins University Press, 1998), 79.

16. Mark Edward Lender and James Kirby Martin, *Drinking in America: A History* (New York: The Free Press, 1987), 98.

17. Burns, *The Spirits of America,* 150.

18. Melvin I. Urofsky, *Dissent and the U.S. Supreme Court* (New York: Pantheon Books, 2015), 101.

19. "There must be," Marshall had reasoned, "a point of time when the prohibition ceases, and the power of the State to tax commences; we cannot admit that this point of time is the instant that the articles enter the country. . . . [I]t is sufficient for the present to say, generally, that when the importer has so acted upon the thing imported that it has become incorporated and mixed up with the mass of property in the country, it has, perhaps, lost its distinctive character as an import, and has become subject to the taxing power of the State; but while remaining the property of the importer, in his warehouse, in the original form or package in which it was imported, a tax upon it is too plainly a duty on imports to escape the prohibition in the Constitution."

20. Robert J. Miller and Maril Hazlett, "The 'Drunken Indian': Myth Distilled into Reality Through Federal Indian Alcohol Policy," *Arizona State Law Journal* 28, no. 1 (1996): 261.

21. See Peter Charles Hoffer, William James Hull Hoffer, and N. E. H. Hull, *The Supreme Court: An Essential History* (Lawrence: University Press of Kansas, 2007), 133–134.

22. Kenneth M. Murchison, *Federal Criminal Law Doctrines: The Forgotten Influence of National Prohibition* (Durham, NC: Duke University Press, 1994), 127.

23. Iain Gately, *Drink: A Cultural History of Alcohol* (New York: Gotham Books, 2008), 318.

24. Wayne Curtis, *And a Bottle of Rum: A History of the New World in Ten Cocktails* (New York: Three Rivers Press, 2006/2007), 153.

25. Michael A. Lerner, *Dry Manhattan: Prohibition in New York City* (Cambridge, MA: Harvard University Press, 2007), 51.

26. Okrent, *Last Call,* 118.

5. THE FULLER ERA

1. The label referred not to Cleveland's taste or capacity for whiskey but to his political party status as probusiness Republican in all but name—and of an aristocratically reactionary mien to boot. The GOP so dominated American national politics during the late nineteenth through early twentieth centuries that the only presidential candidates put forward by the Democratic Party were those who ideologically aligned with and fully promoted political conservatism and laissez-faire capitalism.

2. Daniel Okrent, *Last Call: The Rise and Fall of Prohibition* (New York: Scribner, 2010), 26; Lisa McGirr, *The War on Alcohol: Prohibition and the Rise of the American State* (New York: Norton, 2015), 14–16.

3. James W. Ely, *The Chief Justiceship of Melville W. Fuller, 1888–1910* (Columbia: University of South Carolina Press, 1995), 35.

4. Clare Cushman, *Courtwatchers* (Lanham, MD: Rowman & Littlefield Publishers, 2011), 42.

5. Ely, *The Chief Justiceship*, 39.

6. Ibid.

7. Cushman, *Courtwatchers*, 96.

8. In any case, the practice ended after a leak in an important economic case caused a panic on Wall Street, and the tradition of the junior justice as conference room doorkeeper thus began.

9. Ely, *The Chief Justiceship*, 14.

10. Ibid., 9.

11. Ibid., 10.

12. Cushman, *Courtwatchers*, 216, quoting a nineteenth century law clerk of justice John Marshall Harlan, as to how the clerk adjusted his work hours to accommodate his justice's active social life. See also Cushman 50–51; 54–55.

13. Ely, *The Chief Justiceship*, 54.

14. Ibid.

15. Ibid., 52.

16. Stanley Clisby Arthur, *Famous New Orleans Drinks and How to Mix 'Em* (Gretna, LA: Pelican Books, 1937, 1977), 22.

17. Retaining its association with President William McKinley, the name commemorates the USS *Maine*, the battleship McKinley had dispatched to Havana harbor to protect American interests in Cuba, which promptly exploded under suspicious circumstances and incited the Spanish-American War. Philip Greene, *The Manhattan: The Story of the First American Cocktail* (New York: Sterling Epicure, 2016), 161.

18. Greene, *The Manhattan*, 75–76.

19. David Wondrich, *Imbibe!* (New York: Perigee Books, Penguin, 2007, 2015), 174, 271.

20. Other stories of the daiquiri's birth cite its context as Teddy Roosevelt's campaign for San Juan Hill in 1898, during the Spanish-American War.

21. Wayne Curtis, *And a Bottle of Rum: A History of the New World in Ten Cocktails* (New York: Three Rivers Press, 2006/2007), 172.

22. Wondrich, *Imbibe!*, 72.

23. David Wondrich and Jeff Berry, "Members Only: Club Cocktails in History," seminar presentation at the annual meeting of Tales of the Cocktail, New Orleans, LA, July 21, 2016.

24. Arthur, *Famous New Orleans Drinks*, 49.

25. Indeed, this variation strongly suggests the martini's reputed source of origin in the Martinez cocktail, whose classic recipe first appeared in O. H. Byron's 1884 *Modern Bartenders' Guide*. What ties the lesser-known Martinez to its Waite era past is its use of sweet-style Holland (or Old Tom's) gin and Italian sweet vermouth. It shows its transitional identity, nonetheless, by sharing one quality with the Fuller era's totemic drink, McKinley's Delight, in the use of an elegant and relatively novel cherry-based spirit. (Maraschino liqueur for the Martinez, as in Jerry Thomas's 1887 edition, whereas McKinley's Delight takes a dash of the newly introduced Cherry Heering.) However, other accounts say that the more commonly available orange curaçao was the original sweet ingredient for the Martinez recipe of the 1870s.

26. Wondrich, *Imbibe!*, 237–42; Arthur, *Famous New Orleans Drinks*, 18.

27. Christine Sismondo, *America Walks into a Bar: A Spirited History of Taverns and Saloons, Speakeasies and Grog Shops* (New York: Oxford University Press, 2011), 201.

28. William Schmidt (The Only William), *The Flowing Bowl: What and When to Drink* (New York: Charles Webster & Co., 1892; Middletown, DE: Vintage Cocktail Books, 2008), xiv.

29. Mark Edward Lender and James Kirby Martin, *Drinking in America: A History* (New York: The Free Press, 1987), 98.

30. Catherine Gilbert Murdock, *Domesticating Drink: Women, Men, and Alcohol in America, 1870–1940* (Baltimore, MD: The Johns Hopkins University Press, 1998), 43.

31. Murdock, *Domesticating Drink*, 52, 56.

32. Ibid., 62, 66.

33. Eric Burns, *The Spirits of America: A Social History of Alcohol* (Philadelphia, PA: Temple University Press, 2004), 149.

34. *The Flowing Bowl*'s section on "Some Sample Menus" reproduces a lavish spread put on by Delmonico's for the City Court of New York "Hale and Farewell Banquet tendered to the Incoming and Outgoing Justices," on De-

cember 22, 1890. The nine-course meal featured wine pairings for each menu item, including Chablis, amontillado sherry, German liebfraumilch, Mumm's and Pommery dry champagnes, a Grand Cru Bordeaux, and a Grand Cru Burgundy. Also listed on the menu to follow the entrée course was "cigarettes," the newfangled and prerolled variety, which was a luxury item. The same source reports the menu for another decadent banquet at Delmonico's, for the New York Board of Trade and Transportation in 1891, where The Only William notes as the bottom, "At this banquet, the Honorable William Wisdom, Secretary of the Treasury, died."

35. Murdock, *Domesticating Drink,* 76.

36. Ibid., 108.

37. Ibid., 85.

38. Burns, *The Spirits of America,* 160–61.

39. Ibid., 178.

40. Murdock, *Domesticating Drink,* 13.

41. Okrent, *Last Call,* 36–7, 40–41.

42. Okrent, *Last Call,* 42 ff.; McGirr, *The War on Alcohol,* 20–21; 27–29.

43. Lender and Martin, *Drinking in America,* 127.

44. Peter Charles Hoffer, William James Hull Hoffer, and N. E. H. Hull, *The Supreme Court: An Essential History* (Lawrence: University Press of Kansas, 2007), 189.

45. Robert B. Highsaw, *Edward Douglass White: Defender of the Conservative Faith* (Baton Rouge: Louisiana State University Press, 1981), 78.

46. Acknowledging that "in some of the states, authority to proceed in respect of liquors, without warrant in the first instance, is expressly given by statute, but is accompanied by the provision that when the seizure is so made, the property seized is to be kept in safety for a reasonable time until a warrant can be procured. . . . Should the officer neglect to obtain a warrant within such time, he will be liable as a trespasser." South Carolina's Dispensary Act could not override its constitution's Fourth Amendment equivalent.

47. This view would resurface, again and again, even after alcohol became subject to the post–Repeal of Prohibition regime of pervasive governmental regulation. Fuller era commerce jurisprudence would finally triumph over state antialcohol moralism and free market restriction in the late Rehnquist era decision of *Granholm v. Heald* in 2005.

48. The year 1905 saw yet another decisional update to the perennial litigation involving South Carolina's liquor laws. The state had engaged in the liquor business itself by establishing dispensaries for the wholesale and retail sale of spirituous liquor, and then prohibiting sale by other than the dispensers. This feature of state regulation had animated the overly aggressive constables in *In re Swan* and *Scott v. Donald.* In *State of South Carolina v. United States,* the

6–3 Fuller Court held that license taxes charged by the federal government on persons selling liquor were not invalidated by the fact that those sellers were the agents of the state—moving Associate Justice White to object in dissent, on behalf of state sovereignty.

49. Ely, *The Chief Justiceship*, 34.

50. Highsaw, *Edward Douglass White*, 115.

51. Marcia Yablon, "The Prohibition Hangover: Why We Are Still Feeling the Effects of Prohibition," *Virginia Journal of Social Policy and the Law* 13, no. 3 (2006): 582–83.

52. Okrent, *Last Call*, 56–59.

53. Quoted in McGirr, *The War on Alcohol*, 29.

54. Judicial oenophilia was even extended to sake in *Komada and Co. v. U.S.* in 1910 where the court upheld its classification as a still wine and not a distilled spirit, for the purposes of import duties owed.

6. THE WHITE ERA AND THE PROHIBITION AMENDMENT

1. Wilson, who enjoyed the occasional Scotch highball, thought moderation an acceptable form of temperance, although he did appoint two noted dries to his cabinet: Secretary of the Navy Josephus Daniels, who outlawed the officers' "wine mess" at U.S. naval installations, and Secretary of State William Jennings Bryan, whose first formal diplomatic function, held in the Presidential Suite of the Willard Hotel, was an alcohol-free luncheon. Daniel Okrent, *Last Call: The Rise and Fall of Prohibition* (New York: Scribner, 2010), 77.

2. Eric Burns, *The Spirits of America: A Social History of Alcohol* (Philadelphia, PA: Temple University Press, 2004), 178–79.

3. Burns, *The Spirits of America*, 165.

4. Mark Edward Lender and James Kirby Martin, *Drinking in America: A History* (New York: The Free Press, 1987), 129; Lisa McGirr, *The War on Alcohol: Prohibition and the Rise of the American State* (New York: Norton, 2015), 32–33.

5. Garrett Peck, *Prohibition in Washington, D.C.: How Dry We Weren't* (Charleston, SC: The History Press, 2011), 88.

6. Okrent, *Last Call*, 128.

7. When quoted in Jeffrey W. Linkenbach, "Perceptions, Policies, and Social Norms: Transforming Alcohol Cultures over the Next 100 Years," in *Social and Economic Control of Alcohol: The 21st Amendment in the 21st Century*, ed. Carole L. Jurkiewicz and Murphy J. Painter (Boca Raton, FL: CRC Press, 2008), 142–43, this statement was attributed to a Midwestern senator of the period, sometime in the early 1900s. The source for this information was listed

as R. Svendsen, "Chemical Health: A Planning Guide for Congregations in Response to Alcohol and Other Drugs Issues," *A Publication of the Division for Life and Mission in the Congregation of the American Lutheran Church* (1986). Additional verification suggests that it originated with a speech delivered in 1952 on the floor of the Mississippi state legislature, by Judge Noah S. "Soggy" Sweat Jr., as the state considered the repeal of its own post-Prohibition dry laws. Renowned for the grand rhetorical terminology with which it seems to come down firmly and decisively on both sides of the liquor question, the "if-by-whiskey" speech encapsulates the duplicity that existed around the American prohibition of alcohol—whatever the time period.

8. Stanley Clisby Arthur, *Famous New Orleans Drinks and How to Mix 'Em* (Gretna, LA: Pelican Books, 1937, 1977), 1972 edition, 45.

9. David Wondrich, *Imbibe!* (New York: Perigee Books, Penguin, 2007, 2015), 138–39.

10. Christine Sismondo, *America Walks into a Bar: A Spirited History of Taverns and Saloons, Speakeasies and Grog Shops* (New York: Oxford University Press, 2011), 201.

11. David Wondrich and Jeff Berry, "Members Only: Club Cocktails in History," seminar presentation at the annual meeting of Tales of the Cocktail, New Orleans, LA, July 21, 2016.

12. Wondrich, *Imbibe!*, 139–40.

13. Kerri McCaffety, *Obituary Cocktail: The Great Saloons of New Orleans*, 2nd ed. (New Orleans, LA: Pontalba Press, 2001), 48.

14. Okrent, *Last Call*, 258.

15. Sister Marie Carolyn Klinkhamer, OP, MA, "Edward Douglass White, Chief Justice of the U.S.," (PhD diss., Catholic University of America, 1943), 41.

16. A 1914 menu from New Orleans's Grunewald Hotel contributes the Tulane cocktail, a further homage to its alumnus's era if not specifically to the chief justice himself. The Tulane, essentially a variant on the dry martini, added a bar spoon of the relatively obscure ingredient strawberry brandy, an eau de vie or clear, fruit-essence distilled liquor (as described in Jacques Straub's *Drinks* of 1914). Its proportions appeared to change over time, as the recipe in Ted Saucier's *Bottoms Up* (1951), reflecting a 1936 cocktail daily special from the Roosevelt Hotel (nee the Grunewald), called for a one-third ratio of each ingredient.

Before 1920, White's era and especially White's home city celebrated the popularity and consumption of various continental liquors that fell out of fashion and use during Prohibition: in addition to the aforementioned eau de vie, there was Chartreuse, kümmel, Swedish punsch (like an arrack), and Ojen. Yellow Chartreuse, a French digestive liqueur whose original monastery recipe dates back centuries, had been one of the several, layered spirit and cordial ingredients that made up the Pousse Café—a traditional after dinner drink in nineteenth-century New Orleans that migrated to the elegant dining rooms of America's major cities by the turn of the twentieth century. Chartreuse (the green) was also part of the wider world of pre- to Prohibition-era cocktails, taking a turn with dry gin, Maraschino, and lime in the Detroit Athletic Club cocktail called the Last Word. *Shaking Up Prohibition in New Orleans*, a recently published cocktail book that reproduces a Prohibition-era typescript collection of drink recipes, contributes the judicially inspired Oyez!, a 1:1 stir of Gordon's dry gin and Bols kümmel. See Olive Leonhardt and Hilda Phelps Hammond, *Shaking Up Prohibition in New Orleans: Authentic Vintage Cocktails from A to Z* (Baton Rouge: Louisiana State University Press, 2015), 33. Ojen, too, was huge in New Orleans, especially during Mardi Gras, where it was served like absinthe (which it resembles), a la frappe. An apocryphal story is told of a member of the New Orleans carnival krewe of Rex cornering the last batch of Ojen before its original twentieth-century formula went out of production.

These unusual spirits only returned to the American bar, other than fleetingly and spottily (see, for instance, their occasional use in the older recipes of the 1951 *Bottoms Up*), with the craft cocktail movement and vintage cocktails renaissance of the 2000s.

17. Walter E. Joyce, "Edward Douglass White: The Louisiana Years, Early Life and On the Bench," *Tulane Law Review* 41, no. 4 (1967): 768, 751.

18. Miceli's history of the club lists "White, Edward D." as a "Resident" member, whose membership dated from September 23, 1891; Augusto Miceli, *The Pickwick Club of New Orleans* (New Orleans, LA: Pickwick Press, 1964; Hauser Printing Co., 1992), appendix A.

19. Miceli's history of the club lists "White, Edward D." of the 1st Louisiana Infantry, as among the "Members Listed in Units Participating in the 'Battle' of Liberty Place, Sept. 14, 1874" (Miceli, *The Pickwick Club*, appendix J).

20. Justin A. Nystrom, *New Orleans after the Civil War: Race, Politics, and a New Birth of Freedom* (Baltimore, MD: The Johns Hopkins University Press, 2010), 164–65.

21. Umbreit in his *History of the Supreme Court in Terms of Their Personalities* expresses being "inclined to think that [White] participated to some extent in the activities of the secret societies" like the White League and attributes his early success as a state senator in the aftermath of Reconstruction to the support of the secret societies; Kenneth B. Umbreit, *Our 11 Chief Justices: A History of the Supreme Court in Terms of Their Personalities*, vols. 1 and 2 (Port Washington, NY: Kennikat Press, 1938), 373–74. There is further circumstantial evidence of White's Old South affinities. In the pre–Civil Rights

era, he was the subject of a curiously romantic homage-to-the-noble-lost-cause series of biographies: in addition to the unabashedly honorific Klinkhamer 1943 dissertation (which was animated by and celebrative of White's strong Jesuit connection), he was lionized in a children's book published in 1962 (*The Man on the Bench*, available from the Supreme Court Historical Society), and in a truly weird play "Father Chief Justice" produced at Louisiana State University in 2001 and based on a 1911 tribute published in the *American Law Review*; see Robert B. Highsaw, *Edward Douglass White: Defender of the Conservative Faith* (Baton Rouge: Louisiana State University Press, 1981), 6–7.

22. David E. Kyvig, *Repealing National Prohibition* (Kent, OH: The Kent State University Press, 2000), 25.

23. https://imbibekc.com/2015/08/06/pickwick-club/.

24. Peter Charles Hoffer, William James Hull Hoffer, and N. E. H. Hull, *The Supreme Court: An Essential History* (Lawrence: University Press of Kansas, 2007), 192.

25. Umbreit, *Our 11 Chief Justices*, 383–84.

26. Highsaw, *Edward Douglass White*, 179; Umbreit, *Our 11 Chief Justices*, confirms this, 383.

27. Klinkhamer, "Edward Douglass White," 65.

28. Who Urofsky claims "heartily disliked" White; Melvin I. Urofsky, *Dissent and the U.S. Supreme Court* (New York: Pantheon Books, 2015), 135.

29. Highsaw, *Edward Douglass White*, 184.

30. Hoffer, Hoffer, and Hull, *The Supreme Court*, 199.

31. For a case that concerns a lighter-hearted side of this jurisprudence, as well as concerning a substance that would become both a popular mixer and a spirituous liquor substitute, see Hughes's opinion for the court in *U.S. v. Forty Barrel and Twenty Kegs of Coca Cola* (1916).

32. Kyvig, *Repealing National Prohibition*, 9.

33. Burns, *The Spirits of America*, 173.

34. Kyvig, *Repealing National Prohibition*, 11.

35. Kenneth M. Murchison, *Federal Criminal Law Doctrines: The Forgotten Influence of National Prohibition* (Durham, NC: Duke University Press, 1994), 7–8.

36. Okrent, *Last Call*, 120–21.

37. Kyvig, *Repealing National Prohibition*, 16.

38. *Jacob Rupert v. Caffey* (1920) held that even nonintoxicating beer beverages could be prohibited in the interest of preventing traffic in alcohol. *U.S. v. Standard Brewery* (1920) supported this conclusion.

39. Murchison, *Federal Criminal Law Doctrines*, 112.

40. Ibid., 19.

41. In the words of Justice Clarke's opinion for the court: "The contention that the constitutional rights of defendant were waived when his wife admitted to his home the government officers, who came, without warrant, demanding admission to make search of it under government authority, cannot be entertained. We need not consider whether it is possible for a wife, in the absence of her husband, thus to waive his constitutional rights, for it is perfectly clear that under the implied coercion here presented, no such waiver was intended or effected."

42. Theodore B. Lacey, "The Supreme Court's Fluctuating Reaction to National Prohibition in Fourth Amendment Decisions from 1920–1933" (senior thesis, Princeton University, 2005), ch. 5.

43. White passed away in office in May of 1921, and Taft assumed his seat in late June of that same year. The opinion of the Court in *Burdeau* (from which Brandeis and Holmes dissented) was actually issued after White's death but before Taft had taken part in any of the Supreme Court's cases.

44. Murchison, *Federal Criminal Law Doctrines*, 131–32.

7. THE TAFT ERA OF LAW, ORDER, AND BOOTLEGGING

1. Wilson ultimately nominated Louis Brandeis, who would be Chief Justice Taft's future colleague and fellow Prohibition supporter on the bench—somewhat awkwardly, in that Taft had tried to intervene against Brandeis's confirmation by the Senate, calling him not fit to serve. Later that same year, Wilson was tasked with replacing departing associate justice, and future chief justice, Charles Evans Hughes, whom President Taft had appointed and who resigned in order to run on the Republican ticket against incumbent Wilson. Hughes lost, narrowly. Wilson appointed John H. Clarke to his vacant seat; Clarke would be a vigorous opponent of Prohibition during Chief Justice Taft's early years on the court.

2. Robert Post, "Federalism, Positive Law, and the Emergence of the American Administrative State: Prohibition in the Taft Court Era," *William and Mary Law Review* 48, no. 1 (2006): n. 309.

3. Post, "Federalism," n. 311.

4. Lewis Gould, *Chief Executive to Chief Justice: Taft Betwixt the White House and the Supreme Court* (Lawrence: University Press of Kansas, 2014), 167, 171.

5. Ishbel Ross, *An American Family: The Tafts, 1678–1964* (Cleveland and New York: World Publishing Co., 1964), 325.

6. Daniel Okrent, *Last Call: The Rise and Fall of Prohibition* (New York: Scribner, 2010), 216.

7. Iain Gately, *Drink: A Cultural History of Alcohol* (New York: Gotham Books, 2008), 391, n. 65.

8. See Ross, *An American Family*, 344.

9. Okrent, *Last Call*, 2.

10. Ibid., 93.

11. Ibid., 131.

12. Ibid., 220. The Taft Court would add its imprimatur to the policy in 1923, holding in *Cunard SS Co. v. Mellon* that the Volstead Act covered international shipping of intoxicating liquors. Kenneth M. Murchison, *Federal Criminal Law Doctrines: The Forgotten Influence of National Prohibition* (Durham, NC: Duke University Press, 1994), 19.

13. Garrett Peck, *Prohibition in Washington, D.C.: How Dry We Weren't* (Charleston, SC: The History Press, 2011), 98.

14. Peck, "The Man in the Green Hat," *Prohibition in Washington*, 125–34.

15. Gately, *Drink*, 379.

16. Peck, *Prohibition in Washington*, 105.

17. Gately, *Drink*, 377.

18. Catherine Gilbert Murdock, *Domesticating Drink: Women, Men, and Alcohol in America, 1870–1940* (Baltimore, MD: The Johns Hopkins University Press, 1998), 106.

19. Okrent, *Last Call*, 337.

20. Gould, *Chief Executive*, 116.

21. Murchison, *Federal Criminal Law*, 15.

22. Frederick C. Hicks, *William Howard Taft: Yale Professor of Law and New Haven Citizen* (New Haven, CT: Yale University Press, 1945), 146–47.

23. Post, "Federalism," n. 314.

24. Ross, *An American Family*, 347, 350–51.

25. David Wondrich, *Imbibe!* (New York: Perigee Books, Penguin, 2007, 2015), 319.

26. Susan Cheever, *Drinking in America: Our Secret History* (New York: Twelve, Hachette Book Group, 2015), 211.

27. Peck, *Prohibition in Washington*, 111–13.

28. Ted Haigh, *Vintage Spirits and Forgotten Cocktails* (Beverly, MA: Quarry Books, 2009), 248.

29. Lucius Beebe, *The Stork Club Bar Book* (Mansfield Centre, CT: Martino Publishing, 2015), 74.

30. Murdock, *Domesticating Drink*, 129.

31. Extended from the original three nautical mile limit that demarcated international waters under the Law of the Seas. That issue was merely one that complicated the prohibition enforcement case of *Ford v. U.S.* in 1927. Crew of the British-flagged vessel the *Quadra* were charged with attempting to illegally

import and conspiracy to illegally import liquor into the United States by running smaller boats loaded with liquor from their ship "hovering" outside U.S. territorial waters in San Francisco Bay. The convictions under the Prohibition Act were affirmed in the technically complicated case, which involved the international law of treaties as well as the application of the Tariff Act and definitions of criminal conspiracy.

32. Haigh, *Vintage Spirits*, 270–71.

33. Garrett Peck, *The Prohibition Hangover: Alcohol in America from Demon Rum to Cult Cabernet* (Rutgers, NJ: Rutgers University Press, 2009), 13.

34. Gately, *Drink*, 376; see Lisa McGirr, "Gestures of Daring, Signs of Revolt," in *The War on Alcohol: Prohibition and the Rise of the American State* (New York: Norton, 2015), 103–20.

35. Eric Burns, *The Spirits of America: A Social History of Alcohol* (Philadelphia, PA: Temple University Press, 2004), 202.

36. Melvin I. Urofsky, *Dissent and the U.S. Supreme Court* (New York: Pantheon Books, 2015), 199.

37. Okrent, *Last Call*, 139.

38. Murchison, *Federal Criminal Law*, 17–18.

39. Post, "Federalism," n. 294.

40. Interestingly, this reasoning is from the majority opinion of Justice McReynolds who, as we shall see later in this chapter, would prove to be no great friend of the Prohibition regime.

41. Stephanie L. Slater, "Edward T. Sanford's Tenure on the Supreme Court," *Journal of the Supreme Court Historical Society* 41 (2016): 197.

42. John M. Scheb II, "Edward T. Sanford—Knoxville's Justice," *Journal of the Supreme Court Historical Society* 41 (2016): 181.

43. Clare Cushman, "Beyond Knox: James C. McReynolds's Other Law Clerks, 1914–1941," *Journal of the Supreme Court Historical Society* 41 (2016): 159.

44. This illicit alcohol source would be targeted by the Treasury Department as a potential problem for prohibition enforcement, leading to Agriculture Department inspections that required additional ginger solids that made the substance unpalatable. In efforts to fool inspectors, bootleggers added other adulterants that would pass the tests but not impair drinkability. Some of these additives turned out to be quite toxic, resulting in a form of paralysis known as "Jake walk" or "Jake leg." The epidemic really took hold in 1930, and several blues songs of the period immortalized the condition. An additional cultural reference is found in the character Eddie, played by Walter Brennan in Howard Hawks's *To Have and Have Not*, who is a "rummy"—an old alcoholic—whom Brennan endows with a peculiar gait that may be meant to suggest Jake leg. The film is set in Martinique in 1940, although the Ernest Heming-

way novel that inspired it is set in Depression-era Key West, a context in which
the affliction of alcoholic sidekick Eddie makes more sense.

The harmful qualities of doctored Jake paled in comparison to the lethal
nature of denatured or industrial alcohol, peddled as drinkable liquor by some
unscrupulous bootleggers. *Selzman v. U.S.* in 1925 upheld a Volstead conviction for selling unlabeled denatured alcohol "under circumstances from which
the seller may reasonably infer the intention of the purchaser to use it for
[beverage] purpose." Taft's unanimous opinion rejected as "without force" the
defendant's argument that the Eighteenth Amendment was intended to prohibit only *good* beverage alcohol such as "spirituous, vinous, malt, or fermented
liquor, liquids, and compounds" and excluded denatured alcohol because it is
not fit for beverage purposes—although it is intoxicating. Having none of it,
and mindful of "the ignorance of some, the craving and the hardihood of
others, and the fraud and cupidity of still others," Taft sanctioned a broad
understanding of Congress's choice of means in enforcement under the
amendment. "It helps [its] main purpose," the chief justice instructed, "to
hedge about the making and disposition of the denatured article every reasonable precaution and penalty to prevent the proper industrial use of it from
being perverted to drinking it."

The court also weighed in on the issuance of permits to distill denatured
alcohol. *Ma-King Products v. Blair* (1926) held that the Prohibition Act authorized the Commissioner of Internal Revenue "as the administrative officer directly charged with the enforcement of the law, a responsibility in the matter
of granting the privilege of dealing in liquor for non-beverage purposes, which
requires him to refuse a permit to one who is not a suitable person to be
entrusted, in a relation of such confidence, with the possession, of liquor sus-
ceptible of division to beverage uses." The commissioner's discretionary denial
of the permit was upheld.

45. David J. Danelski, "The Influence of the Chief Justice on the Decisional
Process of the Supreme Court," in *The Chief Justice: Appointment and Influ-
ence,* ed. David J. Danelski and Artemus Ward (Ann Arbor: University of
Michigan Press, 2016), 26.

46. It was said of Sutherland that "he personally approved 'of abstinence
from alcoholic beverages and of prohibition by local option.'" But he also
disliked Prohibition because he regarded it as a violation of personal liberty.
Post, "Federalism," n. 268, n. 292.

47. Post, "Federalism," n. 9; Danelski, "The Influence of the Chief Justice,"
34.

48. Theodore B. Lacey, "The Supreme Court's Fluctuating Reaction to National Prohibition in Fourth Amendment Decisions from 1920–1933" (senior
thesis, Princeton University, 2005), ch. 5.

49. As the White Court had done with respect to private actors' seizure of incriminating evidence that was later utilized for a grand jury indictment, in *Burdeau v. McDowell* (1921).

50. Another future chief justice, elevated after the Repeal of Prohibition, and also no friend of an empty wine cabinet, personally speaking.

51. Okrent, *Last Call*, 285.

52. Post, "Federalism," n. 560.

53. Post, "Federalism," n. 565.

54. Burns, *The Spirits of America*, 273.

55. Okrent, *Last Call*, 284.

56. Lacey, "The Supreme Court's Fluctuating Reaction," ch. 5.

57. Post, "Federalism," n. 110, n. 113.

58. Okrent, *Last Call*, 283.

59. See Murchison, *Federal Criminal Law*, 132.

60. Murchison, *Federal Criminal Law*, 160.

61. Ibid., 185.

62. Okrent, *Last Call*, 265; McGirr, *The War on Alcohol*, 206.

63. Murchison, *Federal Criminal Law*, 114.

64. McGirr, *The War on Alcohol*, 358, 982 (ibook).

65. Murchison, *Federal Criminal Law*, 116.

66. Ibid., 19.

67. Okrent, *Last Call*, 282.

68. Although one year earlier, and with only Brandeis dissenting, the court had held that the records-keeping requirement of the Volstead Act applied only to those authorized to legally manufacture and sell liquor. It did not also apply to and constitute an independent crime on the part of bootleggers who likewise failed to keep records of their illegal transactions (*U.S. v. Katz*, 1926).

69. Murchison, *Federal Criminal Law*, 18.

70. Ibid., 183.

71. Ibid., 192.

72. Chief Justice Taft also led the effort to establish a judicial conference that would contribute to the more efficient administration of the lower federal courts; moreover, he and a committee of justices drafted legislation intended to ease the caseload of the Supreme Court by removing much of its mandatory appellate jurisdiction and creating a discretionary reviewing power. Passed by Congress as the Judges' Bill of 1925, this reform allowed the justices to shape their docket and select for decision those cases they considered of greatest legal or policy significance. Such discretion enhanced the legal policy making power of the court; it also removed from future courts' scrutiny a great many run-of-the-mill but still colorful disputes involving alcohol.

73. McGirr, *The War on Alcohol*, 1103 (iBook).

74. Ibid., 1174 (iBook).

75. Post, "Federalism," n. 406.

76. Detailed, for example, in Michelle Alexander's *The New Jim Crow: Mass Incarceration in the Age of Colorblindness* (New York: New Press, 2010).

8. THE GIN COCKTAIL PARTY OF THE HUGHES ERA

1. Garrett Peck, *Prohibition in Washington, D.C.: How Dry We Weren't* (Charleston, SC: The History Press, 2011), 145.

2. Kenneth B. Umbreit, *Our 11 Chief Justices: A History of the Supreme Court in Terms of Their Personalities*, vols. 1 and 2 (Port Washington, NY: Kennikat Press, 1938), 470.

3. Rhode Island was the only state never to ratify the Eighteenth Amendment. Its liquor interests launched a constitutional challenge in the Supreme Court in *Rhode Island v. Palmer* (1920), "claiming that the dry law impermissibly 'completely alters and transforms' the structure of the Constitution by transferring police powers from the states to the federal government. Reminding the nation that it had ratified the Constitution only after receiving assurances that the Constitution would not intrude upon state sovereignty, Rhode Island also contended that the dry law was inconsistent with the Tenth Amendment. These challenges were based on legal theories drawn from yesteryear." Yet, as one law review source on the state's legal action noted, "Rhode Island raised foundational constitutional questions that troubled lawyers of the era." Henry S. Cohn and Ethan Davis, "Stopping the Wind That Blows and the Rivers That Run: Connecticut and Rhode Island Reject the Prohibition Amendment," *Quinnipiac Law Review* 27, no. 2 (2009): 354. Hughes's brief representing prohibitionist interests made the lawyerly argument that the substantive validity of any constitutional amendment was a political question and not subject to judicial review: "Rhode Island raises nothing but a question of policy—a question which is not justiciable and hence has no place in this Court." Cohn and Davis, "Stopping the Wind," 367. The Supreme Court under Chief Justice White dealt with the Rhode Island challenge as part of its decision in the consolidated *Prohibition Cases* of 1920.

4. Betty Glad, *Charles Evan Hughes and the Illusions of Innocence* (Champaign: University of Illinois Press, 1966), 82–83.

5. Umbreit, *Our 11 Chief Justices*, 478.

6. Glad, *Charles Evan Hughes*, 104.

7. Umbreit, *Our 11 Chief Justices*, 482.

8. Glad, *Charles Evan Hughes*, 319–20.

9. Garrett Peck, *The Prohibition Hangover: Alcohol in America from De-mon Rum to Cult Cabernet* (Rutgers, NJ: Rutgers University Press, 2009), 24, says it was a dirty martini, but this fact is not confirmed by other sources.

10. Clare Cushman, *Courtwatchers* (Lanham, MD: Rowman & Littlefield Publishers, 2011), 87. For further discussion of Douglas, his own martini reci-pe, and his general contributions to cocktail culture, see chapter 11, "The Warren Era: Swanky Swilling."

11. Kenneth M. Murchison, *Federal Criminal Law Doctrines: The Forgot-ten Influence of National Prohibition* (Durham, NC: Duke University Press, 1994), 16.

12. Glad, *Charles Evan Hughes*, 108.

13. Ibid., 98.

14. Michael A. Lerner, *Dry Manhattan: Prohibition in New York City* (Cambridge, MA: Harvard University Press, 2007), 51.

15. Lowell Edmunds, *Martini, Straight Up* (Baltimore, MD: The Johns Hopkins University Press, 1998), 84.

16. Peck, *Prohibition in Washington*, 122.

17. Catherine Gilbert Murdock, *Domesticating Drink: Women, Men, and Alcohol in America, 1870–1940* (Baltimore, MD: The Johns Hopkins Univer-sity Press, 1998), 169.

18. Eric Burns, *The Spirits of America: A Social History of Alcohol* (Phila-delphia, PA: Temple University Press, 2004), 285; Edmunds, *Martini*, 89.

19. Edmunds, *Martini*, 84.

20. Ibid., 89.

21. Burns, *The Spirits of America*, 251.

22. Edmunds, *Martini*, 123.

23. Ibid.

24. As a policy he believed it "unwise and impracticable." James F. Simon, *FDR and Chief Justice Hughes: The President, the Supreme Court, and the Epic Battle over the New Deal* (New York: Simon and Schuster, 2012), 117.

25. Simon, *FDR and Chief Justice Hughes*, 332.

26. Ibid., 314.

27. Ibid., 341.

28. Daniel Okrent, *Last Call: The Rise and Fall of Prohibition* (New York: Scribner, 2010), 349.

29. Theodore B. Lacey, "The Supreme Court's Fluctuating Reaction to Na-tional Prohibition in Fourth Amendment Decisions from 1920–1933" (senior thesis, Princeton University, 2005), ch. 9.

30. Robert Post, "Federalism, Positive Law, and the Emergence of the American Administrative State: Prohibition in the Taft Court Era," *William and Mary Law Review* 48 (2006): n. 412.

31. Murchison, *Federal Criminal Law*, 38–41.

32. Ibid., 21.

33. Ibid., 140–43.

34. Ibid., 149.

35. Ibid., 258, n. 90.

36. Ibid., 21.

37. Simon, *FDR and Chief Justice Hughes*, 358.

38. David E. Kyvig, *Repealing National Prohibition* (Kent, OH: The Kent State University Press, 2000), 198.

39. David E. Kyvig, *Law, Alcohol, and Order: Perspectives on National Prohibition* (Westport, CT: Greenwood Press, 1985), 16.

40. Clement E. Vose, "Repeal as a Political Achievement," in *Law, Alcohol, and Order: Perspectives on National Prohibition,* ed. D. Kyvig (Westport, CT: Greenwood Press, 1985), 103–4.

41. Vose, "Repeal as a Political Achievement," 111–12.

42. Ibid., 111, 115: Lisa McGirr, *The War on Alcohol* (New York: Norton, 2015), 233; 246.

43. McGirr, *The War on Alcohol*, 1164–65 (iBook); see also Kyvig, *Repealing National Prohibition*, 189.

44. McGirr, *The War on Alcohol*, 1167 (iBook).

45. It was this disinclination that fueled states' restriction on so-called brew-pubs, or taprooms as part of licensed breweries—a restriction that only began to be lifted in the last decade or so. Evan T. Lawson, "The Future of the Three-Tiered System as a Control of Marketing Alcoholic Beverages," in *Social and Economic Control of Alcohol: The 21st Amendment in the 21st Century,* ed. Carole L. Jurkiewicz and Murphy J. Painter (Boca Raton, FL: CRC Press, 2008), 33.

46. Carole L. Jurkiewicz and Murphy J. Painter, "Why We Control Alcohol the Way We Do," in *Social and Economic Control of Alcohol: The 21st Amendment in the 21st Century,* ed. Carole L. Jurkiewicz and Murphy J. Painter (Boca Raton, FL: CRC Press, 2008), 7.

47. Jurkiewicz and Painter, "Why We Control Alcohol," 9.

48. Douglas Glen Whitman, *Strange Brew: Alcohol and Government Monopoly* (Oakland, CA: The Independent Institute, 2003), 2.

49. Whitman, *Strange Brew*, 23.

50. Although Mississippi remained totally dry until 1966, and several states chose a local option system that allowed for dry counties within the state.

51. Mark Keller, "Alcohol Policies and Problems in Historical Perspective," in *Law, Alcohol, and Order: Perspectives on National Prohibition,* ed. D. Kyvig (Westport, CT: Greenwood Press, 1985), 163; see also Mark Edward Lender

and James Kirby Martin, *Drinking in America: A History* (New York: The Free Press, 1987), 186.

52. Peck, *The Prohibition Hangover*, 17.

53. And simply because Prohibition was ending did not mean that over-the-top governmental enforcement efforts ceased. Rather, violation of Fourth Amendment niceties due to wiretapping of phone lines continued in the prosecution of suspected evasion of the new federal alcohol revenue laws, as *U.S. v. Nardone* in 1937 illustrates. Justice Sutherland's dissent, joined by McReynolds, reacted strenuously and negatively to *Nardone*'s castigation of the federal agents for their invasive actions: "The decision just made will necessarily have the effect of enabling the most depraved criminals to further their criminal plans over the telephone, in the secure knowledge that even if these plans involve kidnapping and murder, their telephone conversations can never be intercepted by officers of the law and revealed in court." That "the most depraved criminals" in *Nardone* were alcohol smugglers must have been simple hyperbole, although both justices had been part of Taft's majority in *Olmstead,* in spite of their other, more libertarian Prohibition era Fourth Amendment votes. *Scher v. U.S.* in 1938 was another ruling about the tactics used in enforcing alcohol revenue laws, but one in which the case's Fourth Amendment challenge was rejected by the Hughes Court. In *Scher*, the alleged violation was a warrantless search of an automobile that uncovered liquor being transported without the requisite tax stamps. McReynolds's brief opinion for the unanimous court summarily noted that the legality of the officers' action depended upon what they saw and heard take place in their presence—including the petitioner admitting when stopped that he was indeed hauling liquor, "just a little for a party." In the back of the car were eighty-eight unstamped bottles of whiskey.

Other transitional growing pains were evident, as the Hughes Court considered how other Prohibition era enforcement practices should be employed in the new regime of alcohol regulation. In dissent in *U.S. v. One 1939 Model Ford* (1939), Justice Douglas, joined by Black and Frankfurter, had this to say about remitting the forfeiture of automobiles used in alcohol revenue violations: "The problem here involved the question of the duty of automobile finance companies to investigate those who purchase cars from dealers, financed by those companies, in order to determine whether the ostensible purchasers are in reality straw men for bootleggers. Here the dealers knew that the named purchasers were only nominal purchasers; and they also knew the identity of the real purchasers. But the finance companies made no inquiry whatsoever of the dealers to ascertain if those purchasers were straw men. They made no inquiry in spite of the fact that the use of straw men by bootleggers was not novel. They made no inquiry in spite of the intimate business relations which exist between them and the dealers and the presumption of availability of such information which that relationship creates." The United States lost its appeal, and the claimed forfeiture, and the dissenters lamented that "this specific bootleg hazard" would be allowed to continue.

Finally, some serious hairsplitting animated the 1940 decision in *U.S. v. Falcone*, which upended a conviction for conspiring to violate federal revenue laws by operating an illegal still. In a verdict worthy of Solomon, the Hughes Court held that someone who sells materials knowing that they are intended for use, or will be used, in the production of illicit distilled spirits, but not knowing of a conspiracy to commit the crime, is not chargeable as coconspirator.

54. Okrent, *Last Call*, 375.

55. This language has been a favorite phrasing of the proalcohol regulation justices on the Supreme Court, coming as it does from Justice Hugo Black's 1964 vigorous dissent in *Hostetter v. Idlewild Bon Voyage Liquor Corp.*, and then quoted again with approval in Justice Stevens's more recent dissent in the late Rehnquist Court era decision in the "free the vine" *Granholm v. Heald* case.

56. Jonathan M. Rotter and Joshua S. Stambaugh, "What's Left of the 21st Amendment?" *Cardozo Public Law, Policy, and Ethics Journal* 6, no. 3 (2008): 602.

57. *Collins* would have important implications some thirty-five years later when the Burger Court considered a state liquor tax that fell on military base commissaries' purchases of alcohol. The Burger Court would also uphold a national supremacist reading of the situation, in *U.S. v. Mississippi Tax Commission*.

58. Murdock, *Domesticating Drink*, 165.

59. Peck, *The Prohibition Hangover*, 20.

60. Iain Gately, *Drink: A Cultural History of Alcohol* (New York: Gotham Books, 2008), 419.

9. THE STONE ERA

1. Rum, the signature spirit of this era, was a shortened form of its original longer name "rumbullion." As the webpage Britishfoodinamerica.com says in its entry "Rum, the spirit of the Indies":

> In 1650 an unknown Barbadian despaired that "[t]he chief fudling they make in this Iland is Rumbullion, alias Kill Divill, and this is made of Suggar cones distilled; a hot hellish and terrible liquor." The

derivation of rumbullion, shortened in a few years to rum, is conjec-
tural and has been ascribed to various sources. The likeliest is 'rumbustion,' in seventeenth century usage as rumpus or tumult, the state
that drinkers of it quickly acquired. (emphasis added)

As we will see in this chapter, the Stone justices were capable of a good deal of
rumbustion of their own—with or without the addition of rum itself.

2. *Hirabayashi v. U.S.* (1943) and *Korematsu v. U.S.* (1944); *West Virginia
Board of Education v. Barnette* (1943). An earlier decision on the Jehovah's
Witnesses' civil liberties, *Minersville School District v. Gobitis* (1940), came at
the very close of the Hughes era and found the future chief justice dissenting
from the majority's supporting of the national security objectives of the compulsory flag salute law.

3. Wayne Curtis, *And a Bottle of Rum: A History of the New World in Ten
Cocktails* (New York: Three Rivers Press, 2006/2007), 219.

4. Martin Cate and Rebecca Cate, *Smuggler's Cove: Exotic Cocktails,
Rum, and the Cult of Tiki* (Berkeley, CA: Ten Speed Press, 2016), 27.

5. Curtis, *And a Bottle of Rum*, 218.

6. Tiki culture blossomed after the war, a "fusion that did not represent
any real place in the world, but one that undoubtedly looked to the Pacific Rim
for inspiration: Polynesian women, Caribbean rum, Silk Road spices, and a
large dose of American fantasy." Garrett Peck, *The Prohibition Hangover: Alcohol in America from Demon Rum to Cult Cabernet* (Rutgers, NJ: Rutgers
University Press, 2009), 19.

7. Tahitian for "out of this world—the best." Cate and Cate, *Smuggler's
Cove*, 262.

8. Curtis, *And a Bottle of Rum*, 229.

9. Cate and Cate, *Smuggler's Cove*, 34.

10. Matthew Hofstedt, "Acquisitions Committee Highlights: Part I,
2014–2015," *Quarterly of the Supreme Court Historical Society* 38, no. 2
(2016): 10.

11. Clare Cushman, *Table for 9: Supreme Court Food Traditions and Recipes* (Washington, DC: Supreme Court Historical Society Publication, 2017),
80.

12. Harlan F. Stone Papers, Jones Library Special Collections, Amherst,
MA, Box 87, "Recipes" folder.

13. Todd A. Price. "World War II Changed How American Drank: Live
from Tales of the Cocktail," (July 16, 2015), nola.com.

14. Iain Gately, *Drink: A Cultural History of Alcohol* (New York: Gotham
Books: New York, 2008), 408.

15. "Mexican tequila," they add, "also made inroads during the war. Side-cars made with tequila became popular, and that drink, with a salt rim added, was eventually renamed a Margarita." See Joseph M. Carlin, *Cocktails: A Global History* (London: Reaktion Books, 2012), 49, for more on the margarita's creation. See also the discussion in chapter 13, *The Rehnquist Era of Neo-Temperance.* The Singapore Sling, which Wondrich and Berry prepared and served at their 2015 Tales of the Cocktail seminar, was also popular throughout the world during the middle of the twentieth century. A product, however, of an earlier orientalist and colonial fantasy, its heritage is much older, being universal in Singapore from at least 1897; its proper construction was a subject of debate as early as 1930. David Wondrich, *Imbibe!* (New York: Perigee Books, Penguin, 2007, 2015), 152–54.

The most memorably named beverage of the "tiki diaspora" has to be the Suffering Bastard, which began its life as a hangover remedy (!) dreamed up in 1942 by able barkeep Joe Scialom at the Shepheard's Hotel in Cairo. A favorite watering hole of British officers and war correspondents stationed in Egypt for the Africa campaign, Shepheard's was a colonial palace of Pharaonic magnificence that did not survive Nasser's nationalist revolution. Shepheard's accomplished bartender, however, succeeded in plying his trade all around the world, thanks to the patronage of hotelier Conrad Hilton. Less a tropical concoction than a tiki alternate, the original Bastard deployed bourbon or brandy with gin, lime juice, and ginger beer; later Trader Vic variants and successive Scialom spin-offs (the Dying Bastard, the Dead Bastard) incorporated rum, or used bourbon and brandy, or melded all three amber spirits with the gin and ginger beer. The story and the recipes are recounted with verve by the drinking blog "The Alcohol Professor: The Class You Always Wanted to Take" (alcoholprofessor.org).

Not a refreshment Professor Stone would likely have sought—in spite of his travails as chief justice.

16. Peck, *The Prohibition Hangover*, 110.
17. Ibid., 19.
18. Curtis, *And a Bottle of Rum*, 206.
19. Ibid., 178.
20. Ibid., 223; Cate and Cate, *Smuggler's Cove*, 30.
21. Stone Papers, Box 85, "Menus" folder.
22. Stone Papers, Box 87, "Wine Lists" folder.
23. Curtis, *And a Bottle of Rum*, 180–81.
24. Lucius Beebe, *The Stork Club Bar Book* (Mansfield Centre, CT: Martino Publishing, 2015), 182.
25. Wondrich and Berry, in their 2016 Tales of the Cocktail seminar on Club Cocktails, talk about the "myth making of getting in" that sustained the

mystique of former speakeasy, midcentury Manhattan establishments like the Stork Club and the 21 Club.

26. See the photos in "The Stork Club Story," on The Stork Club website, www.storkclub.org.

27. The headnotes in Lucius Beebe's 1946 *Stork Club Bar Book* are just as captivating as the drinks themselves, such as this for its frozen daiquiri: "The Stork will compound as many drinks with Cuban rums as there are days in the year, but the three which are dominant in their field. . . are. . . Frozen Daiquiri. . . Cuba Libre. . . & 'MacArthur Cocktail.'" The daiquiri is self-explanatory; its frozen variant is as old as the electric blender, and almost as old as the classic cocktail itself. The Cuba Libre is of course a lime forward, exoticized version of the humdrum rum and Coca-Cola. The MacArthur Cocktail, a period homage to the World War II general, is a drink that consists of Cointreau, fresh lime juice, egg white, white rum, and a dash of dark rum.

The Stork Club produced its own eponymous cocktail, allegedly invented during Prohibition. The blog *Cold Glass* has this to say about it:

> Beebe attributes the Stork Club Cocktail to the Stork's service captain, Eddie Whittmer. Its basic ingredients would have been very familiar in the Prohibition era: gin, and sweet, flavorful OJ to cover up the gin's potentially dodgy character.

> **The Stork Club Cocktail**
>
> > 1 1/2 oz gin (Hayman's Old Tom)
> > Juice of 1/2 orange (1/2–1 oz orange juice)
> > Dash lime juice (bar spoon lime)
> > Dash triple sec (bar spoon Cointreau)
> > Dash Angostura bitters
>
> *Shake lightly, or stir, with ice until cold. Strain into a chilled cocktail glass. Optionally express and garnish with orange.*

Storiedsips.com offers this slightly contrasting tale and recipe:

> Chief barman Nathaniel "Cookie" Cook and his crew invented dozens of drinks, including the club's signature libation, the Stork Club Cocktail. Featuring sweetened old Tom gin, along with freshly squeezed orange and lime juices, Cointreau, and bitters, the drink is pleasantly tangy and endlessly quaffable.
> The tangerine-hued cocktail added a splash of color to the club's dark-paneled formal dining room, sipped by executives in their tuxedoes and debutantes and fashion models in their strapless gowns. At

this temple to café society, the Stork Club cocktail was the most stylish glass to raise.

Stork Club Cocktail

1 1/2 ounces Hayman's Old Tom gin
1 ounce freshly squeezed orange juice
1/4 ounce lime juice
1/4 ounce Cointreau
Dash Angostura bitters
Glass: coupe
Garnish: orange twist

Fill a coupe with ice to chill. To an ice-filled shaker, add all ingredients and shake for about 15 seconds. Empty coupe and strain cocktail into it. Garnish with an orange twist.

28. Only Douglas's is dated, as 1955. Reproduced in "Personal Letters" on The Stork Club website, www.storkclub.com.

29. Ralph Blumenthal, *Stork Club: America's Most Famous Nightspot and the Lost World of Café Society* (Boston and New York: Little Brown, 2000). For further discussion of Justice Clark's patronage of The Stork Club, see Chapter 10, "The Old-Fasioned Vinson Era."

30. Daniel Okrent, *Last Call: The Rise and Fall of Prohibition* (New York: Scribner, 2010), 281.

31. Robert Post, "Federalism, Positive Law, and the Emergence of the American Administrative State: Prohibition in the Taft Court Era," *William and Mary Law Review* 48, no. 1 (2006): n. 269.

32. Stone Papers, Box 85, "Menus" folder.

33. Alpheus Thomas Mason, *Harlan Fiske Stone: Pillar of the Law*(New York: Viking Press, 1956), 726–33.

34. Clare Cushman, *Courtwatchers* (Lanham, MD: Rowman & Littlefield, 2011), 209.

35. Bennett Boskey, "The Family of Stone Law Clerks," in *In Chambers: Stories of Supreme Court Law Clerks and Their Justices*, ed. Todd C. Peppers and Artemus Ward (Charlottesville: University of Virginia Press, 2012), 99.

36. Melvin I. Urofsky, *Division and Discord: The Supreme Court under Stone and Vinson, 1941–1953* (Columbia: University of South Carolina Press, 1997), 28.

37. Rod Phillips, *Alcohol, a History* (Chapel Hill: University of North Carolina Press, 2014), 299.

38. Phillips, *Alcohol*, 295.

39. Urofsky, *Division and Discord*, 93.

40. Bruce Allen Murphy, *Wild Bill: The Legend and Life of William O. Douglas* (New York: Random House, 2003), 208.

41. Ibid., 208–210.

42. This states' rights cri de coeur would reoccur decades later, in the person of Burger Court–era associate justice (and future chief justice) William Rehnquist, and his crusade to resuscitate a Tenth Amendment restriction on the commerce powers of the federal government. Indeed, the issue of *New York* case was going to be a very important future inroad to a significant revision of constitutional federalism and the balance of national and state powers, a revision brought about by Rehnquist's Supreme Court in another *New York v. U.S.* in 1992.

10. THE OLD-FASHIONED VINSON ERA

1. Melvin I. Urofsky, *Division and Discord: The Supreme Court under Stone and Vinson, 1941–1953* (Columbia: University of South Carolina Press, 1997), 149.

2. John D. Fassett, "Clerking for Stanley Reed," in *Of Courtiers and Kings: More Stories of Supreme Court Law Clerks and Their Justices*, ed. Todd C. Peppers and Clare Cushman (Charlottesville: University of Virginia Press, 2012), 163.

3. Daniel Okrent, *Last Call: The Rise and Fall of Prohibition* (New York: Scribner, 2010), 262.

4. Clare Cushman, *Courtwatchers* (Lanham, MD: Rowman & Littlefield Publishers, 2011), 59.

5. Urofsky, *Division and Discord*, 152.

6. Ibid., 211, n. 95.

7. Melvin I. Urofsky, *Dissent and the U.S. Supreme Court* (New York: Pantheon Books, 2015), 220.

8. Urofsky, *Division and Discord*, 149.

9. Ibid., 151.

10. Peter Charles Hoffer, William James Hull Hoffer, and N. E. H. Hull, *The Supreme Court: An Essential History* (Lawrence: University Press of Kansas, 2007), 308.

11. Arthur R. Seder Jr., "Law Clerk for Chief Justice Vinson," in *Of Courtiers and Kings: More Stories of Supreme Court Law Clerks and Their Justices,* ed. Todd C. Peppers and Clare Cushman (Charlottesville: University of Virginia Press, 2012), 209.

12. Ralph Blumenthal, *Stork Club: America's Most Famous Nightspot and the Lost World of Café Society* (Boston and New York: Little Brown, 2000), 16–17.

13. Rod Phillips, *Alcohol, a History* (Chapel Hill: University of North Carolina Press, 2014), 300.

14. Ted Saucier, *Bottoms Up* (Mansfield Centre, CT: Martino Publishing, 1951, 2011), 182.

15. David A. Embury, *Fine Art of Mixing Drinks* (New York: Mud Puddle, Inc., 1948, 1986), 123–24.

16. Embury, *Fine Art*, 32.

17. Marcia Yablon, "The Prohibition Hangover: Why We Are Still Feeling the Effects of Prohibition," *Virginia Journal of Social Policy and the Law* 13, no. 3 (2006): 564.

18. Christine Sismondo, *America Walks into a Bar: A Spirited History of Taverns and Saloons, Speakeasies and Grog Shops* (New York: Oxford University Press, 2011), 243.

19. Indeed, the *Goesaert* precedent has never officially been gainsaid by the U.S. Supreme Court, although its rule with regard to female bartending was rejected by California Supreme Court in the 1971 decision of *Sail'er Inn v. Kirby*.

20. Lisa McGirr, *The War on Alcohol* (New York: Norton, 2015), 1169 (iBook).

21. David E. Kyvig, *Law, Alcohol, and Order: Perspectives on National Prohibition* (Westport, CT: Greenwood Press, 1985), 4, quoting Richard Hofstadter's 1955 Pulitzer Prize–winning *Age of Reform*.

I I. THE WARREN ERA

1. Laird Borrelli-Persson, *The Cocktail Dress* (New York: Collins Design Publishers, 2009).

2. The justices are now invited individually to White House functions. Clare Cushman, *Courtwatchers* (Lanham, MD: Rowman & Littlefield Publishers, 2011), 85.

3. Ted Haigh, *Vintage Spirits and Forgotten Cocktails* (Beverly, MA: Quarry Books, 2009), 215; Wayne Curtis, *And a Bottle of Rum: A History of the New World in Ten Cocktails* (New York: Three Rivers Press, 2006/2007), 211.

4. David A. Embury, *Fine Art of Mixing Drinks* (New York: Mud Puddle, Inc., 1948, 1986), 81.

5. Curtis, *And a Bottle of Rum*, 210.

6. Garrett Peck, *The Prohibition Hangover: Alcohol in America from Demon Rum to Cult Cabernet* (Rutgers, NJ: Rutgers University Press, 2009), 58.

7. At least, a *segment* of his Democratic Party's liberal progressivism on civil rights. The Southern wing of the party was decidedly not in favor of expanded federal power to enforce such reforms.

8. Peck, *The Prohibition Hangover*, 24; Earl C. Dudley Jr., "A Two-For Clerkship: Stanley F. Reed and Earl Warren," in *Of Courtiers and Kings: More Stories of Supreme Court Law Clerks and Their Justices*, ed. Todd C. Peppers and Clare Cushman (Charlottesville: University of Virginia Press, 2015), 248.

9. When 'Ol' Blue Eyes' was not knocking back a bottle of Jack (Daniels), that is.

10. Jesse H. Choper, "Clerking for Chief Justice Earl Warren," in *In Chambers: Stories of Supreme Court Law Clerks and Their Justices*, ed. Todd C. Peppers and Artemus Ward (Charlottesville: University of Virginia Press, 2012), 273–74.

11. Ibid., 275.

12. Dudley, "A Two-For Clerkship," 237.

13. Bob Woodward and Scott Armstrong, *The Brethren* (New York: Avon Books, 1979), 4.

14. Bruce Allen Murphy, *Wild Bill: the Legend and Life of William O. Douglas* (New York: Random House, 2003), 471.

15. Among other sordid details Murphy (2003) reveals: Tommy Corcoran got Douglas invited to FDR's regular poker games beginning in 1939, and Douglas quickly became a favorite for "his ability to drink with the best of them" (185); in 1950 he also palled around with Joseph Kennedy at his Palm Beach estate, which included "a steady diet of drinking" (179); and Douglas kept an ample supply of booze in his office, in the desk drawer. His physical decline accelerated after he suffered a stroke, which did not happen until the tenure of Chief Justice Burger, in 1974/1975.

16. Murphy, *Wild Bill*, 295.

17. Clare Cushman, *Table for 9: Supreme Court Food Traditions and Recipes* (Washington, DC: Supreme Court Historical Society Publication, 2017), 102.

18. Murphy, *Wild Bill*, 393.

19. Although earlier signs of the link between sickness and alcohol can be found in the public health, sanitation, and social work movements that were part of Progressive social reform measures. For instance, a 1915 document, the "Dutchess County (NY) Survey of Sickness," reports the need to solve the problems presented by the alcoholic, who is grouped with "the feeble minded, the defective, the epileptic," and "the tuberculous." Among the preventive public health measures recommended is "that alcohol and excessive fatigue are

not allowed to undermine health." Illustrations in the report included "Anti-Alcohol Arguments in Silhouette," with stern warnings from all manner of experts ranging from "Life Insurance Men" to Red Cross nurses to ballplayer Ty Cobb. *Survey Associates Inc.* (October 18, 1915).

20. Mark Edward Lender and James Kirby Martin, *Drinking in America: A History* (New York: The Free Press, 1987), 186–87.

21. Vodka has a role to play here as well, for its odorlessness as a spirit made it ideal for undetected, secret boozing. No opaque coffee cup, a la the backroom speakeasy, was needed to conceal: colorless as water when added to innocuous-looking soft drinks, vodka also leaves little trace of liquor on the breath. A further less-than-pleasant association of vodka with the Warren period is found in Barbara Leaming's 2014 biography of Jacqueline Kennedy, whom she describes after her husband's assassination as "self-medicating with vodka, tyrannized by flashbacks and nightmares." Quoted in Anthony Lane, "Wives and Husbands," *The New Yorker*, December 5, 2016.

22. Dudley, "A Two-For Clerkship," 245–46.

23. "A wholesale liquor dealer compelled retailers to buy certain brands of alcoholic beverages which they did not desire in order to obtain other brands which they did desire"; this was held to exact a "'quota' from the retailers and, to that extent, excluded sales by competing wholesalers, in violation of sec. 5 of the Federal Alcohol Administration Act, and it subjected the offending wholesaler to a suspension of its wholesale liquor permit issued under the Act." Additionally, a technical certification issue that the Warren Court summarily dismissed in 1957 suggests early craft infusion practices—or perhaps just fraudulent watering of liquor for sale by the bottle. A regulation promulgated by the Secretary of the Treasury under the authority of the Internal Revenue Code of 1939, provided that "[n]o liquor bottle shall be reused for the packaging of distilled spirits for sale, nor shall the original contents, or any portion of such original contents, remaining in a liquor bottle be increased by the addition of any substance." The Court of Appeals for the Eighth Circuit certified to the U.S. Supreme Court the following question: "Does the phrase 'any substance' include tax paid distilled spirits?" See *Wisniewski v. U.S.* (1957).

24. The ruling can be contrasted with that in *Burke v. Ford* in 1967, which upheld application of the Sherman Act to a statewide market division by territories and brands by Oklahoma liquor wholesalers. As there were at the time no distilleries within Oklahoma, out-of-state liquor was shipped in substantial volume to wholesalers' warehouses and held there until purchased by retailers. The market division adversely affected interstate commerce and reduced competition, and so was enjoined per curiam.

25. The facts in the case were indeed grisly. In 1951, a truck driven by Paul Breithaupt collided with another vehicle while driving on a highway near

Carlsbad, New Mexico. Three passengers in Breithaupt's truck were killed, and Breithaupt was taken to a local hospital to treat serious injuries. Responding officers found a nearly empty one-pint bottle of whiskey in the truck's glove compartment. While Breithaupt lay unconscious in the emergency room, officers ordered physicians to take a sample of his blood. A chemical analysis of this blood sample determined that Breithaupt was under the influence of alcohol when the sample was taken. This blood sample was admitted into evidence at trial, and Breithaupt was ultimately convicted of involuntary manslaughter.

26. *Delli Paoli v. U.S.* (1957), which involved a joint trial for a federal charge of conspiring to deal unlawfully in alcohol, also illustrates the same. Detailed facts of the incident are recounted in the court's opinion:During December 1951, the service station often was used as a meeting place for Margiasso, Pierro and petitioner. . . . Margiasso drove King's car to the garage and returned with it heavily loaded. King then drove it away. Government agents followed him until he stopped in Harlem. There they arrested him and took possession of 19 5-gallon cans of unstamped alcohol found in his car. Later in the evening, Margiasso took Whitley's car to the garage and was arrested in it when leaving the still open garage. The agents thereupon seized 113 5-gallon cans of unstamped alcohol they found in the garage. Whitley, who had been waiting for Margiasso at the service station with $1,000 in a paper bag, was arrested on the agents' return with Margiasso.

Another minor, statutory case, *U.S. v. Dixon* (1954), which made it a criminal offense to possess property intended for use in producing liquor without the payment of taxes in violation of the Internal Revenue Code, also shows the era's stubborn proximity to the Prohibition era. In especially stilted prose, the court noted the similarity of the statute's language to sections of the old Prohibition Act, finding it "most persuasive that the courts consistently upheld criminal prosecutions brought under these sections for the analogous act of possessing property designed for the manufacture of liquor intended for use in violation of Title II of the Prohibition Act." Justice Clark's was a long way of saying that possessing 800 lbs. of sugar and parts of a still were considered evidence of the intention to produce liquor.

27. See also *Jones v. U.S.* in 1958, infra.

28. Lisa McGirr, *The War on Alcohol: Prohibition and the Rise of the American State* (New York: Norton, 2015), 629, iBook.

12. THE BURGER ERA

1. Iain Gately, *Drink: A Cultural History of Alcohol* (New York: Gotham Books: New York, 2008), 441.

2. Todd C. Peppers, "A Family Tradition: Clerking at the U.S. Supreme Court," in *Of Courtiers and Kings: More Stories of Supreme Court Law Clerks and Their Justices*, ed. Todd C. Peppers and Clare Cushman (Charlottesville: University of Virginia Press, 2015), 373.

3. Mark Will-Weber, *Mint Juleps with Teddy Roosevelt: The Complete History of Presidential Drinking* (Washington, DC: Regnery Publishing, 2014), 300.

4. As Anthony Hopkins also brought out in his performance in director Nicholas Stone's 1995 film *Nixon*. Susan Cheever, *Drinking in America: Our Secret History* (New York: Twelve, Hachette Book Group, 2015), 200–207.

5. Cheever, *Drinking in America*, 206–7.

6. Rebecca Hurley, "In the Chief's Chambers: Life as a Law Clerk for Warren Earl Burger," in *Of Courtiers and Kings: More Stories of Supreme Court Law Clerks and their Justices*, ed. Todd C. Peppers and Clare Cushman (Charlottesville: University of Virginia Press, 2015), 287, 294.

7. Essentially a Screwdriver with a float of the sweet Italian liqueur Galliano, the Harvey Wallbanger has an interesting if corporate history. Cocktail historian David Wondrich (*Imbibe!*) emphasizes the role of McKesson Imports Company and its marketing team for developing the drink and the efforts of McKesson executive George Bednar in promoting the drink as a means of selling its component, neon-yellow Galliano liqueur. *Saveur* notes that by 1976, Holland House was putting out a Wallbanger dry mix (o, the horror!) and preblended bottles of the cocktail were sold. The Harvey Wallbanger takes a lot of knocks, but made properly, with the original formula and complexly herbal Galliano L'Autentico, it is really not that bad. Certainly it is more redeemable than later, derivative excrescences such as Fuzzy and Hairy Navels and Sex-on-the-Beach—"cocktails" in name only. All the alcoholic beverages in the Wallbanger pantheon are built in more or less the same way: orange juice, vodka, and some sweet, strongly flavored, and brilliantly hued liqueur. They are designed for both ease of preparation (thus requiring very little mixology skill) and easy drinking (self-explanatory)—not to mention their neon "black lit" visual appeal.

As another 1970s cultural aside, in CB lingo, a Harvey Wallbanger is a drunk driver; specifically, one who continually drifts across the road from one shoulder to the other and back.

8. This high-octane highball derives the amber color and simulated flavor of its namesake from a base blending of Coca-Cola and sour mix. Its effect is notoriously sneaky—and lethal. Bartender Robert "Rosebud" Butt claims to have invented the emulsion of tequila, vodka, light rum, and gin (oh!) as an entry in a 1972 beverage industry contest to create a new mixed drink includ-

ing Triple Sec, while he worked at the Oak Beach Inn on Long Island, New York.

9. Garrett Peck, *The Prohibition Hangover: Alcohol in America from Demon Rum to Cult Cabernet* (Rutgers, NJ: Rutgers University Press, 2009), 23.

10. Peck, *The Prohibition Hangover*, 26.

11. Mark R. Daniels, "Toward Liquor Control: A Retrospective," in *Social and Economic Control of Alcohol: The 21st Amendment in the 21st Century*, ed. Carole L. Jurkiewicz and Murphy J. Painter (Boca Raton, FL: CRC Press, 2008), 224.

12. Clare Cushman, *Courtwatchers* (Lanham, MD: Rowman & Littlefield Publishers, 2011), 200.

13. As mentioned in the previous chapter, Douglas had an aperitif wine for the occasion, as "it was about all he could drink; he had an allergic [*sic*] reaction to other liquors." Bob Woodward and Scott Armstrong, *The Brethren* (New York: Avon Books, 1979), 411. He had developed that "allergic reaction" after decades of Warren era vodka drinking.

14. Woodward and Armstrong, *The Brethren*, 456.

15. Ibid., 424.

16. Cushman, *Courtwatchers*, 225.

17. Memo cited in Woodward and Armstrong, *The Brethren*, 100.

18. Woodward and Armstrong, *The Brethren*, 317.

19. Ibid., 337–38.

20. Bruce Allen Murphy, *Wild Bill: The Legend and Life of William O. Douglas* (New York: Random House, 2003), 499.

21. Cushman, *Courtwatchers*, 245.

22. Woodward and Armstrong, *The Brethren*, 171–72.

23. Which would rename itself Students Against Destructive Decisions and champion total abstinence; see Thomas Vander Ven, *Getting Wasted: Why College Students Drink Too Much and Party So Hard* (New York: New York University Press, 2011), 157.

24. Gately, *Drink*, 455–57.

25. Michael J. Graetz and Linda Greenhouse, *The Burger Court and the Rise of the Judicial Right* (New York: Simon and Schuster, 2016), 7.

26. Woodward and Armstrong, *The Brethren*, 479–81.

27. The latter concern fueled the constitutional controversy over the breadth of Fourth Amendment protections for digital cell phone data in *Carpenter v. U.S.* in 2018.

28. See also *City of Kenosha v. Bruno* (1973) in which the appellees claimed deprivation of procedural due process arising from the cities' failure to hold full-blown adversary hearings before refusing to issue liquor license renewals and the unconstitutionality of the local licensing scheme.

29. Jonathan M. Rotter and Joshua S. Stambaugh, "What's Left of the 21st Amendment?" *Cardozo Public Law, Policy, and Ethics Journal* 6, no. 3 (2008): 611–12.

30. A more minor and technical due process inquiry, again surrounding the procedures in DWI protocols and motorists' opportunity to challenge their arrests, occurred in *Illinois v. Batchelder* (1983) and was settled per curiam.

31. By contrast, a torturously split court in 1983 could hardly have been less clear on Fifth Amendment parameters in the drunk driving manslaughter case of *Oregon v. Bradshaw*. The defendant's original arrest, which provided the *Miranda* situation, was for furnishing liquor to a minor.

13. THE REHNQUIST ERA OF NEOTEMPERANCE

1. Reagan's neocon advisors would lead his administration in its ultimately victorious confrontation with "the Evil Empire" (the by-that-time sclerotic Soviet Union of the mid-1980s)—their willingness to practice a muscularly interventionist foreign policy showing how very "neo" they were compared to the isolationist, traditional American conservatives of the post–World War II GOP.

2. Rebecca Hurley, "In the Chief's Chambers: Life as a Law Clerk for Warren Earl Burger," in *Of Courtiers and Kings: More Stories of Supreme Court Law Clerks and Their Justices*, ed. Todd C. Peppers and Clare Cushman (Charlottesville: University of Virginia Press, 2015), 296.

3. Todd C. Peppers, "A Family Tradition: Clerking at the U.S. Supreme Court," in *Of Courtiers and Kings: More Stories of Supreme Court Law Clerks and Their Justices*, ed. Todd C. Peppers and Clare Cushman (Charlottesville: University of Virginia Press, 2015), 364.

4. Harry A. Blackmun Papers, Box 1406, Folder 10, Library of Congress.

5. See Garrett Peck, *The Prohibition Hangover: Alcohol in America from Demon Rum to Cult Cabernet* (Rutgers, NJ: Rutgers University Press, 2009), 27, 29; Joseph M. Carlin, *Cocktails: A Global History* (London: Reaktion Books, 2012), 48–49.

6. David Wondrich, *Imbibe!* (New York: Perigee Books, Penguin, 2007, 2015), 129.

7. See chapter 7, "The Taft Era of Law, Order and Bootlegging."

8. Mark R. Daniels, "Toward Liquor Control: A Retrospective," in *Social and Economic Control of Alcohol: The 21st Amendment in the 21st Century*, ed. Carole L. Jurkiewicz and Murphy J. Painter (Boca Raton, FL: CRC Press, 2008), 225.

9. Edward Lazarus, *Closed Chambers: The Rise, Fall, and Future of the Modern Supreme Court* (New York: Penguin Books, 1998), 36.

10. Bob Woodward and Scott Armstrong, *The Brethren* (New York: Avon Books, 1979), 489.

11. His favorite soft drink beverage, at any rate. See Woodward and Armstrong, *The Brethren*, 490.

12. Artemus Ward, "Making Work for Idle Hands: William H. Rehnquist and His Law Clerks," in *In Chambers: Stories of Supreme Court Law Clerks and Their Justices*, ed. Todd C. Peppers and Artemus Ward (Charlottesville: University of Virginia Press, 2012), 375.

13. The phrase coming of course from the brand's hummable advertising jingle, "If you've got the time, we've got the beer . . . Miller Beer. Mil-ler, tastes too good to hurry through." "Miller Time" came to evoke happy hour, afterwork relaxing—but in a measured, good-natured fashion. The rest of the original ad campaign was somewhat more consonant with an earlier era's sensibility with respect to consumption, for as the lyrics continue: "So when it's time to relax, Mil-ler stands clear, *beer after beer*" (emphasis added). The television commercial first aired in 1971.

14. Quoted in Iain Gately, *Drink: A Cultural History of Alcohol* (New York: Gotham Books: New York, 2008), 456–57.

15. See Arthur Helman, "The Shrunken Docket of the Rehnquist Court," *The Supreme Court Review* (1996) on the "shrunken docket" of the Rehnquist Court. The court's docket continued to shrink, whittled down to just seventy-seven cases decided with full opinion in Rehnquist's last year as chief—a number that has basically been maintained by the successor Roberts Court. See Ryan Owens and David Simon, "Explaining the Supreme Court's Shrinking Docket," *William and Mary Law Review* 53, no. 4 (March 2012): 1219–83.

16. As she would throughout her tenure on the Rehnquist Court, and joined as usual by the Chief Justice, Sandra Day O'Connor objected to the Supreme Court's weakening of states' Twenty-First Amendment power over the alcohol trade. "Once again today," she scolded, "the Court ventured still further from the intent of the Twenty-first Amendment by adopting an unprecedented test that focuses on the *wisdom* of the State's exercise of its 2 powers" (emphasis added).

17. Compare this approach to that in the *Gardner* case of 1977; see chapter 12, "The Burger Era: Twilight of the Cocktail Lounge."

18. The Ginsburg concurrence provided the fifth vote and commented, in a more technical vein: "as the plurality, Justice O'Connor and Justice Souter agree, it is within the legislature's province to instruct courts to treat a sober person and a voluntarily intoxicated person as equally responsible for conduct—to place a voluntarily intoxicated person on a level with a sober person."

19. Also decided in what was that banner year for alcohol-related decisions.

20. Peck, *The Prohibition Hangover*, 143.

21. Ibid., 232.

22. Ibid., 32.

23. Gately, *Drink*, 495.

24. Elizabeth Norton, "The 21st Amendment in the 21st Century: Reconsidering State Liquor Controls in Light of *Granholm v. Heald*," *Ohio State Law Journal* 67, no. 6 (2006): 1480.

25. Evan T. Lawson, "The Future of the Three-Tiered System as a Control of Marketing Alcoholic Beverages," in *Social and Economic Control of Alcohol: The 21st Amendment in the 21st Century*, ed. Carole L. Jurkiewicz and Murphy J. Painter (Boca Raton, FL: CRC Press, 2008), 50.

26. Marcia Yablon, "The Prohibition Hangover: Why We Are Still Feeling the Effects of Prohibition," *Virginia Journal of Social Policy and the Law* 13, no. 3 (2006): 592.

27. Or—somewhat discomfortingly—abstinence is assumed to be motivated by alcoholism. Here, the attitude of recreational drinkers toward nondrinkers is more squeamish than disparaging.

28. Peck, *The Prohibition Hangover*, 153.

29. Lawson, "The Future of the Three-Tiered System," 42.

14. THE RETRO ROBERTS ERA

1. Andrew Barr, *Drink: A Social History of America* (New York: Carroll and Graf, Publishers, 1999), 385.

2. Christine Sismondo, *America Walks into a Bar: A Spirited History of Taverns and Saloons, Speakeasies and Grog Shops* (New York: Oxford University Press, 2011), 270.

3. See David Wondrich, *Imbibe!* (New York: Perigee Books, Penguin, 2007, 2015), 122.

4. The cocktail magazine *Punch* devoted a segment of its June 2016 issue to a discussion of "The New DIY Grenadine," noting "While diehards prefer to juice their own pomegranates for the syrup's base, virtually everyone agrees that using bottled POM Wonderful 100-percent juice is an excellent substitute."

5. See chapter 13, "The Rehnquist Era of Neotemperance," for a more precise chronology of this drink's date of origin and popularity peak. *Sex in the City* itself ran as a cable television series from 1998 to 2004; the first movie version of the show was released in 2008.

6. See Wondrich, *Imbibe!*, 319.

7. Peck rendered this verdict in 2009, with the margarita firmly ensconced in American drinking habits, by this time for several decades.

8. Garrett Peck, *The Prohibition Hangover: Alcohol in America from Demon Rum to Cult Cabernet* (Rutgers, NJ: Rutgers University Press, 2009), 27.

9. Indeed, such connoisseurship can be applied to the commonest of cocktails. Consider the lowly Bloody Mary, favorite and reassuringly simple hangover remedy for decades. Its garnishes nowadays—to say nothing of its core ingredients—are often more gourmet than the brunch menus its variants adorn.

10. Irin Carmon and Shana Knizhnik, *Notorious RBG: The Life and Times of Ruth Bader Ginsburg* (New York: Dey St./William Morrow Publishers, 2015), 22.

11. Chris Mondics, "Scalia's Former Clerks Recall His Charm, as Well as His Intellectual Rigor," *The Philadelphia Inquirer*, February 16, 2016, http://www.philly.com/philly/business/20160216_Scalia_s_former_clerks_recall_his_charm__as_well_as_his_intellectual_rigor.html#cAhyRe8q3MdpuaXc.99.

12. Noah Feldman, "Justice Scalia Came Close to Greatness," *Bloomberg View,* February 13, 2016, https://www.bloomberg.com/view/articles/2016-02-14/justice-antonin-scalia-came-close-to-greatness.

13. Thus, the businessman chief executive who enters the annals of American political history during the Roberts period is also closely associated with wine, at least commercially. The family owned and run Trump Winery located outside of Charlottesville, Virginia, produces a range of red and white wines—although its most celebrated are its prize-winning sparkling wines.

14. See generally Gary Regan, *The Negroni: Drinking to La Dolce Vita* (New York: Penguin Random House, 2014).

15. Some might counter that hypocrisy about drinking persists, with the current legal and policy views of alcohol "abuse" possessing some of the same class cues as the crusade against the rough antics of the saloon in the late nineteenth century. In other words, nice, middle-to-upper-class wine-tasting and twee cocktail savoring is to be contrasted—and contrasted most fastidiously—with uncouth drunken partying, with drinking (mass-produced!) booze in mass quantities, to get drunk. Evidence of an "alcohol lifestyle" divergence is found in the burgeoning literature chastising the binge drinking culture at the nation's colleges and universities; one such representative title says it all: *Getting Wasted: Why College Students Drink Too Much and Party So Hard* (2011, New York University Press). The 2006 *Smashed: The Story of a Drunken Girlhood* is also part of this genre of neo-Victorian morality tales of alcohol abuse—or, as Gately's Roberts-era *Drink* labels it "a revival in temperance noir." Iain Gately, *Drink: A Cultural History of Alcohol* (New York: Gotham Books, 2008), 492.

16. Its holding aside, the oral arguments in *Birchfield* also supplied the kind of technological context-of-the-times that future historians will likely find

amusing. Colloquy with the justices found the amicus solicitor general referring to something called a "BAT mobile": the blood-alcohol testing mobile unit
that can perform its function at the side of the road. But as these units are not
available in all jurisdictions and their results are often not admissible in court
for a DUI conviction, later breathalyzer analysis done after arrest and at the
police station is usually the evidence desired and utilized. Still, the specter of a
black-winged BAT mobile lurking on the shoulder of the nation's highways
should linger in the imagination of every prospective drunk driver.

17. Various members of the *Powell* court did note that the defendant's
poverty meant that he lacked secure, private spaces within which to confine his
indulging. Similarly, both Sotomayor's partial concurrence/partial dissent and
Alito's majority opinion acknowledged (Alito's somewhat grudgingly) that in
sparsely populated, rural states such as the Dakotas, having a car and driving
were essential to earning a living and living a meaningful public and social life.
Not that this fact excused getting behind the wheel after having had a few
drinks down at the friendly tavern. Rather, the mandatory nature of a driver's
license made the states' particular conditioning of its use highly questionable.

18. *Porter*'s per curiam opinion was essentially confirming the principle
affirmed more iffily by a narrow majority in *Rompilla v. Beard* (2005), a late
Rehnquist era decision. In that case, the Souter-led majority found ineffective
assistance by his trial counsel as a result of the failure to present significant
mitigating evidence about Rompilla's childhood problems potentially related to
fetal alcohol syndrome, mental capacity and health, and alcoholism. *Rompilla*
also had an especially gruesome set of liquor-related case facts, as the opening
to Kennedy's dissenting opinion recounted:Rompilla stood accused of a brutal
crime. In January 1988, James Scanlon was murdered while he was closing the
Cozy Corner Cafe, a bar he owned in Allentown, Pennsylvania. Scanlon's body
was discovered later the next morning, lying in a pool of blood. Scanlon had
been stabbed multiple times, including sixteen wounds around the neck and
head. Scanlon also had been beaten with a blunt object, and his face had been
gashed, possibly with shards from broken liquor and beer bottles found at the
scene of the crime.

Both the *Porter* and *Rompilla* rulings sat somewhat uneasily with *Schriro v.
Landrigan* of 2007, where failure to present mitigating evidence of fetal alcohol exposure at sentencing in capital murder trial was *not* ineffective assistance
of counsel, because the defendant had instructed his lawyer not to present
such evidence.

19. See Nancy Maveety, *Picking Judges* (Presidential Briefings Series) (New
Brunswick, NJ: Transaction Publishers, 2016).

EPILOGUE

1. That component was both nonexercised for the Supreme Court nomination made by lame-duck president Obama, and weaponized as "nuclear" by the Republican majority that eliminated in April 2017 the filibuster obstruction tactic deployed by the Senate's Democratic minority in objecting to the confirmation of Trump's subsequent replacement to fill the vacant (or to some, the "stolen") seat on the High Court.

2. See chapter 14, "The Retro Roberts Era: Running a Tab."

3. David Wondrich, *Imbibe!* (New York: Perigee Books, Penguin, 2007, 2015), 321; 128.

4. David A. Embury, *Fine Art of Mixing Drinks* (New York: Mud Puddle, Inc., 1948, 1986), 130.

5. But seldom getting credit for their recipes—although not, it should be noted, in the case of Marshall's Quoit Club Punch. Its African American author, Jasper Crouch, is rightly acknowledged in cocktail annals. See also Clare Cushman, *Table for 9: Supreme Court Food Traditions and Recipes* (Washington, DC: Supreme Court Historical Society Publication, 2017), 9–10.

6. One bona fide recipe that somehow failed to make the rounds of social media was the *El Presidente*, first mixed to honor pre–Cuban Revolution president (and some-time autocrat) Gerardo Machado. Created by an American bartender at the Jockey Club in Havana, the El Presidente combined white rum with dry vermouth, a dash of curaçao, and another dash of that ol' Roberts era favorite, grenadine. It, like the Cuban rum it featured, was a Prohibition specialty, just as President Machado specialized in aligning his island's touristic offerings to cater to thirsty Prohibition-era *Yanquis*. A midcentury, midday favorite at New York City hotspots like the Stork Club, the allusive El Presidente seems destined for much-deserved renewed fame as the only suitable salute to that scion of Queens and Manhattan arriviste, President Donald J. Trump.

7. Andrew Sullivan, "Reactionaries Must Be Taken Seriously," in "Beyond Alt: The New Reactionary Counterculture," *New Yorker Magazine*, May 1, 2017, 32.

8. Mark Will-Weber, *Mint Juleps with Teddy Roosevelt: The Complete History of Presidential Drinking* (Washington, DC: Regnery Publishing, 2014), 187, 192.

9. Will-Weber, *Mint Juleps*, 229.

BIBLIOGRAPHY

Arthur, Stanley Clisby. *Famous New Orleans Drinks and How to Mix 'Em.* Gretna, LA: Pelican Books, 1937, 1972.

Barr, Andrew. *Drink: A Social History of America.* New York: Carroll & Graf Publishers, 1999.

Beebe, Lucius. *The Stork Club Bar Book.* Mansfield Centre, CT: Martino Publishing, 1946, 2015.

Blackmun, Harry A. Papers. Library of Congress, Washington, DC.

Blocker, Jack S. "Tidy Pictures of Messy Behavior." Review of *Rum Punch and Revolution*, by Peter Thompson. *Journal of Urban History* 29 (2003): 472–82.

Blumenthal, Ralph. *Stork Club: America's Most Famous Nightspot and the Lost World of Café Society.* Boston and New York: Little Brown, 2000.

Borrelli-Persson, Laird. *The Cocktail Dress.* New York: Collins Design Publishers, 2009.

Boskey, Bennett. "The Family of Stone Law Clerks." In *In Chambers: Stories of Supreme Court Law Clerks and Their Justices*, edited by Todd C. Peppers and Artemus Ward, 98–108. Charlottesville: University of Virginia Press, 2012.

Burns, Eric. *The Spirits of America: A Social History of Alcohol.* Philadelphia, PA: Temple University Press, 2004.

Carlin, Joseph M. *Cocktails: A Global History.* London: Reaktion Books, 2012.

Carmon, Irin, and Shana Knizhnik. *Notorious RBG: The Life and Times of Ruth Bader Ginsburg.* New York: Dey St./William Morrow Publishers, 2015.

Cate, Martin, and Rebecca Cate. *Smuggler's Cove: Exotic Cocktails, Rum, and the Cult of Tiki.* Berkeley, CA: Ten Speed Press, 2016.

Cheever, Susan. *Drinking in America: Our Secret History.* New York: Twelve, Hachette Book Group, 2015.

Choper, Jesse H. "Clerking for Chief Justice Earl Warren." In *In Chambers: Stories of Supreme Court Law Clerks and Their Justices*, edited by Todd C. Peppers and Artemus Ward, 263–83. Charlottesville: University of Virginia Press, 2012.

Cohn, Henry S., and Ethan Davis. "Stopping the Wind That Blows and the Rivers That Run: Connecticut and Rhode Island Reject the Prohibition Amendment." *Quinnipiac Law Review* 27, no. 2 (2009): 327–74.

Curtis, Wayne. *And a Bottle of Rum: A History of the New World in Ten Cocktails.* New York: Three Rivers Press, 2006/2007.

Cushman, Clare. "Beyond Knox: James C. McReynolds's Other Law Clerks, 1914–1941." *Journal of the Supreme Court Historical Society* 41 (2016): 147–75.

———. *Courtwatchers: Eyewitness Accounts in Supreme Court History.* Lanham, MD: Rowman & Littlefield Publishers, 2011.

———. *Table for 9: Supreme Court Food Traditions and Recipes*. Washington, DC: Supreme Court Historical Society Publication, 2017.

Danelski, David J. "The Influence of the Chief Justice on the Decisional Process of the Supreme Court." In *The Chief Justice: Appointment and Influence*, edited by David J. Danelski and Artemus Ward, 19–46. Ann Arbor: University of Michigan Press, 2016.

Daniels, Mark R. "Toward Liquor Control: a Retrospective." In *Social and Economic Control of Alcohol: The 21st Amendment in the 21st Century*, edited by Carole L. Jurkiewicz and Murphy J. Painter, 217–32. Boca Raton, FL: CRC Press, 2008.

Dudley, Earl C., Jr. "A Two-For Clerkship: Stanley F. Reed and Earl Warren." In *Of Courtiers and Kings: More Stories of Supreme Court Law Clerks and Their Justices*, edited by Todd C. Peppers and Clare Cushman, 231–50. Charlottesville: University of Virginia Press, 2015.

Edmunds, Lowell. *Martini, Straight Up*. Baltimore, MD: The Johns Hopkins University Press, 1998.

Ely, James W. *The Chief Justiceship of Melville W. Fuller, 1888–1910*. Columbia: University of South Carolina Press, 1995.

Embury, David A. *Fine Art of Mixing Drinks*. New York: Mud Puddle, Inc., 1948, 1986.

Fassett, John D. "Clerking for Stanley Reed." In *Of Courtiers and Kings: More Stories of Supreme Court Law Clerks and Their Justices*, edited by Todd C. Peppers and Clare Cushman, 152–69. Charlottesville: University of Virginia Press, 2012.

Feldman, Noah. "Justice Scalia Came Close to Greatness." *Bloomberg View*, February 13, 2016. https://www.bloomberg.com/view/articles/2016–02–14/justice-antonin-scalia-came-close-to-greatness.

Gately, Iain. *Drink: A Cultural History of Alcohol*. New York: Gotham Books, 2008.

Glad, Betty. *Charles Evan Hughes and the Illusions of Innocence*. Champaign: University of Illinois Press, 1966.

Glick, Joshua. "On the Road: The Supreme Court and the History of Circuit Riding." *Cardozo Law Review* 24, no. 4 (April 2003): 1753–843.

Graetz, Michael J., and Linda Greenhouse. *The Burger Court and the Rise of the Judicial Right*. New York: Simon and Schuster, 2016.

Graves, Suzanne. "Checkpoints and the Fourth Amendment: Saving Grace or Constitutional Martyr?" *Connecticut Law Review* 32, no. 4 (Summer 2000): 1487–520.

Greene, Philip. *The Manhattan: The Story of the First American Cocktail*. New York: Sterling Epicure, 2016.

Gould, Lewis L. *Chief Executive to Chief Justice: Taft Betwixt the White House and the Supreme Court*. Lawrence: University Press of Kansas, 2014.

Griffen, Thomas B. "Zoning Away the Evils of Alcohol." *Southern California Law Review* 61, no. 5 (July 1988): 1373–416.

Haigh, Ted. *Vintage Spirits and Forgotten Cocktails*. Beverly, MA: Quarry Books, 2009.

Helman, Arthur. "The Shrunken Docket of the Rehnquist Court." *The Supreme Court Review* (1996): 403–38.

Hicks, Frederick C. *William Howard Taft: Yale Professor of Law and New Haven Citizen*. New Haven, CT: Yale University Press, 1945.

Highsaw, Robert B. *Edward Douglass White: Defender of the Conservative Faith*. Baton Rouge: Louisiana State University Press, 1981.

Hoffer, Peter Charles, William James Hull Hoffer, and N. E. H. Hull. *The Supreme Court: An Essential History*. Lawrence: University Press of Kansas, 2007.

Hofstedt, Matthew. "Acquisitions Committee Highlights: Part I, 2014–2015." *Quarterly of the Supreme Court Historical Society* 38, no. 2 (2016): 10.

Hurley, Rebecca. "In the Chief's Chambers: Life as a Law Clerk for Warren Earl Burger." In *Of Courtiers and Kings: More Stories of Supreme Court Law Clerks and Their Justices*, edited by Todd C. Peppers and Clare Cushman, 287–99. Charlottesville: University of Virginia Press, 2015.

Joyce, Walter E. "Edward Douglass White: The Louisiana Years, Early Life and On the Bench." *Tulane Law Review* 41, no. 4 (June 1967): 751–84.

Jurkiewicz, Carole L., and Murphy J. Painter. "Why We Control Alcohol the Way We Do." In *Social and Economic Control of Alcohol: The 21st Amendment in the 21st Century*, edited by Carole L. Jurkiewicz and Murphy J. Painter, 1–18. Boca Raton, FL: CRC Press, 2008.

Katz, Lewis B. "'Lonesome Road': Driving Without the Fourth Amendment." *Seattle University Law Review* 36, no. 3 (Spring 2013): 1413–71.

Keller, Mark. "Alcohol Policies and Problems in Historical Perspective." In *Law, Alcohol, and Order: Perspectives on National Prohibition*, edited by D. Kyvig, 139–58. Westport, CT: Greenwood Press, 1985.

Klinkhamer, Sister Marie Carolyn, OP, MA. "Edward Douglass White, Chief Justice of the U.S." PhD diss., The Catholic University of America, 1943 [avail. Collection of the Supreme Court Historical Society].

Kyvig, David E. *Law, Alcohol, and Order: Perspectives on National Prohibition*. Westport, CT: Greenwood Press, 1985.

———. *Repealing National Prohibition*. Kent, OH: The Kent State University Press, 2000.

———. "Sober Thoughts: Myths and Realities of National Prohibition after 50 Years." In *Law, Alcohol, and Order: Perspectives on National Prohibition*, edited by D. Kyvig, 3–20. Westport, CT: Greenwood Press, 1985.

Lacey, Theodore B. "The Supreme Court's Fluctuating Reaction to National Prohibition in Fourth Amendment Decisions from 1920–1933." Senior thesis, Princeton University, 2005.

Lawson, Evan T. "The Future of the Three-Tiered System as a Control of Marketing Alcoholic Beverages." In *Social and Economic Control of Alcohol: The 21st Amendment in the 21st Century*, edited by Carole L. Jurkiewicz and Murphy J. Painter, 31–55. Boca Raton, FL: CRC Press, 2008.

Lazarus, Edward. *Closed Chambers: The Rise, Fall, and Future of the Modern Supreme Court*. New York: Penguin Books, 1998.

Lender, Mark Edward, and James Kirby Martin. *Drinking in America: A History*. New York: The Free Press, 1987.

Leonhardt, Olive, and Hilda Phelps Hammond. *Shaking Up Prohibition in New Orleans: Authentic Vintage Cocktails from A to Z* (1929 typescript). Baton Rouge: Louisiana State University Press, 2015.

Lerner, Michael A. *Dry Manhattan: Prohibition in New York City*. Cambridge, MA: Harvard University Press, 2007.

Lewis, H. H. Walker. *Without Fear or Favor: A Biography of Chief Justice Roger Brooke Taney*. New York: Houghton Mifflin, 1965.

Linkenbach, Jeffrey W. "Perceptions, Policies, and Social Norms: Transforming Alcohol Cultures over the Next 100 Years." In *Social and Economic Control of Alcohol: The 21st Amendment in the 21st Century*, edited by Carole L. Jurkiewicz and Murphy J. Painter, 139–57. Boca Raton, FL: CRC Press, 2008.

Lotito, Michael F. "Unsteady on Its Feet: Sobriety Checkpoint Reasonableness." *Washington and Lee Law Review* 67, no. 2 (Spring 2010): 735–85.

Magrath, C. Peter. *Morrison Waite: The Triumph of Character*. New York: Macmillan, 1963.

Mason, Alpheus Thomas. *Harlan Fiske Stone: Pillar of the Law*. New York: Viking Press, 1956.

Maveety, Nancy. *Picking Judges*. Presidential Briefings Series. New Brunswick, NJ: Transaction Publishers, 2016.

McCaffety, Kerri. *Obituary Cocktail: The Great Saloons of New Orleans*. New Orleans, LA: Pontalba Press, 2001.

McGirr, Lisa. *Prohibition and the War on Alcohol: The Rise of the American State*. New York: Norton, 2015.

Miceli, Augusto. *The Pickwick Club of New Orleans*. New Orleans, LA: Pickwick Press, Hauser Printing Co., 1964, 1992 [avail. Rare Books, Howard Tilton Memorial Library, Tulane University].

Miller, Robert J., and Maril Hazlett. "The 'Drunken Indian': Myth Distilled into Reality Through Federal Indian Alcohol Policy." *Arizona State Law Journal* 28, no. 1 (Spring 1996): 223–98.

Mondics, Chris. "Scalia's Former Clerks Recall His Charm, as Well as His Intellectual Rigor." *The Philadelphia Inquirer*, February 16, 2016. http://www.philly.com/philly/business/20160216_Scalia_s_former_clerks_recall_his_charm__as_well_as_his_intellectual_rigor.html#cAhyRe8q3MdpuaXc.99.

Murchison, Kenneth M. *Federal Criminal Law Doctrines: The Forgotten Influence of National Prohibition.* Durham, NC: Duke University Press, 1994.

Murdock, Catherine Gilbert. *Domesticating Drink: Women, Men, and Alcohol in America, 1870–1940.* Baltimore, MD: The Johns Hopkins University Press, 1998.

Murphy, Bruce Allen. *Wild Bill: The Legend and Life of William O. Douglas.* New York: Random House, 2003.

Niven, John. *Salmon P. Chase: A Biography.* New York: Oxford University Press, 1995.

Norton, Elizabeth. "The 21st Amendment in the 21st Century: Reconsidering State Liquor Controls in Light of *Granholm v. Heald.*" *Ohio State Law Journal* 67, no. 6 (2006): 1465–93.

Nystrom, Justin A. *New Orleans after the Civil War: Race, Politics, and a New Birth of Freedom.* Baltimore, MD: The Johns Hopkins University Press, 2010.

Okrent, Daniel. *Last Call: The Rise and Fall of Prohibition.* Baltimore, MD: Scribner, 2010.

Owens, Ryan, and David Simon. "Explaining the Supreme Court's Shrinking Docket." *William and Mary Law Review* 53, no. 4 (March 2012): 1219–83.

Peck, Garrett. *The Prohibition Hangover: Alcohol in America from Demon Rum to Cult Cabernet.* Rutgers, NJ: Rutgers University Press, 2009.

———. *Prohibition in Washington, D.C.: How Dry We Weren't.* Charleston, SC: The History Press, 2011.

Peppers, Todd C. "A Family Tradition: Clerking at the U.S. Supreme Court." In *Of Courtiers and Kings: More Stories of Supreme Court Law Clerks and their Justices,* edited by Todd C. Peppers and Clare Cushman, 342–83. Charlottesville: University of Virginia Press, 2015.

Phillips, Rod. *Alcohol, a History.* Chapel Hill: University of North Carolina Press, 2014.

Post, Robert. "Federalism, Positive Law, and the Emergence of the American Administrative State: Prohibition in the Taft Court Era." *William and Mary Law Review* 48, no. 1 (October 2006): 1–182.

Priebe, Gregory, and Nicole Priebe. *Forgotten Maryland Cocktails: A History of Drinking in the Free State.* Charleston, SC: American Palate, The History Press, 2015.

Ray, Laura Krugman. "Judicial Fictions: Images of Supreme Court Justices in the Novel, Drama, and Film." *Arizona Law Review* 39, no. 4 (Winter 1997): 151–203.

Regan, Gary. *The Negroni: Drinking to La Dolce Vita.* New York: Penguin Random House, 2014.

Rorabaugh, W. J. *The Alcoholic Republic: An American Tradition.* New York: Oxford University Press, 1979.

Ross, Ishbel. *An American Family: The Tafts, 1678–1964.* Cleveland and New York: World Publishing Co., 1964.

Rotter, Jonathan M., and Joshua S. Stambaugh. "What's Left of the 21st Amendment?" *Cardozo Public Law, Policy, and Ethics Journal* 6, no. 3 (Spring 2008): 601–50.

Rubin, Elizabeth. "Trying to Be Reasonable about Drunk Driving: Individualized Suspicion and the Fourth Amendment." *University of Cincinnati Law Review* 62, no. 3 (Winter 1994): 1105–33.

Saucier, Ted. *Bottoms Up.* Mansfield Centre, CT: Martino Publishing, 1951, 2011.

Scheb, John M., II. "Edward T. Sanford—Knoxville's Justice." *Journal of the Supreme Court Historical Society* 41 (2016): 176–85.

Schmidt, William (The Only William). *The Flowing Bowl: What and When to Drink.* New York: Charles Webster & Co., 1892; Middletown, DE: Vintage Cocktail Books, 2008.

Seder, Arthur R., Jr. "Law Clerk for Chief Justice Vinson." In *Of Courtiers and Kings: More Stories of Supreme Court Law Clerks and Their Justices*, edited by Todd C. Peppers and Clare Cushman, 201–10. Charlottesville: University of Virginia Press, 2012.

Severn, Bill. *John Marshall: The Man Who Made the Court Supreme.* New York: McKay Co., 1969.

Simon, James F. *FDR and Chief Justice Hughes: The President, the Supreme Court, and the Epic Battle over the New Deal.* New York: Simon and Schuster, 2012.

Sismondo, Christine. *America Walks into a Bar: A Spirited History of Taverns and Saloons, Speakeasies and Grog Shops.* New York: Oxford University Press, 2011.

Slater, Stephanie L. "Edward T. Sanford's Tenure on the Supreme Court." *Journal of the Supreme Court Historical Society* 41 (2016): 186–220.

Sokoloff, Alice Hunt. *Kate Chase for the Defense: A Biography.* New York: Dodd Mead and Co., 1971.

Standard, Mary Newton. *John Marshall and His Home.* Richmond, 1913 (1st printing) [avail. Collection of the Supreme Court Historical Society].

Stone, Harlan F. Papers. Jones Library Special Collections, Amherst, MA.

Sullivan, Andrew. "Reactionaries Must Be Taken Seriously." In "Beyond Alt: The New Reactionary Counterculture." *New Yorker Magazine*, May 1, 2017.

Swisher, Carl Brent. *Roger B. Taney.* New York: MacMillan, 1935.

Umbreit, Kenneth B. *Our 11 Chief Justices: A History of the Supreme Court in Terms of Their Personalities,* vols. 1 and 2. Port Washington, NY: Kennikat Press, 1938.

Urofsky, Melvin I. *Dissent and the U.S. Supreme Court.* New York: Pantheon Books, 2015.

———. *Division and Discord: The Supreme Court under Stone and Vinson, 1941–1953.* Columbia: University of South Carolina Press, 1997.

Vander Ven, Thomas. *Getting Wasted: Why College Students Drink Too Much and Party So Hard.* New York: New York University Press, 2011.

Vose, Clement E. "Repeal as a Political Achievement." In *Law, Alcohol, and Order: Perspectives on National Prohibition,* edited by D. Kyvig, 97–122. Westport, CT: Greenwood Press, 1985.

Ward, Artemus. "Making Work for Idle Hands: William H. Rehnquist and His Law Clerks." In *In Chambers: Stories of Supreme Court Law Clerks and Their Justices,* edited by Todd C. Peppers and Artemus Ward, 350–90. Charlottesville: University of Virginia Press, 2012.

Wesser, Robert F. *Charles Evan Hughes: Politics and Reform in New York, 1905–1910.* Ithaca, NY: Cornell University Press, 1967.

White, G. Edward. *The Marshall Court and Cultural Change, 1815–1835.* New York: Oxford University Press, 1991.

Whitman, Douglas Glen. *Strange Brew: Alcohol and Government Monopoly.* Oakland, CA: The Independent Institute, 2003.

Will-Weber, Mark. *Mint Juleps with Teddy Roosevelt: The Complete History of Presidential Drinking.* Washington, DC: Regnery Publishing, 2014.

Wondrich, David. *Imbibe!* New York: Perigee Books, Penguin, 2007, 2015.

———. *Punch: The Delights (and Dangers) of the Flowing Bowl.* New York: Perigee Books, Penguin, 2010.

Wondrich, David, and Jeff Berry. "Members Only: Club Cocktails in History." Seminar presentation to the annual meeting of Tales of the Cocktail, New Orleans, LA, July 21, 2016.

Woodward, Bob, and Scott Armstrong. *The Brethren.* New York: Avon Books, 1979.

Yablon, Marcia. "The Prohibition Hangover: Why We Are Still Feeling the Effects of Prohibition." *Virginia Journal of Social Policy and the Law* 13, no. 3 (Spring 2006): 552–95.

Young, James Sterling. *The Washington Community, 1800–1828.* New York: Columbia University Press, 1966.

INDEX

ABC. *See* alcohol beverage control system

Abington v. Schempp, 215

abolitionism, 43

Acheson, Dean, 42–43

Act for the Suppression of Drinking Houses and Tippling Shops, Maine, 39

Adams, John, 14

Adams Express Co. v. Kentucky, 9, 106–107

alcohol: abuse, 205, 222; American Medical Association on, 109; Brandeis on medicinal, 140; Constitution and, 2, 4; Federal Alcohol Control Administration, 160; in Indian territories, 31–32; industrial use of, 173; Marshall Court consumption, 28; in political culture, 1–2; shipment of, in Taft Court, 130–131; Stone Court decisions, 180–186; war on, 145. *See also specific topics*

Alcohol Beverage Control Law, 243

alcohol beverage control system (ABC), 229–230, 231, 250, 263

Alcoholics Anonymous, 122, 180

alcoholism, 205, 205–206, 259; National Institute on Alcohol Abuse and Alcoholism, 222

Alito, Samuel, 283, 287, 288

An American Family (Ross), 118

American enterprise, 2

American Express v. Iowa, 86–87

American Fur Co. v. U.S., 31–32

American Medical Association, 109, 140, 205

American Temperance Society, 36

Amos v. U.S., 114

Anderson, Larz, 119

Anheuser-Busch Brewing Assoc. v. U.S., 95

Anti-Saloon League (ASL), 3, 48, 79–80, 98; as special interest, 108; support by, 136; Taft and, 117; Wheeler and, 119

articles of necessity, 71

ASL. *See* Anti-Saloon League

ATF. *See* Bureau of Alcohol, Tobacco, and Firearms

automobile searches, 137–138, 139, 195, 271

Bacardi Corp. v. Domenech, 166–168

Bacchus Imports, Ltd. v. Dias, 239–241, 242, 262

Bamboo Cocktail, 71

Barnes v. Glen Theater, 264

Barr, Andrew, 37

bars: in Burger Court, 222; dive bars, 298; fern bars, 221, 256; hotel, 71, 77, 79; in Rehnquist Court, 262; in Roberts Court, 286; in Vinson Court, 193, 196

Bartemeyer v. Iowa, 59–60, 61, 68–69, 127

bathtub gin, 120

ABOUT THE AUTHOR

Nancy Maveety is professor of political science at Tulane University, specializing in U.S. Supreme Court studies, judicial decision making, and comparative judicial politics.